W9-BWR-880

Released from DPL

Our Right to Choose

OUR RIGHT TO CHOOSE
Toward a New Ethic of Abortion

Beverly Wildung Harrison

Beacon Press   Boston

The lines from the poem "Dark Testament" by Pauli Murray are reprinted by permission of the author. Copyright © 1970 by Pauli Murray.

Grateful acknowledgment is given to Dorothee Soelle
for permission to reprint the lines from the poem "Play Me a Song about Rosa, Anna, and Rosa" from *Of War and Love,* reprinted from *Of War and Love* copyright © 1983 by Orbis Books.

Beacon Press books are published under the auspices of the Unitarian Universalist Association of Congregations in North America, 25 Beacon Street, Boston, Massachusetts 02108

Published simultaneously in Canada by
Fitzhenry & Whiteside Limited, Toronto

Printed in the United States of America

(hardcover) 9 8 7 6 5 4 3 2 1
(paperback) 9 8 7 6 5 4 3 2 1

Library of Congress Cataloging in Publication Data

Harrison, Beverly Wildung, 1932-
  Our right to choose.

  Includes index.

  1. Abortion — Moral and ethical aspects. 2. Abortion — Religious aspects — Christianity. 3. Abortion — Political aspects — United States. 4. Pro-choice movement — United States. 5. Feminism. I. Title.
HQ767.3.H37 1983   1979'.76   81-70488
ISBN 0-8070-1508-3
ISBN 0-8070-1509-1 (pbk.)

PRÉ

To Adahlia Margaret Wildung
and
Beverly Rankin Ellison
In gratitude for
A life well lived, A life begun.
And for the particularity of
women's lives.

Acknowledgments

When one has written on a controversial subject, adopting a stance which itself is bound to be controversial, it is wise to begin where acknowledgments usually end, by accepting all responsibility for what follows in the book. I gladly do so, since the factual and moral claims, the ethical and religious premises, and the conclusions it contains are my own. Its limitations and errors also are mine alone. However, it is a far better book than it would otherwise have been because of the help of many people. Shirley Cloyes, a dear friend and colleague, bears considerable credit for enhancing its readability; she worked with me on the final draft, helping me shape the unwieldy text and mitigating my complex, Germanic prose. Carter Heyward has been my beloved companion in the process of its writing, extending encouragement and tangible support in ways that words cannot convey. Her faith in the critical importance on the project never waned when my own conviction about it flagged. She also read the manuscript and made numerous helpful suggestions.

Fay Ellison deserves special gratitude for several important reasons. It was her work on abortion a number of years ago that initiated my awareness of its urgency as a social ethical issue central to women's lives. Her research and writing on the question has been a source of much of my own insight. In addition, she and Marvin Ellison have extended love and support in numerous ways, not least through the gift of conferring my name upon their beautiful daughter, Beverly. It is to her, and to my wonderful mother, that *Our Right to Choose* is dedicated.

Many others have extended help in identifying sources for my research, including Eleanor Bader, Anne Barstow, Ruth Evans, Kate Cannon, Annette Daum, Donna Day-Lower, Lon Weldon Palmer, Mary Pellauer, and Judith Plaskow. Conversations or correspondence with many of these friends, and numerous others, have clarified my thinking on technical or theoretical aspects of my work. Carol Robb, Janet Gallagher, Rhonda Copelon, James Nelson, James Harrison, and many of the wonderful sisters in the Feminist Ethics Colloquium have been sources of insight and stimulation on specific topics, methodological issues, and style. Librarians Sandra Boyd, Betty Bolden, Karen Whittlesly-First, and Noreen Carter have generously aided my work.

I also have been uncharacteristically blessed by a group of typists over the two years it took to draft and revise the manuscripts, who not only struggled with my often difficult texts, but took the subject of the book to heart, offering responses that improved it and, at times, enabled me to sense what other readers would make of it. This list includes Keta Jones, Toni Minett, Julie Norton, Coryl Larsen, Sherry Horn, Connie Benson, Brian D'Agostino, and Taeko Tsujimoto. Taeko, the secretary of the Theological Field at Union Seminary in New York, where I teach, also helped to relieve me of other work, and to keep the telephone at bay, so this book could get done. At the end, Sydney Howell, Bob Antley, and Anne Gilson joined Shirley, Carol, Carter, and me in the tedious work of reading galleys.

The entire staff at Beacon Press was unfailingly helpful. I am grateful to Marie Cantlon for her patience, friendship, encouragement, and editorial judgment, and to Jeff Smith and Judith Rosen for their collaboration.

Barbara Flanagan was the sort of copy editor for whom every author longs and Nancy Donovan's indexing greatly improved the usefulness of the book.

Joining all of these people in the circle to which my gratitude extends are those hundreds of women and men I have come to know in the work of the pro-choice movement. Many of the organizations which comprise this movement are mentioned in the pages that follow. Here, a special word of appreciation is in order for the work of the Religious Coalition on Abortion Rights. After this book was completed, word came of the untimely death of Patricia Gavett, the energetic and perceptive Executive Director of RCAR for over six years. I am mindful that it was Pat who first prevailed upon me to write a book addressing the abortion issue. This acknowledgment would be deeply flawed without a memorial word of gratitude for her life. She did as much as any one woman could to shape our right to choose as a genuine religious and moral sensibility.

Preface

Book titles are best when brief, yet this one, encompassing a complex political, moral, and religious matter, could, by its brevity, mislead. The "choice" which receives moral defense in these pages is women's right to the *conditions for procreative choice*, not merely the narrower option of elective abortion. Here, my effort to identify the reasons why this claim to procreative choice gets so little hearing in the morality of abortion debate has required me to enter to a forceful caveat against much that passes as unquestioned wisdom in Christian tradition and teaching — on women's nature, on procreation, *and* on abortion.

Responses to pieces I published earlier on this subject make me aware already of the incredulity, not to say, hostility, which my thesis provokes amongst some of my colleagues in the field of Christian ethics. Several commentators have been quick to point out the "more than a hint of anger" with which I pressed my earlier case. No doubt it may be difficult for some men, perhaps especially some Christian moralists, to hear me when I say that researching Christian teaching on abortion is often a brutalizing experience for an aware woman. What I, and many other women, hear in much Christian morality of abortion discussion does indeed engender some anger. Until our opponents consent to examine not merely conclusions but unspoken premises, this state of affairs will not change. At present, the demand to speak judiciously falls exclusively upon us, while the accountability of the discussion to women's well-being easily can be evaded. Certitude, even complacency, in the presence of unprobed assumptions often bequeaths an aura of judiciousness. Under the circumstances, to say bluntly, as I do here, that this complacency is misplaced is, I suppose, bound to be construed as rage by some. Nevertheless, as a practicing Christian woman, I take no pleasure in my conclusions about the inadequacies of my tradition on these matters. My life and professional work are a pledge of my hope and faith that a non-misogynist Christianity is a possibility. Be that as it may, though, a formulation of the ethics of abortion which is fair to women's reality is a moral necessity. Ethics is a *critical* discipline, one that demands rigorous honesty about religious and moral traditions and conventions in the service of concrete good. As I understand the matter, its requirements can never be suspended in the service of presumed piety. In any case, *Our Right to Choose* aims to make it harder for *anyone* to speak of abortion as "a moral dilemma," without giving women's well-being central standing in the discussion. If anything I say here advances that agenda, the burdens of doing this book — and there have been burdens, as well as joys — will be well justified.

CONTENTS

Our Right to Choose

1

The Abortion Controversy: Who Shall Control the Power to Reproduce the Species?

The debate over abortion has moved outside the stream of "normal" political process and has pressed us into bitter social discord. The disagreement about abortion is multifaceted and deep, and all participants contend that human lives are at stake. To be sure, morally sensitive people on both sides of the political controversy seek to minimize its vitriolic quality. Even so, a not insignificant number of persons opposed to legal abortion have moved beyond the "art" of politics as persuasion to coerce those who seek abortions. Bombing of abortion clinics has occurred; those wanting access to abortion have found facilities blocked by angry pickets; telephone harassment of those who have had abortions has been widespread.[1] And if anti-abortion politics succeed, numerous women, believing they have the right to determine whether to bear children, will turn to acts of civil disobedience — that is, they will seek illegal abortions. Because women's lives are rarely understood to have profound public import, few recognize that prior to legalized abortion socially aware women often understood themselves to be engaged in serious acts of political resistance. Be that as it may, anti-abortionists and many women experience the current situation as a genuine state of civil war.

Some moralists are appalled by the prevailing state of affairs. Hand-wringing about the situation is not infrequent among moral philosophers and religious ethicists in particular. I write as one of the latter group, a religiously committed social ethicist who, nevertheless, finds the present situation not very surprising. I believe, like most people, that the political institutions of this society are not well suited to adjudicate deep social, moral, and religious conflicts. This is especially true if such moral conflicts intersect with lines of social class and caste. Ours is a deeply class-stratified society, and the rigidities of caste divide white Europeans from racial and ethnic persons. Less frequently acknowledged, however, is that gender too has a castelike quality, a critical factor in the abortion controversy. Only women can get pregnant, yet men, almost exclusively, interpret the morality of and make the laws about abortion. The political conflict over abortion is so intense partly because the population at risk from the effects of public policy is all but excluded from a direct voice in the policy-making process. Whenever such politics of exclusion obtain, it is predictable that those who make the policy, or favor it, will focus on the intensity rather than the substance of the conflict.

The magnitude of the conflict is also an indication of how much is at stake. Few have paused to note that the abortion controversy is a part of the larger question of who shall control a most precious human resource — the power to reproduce the species. Especially in affluent industrial countries, as birth rates have fallen and as women have begun to assume freedom from the capriciousness associated with their biological capacity to bear children, many have become distressed by these changes. The volatility of the abortion question is not unrelated to the fact that safe, legal abortion has finally assured that bearing children is an option rather than a necessity for fertile, heterosexually active women who have access to abortion. What other contraceptive techniques do imperfectly, abortion does irrevocably — that is, it makes pregnancy avoidable. While safe, legal abortion is not yet available to many women, the aspiration for procreative choice is sweeping the globe and certainly spreading faster than effective contraceptive technology.

Opponents of abortion share with many proponents an awareness, on some level, of this fundamental change in human history. The expectation that women's lives may, and even should, assume procreative choice is radically new. Nothing in our lives will remain unaffected by this movement toward procreative choice. Ancient ideas about women and the parameters of female existence were conditioned by the inevitability of procreation, even in cultures where fairly effective contraceptive controls existed. Those whose self-interest rests with the status quo have sensed the depth of change in human history implied by the emergence of a technology that assures procreative choice. Indeed, this awareness has much to do with the warlike zeal of the current controversy.

We are only at the beginning of the public, political dispute over procreative choice in human history. If we do not obliterate ourselves with other, life-destructive technologies in the meanwhile, the abortion debate probably will continue in one form or another for decades, perhaps for generations. This is because all the intricate social systems that characterize human life — our institutions, mores, and customs and all the varied religious sacralizations of these systems through all recorded history — have been shaped inherently *to control women's procreative power.* This control will not be relinquished without a struggle.

All the more reason, then, why the tiny minority of women like myself — affluent, usually white — who have so far gained a toehold on the new horizon of procreative freedom should not imagine that abortion politics is merely a "private" matter of individual choice. As everybody knows perfectly well, economically advantaged white women in the United States, including the wives and daughters of those political and economic leaders who are gaining political mileage by opposing legal abortion, will have access to medically safe abortions, legal or not. If our world survives the dangers of the present, we may be absolutely certain that women who are *related to ruling-class males* always will obtain the goods and services they and their male partners need to enhance their personal lives. Among most social elites, procreative choice is, and will remain, a taken-for-granted option, more costly if illegal but still accessible.

A thesis of this book is that we cannot begin to formulate an adequate moral approach to abortion without affirming that what socially elite women have come to expect for themselves — the capacity to shape their procreative power rather than to live at the caprice of biological accident — is, in fact, a social good that all women require. Yet we cannot assume that simply extending the availability of legal abortion to more women will lead per se to genuine procreative choice.

THE FUNDAMENTAL, NEGLECTED MORAL DILEMMA: THE WELL-BEING OF WOMEN IN SEXIST SOCIETY

Despite the intensity of the social conflict over abortion, we may observe the waning of questions about the morality of abortion in the immediate future, not because the moral issue has been resolved or our social policy clarified, but because other crises and historical problems may render the abortion controversy moot for a time. The present political and economic crisis will be a long-term one. All people — but women and men of color and working-class men in particular — are being pressured to desist from protest and to adopt disciplines of self-sacrifice willingly and without complaint. Everywhere we are prevailed upon to eschew hopes of personal fulfillment and to return to "traditional values." Abortion politics may fade for a time because, given other pressures and adversities, people may grow weary of all moralizing and pragmatically accept new legal restraints on abortion as the least objectionable option. The outcome of the present politics of abortion, then, could lead either to the tightening of the restrictions or to the continuance of the status quo. The deeper moral and religious challenge of clarifying what is at stake for the well-being of people and society, however, will not quickly disappear, whatever the political resolution.

This book is written especially for those who have sensed the serious need to weigh the abortion controversy in a moral context that both affirms and advocates women's well-being. These people have grasped that the controversy over abortion is but one dimension of that far broader world historical struggle to enable us to "become the subjects of our lives."[2] I will argue that once the material historical conditions exist to make procreative choice possible, there are excellent moral reasons for viewing it as a right all women should possess. No society is adequate morally which does not organize its life to encourage the existence and extension of procreative choice. I also will argue that gains in conditions for genuine procreative choice for women are not to be expected soon. Safer contraception, greater economic and social security, stronger support for childrearing, lessening of racial brutality, reduction of violence against women (including incest, rape, and sterilization abuse) are not on the horizon. It is not a promising time for enhancing the quality of most women's lives.

Unfortunately, most "pro-choice" supporters have little awareness of the numerous means anti-abortion proponents have at their disposal to close off options for safe, legal abortion. Even as ill-considered efforts wane to pass a constitutional amendment granting fetal life full citizenship (a status that women as a group do not have, given the defeat of the ERA) and as abortion politics shift to a state's rights approach through strategies such as the Hatch Amendment, new and numerous patterns of social coercion to limit access to abortion are evolving. Success in denying the use of any federal funds to finance abortions for poor women augurs a similar outcome for state and local funding. A panoply of legal and extralegal tactics will continue to be used. Let no one imagine that the effort to recriminalize abortion and to make women who choose abortion, and physicians who perform abortions, felons under the law will soon end or that efforts to curtail legal abortions will abate. Neither will there be a cessation in the availability of abortion or in the ongoing struggle to secure procreative choice. To be sure, if anti-abortion legislation succeeds, the abortion industry will go underground; nevertheless it will continue. And it is not likely that authorities will find enforcement of anti-abortion laws either easy or palatable. More important, such law enforcement, like all law enforcement in U.S. society when it occurs, will be aimed chiefly at poor or nonwhite women.

I write convinced that in a protracted political conflict such as this one it is particularly urgent that we get our moral bearings straight. Some approaches to ethics and morality draw a sharp distinction between politics and morality. My own view is that they are, in fact, intimately related and that they should be. Furthermore, I believe that all political arrangements which violate minimal moral conditions — that is, conditions for human well-being — are *inherently* unstable. People find ways to resist political and social orders that coerce them and threaten their well-being, and I believe they are morally right to do so. I fully agree with many abortion opponents that we owe it to each other to shape our common life as effectively as possible around "the moral point of view."[3] In any case, morality always enters into politics one way or another, and deep political conflict is always simultaneously basic value conflict about what constitutes human well-being. A moral analysis offers those engaged in political conflict an opportunity to both clarify and commend to others their goals and reasons for judgment. It also encourages self-reflective criticism and self-assessment. Most of us evade moral analysis in politics, as often as not to avoid such self-reflective evaluation and also *to avoid others' careful scrutiny of our reasons for our actions.* Moral reasoning is inherently dialogical; it involves the effort to communicate to others. Those in political control in society often wish to evade accountability. Hence, "morality" either is construed as antithetical to politics or is bandied around as rhetorical window dressing. But we eschew moral analysis at the risk of failing to understand what it is we are actually doing through political choices and social policies.

As a political activist and a partisan in abortion politics and controversy, I can testify that most pro-choice women are eager to clarify the moral foundations of their position, in anticipation of the turbulent period that lies ahead. So much has been written about the so-called ethics of abortion that, recently, one well-respected Christian ethicist commented that the debate had become ritualistic.[4] It seems that both sides already know and can refute all arguments of the other side, as if nothing new could be said on the subject. By contrast, I find that almost nothing, especially in the literature in Christian ethics, has been written specifically on the morality of abortion that fully reflects women's experience, and I have found no adequate refutation of my arguments in Christian ethics. Nor has there been any book-length ethical study that systematizes a feminist moral perspective on abortion.

Pro-choice women have entered the political struggle valiantly and the political debate eloquently.[5] But the impression is left that "the ethics" of the issue are "owned" by anti-abortion proponents. In spite of this assumption that morality rests with the anti-abortion side, women have mounted a strong if sometimes *ad hoc* ethical case for choice. Nevertheless, through my research and reflection on this question, I have come to believe that some efforts to develop a moral understanding of the abortion dilemma may be hampered by an uncritical adoption of certain dominant political theories and also by our failure to understand the structural nature of women's social oppression. So while the chief critical polemic in what follows is directed against dominant trends in Christian theological ethics and moral philosophy, I am concerned also to identify approaches to abortion employed by pro-choice advocates that I believe are inadequate from the moral point of view.

REVISIONING THE ETHICS OF PROCREATIVE CHOICE AND ABORTION: A TWOFOLD TASK

When I began research on this study in 1979, I was motivated by a growing distress at the lack of critical awareness exhibited in the abortion debate by writers in my own field of Christian ethics and also by some moral philosophers.[6] My assessment of the shortcomings of the professional Christian ethical discussion about abortion led me to envision two tasks for my study: a critique of the misogynist bias of theological and moral tradition on abortion and an elaboration of the elements essential to an ethic of procreative choice. These tasks, I am now persuaded, were the right ones. The research tasks related to that goal are endless, and I have not pursued all lines of inquiry to my satisfaction. Even so, since I believe that ethical analysis best proceeds through public discussion, I submit my claims regarding the problems within the Christian moral tradition on abortion as an invitation to more critical sensibility from my peers. The lines of argument I advance toward women's re-visioning communally a constructive ethic of our procreative power are less provisional, but they are not the end, but the beginning, of moral dialogue. We must insist on doing this for ourselves, even though we should welcome critical and sympathetic support from men.

My first task is to open the way for a moral reevaluation of abortion as an act and of legal abortion as a social practice or policy. In particular, I apply intellectual-critical insights gained from a decade of feminist scholarship to assumptions of Christian ethicists and theologians about the morality of abortion. This new feminist critical work is of fundamental intellectual significance for a reinterpretation of all western history, philosophy, and theology. Furthermore, all academic disciplines, especially all religious ethical and moral philosophical perspectives, ignore this work at the peril of intellectual provincialism and moral insensitivity. Many religious ethicists, moral theologians, and moral philosophers, mostly male, have discussed the morality of abortion, or of social policy relating to abortion, without reference to contemporary scholarly evidence that the disvaluation of women is deeply embedded in western culture and constitutes an unacceptable moral heritage that requires correction. Unfortunately, the growing impact of feminist scholarship on many academic disciplines is almost absent in Christian theology, which remains perhaps the most misogynist of disciplines.[7] In any case, feminism is fundamentally a moral claim.[8] The contention that women as a group ought to have the same basic standing as "rational moral agents" as do men, with all the rights and responsibilities attendant to that status, has deep implications for theology and ethics. One of the aims of this study is to demonstrate that the absence of a feminist moral perspective has seriously flawed Christian discussions of the abortion issue. To assert that discounting women's standing as moral agents has been not only a historical, logical, and theological error but also a moral failing is to insist that it has eviscerated what in ethics is called the "normative ethical sensibility" of professionals in the field, at least in relation to the issue of abortion.

Since my research began, some professional religious moralists have emerged who discuss the topic with awareness that women are, after all, the persons most at risk in whatever social policy this nation makes about abortion.[9] This development is most welcome, but we still are very far from the historically integrated and wholistic perspective needed on this issue in Christian ethics and theology. Of course, I do not claim that the moral insensitivity against which I contend is due simply to the genitalia possessed by those who, until now, have written most of the Christian ethics of abortion. The disvaluation of women as full, morally competent members of the human species is a moral ill that afflicts both men and women, some more than others. The reasons for the failure of Christian ethicists and moral theologians in this area are, as we will see, complex and numerous. I would be less than candid, however, if I did not acknowledge what years of work in theological education and the churches have taught me — that males at the center of dominant religious communities, especially those from religious communities that consign women to the periphery, are inclined to transmit inherited patterns of misogyny unawares. Much of the substance of this book documents this allegation. The challenge of eliminating misogyny from Christian abortion teaching is one that I most urgently press upon professional colleagues, female and male.

The moral intuition that many share of a connection between the availability of legal abortion and other social justice issues requires development and elaboration. The greater part of this study, then, aims to make a contribution to this longer-term, constructive normative moral project.

I do not believe that "doing ethics" or "doing moral reasoning" is a task merely for individuals or chiefly for experts. My indebtedness to others will be obvious to those familiar with the new feminist scholarship. In initiating steps to bring this new perspective into critical relation with the existing ethics of procreative choice and abortion, I hope to demonstrate the ethical importance of feminist methodology. The critical materials exposing the distorting effects of the disvaluation of women in existing theological and moral approaches to procreation and abortion may help to gain a new hearing for this moral defense of procreative choice, including the availability of safe, legal abortion. The terms of the moral debate are already so entrenched that only a critical exposé will make clear how badly we need a new moral approach.

Most professional ethicists would insist that an optimal moral point of view and an adequate historical and theological analysis of any moral problem require that we clarify *concretely* the moral dilemma we seek to evaluate as it arises in the context of real-world decision making. In discussions of abortion, however, there is a noticeable absence of critical sense about whether existing formulations of the morality of abortion even pose the moral dilemma accurately. This methodological weakness is rooted in insensitivity to women's lives. Most Christian "ethics of abortion," more by accident than by design, treat abortion as if it were an isolated act or deed having no relation to the lived world other than its involvement with prospective birth. Few even pause to notice that the question of whether to seek an abortion arises concretely within the life of a woman only under specific circumstances — circumstances that are not mere "externals" to the consideration of abortion but are integral to the full meaning of the dilemma. The abortion dilemma arises, in nearly all cases,[10] because of an unwanted pregnancy. From the standpoint of a woman's experience, a more basic and prior moral question operates: "What am I to do about the procreative power that is mine by virtue of being born female?" The question of abortion arises only in this wider human context. In one sense, abortion is a negative, therapeutic, or corrective act, not an act of positive moral agency at all. A woman's basic constructive line of moral action is responsible life planning in relation to her procreative power. The habit of discussing abortion as if it were a "discrete deed" is a way of formulating the abortion issue as a moral question abstracted out of, and hence irrelevant to, the way it arises in women's lives.[11]

This tendency to abstraction is reinforced in current religious ethics because most professional ethical analyses, including those by Christians, occur within medical settings where a biomedical ethical perspective is assumed. As a result, current discussion of abortion ethics is permeated by the context and the ethos of *medical* choice. *Choice* in a medical context usually is construed as an individual "case" problem and treated as an issue of professional discernment. Doctors and other health-care professionals frequently view social reality as external to a technical medical context and biological considerations as abstractable from the deeper social setting.[12] This strongly reinforces the "discrete-deed" approach already ideologically embedded in reigning religious and moral approaches to abortion. I do not, of course, mean to suggest that we have nothing to learn from the moral philosophy and religious ethics being done in contemporary biomedical settings. On the contrary, some of the most elegant current moral philosophy and religious ethics emerge through biomedical work, perhaps because moral factors are easier to identify in individual biomedical cases than in a complex social setting. Even so, biomedical discussions of abortion tend to lack genuine critical consciousness of the effects of disvaluing women in the moral debate.

The line of moral argument developed here, then, assumes that the moral evaluation of abortion must proceed from the prior and appropriate question of how women are to secure, shape, and use their procreative power, a social power that only women possess, although not all women possess it. The effort of women to claim this power fully is new. In our western biomedical, theological, and moral traditions, women consistently have been cast as passive vessels through which the power of male generation flows. Male control of procreative power has never before been challenged institutionally on the scale at which women are challenging it today. Men, out of innocence or self-interest, may perhaps evade awareness of the ideological implications of this challenge. For many women the human stakes are too high for such evasions.

ACCOUNTABILITY TO WOMEN

It is to my sisters' collective judgment that I submit my work in this book. I do not imagine that every woman will agree with the way I formulate the issues here or with all the moral judgments I have arrived at, but I hope that all may understand the importance of the discussion, for women's lives are at stake in the outcome of the abortion controversy.

To insist that my accountability for making moral sense on this issue is chiefly to women does not deny the relevance of all "male-stream"[13] moral theory and reasoning to the needed revisioning, nor does it imply that nothing is to be learned from men's theological and historical discussions of abortion. To insist on a clear-eyed critique of the antiwoman bias in our intellectual tradition does not imply for me a total rejection of that heritage. I do not believe that what is tainted by patriarchy is thereby totally distorted,[14] although a strong corrective is now in order in all scholarship involving women, a corrective that must be launched even in the face of charges of bias and partiality. I concur with Mary O'Brien's brilliant characterization of the requirements of feminist scholarship. Her aim is a feminist corrective in political theory, and mine is in ethics, but her hermeneutic, or principle of interpretation, is apt in every detail and deserves extensive quotation:

> Feminist theory has to be biased because it is anti-bias. We have to correct a profound and long-sustained imbalance, and this cannot be done without jumping rather brutally and without invitation on the end of the philosophical see-saw which has lingered too long in the rarefied heights of the complacent taken-for-grantedness of male conceptions of human nature. Perhaps more important than these considerations, however, is the presupposition which informs the whole exercise: it is posited that there is such a thing as a "feminist perspective." It is also assumed that this perspective must carve out its own subject matter, and in so doing can provide new and illuminating reappraisals of the more encrusted tenets of the male-stream thought. Meantime, we may quite cheerfully borrow from that tradition any contributions in terms of theory and methodology which are needed for the development of feminist theory. In this way, we avoid slavish and ultimately inappropriate devotion to any particular set of theoretical beliefs. We do not say that the tradition must be rejected in a wholesale way. . . . What we do, therefore, is to work in a dialectical way. We seek to uncover contradictions in traditional thought; to root these contradictions in the reality of male experience; to point out that they have been valid in specific historical circumstances; to say why they are not longer valid; to conserve what is valuable and to transcend what is not; to create something new which is none the less continuous with history and a creative future. If one wants a metaphor for this process, women do not have very far to look. We are laboring to give birth to a new philosophy of birth . . . It will be unlike the tradition in that the genderic perspective brought to bear is one which has historically been excluded from the human history, and human history perceived as a social process which has as its absolutely and inescapably necessary substructure the process of human reproduction.[15]

I would add only that this same substructure also has been the source of women's historical subjugation. From a moral point of view, it is time to make the connections between abortion politics and these realities.

AN APPROACH TO MORAL THEORY

In what follows, the reader will find any technical terminology of ethics or theology either defined briefly in the text or, where it seems necessary to do so, elaborated in notes. For those interested in the more technical aspects of moral theory, I will briefly identify my own approach before proceeding. One need not be sophisticated in moral theory to make conscientious life choices, but moral theory can provide a check on our ethical reasoning. Moral theories are proposals about what sorts of considerations should count as "good reasons" morally for actions and evaluations. Moral theories may also be understood as proposals for styles of ethical reasoning. Professionally, I am a "mixed theorist." That is, I believe actions, strategies, and judgments are morally right and wrong, or good and bad, by virtue of *several different* characteristics they may possess rather than only one. No single moral criterion, principle, or standard of moral value is applicable to all cases. Part of the work of ethics is to consider how an act, policy, or institution appears in light of some moral criterion, principle, or value. A mixed theorist "tries on" a range of moral reasons in any given case.

One way is through the use of principles and rules, what moralists call "action guides," that identify values or established patterns of practice to be expressed or avoided when we act. In the case of the principle "respect human life," for example, we are directed to act in a certain way when a specific value is present. Some principles, then, function to call attention to values. Principles and rules have other functions as well. They may identify features of actions that in moral discourse we call "obligations." To say that something is an obligation means that, on reflection, it is what we owe to others in our social relations. For example, "tell the truth" is an action guide that identifies truth-telling as a right-making property in social relations. As I will indicate later, there are different ways we may employ principles and rules in moral reasoning. Some Protestant Christian ethicists of the last generation dismissed the role of action guides, or rules and principles, in ethics.[16] I believe that that rejection grew out of confusion about the logic and function of action guides in our moral reasoning. Some people abuse and misuse principles and rules, as we will see; nevertheless, principles and rules have several important roles in moral reasoning and we cannot do without them.

Theorists who appeal exclusively to established understanding of correct principles to determine the rightness and wrongness of acts are called "deontologists." There are many types of deontology. Some moral philosophers suppose that we possess a moral sense or conscience that enables us to "intuit" the moral quality or intrinsic value of things. Others claim that our capacity to identify intrinsic value is the product of revelation requiring no further rational justification (a view I criticize in Chapter 3). Yet other deontologists assert that there are a few logically grounded moral principles so uncontestable that no existing, historical reason could ever refute them. Deontologists, then, insist that prescriptions or action guides can be fully valid apart from what results from their application. Nondeontologists also appeal to principle and prescription, but not as unchallengeable phenomena. Many moral dilemmas cannot be resolved by such appeals to principle, either because several principles may be related to a specific decision, judgment, or policy or because the relevance of intrinsic value claims to an action is sometimes neither direct nor clear. Notoriously vague as foundational values and principles are, it is not clear to me how anyone could consistently adjudicate moral dilemmas only in deontological terms. For this and other reasons, I agree with most "normative ethicists" (that is, those who attempt to make a case for the moral appropriateness of specific actions and policies) that it is better to evaluate the morality of actions and policies from mixed-theory assumptions.

Another sort of morally significant test for the goodness or evil of actions involves weighing the consequences or probable results of proposed actions. Those who evaluate actions exclusively or chiefly by their consequences are called, broadly, "teleologists." When people argue about consequences of actions, they often have entirely different contexts in view, so there are, in fact, several types of teleologists. Some religious ethicists, myself included, believe that it makes sense to evaluate actions in one dimension, in terms of their "telos" or end — that is, in terms of how they fit into a theological vision of life. One such dimension of evaluation in theological ethics, for example, consists of how an act or strategy of action fits into our hope for human life as part of God's "commonwealth."[17] Other teleologists believe that a theological conception of the goal or end of life should be the primary source of our moral ideals. Both sorts of theological teleology yield notions of consequences that do not relate so much to the here and now as to our moral horizon. Religious ethical approaches, then, are often teleological in this visionary sense.[18]

In current philosophical discussion, the interest in consequences focuses more distinctly on the rightness and wrongness of acts in terms of how they shape specific, historical consequences. Those who justify acts and policies in this way are often called "utilitarians." Utilitarians in moral theory, then, are those who hold that the measure of rightness and wrongness of acts, strategies, and judgments is in the effects the acts have on our actual social welfare. Classic utilitarianism, elaborated by nineteenth-century philosopher Jeremy Bentham, conceived of social welfare as consisting of the cumulative pleasure of individuals. Social welfare, he assumed, could be calculated rather simply by following the principle of "the greatest good for the greatest number." Telling criticisms of this "classic" version of utilitarianism are numerous. It is easy to show that the use of "hedonic calculus" (that is, its simplistic pain/pleasure psychology) in the application of its central principle led to morally dubious results. Quantifying social welfare in a simplistic way can lead to the presumably moral justification of cruel actions against a minority. Recent formulations of this theory have made clear that one can avoid such results by employing principles not as indicative of uncontestable intrinsic value but as social welfare-shaping pre-scriptions that evoke good consequences in the long run. The fact is that the basic logic of utilitarianism — that social consequences are a good measure for determining the morality of acts — really has not been discredited.[19] Those who do not weigh the consequences of the acts their principles seem to endorse often do evil and call it good.

The truth is that *both* deontological and utilitarian moral reasoning carried to their logical conclusions, without the corrective of the other, can lead to actions that offend people's moral intuitions.[20] The complaint that utilitarians can be tempted too readily by pragmatic resolutions to moral dilemmas needs to be taken seriously. Less often observed, however, is the possibility that a deontologist, adhering to a fixed principle, might refuse the death of one person at the cost of thousands of other deaths. If premature compromise is the tempter of utilitarians, excessive rigidity and moralism are the hobgoblins of deontology. Neither line of moral theory deserves to be canonized as an infallible guide to moral action, but both can be helpful in assessing moral responsibility.[21]

Human Social Relations and Women's Personal Moral Choice

An adequate ethic not only clarifies dilemmas of personal choice but also illuminates the question "What practices and policies ought to characterize a genuinely moral or good society?" An appropriate ethic of procreative choice must illuminate both questions, because life is inherently social and what government does or does not do affects everyone. Even so, it is important to affirm at the outset that it is more critical for women to face together and agree on the latter question — "What is a humane social policy regarding abortion?" — than to reach consensus on the question of the morality of the act of abortion itself. Differing personal commitments, all justifiable from a moral point of view, yield different conclusions about choosing abortion.

I firmly believe that many women share a historically shaped gift of moral sensibility such that they do not find it easy to prescribe morality for others, especially when life-shaping questions are at issue.[22] Respecting this reluctance and recognizing its wisdom, I have tried to be sensitive to the diversity of moral judgments among women regarding the act of abortion itself. I do not attempt to develop specific criteria for responsible individual decisions in relation to abortion. One person cannot adequately clarify the range of values and contingencies that must be incorporated in these deliberations, given the diversity of women's life situations. I do pursue, however, my conviction that values and principles are appropriately invoked to justify choices for abortion in numerous circumstances. I do not assume that this conviction will be convincing to women who believe that for themselves the individual choice for abortion could be justified only in the most extreme circumstances, if at all. Although I respect this viewpoint, I do not share it.

It is important for women to recognize that if we did not have to consider the matter of procreative choice in its historical context where strong abortion taboos obtain, the focus of our discussion would be quite different. In such an "ideal" context, the basic moral issue for women would be how we might responsibly use the procreative power our gender bequeaths us. Given the politics of abortion, women have had little psychological space to pursue this question, which in the last analysis may be the greatest tragedy of all. For women need desperately to understand that we do possess a strong, creative social power and that we are genuinely morally accountable for how we use that power. The current context of debate makes it incredibly difficult for us to put this fact of our social accountability in perspective. Until and unless procreative choice is understood as a basic moral value in our society, women's full capacity as moral agents will not come to fruition.

So while for me moral wisdom entails the acceptance of a certain provisionality about the moral criteria that can justify a personal choice about abortion, I am not in the least a pluralist with respect to social policy. From women who rationally deliberate the issues, I confidently expect agreement that women as a group must be considered competent moral agents and that an optimal social policy places the decision about abortion with women. It is one thing to have moral scruples about abortion as an act and quite another to support coercive public policies. The prohibition of legal abortion will mean not only that many women must bear children against their will but that state power will be directed against the well-being and standing of women as moral agents.

Actually, I perceive a consensus favoring the legal availability of safe surgical abortion as good public policy, at least in the earlier periods of pregnancy.[23] Many people may deny what I hold to be true: that the act of abortion is sometimes, even frequently, a positive moral good for women; but those who empathize with the realities of women's lives usually recognize that a specific choice for abortion is often the least wrong act under the circumstances. What follows, then, is an unequivocal defense of a social policy of legal abortion and a more tentative case for the morality of abortion as a specific act in many circumstances.

Concerning the Value of Fetal Life

My argument that abortion is not what moralists call an intrinsically wrong act is developed in Chapter 7. A chief source of moral disagreement on this point is varying judgments about how the value of fetal life should be viewed. Some readers may be surprised, perhaps even offended, by my decision to delay a full discussion of this key issue. I would not defer this question if I agreed with the premise most moralists assume — that the status of fetal life is *the* determining issue in the moral debate about abortion. In fact, I believe that whenever we encounter this view we should be aware that the line of moral reasoning sustaining it is intrinsically sexist. The well-being of a woman and the value of her life plan always must be recognized as of intrinsic value in any appeal to intrinsic value in a moral analysis of abortion. Although I agree that the value of fetal life is an important dimension of the moral question about abortion, it is not the sole or singular issue. Furthermore, I argue that noncoercion in childbearing is a foundational social good.

In a recent book, an able moral philosopher noted the widespread failure of participants on all sides of the abortion debate to justify or "give reasons" for all their claims about the status of fetal life.[24] I concur that this is a serious weakness overall in the moral reasoning in the abortion controversy. I have protested that many Christian ethicists and moral theologians simply assert the equation of fetal life with full human life without defending the position, deferring evidently to established ecclesiastical teaching on the matter. The literature on abortion, especially that written by those in Christian ethics, abounds with evasions and equivocations on this point. Moral objections to abortion are often conveyed merely by reference to the fetus even at conception as a "child" or a "baby," without a word of justification for the use of that language.[25] Proponents of safe, legal abortion, by contrast, often remain silent on the question of the value of fetal life.

Like the issue of criteria for choosing abortion, the question about the status of the fetus is one over which morally sensitive people can and will disagree. The reason most people look "beyond morality" per se to answer this question is that most of us sense the direct relationship between our answer and our envisagements, not only of what constitutes a good community but also of what we most value and hold most sacred. The question of the value of fetal life can indeed be construed as a religious or theological question, although that surely does not mean that we can answer the question dogmatically. It is religious because our answer reveals our deepest sense of bondedness, that is, our most basic sense of connectedness, which is what the Latin term for *religion* originally meant. It is not surprising, therefore, that theological teaching most often comes into play, explicitly or covertly, in the abortion debate. Of course, nonreligious people can reach a reasoned, justifiable judgment about the value of fetal life quite apart from religious sensibility. The answers given by religious communities, however, have a powerful personal and social impact on people's moral sensibilities, often even after people have ceased religious practice or affiliation.

Abortion as a Moral Issue

Through all my years of involvement in pro-choice abortion politics, I have never heard a woman suggest either that a specific abortion decision was a simple one morally or that abortion is a morally indifferent matter. I believe most pro-choice proponents are aware that in the best of all worlds we would have the conditions for greater procreative choice, including safe and reliable means of contraception, which would preclude the necessity for frequent abortions. Men and women would share responsibility not only for procreative choice, including contraception, but also for the overall well-being of children, and there would be no sexual violence or sexual abuse. In such a utopian world, where women's lives were really valued (a world, let us insist, quite unlike the one we know!), it probably would be possible to adhere to an ethic which affirmed that abortions should be resorted to only *in extremis,* to save a mother's life. The frequent trade-off between fetal life and a woman's life, a trade-off no one welcomes, then would be less often necessary. It is a circumstance devoutly to be hoped for. Much later in my argument, I acknowledge that, for several reasons, our society would be better off if we collectively turned our attention to ways in which abortion might be minimized. (This is, of course, a different moral point than arguing that an act of abortion is always wrong.) Given the status of abortion politics and the debate about the morality of abortion, however, it is necessary to belabor the point that we do not live in the best of all possible worlds. It is all the more accurate to contend, therefore, that the existence of a safe, surgical, legal abortion is often a genuine moral blessing, despite a degree of moral ambiguity that needs to be acknowledged.

INTRODUCTORY NOTES ON THEOLOGY AND MORALITY IN THE POLITICAL PROCESS

Recently, a woman who could not secure an abortion when she needed one on financial grounds sought relief from the courts by claiming that her First Amendment rights to religious liberty were being violated by the Hyde Amendment.

Two kinds of appeal are possible to First Amendment protections of religious liberty. One is a free-exercise claim, the contention that a given law makes it impossible for one to conscientiously fulfill a religious obligation. The other, an establishment of religion claim, is based on the charge that a given law constitutes direct governmental endorsement of a particular theological tradition. In the case that became known as *Harris v. McRae,*[26] the litigant, Cora McRae, contested the Hyde Amendment on several constitutional grounds, including both appeals to the First Amendment. McRae maintained that she conscientiously believed that God willed her to have an abortion and that her free exercise of religion was infringed. Her legal brief argued also that, since many religious groups do not believe that abortion per se is wrong, the Hyde legislation in fact established an interpretation of fetal life belonging to a specific theological tradition. Her appeal carried through the Federal District Court in New York, which agreed, among other things, that her right to free exercise of religion had been infringed. During the litigation, many Christian theologians objected to her legal challenge, railing against those female Christians who supported McRae's First Amendment case. The theologians maintained that it was unwise for Christians to support efforts to limit the freedom of religious groups to shape public policy on the abortion issue.[27] The U.S. Supreme Court overturned the decision of the district court, although it rejected the religious liberty issues on technical, not substantive, grounds. In fact, the high court chose to evade the religious freedom issue vis-à-vis abortion. This evasion may be temporary, however, because the question will certainly arise in future litigation.

When the state prohibits all access to abortion, women who conscientiously believe their faith prescribes abortion in a particular case will appeal on free-exercise grounds. Others whose religious belief does not sustain an anti-abortion stance are bound to make appeals related to the establishment of religion clause. The more direct the involvement of churches in politics, the more likely it is that we will all witness frequent invocation of the First Amendment establishment of religion clause.

A major objection to a Christian's invoking the First Amendment in the *Harris v. McRae* case was that the result might make it more difficult for churches to have a positive impact on the formation of social policy on other matters. These objections seem ill placed to me; for, as I have argued already, all advocacy of religious groups should be constrained by respect for others' rationality. Furthermore, current U.S. anti-abortion sentiments are related directly to this nation's specifically Christian history; non-Christians and Christians who dissent deserve First Amendment protections, for this amendment functions to prevent too-easy equations of particular religious groups' views with a general definition of the public good.

If a decision of a Supreme Court turned out to inappropriately restrain church involvement in public policy, the First Amendment free-exercise clause, we may be sure, would be invoked in defense of such church activity. In any case, we may be certain that unless religious groups voluntarily forgo or moderate their efforts to preclude access to abortion, First Amendment claims will multiply. What other recourse is there for people who find their own religious practice or their theological convictions overridden by the law of the land?

I do not see how anyone can deny that abortion has become a deep source of political and religious conflict and will remain so, because the dominant Christian teaching on abortion involves assumptions many Christians as well as other religious groups do not share. Secular people often find the Christian teachings dubious, and the action guides generated by Jewish tradition on these matters differ greatly from Christian teaching.[28] Furthermore, trends in much Protestant Christian theology (and some Roman Catholic theology) are at definite variance with the sort of Christian teaching so profoundly influential in the abortion debate. We who are Christians, in particular, should not be surprised, therefore, to be perceived as speaking in bad faith if we fail to acknowledge publicly how deeply and definitely our specific theologies have shaped public policy disputes around abortion. We do not need to suspend our theological convictions in political conflict, but we need to be honest about the depth of difference that exists between the Christian and Jewish traditions on abortion, for example, or between conservative Christians and nonreligious people, to say nothing of the differences *within* religious traditions.

We must recognize also that whenever an official church teaching leads to any direct political action, social conflict is always heightened. This should not keep us from engaging in direct political action, but we Christians need not be surprised that our active presence intensifies a conflict. Even so, we need to recognize that within contemporary Christianity most major moral disagreements do not divide Christian denominations very much. The various "schools" of theology, or theological movements, currently cut across denominational lines, not between them. Each major line of theological development is, as we will see, clearly related to moral differences. Because these divisions characterize each Christian denomination, official church teachings on abortion *do not tell the whole story, or even very much of it*, about where individual Christians' minds and hearts are on the abortion issue.

Theological and Moral Dimensions

Much public discussion in the abortion controversy exhibits unnecessary ambiguity about how the political, religious, and moral dimensions are interrelated. Competing claims about whether abortion is a moral issue only, and therefore does not involve religious freedom, or a religious issue, or both, are at loggerheads in the public debate. Much ill will has developed around this question because of the failure to acknowledge the divergent assumptions involved. In the interest of avoiding unnecessary ambiguity, I will identify some of my theoretical assumptions.

Too frequently, moral philosophers and theologians ignore precisely the point I emphasized at the onset — that all *moral* conflict has its source in and is generated by what in modern parlance is defined as either "religious" or "political" conflict. Religions, in all their diversity, are born out of specific historical events and crises. Religious communities not only have histories but are rooted in concrete, value-oriented historical commitments generated by social movements.[29] Because intergroup conflict over time always has a religious dimension, religious and political conflicts in any society invariably interweave and become intermeshed. Conversely, in modern societies, where conflict is understood primarily as political, disputes about what social policies should shape our common life and who should make these policies inevitably tap interreligious disagreement. It is not too much to say that historically conflict in society is rooted in internal religious strife and that moral arguments developed historically as an attempt to settle religiopolitical conflict through persuasion rather than by resort to coercion. Commitment to persuasion or reasoned argument is a dimension of the "moral point of view" itself.

To further appreciate why religious, moral, and social systems in any community are so intricately interrelated, we need to recall a major function of religion in society. All living religious systems (that is, religious systems that are practiced) generate specific ways of living or "religious action guides," as they are called in contemporary moral terminology. Adherents of a given religious community are expected to live in a certain way or to follow certain practices. In earlier, simple societies, all of life was encompassed by a community's religious system. Consequently, no distinction was made originally between religious and moral action guides. "Thou shalt have no other gods before me" and "Honor thy father and thy mother," prescriptions of the Decalogue,[30] were both action guides integral to the religious system. Both were understood to express *religious* obligation, and both had concrete behavioral significance. The former meant, literally, "stay away from the nearby altars of other gods"; the latter meant that a person should feed and clothe his parents into their old age. (*His* is appropriate here; female children did not have full autonomous standing as persons or access to social resources.) Though today we would make a distinction between these action guides, identifying the former as a religious commandment and the latter as a moral rule, both at one time were part of an unbroken system of religious obligation. Morality was completely embedded in the religious system.

In societies where the religious system and social system are undifferentiated to the extent that religion holds a monopoly in the community, a differentiation between basic religious action and moral rules will occur only gradually. The distinction is made only after certain action guides begin to encounter opposition from someone in the society. Even in a society with only a single religious system, however, some religious action guides will eventually become a source of conflict. The question arises of whether a given action guide really is necessary to express the "true" faith of that community. Such conflict ultimately generates not only competing theologies but also, in time, something called "unbelief." The possibility of what we call "secularization" — people's option of detaching their identity and their life practice not merely from a religious action guide or theological interpretation but from the *entire belief system of all existing institutionalized systems of religious obligation* — is rooted, then, in religious and moral conflict.[31] In complex and culturally developed societies, where several religious systems coexist, it becomes possible for people to choose to live free of all action guides that express religious obligation. Furthermore, in such a system over time, at least a provisional distinction between religious action guides and moral action guides evolves.

As this happens, the insight begins to flourish that moral reasoning is not *logically* dependent on existing religious belief. Many reasons for behaving morally seem plausible regardless of whether one professes theological conviction. It should be noted, however, that this view of religion and morals as logically discrete entities is quite modern. For centuries in western society the theological and the moral were not understood to be distinguishable on logical grounds.

In societies with widely divergent religious systems and a secular option as well, there are also diverse value commitments and, inevitably, a great deal of religious, moral, and political conflict. Modern societies, including our own, have sought to depoliticize intragroup religious conflict and to partially insulate the religious and political dimensions by establishing constitutional guarantees of religious freedom such as those expressed in the First Amendment. Often honored more in the breach than in the practice, these guarantees are nevertheless aimed at equalizing the social penalties and benefits of being religious and nonreligious. In societies that presuppose the liberal constitutional provisions of religious freedom, it is now customary to draw a rather sharp legal distinction between religious and theological opinion on the one hand and moral conviction on the other because people can hold moral convictions apart from religious beliefs.

In U.S. legal history the precedent for interpretation of what is religious rather than moral has been poorly drawn. It has usually been claimed that a view is theological only when it involves a specific teaching of a church or religious group, especially a conviction about God or theism. In our legal tradition, matters are assumed to relate chiefly to morality and to be, in principle at least, separable from matters of theology if they relate only to human action or if the state has legitimate secular purposes for acting on an issue. Such distinctions never work smoothly, however, because of the continuing pervasive impact of systems of religious obligation on behavior.

Given the public controversy, the claims about whether or why abortion is a religious or a moral issue are increasingly harder to follow. Working assumptions about abortion as a moral or a theological matter become important for their political implications. Although it is impossible to identify all of the differing assumptions, some observations may be helpful as background to our discussion of the morality of abortion. It is important to note that there are at least two quite different assumptions among those who insist that abortion is a moral, *not* a theological issue and also two differing lines of argument among those who advance the claim that abortion is chiefly a theological issue.

Some who contend that abortion is exclusively or primarily a moral issue base their claim on the set of technical, philosophical assumptions discussed above about the logic of moral reasoning. They mean that because human moral discourse itself has a provisional *logical* autonomy in relation to other systems of discourse, a theological teaching, for example, would never in itself be a sufficient ground for justifying a moral judgment. From their perspective, it is possible for society as a whole to reach a moral judgment, regardless of whether a given theological teaching about fetal life is accepted. In this view, the logical autonomy of moral reason is itself sufficient grounds for not concerning ourselves about undue theological influence in the political debate. The unstated premise of this argument is that because all theological convictions must stand a public political test, wisdom will prevail in the end. Even if some argue that abortion is morally wrong because God forbids it or because their church teaches that abortion is contrary to God's will, we need not be concerned about violations of religious freedom. Evidently some theorists trust that logical considerations can shield us from violations of religious freedom. I do not agree. One may question whether there is a confusion in such reasoning between logic and existence.

To argue that abortion as a moral issue has a provisional moral autonomy does not mean that one's religious conviction, if indeed one is religious, can ever be irrelevant to the question. What the acknowledgment of provisional moral autonomy should imply is that religious and nonreligious people alike enter a political debate open to the possibility that in *the ongoing process of reasoning*, moral argument may shift our perspective, altering our judgments of what we should do. To put the point another way, openness to the moral point of view precludes authoritarian appeals or condemnation of actions and policies without good reasons. Many religious people are confused on this point. They believe that to question and to reason demonstrates a *lack* of religious faith. In actuality, to reason is to show respect for human intelligence and "the moral point of view" and also to demonstrate good faith in the search for public policy for our common life.[32] The most able and sophisticated Protestant and Roman Catholic moralists endorse this understanding of the relation of morals and theology overall.[33]

Many who insist that abortion is chiefly a moral issue rather than a theological one, however, are not so sophisticated. In fact, in appealing to the moral autonomy of the abortion question some people actually are invoking *theological opinion and authority*. This anomaly is possible, of course, because much Christian tradition, including present authoritative Roman Catholic moral theology, has endorsed officially the separation between moral and theological teaching while nevertheless maintaining an official unyielding stance on the morality of abortion. Even if Catholic moral theologians make clear that there can be no infallibility in morals, many who stand within this ecclesiastical tradition frequently embrace a theory of separation but join the numerous Protestants who act as if no rational dissent on moral grounds is possible. The present abortion debate is charged with misunderstanding precisely for this reason.

Unlike Protestant conservatives and fundamentalists, Roman Catholics usually contend that their church's teaching on abortion is in no way related to specific, unique theological assumptions. From one perspective, this is true. Roman Catholic teaching on fetal life does not fall technically within its categorization of revelation or definitive theological truth. The Roman hierarchy's authoritative position on fetal life is, as a Roman Catholic who defends it would insist, a rational judgment about a human issue predicated solely on evaluating scientific knowledge. Where there is little de facto room for dissent within a tradition, however, a formal distinction between theological and moral teaching is, in fact, without much force.

What is really at issue is the existential effect of various churches' influence and massive mobilization in the abortion controversy and the empirical effects of their belief systems on public debate. With respect to Roman Catholicism in particular, the technical claim that abortion is about morals, not theology, seems hollow notwith-standing, because we see not the slightest openness to genuine moral debate within the Roman hierarchy itself.[34] While many Roman Catholic moral theologians compare most favorably with Protestant theologians in the quality of their moral reasoning on abortion, the *formal* power of their church has worked to silence direct dissent on this issue. The public resistance to official teaching has come mostly from women and from laicized males and pastoral priests rather than from theologians.[35]

Because it is not the logical distinction between morality and theology but the existential reality of ecclesiastical power expressed through the political process that is at issue, I believe that any religious people who claim not only that abortion is a *moral* issue but also that it is *not* a theological one owe the rest of us the most scrupulous effort to critically scrutinize, and even to provisionally suspend, the authoritative claims of their own tradition. It is a particular concern of my study to show that special care is needed on the abortion issue precisely because Christian teaching on that question has never been exposed to sustained critical review. The degree of certitude on this question among so many Christian theologians, Protestant as well as Catholic, makes even a modest critical sensibility for perceiving genuine moral difference difficult to achieve. If we are to possess this critical sensibility, we cannot close the door on others' moral evaluations until we have weighed them carefully.

And we must never let our own theological traditions insulate us from the need to recognize possible legitimate grounds for moral dissent by those whose traditions differ from ours.

What, then, of those who insist that abortion is, above all (or exclusively), a religious (theological) issue? Most people who make this claim do not, of course, mean to deny that abortion is also and simultaneously a moral issue. On the contrary, what they frequently mean to say is that questions of human life and meaning implicit in abortion run so deep and are so basic that they press the limits of the moral point of view toward those questions traditionally addressed by theology. The majority of people deliberating the morality of abortion are unaware of the technical logical considerations that lead to provisional separation between the theological and moral frames of reference. Besides, the vast majority of Protestants, and most Roman Catholics as well, assume that it is deeply desirable that one's theological conviction inform, if not dictate, one's "normative" ethical point of view — that is, one's standards for what is morally right and good. In the last analysis, of course, what someone means by saying that abortion is *basically* a theological issue will very much depend on the style of theological approach that person embraces. I review some of the implications of these styles in Chapter 3. I will merely say here that conservative Christians often assume that theology ought to preclude reason giving and analysis by prescribing exactly what is right and wrong to do. Liberals, by contrast, tend to understand theology as a shaping and a conditioning, though not a prescriptive, force in relation to moral choice. Liberal theology is grounded in the belief that "new occasions teach new duties"[36] and in the necessity of always questioning the adequacy of past moral wisdom to serve present human well-being. As we will see, incorporating a provisional suspension of theological authority precisely to test for new moral wisdom may be the defining characteristic of theological liberalism at its best.

This positive sense that abortion is, above all, a theological issue is not shared, of course, by all who contend that abortion is a theological matter. Some nonreligious people voice this claim as a complaint because they notice — and object to — the fact that public arguments about abortion are always suffused with assumptions that people probably would not make if they had not been raised in a Christian or other religious tradition. For these people, then, that abortion is, above all, a theological issue constitutes a protest against having someone else's theological presuppositions forced on them. I have considerable sympathy for secular people who feel this way. It would be palpably dishonest not to acknowledge that the public debate around abortion often exudes the atmosphere of a fundamentalist Christian Sunday school. Statements like "The Bible *ought* to dictate what we believe on these matters" or even "Science teaches us that human life begins at conception" are, it seems, good politics these days. Understandably, a nonreligious person will respond, "Science teaches no such thing. Your church does." Blind theological conviction often suffuses the abortion controversy, in large part because many fundamentalist Protestants and conservative Christians and Mormons, like some precritical Catholics, deny any autonomy to morality. Some even accept the notion that a theological authority ought to control what *science* should teach on the question. This is an instance in which, by virtue of a theological authority, a *moral* question is de facto closed. Undermining of the genuine openness inherent in the moral point of view, such theology is antagonistic to ethics. From the moral point of view, doctrinaire theological appeals to science occupy the same status in moral reasoning as indirect and unacknowledged appeals to religious authority — by definition they violate the integrity of moral reasoning. Such dogmatic views have to be set aside, at least provisionally, to give moral reason space in which to operate.

It is essential to stress again that recognition of the provisional autonomy of moral reasoning does not mean we can or should ignore the theological dimensions of teaching on abortion. Theological perspectives on abortion must be considered, weighed, and evaluated along with the moral wisdom of nonreligious people in any moral discussion. What theology cannot have is a privileged position in public discussion.

ORGANIZATION OF THE BOOK

The organization of this book is shaped by its twofold goal. Furthermore, the method that informs the study dictates an "unfamiliar" pattern of organization in what follows. This chapter and Chapter 2 constitute the sketch of my moral assumptions and basic argument in the context of the politics of abortion. The last two chapters, 7 and 8, return to morality and politics and complete the constructive argument. In between, Chapters 3 and 4 address the contemporary theological background of the debate, and Chapters 5 and 6 the historical/cultural background.

A word about why the historical and cultural analysis follows the contemporary theological analysis is needed. Most reigning method-ologies of Christian social ethics would dictate moving to the present from the past. However, the principles of interpretation I employ are predicated on a different method. The structure of the study may puzzle those unfamiliar with liberation ethics. This ethical method presumes that our commitments in the here and now shape our appropriation of the past. The order of study intends to convey that the sort of critical objection I have to most contemporary Christian theological teaching about women and the role of procreation in relation to sexuality (Chapter 3) yields a more critical reading of the Christian past teaching on abortion (Chapter 5).

A more adequate contemporary theological perspective on ethics (Chapter 4) yields a recognition that we need a more fulsome under-standing of the historical and cultural context in which women coped with their fertility (Chapter 6). This awareness must inform contemporary discussions of the morality of abortion, which is why I defer the question of the valuation of fetal life (Chapter 7) until this wider context has been analyzed.

Beyond sketching the main line of my argument for procreative choice, Chapter 2 aims to make clear why a feminist perspective is necessary to formulate the case for procreative choice. Given the widespread hostility toward feminism in our culture, nonfeminist women often reject this claim, while some feminists conclude that it is unnecessary, or even unwise, to approach abortion as a moral issue at all. I believe it is the better part of wisdom to face directly these sorts of reservations among women and also to clarify why attention to the moral issue supports rather than hinders the political struggle around abortion. I also examine some of the ideological pitfalls that reigning political theory creates for us if we accede to it in developing a strong moral case. In making this "good society" argument prior to evaluating the morality of specific acts, I follow the logic, though not the substance, of traditional natural law ethics, including Roman Catholic ethics, that social justice takes precedence over individual preference in our morality.

The contemporary range of Christian theologies reviewed in Chapter 3, specifically in terms of what they teach or imply about women, sexuality, and procreation, enables us to grasp the lingering misogyny that either overtly or ever so covertly conditions Christian sensibilities on abortion. Knowledge of the theological background is a critical and helpful prologue for everyone involved in the politics of abortion. Because we are, *ipso facto*, awash in the sea of theological ethics when the topic of abortion comes up, even non-religious readers may find this chapter helpful.[37]

The sketch in Chapter 4 of some elements of a constructive "liberating" theological alternative may assist us as women in approaching the abortion dilemma without ignoring the genuine dimensions of spirituality and religious accountability in our lives. Many women recognize the need to rethink the moral issue of abortion in a religious context. As a practicing Christian woman, I affirm this widespread desire among women to keep the ethics of the abortion discussion close to its moorings in theological sensibility. This restatement of a feminist Christian theological perspective is included also to sharpen the theological contrast with some of the dominant Christian theological interpretations criticized in Chapter 3. While I believe that the sort of critical and constructive sketches of Christian theological ethics included in Chapters 3 and 4 are helpful in focusing the moral issues, readers who find theological discussions irrelevant may ignore those included here.

Chapter 5 shifts our attention away from contemporary discussion to the history of Christian teaching on abortion. I seek to show that these recent accounts have created the false impression that an overwhelming and homogeneous, well-reasoned anti-abortion tradition has always characterized Christianity. Historically, the Christian teaching on abortion was far from adequate from a woman's viewpoint, but it was not as rigid and uniform as much current Christian teaching suggests.

The concern of Chapter 6 — how the history of procreative choice, and abortion as a means of access to procreative choice, would appear if the focus of our attention historically had not been on what male theological teachers said about it — becomes urgent only from the standpoint of critical consciousness in the present. We are a long way from being able to reconstruct the history of procreation in women's lives. In Chapter 6 I indicate a few outlines of what we know and what we need to take into account to put the abortion question in the proper cultural and historical context. When we begin to grasp the long struggle women have waged for fertility control as one element of the larger effort to secure survival or well-being in history, the abortion dilemma appears in a different light. Failure to set this moral discussion within the history of the social control of women has flawed even some very elegant philosophical analyses of abortion and obscured understanding of the present vitriolic character of the controversy. I have intentionally deferred to Chapter 7 a specific discussion of the morality of abortion as an act to underscore this point. The evaluation of fetal life is a difficult question, but I make a case that early abortion should never be understood as homicide.

In the conclusion of the book, I return to our political situation and address the question of what constitutes a sound social policy about abortion. Social policy questions are the lifeblood of morality. A society's morality is always present, embedded in and expressed through its social practices. Until we understand the consequences of enforced childbearing for women, it is doubtful whether we will understand, even appreciate, abortion as a genuinely serious moral dilemma, not just for individual women but for the entire society. A central question of this last chapter is whether, and to what extent, morally concerned people can find common ground for social policy even when we make different judgments about the morality of abortion as an act. There have been calls to compromise, but not often from those who appreciate the costs to women of recriminalizing abortion. Can we really work together to enhance and deepen respect for human life, including female human life, in this society? If we are to develop an adequate spirit of compromise, however, we must begin by acknowledging, contrary to the claims of the New Right, that abortion on demand is *not* now the law of the land. Much bad faith has been generated in the politics of abortion by abortion opponents' misrepresentation of the status quo.

If one focuses only on the present social policy conflict around abortion, political compromise seems difficult. The difficulty, it should be emphasized again, resides as much in differing perceptions of what abortion *is* and in genuine moral conflict over it as in the rigidity, ill will, or zeal of those who are at odds on the issue. On the one hand, a woman denied access to an abortion she wants is, de facto, *compelled to childbearing against her will.* On the other hand, for those who believe that a fetal life is *a* human being from conception or from the implantation of the genetic code, termination of pregnancy is *always* homicide, even if sometimes justified, or murder. Proposals for compromise almost invariably obscure the either/or nature of the act itself as defined by the controversy. However, if together we recognize and embrace a broader positive social agenda *for enhancing procreative choice,* we may begin to find lines of strategy that will simultaneously bring about both less reliance on abortion and less resort to coercion of women and enforced childbearing. Nothing less, I argue, would be a genuine moral compromise.

The social policy I propose is highly utopic. Even to imagine a society that would function to prevent a trade-off between fetal life and women's well-being is difficult. I stress throughout that we do not live in a society that cares very much either for the well-being of women or for most of the children women actually bear, much less one that values fetal life. Nor does this society confer worth upon men who are not among the powerful. I insist that some of the roots of these moral ills, including our alienation from and lack of respect for each other, lie in our deep-seated negative attitudes toward women. Chapter 8 also expresses my conviction that anyone who believes that flatly outlawing safe, legal abortion will correct this monstrous moral state of affairs is deeply deluded.

2

The Morality of Procreative Choice

CONSTRUCTING THE MORAL DIMENSIONS OF PROCREATIVE CHOICE: THE TENSIONS AMONG WOMEN

Two separate and antagonistic ideological trends threaten women's capacity to come to grips with the morality of abortion and to formulate an adequate ethic of procreative choice. Addressing the moral meaning of procreative choice in women's lives is the necessary prelude to the evaluation of abortion. Yet sensibilities widely shared by two different groups of women militate against our entering into crucial dialogue on this issue and launching the task of moral reconceptualization. It is necessary, therefore, to unravel the tensions that make it difficult for women to bring abortion into focus as a moral question prior to reconceiving the morality of procreative choice.

One concern, widely voiced by men but also by some women relatively unalienated by the presumed "traditional" role of motherhood, is that any critique of dominant Christian teaching, including abortion ethics, is hostile not only toward men but also toward those women who choose and value marriage and motherhood as central to their lives. The propagandistic claims of the political New Right, cultivating and playing on such fears,[1] have been packaged to convince women that the women's movement agenda, including the pro-choice stance, poses a serious threat to their identity and lifestyle. There are, after all, millions of women in our society who, if they regret anything about their own life choices, certainly do not regret their decision to use their procreative power, personal energies, and creativity to bear children and to make a home for a family.[2]

The propaganda intentionally generated by the New Right to discredit feminism and to link it to those presumed forces currently "destroying" family values is surely one reason why many women have grown wary of feminism. Economic depression has also reinforced the climate of anxiety now widespread among women. Few people pause to notice that the argument that political and social equality weakens "family values" is tantamount to confirming that existing family structure is predicated on social inequality and the exploitation of women and that its values are inherently inimical to women's worth.

The transparent propaganda of the New Right, however, is perhaps no more dangerous than the more subtle, yet pervasive, attack on "feminism" now offered as daily fare in the media and in some "respectable" journals. This more subtle attack equates feminism with man-hating and implies that any strong and clear claim for women's rights results from women's lack of "femininity" and their neuroticism. When so-called reputable major magazines announce, and celebrate, "the death of the women's movement" or openly satirize women struggling to overcome historic oppression, printing without rejoinder, for example, an attack on the "trendiness" of ordaining women clergy,[3] or when personal attacks are made against well-known and courageous feminists, it is not surprising that many women get the (intended) message that other women — that is, feminists — threaten their well-being. Women whose lives have followed a more traditional bent and who have experienced their lives as at least moderately secure and fulfilling find themselves avoiding identification with "feminists" as extreme or perhaps "too radical." In actuality, these women are often far more vulnerable socially and economically than they perceive.

It is hard for many people, including women whose energies have been directed toward motherhood and homemaking, to entertain the possibility that this process of discrediting feminism *is itself an intentional effort to divert the pace of social change away from greater justice for all women.* The multifaceted pressures generated by the women's movement in the last decade have gone well beyond the demand that women receive equal pay for equal work. Feminism spawned the much more radical notion that women's bodies and all of women's work — including housework and child care — should be valued as much as men's lives and work are valued.[4] The effects of these convictions, translated into social practice, would be sufficient to threaten the existing structures of privilege and patterns of distribution of wealth in this society. Hence the need among dominant males and the women they have subjugated to turn back these demands for deep and genuine social equality for women. This leads to the "put-down" of a full, consistent women's liberation agenda. It is important to appreciate in this connection the extent to which procreative choice, and legal abortion as its guarantor, is fundamental to all other justice claims that women make. Failure to see this point may mean a major historical setback for women's struggle for justice. If the availability of safe, legal abortion can be isolated and split off as somehow a "more radical" issue than, for example, the Equal Rights Amendment, women who advocate social equality will witness the very effective derailment of their long-term agenda. It is crucial to develop the understanding that women's support for a so-called pro-life social policy option has the objective result of placing unbearable pressure on other women whose life situations are less favorable, if more typical of the lot of women generally. Many women, however, will change neither their moral position about abortion nor their attitudes toward abortion politics until they are persuaded that a pro-choice position is grounded in a deeper, stronger, more caring moral vision than the anti-abortion political option now articulated with such apparent ethical passion. The outlook of many women who do not yet see the moral wisdom of a pro-choice social policy, for them as well as for all women, will change only as we attempt to adequately frame our case for procreative choice as a moral claim.

The women who embrace and celebrate their own and other women's devotion to childbearing have little difficulty appreciating why abortion is a moral issue, because they recognize and cherish the deep and fundamental values at stake in these decisions. However much some of these women may fail to recognize the extent of social injustice toward women as a group, they well understand and sympathize with the claim that the abortion controversy is a moral one. It is not surprising that they sometimes identify with public leaders who favor curtailing legal abortion, because such politicians frequently mask their position by moral appeals to "family values." The conviction of the "more traditional" women that abortion is a moral issue can be a strong resource for our collective struggle to formulate an adequate ethic of reproductive freedom, provided that we all clarify the concrete connections between procreative choice and social well-being. Whenever we forget traditional women's sensitivity to the value of childbearing and nurturing, we make it harder to reach these women, who are so important to the cause of procreative choice. It is they, after all, who have had the greatest actual degree of experience with the *benefits* of procreative choice. Many such women have received the strong family and social support for the positive exercise of procreative power that makes childbearing and childrearing a joyful experience.

It would be naive, however, to imagine that powerful interests in this society wish women to possess the power of genuine procreative choice. All present proposals for a so-called pro-life (or anti-abortion) social policy involve making the state the controller of procreation. This social policy of state control of women's procreative power almost invariably is favored precisely by people otherwise professing the ideology that state interference in the "private" lives of citizens is wrong! Furthermore, zeal for increased military spending and for capital punishment more often than not thrives among legislators most eager to prevent all legal abortion.[5] Nothing makes clearer how little women count as full, valued persons or as competent moral agents than this dramatic ideological inconsistency on the part of so many anti-abortion advocates. On the one hand they endorse unquestioningly a laissez-faire economic doctrine that assumes (decades of contrary experience notwithstanding) that unrestricted economic activity produces optimal social welfare and that state intervention in the economy for the purpose of justice is a great evil. Simultaneously they insist that the state must intervene to secure sexual conformity and, above all, "procreative morality" — that is, to control women's distinctive social power. This selective ideology about the role of the state is characteristic of many leaders in this society, who espouse whatever social ideology is necessary to justify the perpetuation of their power. It is also critical that women recognize how the active discrediting of the women's movement works to suppress women's potential to work together for all social change, not merely to control procreation. What feminism is and always has been about is *expanding the concrete range of choices available to all women* — to women as a group and to women as individuals.

We must understand, as we discuss the ethics of procreative choice and the morality of abortion, the connection between women's subjugation, historically, and the efforts of male-dominated social institutions and systems to control the critical human social power of procreation. Women's emancipation depends personally and collectively on how societies choose to shape this power. We cannot eschew a feminist analysis without obscuring the real meaning and moral significance of the controversy at hand. As feminist scholars have begun the long, slow, and difficult task of reconstructing the real but suppressed history of women's contribution to human culture and society, it has become evident that in most societies frequent, fundamental social tension has existed between women's and men's cultures precisely over the issue of fertility control. While the origins of the many institutions supporting and maintaining male superiority throughout human history are far from obvious, much speculation about the impetus for patriarchalization focuses on women's power of reproduction, and the threat it posed, as the primary factor in male efforts to channel and control women's lives in various ways.[6] It is also becoming clear, even at this early stage of feminist historical scholarship, that prior to the rise of modern society, even in most male-dominated societies, women's culture frequently harbored whatever knowledge and control were available to shape procreation, often in spite of male-articulated moral prescriptions. A few ancient societies, like modern western societies, developed male-controlled orders of healers, or medical elites, to oversee women's procreation, but in most cultures, including our own until the comparatively recent rise of the medical profession, the power of procreative control was embedded in women's culture and was often channeled by women without undue interference.[7]

We tend to think of modern society as particularly enlightened in matters of procreation. To be sure, modern medical knowledge and practice have delivered us from some of the harsh capriciousness of most women's fertility, but we cannot let this fact obscure another, harsh truth — that the social organization of modern advanced industrial societies, including the professionalization of health care, has worked to destroy women's culture and, with it, many traditional supports both for childbearing and for procreative control previously developed by women and shared intergenerationally. Much female cultural and social power has been lost and many women's support networks displaced in this process. The isolated woman in the nuclear family is, *perhaps more than any other woman in history*, at the mercy of the knowledge and empathy (or lack of it) of an as-yet male-dominated medical profession when it comes to understanding her fertility and its control.[8]

Women, who may make diverse life choices about their procreative power, still need to unite in appreciation of what they have in common. However they view their own biological fertility, freedom in their lives will have no concrete meaning apart from the socially supported conditions that enable them to shape that fertility. Furthermore, a genuine degree of freedom from coercion is important to every woman. This principle of noncoercion could be as critical for women who wish to center their lives in childbearing as for those who do not. Biomedical research into the processes of reproduction has reached a point where some experimenters actually anticipate the day when a biological mother may no longer be necessary to human reproduction. One scientist has authored a work entitled *The Obsolete Mother,* and another has celebrated the prospect of gestation outside the womb as the means by which, at last, males can guarantee that their offspring are their own. Motherhood in our society may decline in value, not because some women choose other options but because technological innovation makes women expendable in the procreative process.[9] Women who have never suffered the pressures of childbearing nevertheless can come to grasp the broader social realities that account for other women's suffering around these issues.

Perhaps this is why women, despite their strong identification with motherhood, always reveal some ambivalence in studies that give them an opportunity to confidentially disclose their real feelings about childbearing. A considerable number of women acknowledge some regret about *whatever* choices they make.[10] And because the formidable social construction of women's lives beckons us to "celebrate motherhood," only later in life do myriad women recognize that their childbearing was not chosen, that it was the result of pervasive social pressure that, they see in retrospect, they had no ability to refuse at the time. No one can deny that traditional female socialization tends to undermine a woman's capacity to know clearly what she wants for herself. Women frequently drift into motherhood only to discover after the fact the high social cost of mothering. This does not mean that such women regret having borne their children. Most live into their ambivalence and overcome it. Many young women also experience their very first, life-changing coming of age when they find themselves unexpectedly pregnant; for many, pregnancy is their first genuine and realistic encounter with adult reality.[11] That some women's first real awareness of the need to take charge of their lives, in the face of very limited social options, comes from unwanted pregnancy is sad. Such psychological innocence is rooted both in female socialization and in young women's social powerlessness.[12] Support for developing psychological maturity is no easier for women, even affluent women, to achieve than is support for social justice. We have reason to be grateful that safe, legal abortion provides at least the *negative* means of assuring the elements of choice, given that far too many of us must still drift into maturity through crisis surrounding our procreative capacity.

To defend the morality of procreative choice for women is not to deny reverence toward or appreciation for many women's deep commitment to childbearing and child nurturance. It does ask that women collectively come to understand that genuine choice with respect to procreative power (not simply choice for the sake of choice) is a necessary condition of *any and all* women's human fulfillment. When the day comes that the decision to bear a child, for all women, is a moral choice — that is, a deliberated, thoughtful decision to act for the enhancement of our own and our society's well-being with full responsibility for all the implications of that action — then and only then, the human liberation of women will be a reality.

FEMINIST RESISTANCE TO ABORTION AS A MORAL ISSUE

A second ideological trend also threatens women's reassessment of the morality of procreative choice. Because conventional moralists have not taken women's lives into account, some women have rejected any moral analysis out of hand. These women see clearly that procreative choice is a necessary condition both for ending women's historical subjugation and for individual women's well-being. But they reject the importance of placing the abortion question, and the social policy issues surrounding it, in a moral context.[13] That women, including some critically oriented feminist women, are skeptical of developing a moral case for abortion is not surprising, given many moralists' hostility to feminism. There are many reasons why such reluctance has evolved and why, on the surface, it makes sense. A certain skepticism about reigning moral wisdom relating to women's lives is certainly in order. A distinguished male philosopher recently conceded that only white males are taken seriously because

> the dominant ideology contains the belief that white males are the one group in society whose members are able to be genuinely detached and objective when it comes to things like an understanding of the place of race and sex in the culture.[14]

Now, however, a few women reverse the ideology: morality is male-generated and therefore no intellectual fairness can be expected where women's lives are concerned.

In addition, many in our culture equate any concern for "morality" with sex-negative and rigid, prohibitory attitudes. Sometimes the term *morality* is used as a euphemism for "traditional rules governing sexuality." Likewise, anti-abortionist "moral" arguments have not been free of the suggestion that the sexual freedom assured for women by the availability of abortion is one of the "moral evils" that must be ended. Women who have embraced the feminist procreative agenda often have been eager to escape the corroding effect of this sex-negative moralism. Furthermore, the either/or split in traditional ethics between personal well-being and moral obligation, often understood as referring only to obligations to others or "other regardingness," encourages women to believe that concern for one's own well-being as a sexual person has nothing to do with morality. These women understand that contraceptive control is one condition, among several, necessary to women's enjoyment of their sexuality, apart from its procreative consequences. But given the dualism of some moral theory, women conclude that the question of personal well-being is unrelated to morality. Even feminists sometimes fail to recognize that sexual expression should be understood as a *positive* moral good that contributes to personal self-respect and dignity. We need to recognize that sexual self-determination is a right, and sexual pleasure is a foundational value that enhances human well-being and self-respect. It is incumbent upon feminists to lead the way in challenging any equation of morality with sex-negative moralism. Failure to do so will prolong the effort to shape a powerful case for the morality of abortion and for the pro-choice social policy women need. In spite of the social trends aimed, under the guise of morality, at reinforcing sexually repressive attitudes toward women who break with traditional patterns of dependence on men, some recent moral, philosophical, and theological work supports transcending the sex-negative bias of past academic and ecclesiastical opinion.[15] The full connection between the sex-negativity of these traditions and their views on abortion has not been explored satisfactorily, however.[16]

Many philosophers and theologians, although decrying gender inequality, still unconsciously assume that women's lives should express a different moral norm than men's, that women should exemplify moral purity and self-sacrifice, whereas men may live by the more minimal rational standards of moral obligation. We must assert that perfection and self-sacrifice are never taken to be a day-to-day moral requirement for any moral agent except, it would seem, a pregnant woman.

The abortion issue is but one illustration of what happens when this popular equation of morality with sexually restrictive attitudes goes unchallenged and is given free reign. To their regret, many theological liberals are discovering belatedly that failure to challenge a simple-minded equation of morality and sexual rigidity can be costly. Recent ecclesiastical debates on homosexuality have actually delivered some denominations into the control of those who define morality in a personalistic, nonsocial way. Thinking to evade divisive conflict, Christian liberals have sidestepped the sexuality issue and ended up giving highly organized, strong neoconservative groups the power to reshape the social justice agendas of their churches. It would be ironic, and genuinely dangerous, to have many feminists, usually among the most humanly open and sensitive persons in society, define themselves out of a moral debate that urgently requires their participation because they unwittingly concede the field to neoconservative, individualistic assumptions about morality.

A further reason why some women are doubtful about formulating their demands for legal abortion as *moral* claims derives from the prevalent confusion about how moral claims relate to religious conviction. Taking at face value the claim that theology grounds teaching on abortion, they feel forced to forgo moral defense of their position. As we will see, some religious groups whose historical praxis has been most oppressive to women frequently tend to *equate* morality and religion. Because of the close identification of fundamentalist and neoconservative theology with moral certitude about abortion, some people give the moral point of view over to such zealots. Young women, in particular, observe the direct existential correlation between the degree of a religious group's discrimination against women and its degree of unqualified moral condemnation of abortion and reject not only religion but morality. I have made clear already that any such close association, even identification, of religion and morality pains many secular moral philosophers as well as a considerable number of other persons of moral passion who do not practice religion but who believe that their morality does not suffer by comparison to the practice of religious people.[17] Even so, the impression persists that a strong commitment to women's rights in particular forces us out of both religious and moral frames of reference. Women go through a process of secularization in relation to religion that also comes to be experienced as a release from morality.

What many women assume, with some validity, is that the politics of feminism — that is, the historical agenda of the women's liberation movement — has to move ahead regardless of reigning moral justifications, because both morality and religion are male-controlled social institutions. They believe that no matter how censorious establishment moralists are, women's historical struggle for liberation must proceed. They expect women who press for full dignity to be denounced under existing mores and social conventions and to be found wanting morally no matter what they do. No one who knows the history of feminism will deny that those who feel this way have much historical precedent on their side.

If, however, women are to undertake the collective task of revisioning the morality of procreative choice, and of legal abortion as a dimension of that choice, we need both the clarity of a critical feminist analysis concerning procreative choice and the constructive wisdom gained from values learned in childrearing. In spite of some good reasons to be cautious about moral entanglements, moral legitimacy needs to be wrested from those who oppose procreative choice. Those who press moral claims while ignoring the concrete well-being of people do not deserve to control the definition of "morality." Nor do those who dismiss or make light of women's need for emancipation deserve the sanction or legitimacy of either religion or morality. It is far too late for anyone to deny the truthfulness of protests against antiwoman bias in established religious and moral traditions, especially as these traditions have shaped views of sexuality, procreation, and abortion.

THE BASIC MORAL ARGUMENTS
FOR PROCREATIVE CHOICE

Dispelling the myth of moral superiority on the so-called pro-life side of the abortion debate commits us to develop our moral arguments more compellingly and also to evaluate critically existing moral theory and moral theology as they bear on the abortion controversy. I must repeat that unless procreative choice is understood as a desirable historical possibility substantively conducive to every woman's well-being, all debate regarding abortion is morally skewed from the outset. Yet no question is more neglected in moral evaluation of abortion than the prior question of whether women should have procreative choice. To say that this is the prior issue is to fly fiercely in the face of the precedent set by earlier discussions of the morality of abortion. Unbelievable as it may seem, many Christian ethicists, *including* proponents of legal abortion, would prefer to ignore or even suppress the fact that abortion is a birth control method. Others imply precisely that women should be condemned for using abortion as a means of birth control.[18] Only when we begin to perceive the importance of procreative choice in women's lives and to face the limitations of other contraception do we have a full context for realizing what it means to deny women access to legal abortion. We can then also better understand why the issue of abortion must never be separated morally from other issues related to the morality of procreative choice, including sterilization abuse, too-ready resort to unnecessary hysterectomies,[19] and broader issues of women's health care and social well-being. That efforts to deny women access to abortion are widely interpreted as acts of moral sanctity while widespread patterns of sterilization abuse go unnoticed[20] bespeaks the ease with which our society distorts the reality of women's lives.

I insisted earlier on the methodological point that any evaluation of a human act that misrepresents its full meaning in human life deserves to be faulted as moral abstractionism. Yet few moralists even recognize that with respect to abortion women do not, in the first instance, choose it at all. Rather, mature women choose to shape their own procreative power within a meaningful life plan. The decision for or against abortion arises either from a failure in such rational life planning owing to circumstances outside a woman's control or from a failure to take responsibility for contraception. Abstractionism in relation to the concrete reality of women's lives is characteristic of much western intellectual life but is overcome when the dilemmas that characterize men's lives are the focus of moral reasoning. Over the centuries, for example, Christian moral theologians have wrestled with the question of the use of violence in war — the so-called just-war issue — and in the process they have demonstrated a remarkable capacity for empathy toward the dilemmas of choice that rulers face in war.[21] They demonstrate no such empathetic casuistry in relation to women's options in the abortion dilemma, which is why I insist that ignoring the life circumstances out of which a woman confronts an abortion dilemma is inherently antifemale, regardless of whether the reasoner intends such gender-negative consequences.

Human pregnancy is in some respects *sui generis* as a human experience. To say that is to acknowledge that pregnancy is not precisely analogous to other human experiences either culturally or biologically.[22] It is a long, complex biological process that, over time, produces a human life. In the process, a woman's body becomes the mediative vehicle for the emergence of that new life. This biological process requires a woman's cooperation. She must adjust her activities, take special care with her diet and her health, and in myriad other ways alter her lifestyle to bring the pregnancy to a successful outcome. There is always genuine physical risk involved and, in some cases, actual physical danger to the pregnant woman, but we must recognize that women bear not only the biological risks but also the cultural, social, and economic consequences of pregnancy and childbearing.

As a result, the misrepresentation of abortion at the level of women's personal lives turns out to be only a minor part of the problem. The distortion in the way the individual dilemma is interpreted is repeated and reinforced at the collective, historical level. Very little written about abortion incorporates a recognition of the distinctive character of the human reproductive process, not merely as a biological reality but also as a historical and cultural one. I have never read a word of moral discussion on abortion that recognizes the complex history of women's efforts to control and shape their own power of reproduction. That few moral philosophers or moral theologians have paid attention to the role of the "politics of reproduction" in human history is not surprising given the unacknowledged depth of antifemale bias in the dominant intellectual tradition. However male moralists respond on this matter, we must underscore the fatefulness for our lives of this failure to set the act of abortion in its proper human context.

There are, of course, no uncontestable grounds for moral claims, just as there are many ways to frame this call for procreative choice so integral to the global "rising of women." I believe, however, that the strongest possible moral argument will focus in the two directions already identified. On the one hand, we should take a cue from our European feminist sisters, especially committed Italian women, who comprehend the importance of appealing to foundational social justice considerations in seeking legal abortion.[23] To rest a claim morally on social justice criteria means that the matter at hand is arguably a part of the basic conditions needed for a good society because they are foundational for the well-being of people. Learning from the wisdom of their Catholic heritage, these European women recognized that the strongest moral grounding for legal abortion rests in the claim that any society has a positive moral obligation to support the conditions for women's well-being. That the basic conditions needed to pursue our own life plans are moral requirements of the just society has been widely recognized in religious ethics and moral philosophy. There is *nothing controversial* about this claim that a good society is one that promotes conditions for this enhancement.

The inability of many people to see that procreative choice is conditional to women's social well-being reflects a failure of moral imagination and empathy. Many simply cannot "take the role of the other"[24] when this involves identifying positively with women's lives. Happily, a few moralists have seen the moral importance of noncoercion in childbearing. Their hypothesis is that if we all had general knowledge of the nature of childbearing prior to awareness of who we would be in society, we would choose to reject social coercion in procreation as a condition for women's lives. It is important to emphasize that pondering the conditions for a good society along these lines helps us see that anyone who faced life with the prospect of childbearing would choose rules accordingly and elect procreative choice. Jewish moral philosopher Ronald Green has contended rightly that men and women alike would opt for a policy of procreative choice as the basis of childbearing if they had to determine the rules for a good society without knowing whether they would be female or male in that society.[25]

Green's sort of contractualist argument for determining the rules for a good society has high standing among philosophical moralists today. The basic notion underlying this approach is that one way to clarify the criteria for social justice is to return ourselves in our imagination to an "original position" in which together we choose rules for society without foreknowledge of what our own concrete situation in that society would be. This paradigm of moral reasoning has been advanced by the work of moral philosopher John Rawls, especially in his much-heralded *Theory of Justice*.[26] This view that rational moral choice should conform to principles we would agree to disinterestedly — in an "original position," free of privilege, under conditions uncorrupted by concrete or specific self-interest — is now widely accepted in moral theory. I share the view that envisaging moral rules for a good society without specific knowledge of who we might be in that society is *one* good way to clarify our sense of foundational moral requirements — that is, our criteria for social justice. It is important to recognize that under the best available conception of disinterestedness in ethics, procreative choice makes sense as a foundational social justice claim. It is a moral ideal that stands the test of current notions of moral rationality.

We need not embrace the current certitude of much moral philosophy that disinterestedness is the most important ingredient or characteristic of moral reason to grasp the importance of such "original position" arguments. In fact, a more adequate perspective on moral reason enables us to see that the greatest value of such arguments is that they do not detach us from specific interest or elevate disinterestedness per se. Rather, they invite our interest in positive moral value, that is, our investment in a fair society in which nobody would be trapped at an irrevocable disadvantage. Rawls and other contractualists like Green who seek to liberate us from the bias of individual self-interest have in fact helped us re-vision the *common* good. They propose a creative method that encourages us to think together about what a fair or just society would entail and that requires an empathy too few of us attempt in evaluating actions. Proceeding this way in considering procreative choice forces men and women alike to enter sympathetically into the life situation of one faced with unwanted pregnancy, to feel as she feels, and to face what she faces. It was just such basic social justice or good society arguments that enabled our Italian sisters, facing the implacable opposition of their church, to nevertheless advance claims for procreative choice persuasively and to convince a clear majority of Italians that they, not the Roman hierarchy, had moral right on their side.

In spite of the strength of original position appeals, however, it is critical not to let our moral case for abortion rest exclusively on abstract, contractualist claims about principles or views of rational choice limited to norms of disinterestedness.[27] Our other line of reasoning must be a strong utilitarian argument emphasizing the actual social vulnerability of women, one rooted in a concrete history of subjugation. This reality also makes the availability of abortion absolutely critical morally. No concern for social justice is genuine if it does not lie close to concrete historical consequences. To enhance the "quality of life" of a society by adopting policies whose consequences deteriorate the life conditions of "the fifty-one percent minority"[28] is bizarre. Regardless of whether people concur that procreative choice falls within the rubric of a good society, we need to challenge them to apprehend the concrete reality of women's historical oppression, especially in relation to childbearing.

As I have already observed, in this nation, and especially elsewhere on the planet Earth, the conditions for procreative choice are hardly available. In the United States, the defeat of the ERA should serve as a continuous reminder that not even formal legal equality between men and women is desired by the powers that be. And formal legal considerations aside, the economic and political inequality between men and women is marked; many recent gains by women are being reversed rapidly. The reality of most women's lives everywhere is constrained by severe economic inequity and by the strong cultural pressures reinforcing inferiority, to which I have already alluded. Given contemporary society's operative values and social dynamics, more and more children born today are very likely to be dependent solely on their mother's emotional and economic support. We need to stress this de facto reality, which includes the fact that most women already live under strong and often coercive pressures either for or against childbearing. It is also surely time to reject the innuendo that most women currently make quick decisions about abortion and casually elect abortion in a morally irresponsible fashion. Such claims really deserve branding as arrogant moralism, especially in light of the contrasting track records of men and of women in relation to moral values and moral concerns overall.

While a majority of people in American society favor some degree of "choice" for women in childbearing, apparently far fewer recognize the precariousness of the social conditions necessary to undergird genuine choice or the breadth and depth of subtle coercive factors, whether for or against choice. My earlier discussion should have made it obvious that many women choose abortion reluctantly in situations of marginal desperation, recognizing realistically that they cannot maintain conditions for their own and a dependent child's survival given the social and economic constraints governing their lives. Some women are overtly pressured, or indirectly lured, into choosing sterilization as a nonreversible means of birth control.[29] Still other women bear children they do not want, or only half-desire, because in a community hostile to any other fate for them, the stigma of abortion would be greater than they could bear. And others choose abortion as a birth control method of last resort because, in a society still contemptuous of women's right to contraception and to active sexuality, they do not have access to safer, more reliable means of contraception. Still others, especially young women, legitimately fear familial and social reprisals or psychological abuse for seeking contraception at all.

Those who continue to claim that feminist argument is morally irrelevant demonstrate contempt for women's lives. A wise ethic protests the moral myopia of any ethical theory incapable of integrating world historical data into its analysis. Of course these lines of argument make sense only to those whose moral sensibilities encompass a concrete refusal of the ancient trivialization of women's lives. Frequently we reach the limits of moral argument precisely because social pressures invite us to relinquish the task of transforming and deepening moral value. And yet it is the confrontation with perpetual moral insensibility that pushes people "beyond morality" into pragmatic and morally cynical politics. Understandably, then, the present political conflict over abortion tempts us to a political stance of "win at any cost." Even as we pursue a vigorous and well-organized strategy for procreative choice, we need to probe continuously the implications of our moral stance for our politics and to increase our sensitivity to the strengths and limits of the ideologies at work in the political arena.

THE MORAL DIMENSIONS OF PRO-CHOICE POLITICAL CLAIMS

The still widely held view that anti-abortion proponents have a monopoly on the moral factors in the abortion controversy remains not merely a substantive moral problem but a strategic one as well. To be sure, part of the "moral legitimacy" adhering to the anti-abortion position rests simply in the way that any appeal to established moral tradition resounds. Such appeals are designed to trigger and restore our confidence in a certain moral weight foundational to established traditions and born of the power of social convention. Ruling ideologies invariably are expressed in an array of religio-moral terminology. An adequate sociology of knowledge discloses[30] that at the outset of any moral conflict, legitimacy invariably appears to reside with the dictates of propriety set by dominant groups within a society.

Gaining perspective on the centuries of ideology generated by male-dominated institutions is not easy. Even many women still believe at a subconscious level that unless women's lives are constrained

by unquestioned and unquarreling assent to our so-called natural destiny — that is, our biological role as childbearers — we will become in
some way "defective" as women. These male-generated theories
claiming that our procreative power is literally our "essence" or
"nature" have become very much a part of who we feel we ought to be.

Clarifying the connections between our socio-moral vision and the
so-called pro-choice political position is especially urgent, precisely
because feminist moral values — those that affirm and respect
women's well-being — have deep implications for all of our lives. As a
result, most women sense that a pro-choice political agenda cannot
be one-issue politics. Equally urgent is that more women come to
appreciate that the considerable power of feminism in the lives of contemporary women is rooted not, as some have claimed, in women's
growing selfishness, preoccupation with self, or even narcissism[31]
but in women's growing self-respect. This self-respect has been
generated over against the many women-negating values, which also
and simultaneously bespeak antihuman values long expressed in the
dominant society. Women, especially feminists, are the ones rightly
demanding a more integrated approach to all of human life, seeking
social policies that place humane values and personal worth at the
center of both our interpersonal relations and our public life. The
slogan "The personal is the political" has meant, among other things,
that we need to seek our social and political ends in a way consistent
with the personal values we espouse; it also means that nothing can
be good for society that concretely negates people.

Because our "moral intuitions" have implications not only for how
we develop our ethics but also for how we struggle for procreative
choice, it is well to observe how deeply feminist conviction runs
counter to prevailing political "wisdom." It is deeply ingrained in the
ethos of this society that good politics permit or even require moral
posturing, but when push comes to shove one should fight for one's
political goals on any terms, giving no quarter to moral considerations. I join many other feminists in identifying this split between
politics and morality as a symptom of patriarchal consciousness.
Many of us believe, probably correctly, that women's lives historically
have been less relationally brutal than men's because women as a
group have not yet capitulated to such deep, value-denying dualism.
Many women would forgo politics rather than be implicated in this
separation.

Some adherents of procreative choice, especially men accepting the political "realist" line, have resorted to morally dubious arguments in support of a pro-choice position. These crass utilitarian arguments take the form, for example, of urging that the availability of legal abortion is desirable because it lowers welfare costs and lightens taxpayers' burdens in caring for the poor or because it reduces illegitimacy. There is surely some political mileage to be gained from the use of such covert racist appeals or appeals to class privilege. Those who are morally serious about the struggle for human liberation, however, are wise to assume that such arguments turn out, in the long run, to be bad politics. Gaining support for abortion by reinforcing race and class hostility is costly to our sense of polis and community, and it further injures many of the very women most desperately in need of conditions for procreative choice. Furthermore, even if crass utilitarian arguments prove effective in the short run, we need to remember that at the moment the other side controls the moral momentum on the issue; it is this reality, not permeable by such arguments, that must shift. Procreative choice is a morally right position because it creates conditions essential to the well-being of over half the human species, not because it allows any of us to live free of our social obligation to provide for the common welfare, especially that of less advantaged people.

The fact remains that political pragmatism — that is, appeal to whatever arguments "work" in political debate — will always characterize good politics for dominant groups in a society. But this sort of short-term expediency is never an option for marginalized, disenfranchised, and disadvantaged citizens in any society; moral power is one of the deepest resources available to subjugated and oppressed people. Women are collectively the most disadvantaged people *within* their own communities and social groups, and their moral courage, often unnoticed, has been decisive for their communities' very survival. We need to make a political case that interrelates the need for legal abortion and the concrete pressures of racial-ethnic and all poor women's lives. The double and triple jeopardy of gender, race, and class must be central to our approach.[32] Our political goal will be genuinely secure only when more people grasp that we cannot prohibit legal, elective, surgical abortions without further violating the well-being of the vast majority of women and the children they bear, especially those most socially vulnerable because of other historic patterns of oppression.

IDEOLOGICAL PITFALLS IN FEMINIST POLITICAL ARGUMENT

One reason our political arguments about abortion fail to cohere to the outlines of a social-justice moral argument such as the one I have sketched is that politically involved women, like most men in political debate, adopt certain ideological assumptions of male-generated political theory without sufficient critical scrutiny. Liberal or mainstream feminism has not struggled deeply enough with the moral implications of dominant political rhetoric.

A look at the political and legal context of the discussion quickly reveals that the debate around abortion is shaped, obviously enough, by terminology appropriate to the nation's political and legal traditions. We need to be aware, however, that the forms of rhetoric appropriate to politics, law, and morals are not, to say the least, always perfectly coordinated. Many people believe that the state should desist from exercising jurisdiction over abortion, relying on the right to privacy held to be implicit in several constitutional amendments. *Privacy* in legal parlance literally means "resting outside the spheres of government control." In the discourse of recent politics and much social theory, however, the term *private* has taken on a somewhat different connotation, stemming from the individualistic assumptions of the reigning social theory. Claiming that something is a "private" matter has come to mean that it is "unrelated to social reality," or that it affects an individual alone and should not be a shared reality. Although it is a fiction that at any point reality is *not* social, our liberal political rhetoric is saturated with such antisocial implications.

When we shift to moral discourse the complexity deepens. In moral terms, anything "private" should be construed as "standing outside the sphere of morality." If anything is private, it is a matter of utter indifference morally. Obviously, then, appeals to abortion as a "private matter" can be and frequently are heard as claims that abortion is "beyond morality." Pro-choice proponents sometimes conflate legal appeals to privacy and moral claims, misleading both sides on this point.

Furthermore, our appeals to "choice" in pro-choice politics sometimes exhibit a similar ambiguity. Our statements are received as an appeal to some abstract value, *choice for choice's sake,* rather than to *procreative choice as a substantive moral good.* Furthermore, whenever we speak casually of choice without sufficiently grounding our language, we seem to imply that governmental noninterference is a good in itself, apart from social consequences. This sort of celebration of abstract choice betrays the heavy hand of the antisocial individualism of nineteenth-century liberalism (today's laissez-faire conservatism). Such political theory makes liberty, rather than justice, the be-all and end-all of the good life. Appeals to liberty often actually mask our desire to prevent others from constraining *our* economic activity so that we may be free from accountability for the effects of our activity on our common life.

Real moral choice is, of course, never abstract. The moral right to procreative choice, including the legal or moral option of abortion, is much more basic than "mere liberty" defined as noninterference or lack of any constraint. Nor are our appeals for choice ever really merely for choice's sake. To claim procreative choice as a right means that it is a foundational condition for our well-being in society. Because there can be no real freedom without such substantive conditions, moral claims are more basic than claims to liberty. To put the point another way, morally we all deserve as much liberty as is consistent with not violating others' basic life conditions. The reason choice or liberty came to be seen as an end or value in itself in early liberal political theory was that the images of the human being and human nature underlying laissez-faire ideology were antisocial. A person or self was conceived of as an isolated monad, a "lone ranger"[33] who can, if he or she wills, live free of social entanglements or "contract" into society at whim.

Zillah Eisenstein has documented that even the best liberal political theory cannot accommodate the full agenda of women's historical liberation, arguing that even a moderate feminist political stance must necessarily carry feminists beyond political liberalism and its individualistic assumptions.[34] Eisenstein's claims about political theory and strategy are even more applicable to feminist moral theory and argument concerning procreative choice and abortion. Morality is, intrinsically, about our social relations, including our social relations to ourselves. The tendency of liberal political theory to image human beings as isolated and discrete entities who may, *if they choose*, enter into society flies in the face of most women's experience. Such libertarian assumptions reflect social privilege, power, and wealth. Women know, especially through childbearing and child-rearing, that our social interrelations are basic even to our biological survival and are not now, nor have they ever been, entirely optional.

From a moral point of view the idea that abortion is and should be a strictly "private" matter does not deserve standing. It implies that childbearing is a purely individual concern, separable from our own and others' well-being, from all our interpersonal obligations, and from the common good. The effect of liberal rhetoric on some mainstream feminist argument is noticeable in the implication that individualism is a more basic value than genuine community. This is simply untrue; when the conditions of community collapse, "individual" centeredness is also threatened. A few proponents of procreative choice may even seem to suggest that women should be able to live free of any accountability in the use of their procreative power. Such libertarianism no doubt appeals to more privileged groups who have every reason to welcome laissez-faire doctrine in social and economic relations, but it is simply not consistent with social reality. Women, like men, have accountability to others for the overall well-being of our common life, no more and no less. To be sure, part of our present moral conflict is due to the fact that, by virtue of women's procreative power, females have been expected to take *more* responsibility for creating and sustaining basic humane conditions than men. Simultaneously, women have been expected *not* to seek or express genuine moral freedom, especially, as I have observed, when it comes to their unparalleled power of procreation.

Even as we recognize the moral inadequacy of treating abortion merely as a private matter, many will continue to make legal claims based on presumed constitutional provisions for "the right to privacy." We need to recognize, however, that grounds for this and other legal appeals are murky. Though many believe that matters involving intimacy and family and domestic relations ought to be protected by the right to privacy provisions that some construe to be implicit, especially in the Ninth and Fourteenth Amendments, the courts have been erratic in sustaining such claims. Nor is misogyny a stranger in the history of other legal provisions relevant to women. Even such critical constitutional provisions as the due process and equal protection clauses of the Fifth and Fourteenth Amendments frequently have been rendered irrelevant whenever woman's "nature" could be invoked to justify differing treatment.[35] In any case, I have made it clear that legal appeals to privacy do not encompass optimal moral concerns directly. To help people who care about social justice hear us more accurately we need to be aware that such legal claims to abortion are not equivalent to our best moral arguments.

From a moral point of view it is appropriate to recognize that our legal claims are somewhat precarious because important basic, foundational moral conditions of life were not recognized as critical by the socially elite men who penned — and later interpreted — the Constitution.[36] Our analysis must not absolutize the U.S. Constitution, which is a somewhat more limited vehicle for grounding human rights than our political rhetoric usually acknowledges. The authors of the Constitution were eager, of course, to guarantee conditions for the *political* participation and social liberty vis-à-vis the state for men like themselves; in the process they secured formal provisions for a number of rights that are genuinely foundational to human well-being. What a feminist analysis must stress, however, is that no direct constitutional provision was made for that most basic foundational requirement on which women's existence as the "social other" of intimacy relations pivots — the right to bodily integrity, including the noninvasion or nonvoluntary manipulation of our bodies by others.[37] While, as we will see, there are common law precedents against bodily invasion, they have never been applied to women as childbearers. The critical need for foundational moral recognition of body-right was surely not apparent to slave-owning white males at a point in history when both slaves and wives were legally their property, but it must be apparent to anyone who cares about social justice in the twentieth century. I elaborate this moral argument in Chapter 7, but here it is important not to overlook the fact that our liberal political heritage puts no great emphasis on this most concrete moral right.

It is also important to examine a related and equally critical point about legal arguments in relation to abortion. The shifting reasoning of the U.S. courts in recent abortion decisions demonstrates that the present legal grounds for procreative choice are far from secure.[38] In the original Supreme Court decision legalizing abortion, *Roe v. Wade*, Justice Harry Blackmun gave women's well-being some centrality in his argument. He claimed the state has a legitimate interest in women's well-being and linked this interest with justification for procreative choice. Since the *Roe-Wade* decision, concern for women's well-being has hardly been mentioned in the Court's reasoning. Furthermore, the state's interest in promoting childbearing has emerged in the discussion. No woman should rest easy when this sort of legal thinking characterizes the judiciary. Given these developments, legal claims to "right of privacy" may be pressed with even greater force. Those who appeal to privacy should be prepared to reject criticism that their appeals imply a lack of moral sensibility on the part of pro-choice proponents. Some of our critics encouraged the confusion between our legal claims and our moral ones, and we can predict that they will continue to try to heighten that confusion.

To recognize the moral limits of political liberalism is not, of course, to reject this society's liberal heritage in toto. My own affinities with theological liberalism should be clear enough already. "Liberalism" has a complex and shifting history, but its current limits are set by its abstract individualism. I am persuaded that the survival of liberalism's best insights is contingent on a total break with laissez-faire ideology and on the integration of substantive social justice concerns, including economic democracy, in the liberal arguments. The "individual as central sensibility,"[39] liberalism's deepest moral fruit, may yet survive if such shifts occur. The deep moral wisdom that people are to be treated as ends, never merely as means,[40] when it is not taken to deny that we are social, interdependent beings, is too precious to lose. Liberal ideology goes astray not because of its concern for people but because of its portrayal of people as individual monads and the overwhelming tendency of liberals, now often among the affluent and privileged, to assume that guarantees for individual welfare are already embodied in our political-social structure. The truth is that in this society one's "individuality" is respected in direct proportion to one's wealth, social standing, race, gender, and age. Even wealth may not give access to social power if one is neither white nor male. Speaking of the morality of abortion as if women were abstract individuals for whom procreation is largely a simple matter or an asocial, nonrelational decision is absurd. And it is this same mystified individualism that motivates some people to perpetuate the serious illusion that genuine procreative choice for women will be ensured merely by securing the legality of abortion. Here, as elsewhere, liberals persistently misperceive and misrepresent the extent and nature of social constraint and control. Freedom *from* political, economic, or legal constraints is held to be a sufficient foundational condition for the actual exercise of human freedom. The *de jure* or legal freedoms of liberal political constitutions are a sufficient condition for de facto freedom *only if one has access* to the various forms of social, political, economic, and personal power.

Disentangling our moral case for procreative choice from assumptions of individualistic liberalism will pave the way for establishing common ground with some of our opponents who also rightly reject such liberalism on moral grounds and out of fear that this "superficial" moral theory, with its dualistic "public" and "private" split between morals and politics, is eroding concern for social justice. To ultimately unite with our opponents over concern for the common good is possible, I believe, precisely because the moral and religious vision underlying a feminist commitment places deep and realistic concern for basic community at the center. Many critics of feminism have branded feminists as rigid and uncompromising in our abortion politics. Yet, given our moral concerns, we exhibit more genuine sympathy for our opponents than those who merely believe that all abortion politics are too zealous and unseemly.

In our present situation many women's almost intuitive recognition of the zero-sum nature of the personal abortion dilemma mitigates efforts to develop strong politics of procreative choice. In spite of the persistent diatribe from the radical Right, most women are only too well aware that, given the life-affirming values they celebrate and wish to exemplify in their own lives, abortion is not only an agonizing dilemma but one that defies simplistic moral definition. If women trust their power of self-interpretation, their reluctance to impose their own convictions on others can be transformed into a positive resource not only for moral reason but for the new sensibilities this nation requires in its political life. Deeply felt and deeply registered awareness of the complexity of life can be a source of both moral and political wisdom.

In insisting that the power of procreative choice be ours, we are necessarily seeking a considerable shift in the distribution of power in society. Far from being a matter of social indifference or a "private affair," procreative choice will alter the dynamics of social power considerably. Our opponents know this, and it is the reason they fight us. Some women, too, find the idea of appropriating our rightful social power threatening, so conditioned have they become to social powerlessness. But such fears cannot be permitted to obscure the issues at hand. With social power comes a necessary social accountability. It is obvious that much of the hysteria generated by the abortion controversy stems from the fear of some people that women cannot be competent historical agents. Though women's moral record historically is probably superior to men's, the irony is that women's ability to exercise social power is perceived as less trustworthy than men's, precisely because of women's historical social disadvantage. If my thesis is correct that procreative choice involves a major historical shift and that it is a great moral good uniquely foundational to women's well-being, then the success of present anti-abortion politics would be a moral disaster for the whole society. It would extend the dubious moral reality of female subjugation and male supremacy. To subvert the conditions for procreative choice is simultaneously to set back women's long struggle to gain all of the other conditions of human dignity that the wisest men, through their moral theories and theologies, have argued constitute human well-being. The institutions of male supremacy have been perhaps fifteen thousand years in the making. The social conditions for the end of this supremacy are only now at hand. We are still far from incorporating them in a way relevant to most women's lives. A society over half of whose members lack the basic conditions for the exercise of rational choice when such conditions are available could not, by any moral standards, be counted as a good society. Not until this simple point also becomes obvious will "the longest revolution" be won.[41]

3

The Theologies Behind the
Moral Debate on Abortion

I have described some of the diverse assumptions about the relation between theology and morality that Christians bring to the public debate over abortion. To fully appreciate the role Christian theological teaching plays, however, it is not enough to assess the more formal connections said to exist between theology and morality outlined in Chapter 1. A fundamental but little examined dimension of theology operates powerfully in discussions of abortion. Few pause to ask how the definitions of women, sexuality, procreation, and the family operative in contemporary Christian theology shape the abortion debate. In public discussion of abortion, theologians invoke God's role in creation or the sacredness of the gift of human life in universal and general terms without awareness of the largely tacit understandings of "proper" social relationships underpinning such abstractions. To clarify the existential connections between contemporary Christian theological positions and their normative stances on abortion, we must focus on the subtext of assumptions about the meaning of human sexuality, the procreative process, and the relationship between men and women.

Chapter 5 makes clear that these same assumptions hinder our interpretation of the Christian past. But here it is important to understand the role that notions of women, sexuality, procreation, and the family play in the configuration of contemporary Christianity. Roughly characterized, contemporary Christian theologies run the gamut from fundamentalist and biblicist-conservative to neoorthodox and liberal. There is, of course, the danger of oversimplification in treating these four types as exemplary of contemporary Christianity. Nevertheless, the typology is useful for identifying the salient features of positions that shape the public policy debate on abortion.

Fundamentalism is the theological conviction that "God's Word" is unchanging and readily identifiable in specific theological formulas, especially in biblical inerrancy. I have noted the extent to which fundamentalist theological rhetoric permeates public debate on abortion.

Some may protest that a critique of popular theological rhetoric has no place in a serious discussion of modern Christian theology and its views on procreation. After all, it may be argued, fundamentalism has little in common with orthodox or genuinely traditional versions of Christianity. Mainstream Christianity, it can be said, affirms both the goodness of the created order and the capacity of human beings to exercise responsible freedom in the world; not so fundamentalism. It is true that most Christian theology espouses loving and life-regarding values and keeps considerable distance from the quasi-magical, control-fixated, sexually repressive mutterings of some New Right fundamentalist spokesmen. And it is equally true that many people who support the so-called pro-life movement are neither fundamentalist nor allied with the political Right. But the crux of the matter remains that fundamentalism not only is a highly influential theological stance but also thrusts into bold relief assumptions about sexuality, procreation, and childbearing that are latent but nevertheless operative in much other Christian theology. It is significant that mainstream Christian theologians have yet to dissociate themselves adequately from fundamentalism's explicit patterns of masculinist superiority. Identifying the basic theological assumptions of New Right/fundamentalist teaching is thus a necessary step in a genuinely critical review of the stance of contemporary Christian theology on women, sexuality, and procreation.

Deification of the male gender and trivialization of women and sexuality are not simply minor subordinate themes in an otherwise enlightened Christian theological world view. For a long time, women have sensed the extent to which their calls for gender justice were thwarted by the pervasiveness of male bias. More than one nineteenth-century leader in the struggle for women's rights learned the lesson Mary Daly rediscovered for many in the twentieth century — that the hold of patriarchal idolatry on Christianity goes to the heart of its story and sense of mission.[1] Many committed nineteenth-century feminists, socially ostracized and vilified especially by churches and clerics, looked upon theological fundamentalism in the United States as the consequence, not the source, of antifeminist sentiment.[2] There is increasing reason to believe they were correct in connecting the rise of fundamentalism with hostility to the women's movement and "sexual permissiveness." Reactionary religion always emerges as a symptom of the loss of social power. What is new today is the link between this sort of theology and the well-financed resources of the political Right.

FUNDAMENTALISM: MASCULINIST
SPIRITUALITY WRIT LARGE

Every contemporary Christian theological stance conveys its sense of the desirable or normative way for religion, ethics, and politics to mix. To be sure, all these theological positions, to some degree, are subject to restraints set by the First Amendment as described in Chapter 1. But other constitutional provisions, such as freedom of speech and freedom of the press, grant considerable leverage to those who, thinking ill of First Amendment freedom of religion provisions, would prefer direct Christian control of the public order. The unprecedented social compact[3] between the well-organized political New Right and formerly apolitical American fundamentalism perhaps has engendered more zeal for a "Christian" state than this republic has witnessed since the ratification of the Bill of Rights. The political New Right seeks to secure a public order in which rule by a "Christian majority" and "Christian" assumptions will shape everyone's lives. In the words of one of the founders of this self-proclaimed "moral majority":

> When the Christian majority takes over this country there will be no satanic churches, no more free distribution of pornography, no more abortion on demand and no more talk of rights for homosexuals. After the Christian majority takes control, pluralism will be seen as immoral and evil and the state will not permit anybody the right to practice evil.[4]

Needless to say, the effort to close the door tightly on legal abortion has high priority among these self-professed Christian "masculinist" crusaders. Fundamentalist rhetoric, riddled with crass Christian imperialist overtones, is pervasive and permeates much public policy debate:

> The unmistakable signs of moral decay are all around us: Sexual promiscuity and perversion, pornography, legalized abortion, the disparaging of marriage, family, and the role of motherhood — all are rampant in our schools, our government and even in many churches . . . We believe that America's rapid decline as a world power is . . . a sign that Satan's strategy is on or ahead of schedule.[5]

In the current fundamentalist scenario, abortion is the linchpin in a panoply of evils. According to its logic, abortion must be abolished because it militates against the male-dominated patriarchal family as the central institution in God's scheme of "personal salvation." Not surprisingly, those who share this theological world view also perceive a threat to "the family" in nonconstraining divorce laws and all legal protections against wife-battering and child abuse. The core of the fundamentalist public policy goals is a legislative package designated as the Omnibus Family Protection Act, which boldly asserts that "God's intended" family is not only male-ruled and patriarchal, but also racially segregated. The act aims to end the integration of schools under the guise of parental control of education. It strives to punish anyone teaching a nonrepressive attitude toward homosexuality or any tolerance of extramarital sexuality. Some of these sentiments already have been translated into public policy by the Reagan administration, which formally supports this bill, though not as fully as the New Right hoped.[6] Any interpretation of theological truth departing from the New Right's unblemished vision is labeled a conspiracy against God and "His" divine plan of salvation, the work of the anti-Christ, or "humanism."[7]

Fundamentalism deems the male-controlled family as sacrosanct because it transmits "spiritual values" over against a hostile society where "worldly" wisdom prevails. Supporting this belief is a conception of women that lies at the heart of fundamentalist theology. This segment of Christianity interprets salvation as a process of deliverance from our *once-bornness* or, in other words, "earthly" and "sinful" existence. Therefore, salvation constitutes being "born again." Though this sort of masculinist theology is quite modern in its sense of family and society (its roots are in the liberal political ideology described earlier), its prototypical religious symbols are ancient. We now know that myriad very diverse societies have generated religious sytems that interpret salvation as a ritual rebirth, delivering its adherents from the given, physical order and the once-bornness of "mere" biological birth. From its incipience, this ritual transcendence of the "flesh" and the material world meant deliverance from women's "natural" power, the ultimate symbol of our "earthly" dependence. A recent powerful feminist analysis of the sociology of religion by Nancy Jay traces this theme of rebirth through blood sacrifice, concluding that the social function of such religion frequently was to shift a society from patterns of matrilineal to patrilineal descent.[8] Jay's study leads us to suspect that where blood sacrifice is a central ritual theme in a religious system, that system has participated in legitimating male control. While not unique to Christianity, such themes are pervasive in its history.

Christian fundamentalism and also, to a degree, Christian orthodoxy, which developed a story of salvation as a process realized through blood sacrifice, replicates this shift of generative power away from "merely physical" women to "spiritual" or mentally superior males. Fundamentalism simply carries to an extreme this latent antibody, antiphysical ideology that, in Christian history over time, shifted spiritual power away from birth through a woman to rebirth through God, *the Father*, and *His Son*. Women, at least *good* women, had a place in this scheme of salvation, but their "spiritual" role changed as the anticarnal and otherworldly motif strengthened in Christianity. Ultimately, women could fulfill their role only through the most ardent obeisance to childbearing, homemaking, and a husband as the true head of the family.

In the modern fundamentalist New Right version of this masculinist theology, the spiritual meaning of life is captured in escape from the physical world into "higher and loftier" realities. And yet this does not prevent the true believer from actively engaging in worldly activities. On the contrary, one is encouraged to pursue enthusiastically efforts that will ensure the best available worldly support for one's "spiritual family." In this way the spiritual believer indirectly supports God's plan of salvation. This enthusiasm for worldly activity in such masculinist theology is, of course, a fruit of the liaison between otherworldly spirituality and capitalism. That this spirituality divinizes male control is evident in a rigid dualism that places mind in a position of control over nature.[9] The most salient function of such spirituality is to empower believers to overcome the fallen condition of humanity — a condition inherent in all by virtue of being once-born of woman. It is obvious how deep the contempt for women runs in this "story of salvation." Such spirituality generates institutions absolutely impervious to women's influence and requires exclusion of women wherever the real spiritual treasure is thought to be centered, that is, in interpreting the truth of "the book," in pronouncing assurance of born-againness, or, in its more orthodox form, in offering the blood sacrifice for the consecration of the "holy mysteries." All such masculinist Christian spirituality is also fixated on the theme of expiation of sin or blemish, specifically by the shedding of male blood as requisite to salvation or deliverance from the pollution of blood preeminently associated with women.

The deepest irony of fundamentalist masculinist spirituality today is that it is embraced by wealthy and powerful men who, while endorsing a vision of salvation exhorting contempt for the existing world, including the processes of nature, simultaneously command and control everything worldly in sight. By way of imposing this world-denying religious system, these powerful, world-commanding men continue to insist that a woman's fate is to submit unquestioningly to her "nature," that the truly womanly woman lives without protest a prescribed biological destiny. The holy woman is the compliant one who dutifully sacrifices herself, accepting the vocation to motherhood in recognition of men's intellectual superiority and their consequent power and right to lead the public world. The morally normative, *sacrificial* behavior expected from women in relation to childbearing and childrearing never applies to the public actions of men. Men's lives are to be governed by strict conformity to "duty" construed narrowly as observing established conventional behavior. Women, by contrast, are expected to achieve a "supererogatory" morality.[10] Although women have moral obligations in relation to procreation, this sort of theology double-binds us. We are admonished to be obedient and passive but simultaneously are told that we were born to be more responsible than men for nurturing human well-being and embodying an ethic of sacrifice. We live in a world where many, perhaps most, of the voluntary sacrifices on behalf of human well-being *are* made by women, but the assumption of a special obligation to self-giving or sacrifice by virtue of being born female, replete with procreative power, is male-generated ideology.

It is clear why, to such a theological imagination, the very thought of abortion conjures up images of women's cosmic rebellion against a divinely prescribed theological and moral destiny. From this perspective, every abortion represents a heinous act of self-assertion, a bloody, wicked renunciation of all that women were created and born to be. In this theological world view, women's blood, if not shed for purely "natural" reasons, is polluting, whereas male sacrificial blood is always salvific. It is no exaggeration to say that in this form of spirituality abortion is, simply put, a *taboo*. Even its availability to the woman who has been raped, or will otherwise die, is suspect. Clearly, abortion is a dangerous power that threatens this entire sacral system.

BARRIERS TO REVISIONING
PROCREATION IN
NONFUNDAMENTALIST THEOLOGIES

Even though one does not daily encounter this sort of theological fare in the worship and teaching of mainstream Christianity, we must engage the Christian tradition skeptically, asking to what extent such views have been perpetuated by nonfundamentalist Christianity. Lingering elements of misogyny have continued to shape even some of the most sophisticated modern theology. An adequate ethic of procreative choice can be developed only through direct recognition of this fact. One cannot easily or readily spot this misogyny simply by going directly to explicit abortion teaching. Basically, one must scrutinize carefully what a given theological stream teaches or assumes about women, sexuality, procreation, and the family and observe how these assumptions shape abortion teaching.

The development of critical reflection on these issues in modern nonfundamentalist Christian theology has been difficult for two reasons. The first concerns the persistence of nonhistorical thinking about procreation, in spite of gains in incorporating a genuine historical outlook throughout the discipline. Given the general trend of theological renewal in Christian theology, the ahistorical treatment of sexuality and procreation has not been readily apparent. In the mid-twentieth century, theological differences formerly thought to definitively divide the various Christian denominations eroded. Theologically, there is not only widespread ecumenical dialogue but even consensus, such that schools of theology cross denominational lines. Between the two world wars, European and North American white mainstream Protestant theology underwent what is often referred to as a neoorthodox renewal, followed by an equally dramatic turn in Catholicism during the post-World War II period. In this process of mainstream Protestant theological development, a style of theology grounded explicitly in modern scriptural exegesis gained preeminence. At a later point, Roman Catholic scholars joined this "biblical theology" movement first generated by neoorthodoxy. Protestants began to take "tradition" more seriously, while Roman Catholic theologians granted to scripture and the study of Christian origins a primacy earlier Roman Catholic theology denied in determining which theological teachings are most essential to continuing Christian identity. Now nearly all biblical theologians emphasize historical-critical approaches to the past, including scripture and earlier

Christian tradition. Yet inspite of this strong disposition to accept historical criticism, Protestant and Catholic theologians alike have tended to exempt questions of women's nature, sexuality, and procreation from the historical-critical scrutiny they otherwise so warmly embrace. While the movement in the last decade toward a Christian theological reconstruction in relation to human sexuality has not been without impact, full appropriation of a genuinely critical consciousness about these issues still lies in the future. Roman Catholic and Protestant theologians continue to perpetuate older natural law notions about women, procreation, and sexuality. Whether they appeal to scripture or to reason, these Christian theologians tend to endorse or assume some ontic[11] distinction between male and female nature. Furthermore, they treat procreation and childbearing as essentially ahistorical, without a past or potential for change in the future.

Nevertheless, through deeper historical-critical understanding, more and more Christian theologians have come to acknowledge that theology is rooted in story, and that appeal to scripture makes Christian theology especially accountable to biblical stories, including those appropriated from the early Jewish community as "the Old Testament." Thus, Hebraic and early Christian writings incorporated officially into the canon[12] figure into Christian theology more powerfully today than ever before. The ecumenical consensus about the centrality of biblical story in the Church's life probably has benefited Christian theology overall. Without a critical historical perspective on women's lives, however, which feminist biblical and historical scholarship only now is beginning to provide,[13] biblical theologians have been guilty of using biblical stories, especially pronatalist ones, in uncritical ways.

The differences existing in modern Christian theology on these matters, then, have more to do with whether theologians bring or fail to bring a critical historical sense to these questions than with how little or how much they appeal to scripture and tradition to support their views. Christian theologians who offer an unbroken endorsement of pronatalist values and a rigidly patriarchal concept of the "good family" usually do so by claiming direct biblical "authority" for their position. A rather simplistic biblicism consequently lingers in much teaching, chiefly in Protestant arguments. Biblicism remains a Protestant "disease." Nonbiblicist Roman Catholic and Protestant theologies do not differ very much in the assumptions they bring to the broader issues of procreative choice. A few

Protestant theologians have appropriated a feminist analysis, but so have a few Catholics. Roman Catholics happen to be saddled with, and some continue to accept, a better-defined negative official stance on contraception, which mainstream Protestant theologians have all but laid to rest intellectually and politically. With respect to the overarching questions before us here, however, there is more continuity than difference between Protestant and Catholic theology.

A second reason why rethinking the issue of procreation is difficult in contemporary theology is that, in spite of the complex history of specific moral teaching, all western Christians, often unawares, assume a *modern* view of sexuality and family relations, one rooted not in scripture, as theologians sometimes suppose, but in theological sensibilities incipient in and shaped after the Reformation.[14] Since the Protestant Reformation and, increasingly, since the total triumph of the modern child-centered family under late eighteenth- and nineteenth-century capitalism,[15] Christian theologians have read the early Israelite stories of origin and even the New Testament through lenses colored by modern institutions of marriage, family relations, and sexuality. Especially with the passing of scholasticism in both Protestant and Catholic theology, interpretations of biblical stories of divine blessing conferred through procreation have merged gradually with rising modern myths of romantic love. In ancient patriarchal societies, children were a concrete expression of both communal survival and male wealth and prosperity. In the modern world, the baby is the "love child," the sign of affective expansiveness, a paradigm of the "miracle" of "divine love," which we are presumed to experience chiefly in the privatized interpersonal family sphere. It would not be hyperbole to suggest that, at least in unguarded moments, many Christian theologians imply that procreation within the context of marriage as a "covenant" or "sacrament" is the primal metaphor for divine blessing of human life.[16] In Catholicism, even though celibacy and asceticism retain status as committed Christian lifestyles, official teaching has appropriated fully a romantic view of marriage, accommodating procreation within this context as an unambiguous sign of God's blessing. Roman Catholics and Protestants alike now celebrate the family (read "the modern nuclear family") as an unparalleled sphere of love and care, genuinely paradigmatic of God's love for "mankind."[17] Furthermore, as secular norms displaced earlier Christian influence on public morality in the political and economic spheres, biological fertility increasingly remained an unchallenged image for God's direct action in human life. Because the birth process seemed so "natural" and "mysterious," it remained sacralized long after most human activity had ceased to be understood as accessible to direct divine intervention. It is not surprising, then, that large sectors of Christianity eventually came to identify their religion with a pronatalist world view. By contrast, in Jewish tradition procreation for its own sake did not acquire the isolated and abstract value it came to have among Christians.[18]

This sentiment about procreation in marriage as a paradigm of direct divine action still permeates modern Christianity; it is a modern view, hardly characteristic of the early Christian movement. The synoptic gospels and other early writings provide evidence that Christians originally were far too preoccupied with an impending crisis related to the inbreaking "Kingdom of God" to develop familial enthusiasm about the family, much less a pronatalist stance.[19] Given their eschatological orientation, early Christian theological metaphors for God's blessing almost exclusively focused on world historical crisis. And the Apostle Paul, whose work so profoundly influenced later Christian theology, did not contribute to the identification of procreation with divine action. Assuredly, his attitudes toward sexuality were complex and inconsistent. Some of his writings reinforced later sex-negative attitudes toward procreation as a necessary evil; but he endorsed directly neither marriage (Christians should marry, if necessary to avoid sin)[20] nor the notion that children were a special sign of divine blessing.

During later historical periods, a powerful and growing antisexual bias rose to prominence in Christianity, and asceticism and repudiation of sexuality through celibacy became primary spiritual ideals.[21] But asceticism and celibacy always stood in some tension with a more body-affirming tradition.[22] Furthermore, after Christianity gained ascendancy with the collapse of the Roman Empire, the ascetic ideal developed alongside a growing emphasis on procreative commitment in marriage. In fact, it has been argued that the church first began to assimilate strong pronatalist passions from the later Roman Empire, learning the lesson of conquest through procreation from the Roman state. Whether or not this claim is true, it took centuries for the celebration of reproduction to be interpreted theologically as a distinctive expression of fidelity to God.

By the Reformation, pronatalist enthusiasm was so strong the ensuing theological revolution only reinforced it. Protestant theologians, disavowing celibacy as an ecclesiastical norm for clergy, endorsed the belief that divine blessing was expressed directly through progeny. God's blessing of "His" people through reproductive fruitfulness became a theological truism for mainstream Protestants. Modern official Roman Catholicism's passionate defense of the companionate nuclear family actually represents accommodation to this Reformation theological ethos. The result is that, even when professing commitment to modern standards of scholarship and historical-critical method, Catholic and Protestant theologians alike frequently invoke prestigious "biblical authority" for some quite modern romantic views of the family and for pronatalist sentiments highly atypical of earlier Christianity.

BIBLICISM IN NEOCONSERVATIVE THEOLOGICAL APPROACHES

While the major schools of contemporary Christian theology all claim historical-critical openness, much mainstream Protestant theology approaches human reproduction with a biblicist, if not fundamentalist, orientation even as it embraces unawares modern views of the family. Norms for marriage, the family, sexuality, and abortion, it is assumed, are clearly formulated in scripture and should be obeyed. These scriptural norms are thought to apply directly to each and every historical epoch and culture. Unlike fundamentalists, neoconservative biblicists do not deny the historical nature of human existence altogether, but they exempt de facto from the realm of change not only human biological reality but human nature itself. "The Bible says . . ." remains sufficient warrant for any moral claim, especially where women and procreation are concerned. Neoconservative biblicists manifest a sex-negative rigidity and permit no recognition for the diversity of traditions about sexuality in biblical literature.[23]

That scripture incorporates varying conditions spanning a millennium of history and culture is not acknowledged; nor is there any tentativeness about the meaning of texts originating in settings about which we have little accurate knowledge. That there are tensions and even contradictions within scripture is never admitted. Furthermore, neoconservative biblicists never acknowledge that scriptural materials frequently reflect moral practices that, having been transcended historically, should no longer be considered adequate from a moral point of view. For example, the ancient story about Sodom and Gomorrah, often cited by biblicists to condemn homosexuality, is actually a story about the ancient Israelites' lack of hospitality to strangers. What the text of this story may disclose, however, is that at one time it was morally acceptable for a man to offer his daughters to troublemakers to protect strangers who were his guests. Moreover, this story also demonstrates that in this historical period incest was practiced.[24] A passage invariably cited by biblicists to condemn homosexuality in fact reveals a cultural acceptance of male control of women. An ancient story with nothing at all to teach about desirable norms for heterosexuality nevertheless is confirmed as evidence that homoeroticism is an unspeakable evil. Biblicist "sexual ethics" are invariably a pastiche of such citations, which reflect dubious and long-transcended patterns of gender oppression.

The one uncontested reference to abortion in Christian scripture well illustrates this problem.[25] One regulation recorded in the collation of early Israelite laws elaborated in the book of Exodus sheds some light on attitudes toward abortion at the time. While accurate translation of this passage is notoriously difficult, a fairly solid consensus supports the rendering that now appears in the Revised Standard Version:

> When men strive together and hurt a woman with child, *so that there is a miscarriage,* and yet no harm follows, *the one who hurt her shall be fined,* according as the woman's husband shall lay upon him; and he shall pay as the judge determines. If any harm follows, then you shall give life for life, eye for eye, tooth for tooth, hand for hand, foot for foot, burn for burn, wound for wound, stripe for stripe. (Italics mine) Exodus 21:22-24

This text, with its checkered history of mistranslations, has had a negative influence on Christian teaching on abortion, as we will see in Chapter 5. Cited regularly by biblicists to "prove" that scripture condemns abortion, in actuality this passage reveals something quite different about the abortion mores of early Israelites. It demonstrates that causing the death of a fetus did *not* constitute a major crime at that time; payment of a fine to a prospective father was considered adequate compensation for the miscarriage. Hurting or maiming a pregnant woman, on the other hand, was a serious penal offense equivalent to other life-denying crimes. The text clearly supports the general trend of Jewish teaching, which values the mother's well-being more than fetal survival.

Biblicist approaches to this text disclose a further limitation of all biblical proof-texting for the purpose of justifying morality. This same text is often cited, appropriately, on the pro-choice side of the debate. Even as we do so, we may bypass a deeper problem. All appeals to this passage obscure the painful fact that the moral ethos revealed in this and many other biblical stories is that of a patriarchal society in which *ownership of women and children by men was not merely assumed but considered morally acceptable.* Exodus 22:25 reflects a world of male prerogative. For the male in question, a miscarriage paled in comparison to damage or loss of "his" wife, but in each event, respectively, financial recompense and "justice" were *owed* to the man. The loss was his, not his wife's. In this connection, the reasons for considering a resulting miscarriage wrong were less related to women's intrinsic value than to definitions of just social relations *between men.* Under the law, a man's valued property, especially his spouse, could not be denied him. Whereas this text and other biblical stories reflecting ancient morality almost always manifest a cultural and moral ethos quite different from our own, this fact goes unnoticed only when gender or sexuality is involved. Consequently, pro-choice proponents need to interpret this text with a critical awareness.

To claim additional "scriptural authority" for their positions, anti-abortionists frequently cite passages in early Jewish scripture that celebrate fertility as a sign of God's blessing and portray infertility as a divine curse.[26] Invoking this ancient material to support more modern pronatalist views is an easy matter, and biblicists reiterate these passages ritualistically to imply unqualified scriptural support for procreation as the result of direct divine action.[27] Several of the finest poets of the ancient Israelite tradition rely heavily on imagery depicting God's passionate love for humankind and the result of creation as preexistent and extending from before conception to beyond death. The Psalmist expresses this conviction in a characteristic way:

> For thou didst form my inward parts,
> thou didst knit me together in my mother's womb.

> I praise thee, for thou art fearful and wonderful.
> Wonderful are thy works!
> Thou knowest me right well;

My name was not hidden from thee,
when I was being made in secret, intricately wrought in the
  depths of the earth

Thy eyes beheld my unformed substance; in thy book were
  written, every one of them,
the days that were formed for me, when as yet there was
  none of them.

Ps. 139:13-16

Such powerful poetic metaphor beautifully conjures up the depth and all-inclusiveness of divine love, and, as a result, this passage has achieved a well-deserved place in both Jewish ritual and Christian liturgy. But biblicists, invoking it as evidence for the full personhood of fetuses, confuse poetry with science and fail to notice that, in the process, they are transmuting imagery and metaphor into causal and propositional modes of discourse.

Not explicitly, but by indirection, they suggest that the presence of such imagery in scripture requires our acceptance of the imagery as an explanatory argument for determining when life begins. Those who do not agree are neither "biblical" nor genuinely Christian. That such imagery fosters a theological sensibility about the radicality of God's love for us is not in dispute. What is questionable is the reduction of this splendid example of metaphorical theology to causal reasoning and the manipulation of its status as scripture to obviate any contemporary moral reconsiderations of the nature of fetal life.

Neoconservative biblicists who substitute scriptural exegesis for ongoing moral reasoning never face the genuine complexity of modern moral dilemmas or their origin in historical change. When Christians find proof-texting sufficient justification for condemning the morality of an act such as abortion, they thereby substitute religious authority for moral reasoning. Unwittingly or not, they falsely portray the past as inherently morally superior to the present by evading the moral inadequacies reflected in scripture.

The dialogue with our moral past always requires a more critical engagement. Even though there are positive elements of moral wisdom in scripture, there are also distortions wrought by as yet unacknowledged historical patterns of oppression. Anyone possessing an adequate theological-moral hermeneutic will attempt to reconstruct the historical background of a current moral problem as it emerges from the life of her religious community. But she will make this attempt not simply for the purpose of finding "the answer" to the present moral dilemma.[28] The positive theological values and moral principles embraced in the past may have continuing claims to make on us. Whether and how they do so must be tackled straight-forwardly. Simultaneously, this process requires that moral authority be ascribed to the demands of human well-being in the present. Often we will discover it necessary to transcend earlier historical limits to our community's actions. In this respect, transcending social relations in which women were considered the property of males, however beloved, represents a positive moral breakthrough not fully envisaged by either ancient Israel or the New Testament Christian community.[29]

Biblicists refuse to face the fact that the ancient moral ethos reflected in scripture is not always noble by our moral standards and has been superseded by a more adequate morality at some stages in later human history. Admitting this fact, however, enables us to acknowledge that scripture does not incorporate vexing dilemmas specific to the modern world. Whether women should resort to abortion as a *safe, elective, surgical procedure,* for instance, is a very recent option posing new questions. As in many other matters, scripture at best addresses analogous, but never identical, issues. While we are always well advised to probe these analogies for genuine correspondence, we must remember that we are never justified in simply deducing standards of moral conduct from scripture. On the contrary, we are responsible for bringing biblical norms into dialogue with new circumstances and weighing the relevance of other moral orientations to the development of our value systems. We have good reason to suspect that when a Christian group decides that doing Christian ethics is only a matter of reiterating a specific moral counsel found in scripture, it has ceased to have a living theological tradition.

POST-BIBLICIST, NEOORTHODOX THEOLOGICAL APPROACHES

Most professional Christian moralists today recognize the general limits of biblicism in ethics, and much has been written to help us avoid such pitfalls.[30] It is still true, however, that the quality of biblical exegesis in post-biblicist theologies leaves much to be desired when sexuality, women, and procreation are at issue. The newer, neoorthodox theologies, unlike neoconservative versions, do not ground their ethics exclusively in appeals to biblical authority, but the ahistorical treatment of these issues remains largely uncorrected. Characteristically, Protestant neoorthodox theological ethics, now also adopted by some Catholic scholars,[31] purport to seek in scripture not a detailed morality or a specific set of prescriptions but a more general framework for what God wills or intends for human life. Such neoorthodox theological ethics are identified in current professional discussion as "Divine Command ethics."[32] This style of Christian theological ethics does not conclude that every detail of human life is elucidated as a product of divine intention, but rather that divine will shapes the main structures or forms of our lives.

Christian theologians have engaged in much internal debate about the form the divine will takes. Several neoorthodox theologians spoke of God's will as shaping "the orders of creation." Others, who objected to such terminology, fearing that the notion of "orders" implied an older, ahistorical, natural law conception of creation, preferred to speak of God's will as expressing itself in "mandates" or "decrees."[33] While theological versions of Divine Command ethics vary greatly, for the most part only the major patterns of life are understood to be shaped by God's active and ongoing intentionality. Not surprisingly, they generally affirm that the forms of our socio-political institutions and the family represent a divine mandate. The most sophisticated versions of Divine Command ethics, such as the version elaborated by Swiss theologian Karl Barth, aimed to historicize government institutions so that *theological legitimation* of any specific form of political order would not automatically occur. Nevertheless, in Barth's analysis the family and male-female relations remain shrouded in ahistorical univeralism.

In much Divine Command ethics, the well-ordered state is one that serves the well-being of its people. Neoorthodox theologies incorporated participatory values into their political ethics so as to mandate only general obedience, that is, participation in politics and general respect for government. The most sophisticated versions of Divine Command ethics did not authoritatively dictate a great deal of normatively specific morality. God's command shaped our lives in a broad way, but our freedom made new forms of action possible. Discussions of the family, however, implied an unchanging need for this primal institution and reinforced the belief that the family (read "modern, child-centered family") was normative for all societies and any community.[34] Women's role, in particular, continued to remain "ahistorical," even though Divine Command ethics interpreted history as the central arena of divine activity and generally affirmed historical change. Furthermore, Divine Command theologians stressed, *ad nauseum*, that a Christian theological ethic should stand in intense critical tension with the spirit of any given human culture. Even so, the neoorthodox Divine Command ethic was conspicuously conservative culturally and nostagically wedded to nineteenth-century romanticism where marriage, the family, women, and sexuality were concerned.

The early Protestant neoorthodox theologians also emphasized repeatedly that Christian theology should never equate the value of human life with mere biological existence. To be sure, neoorthodoxy gradually accommodated to the general and widespread cultural acceptance of family planning and contraception while continuing to affirm procreation in marriage. But, characteristically, twentieth-century Protestant neoorthodoxy did not address directly the question of when human life begins. Theologically, its interest focused on what it meant to say that "man" is created in "God's image." Its exposition of what is normatively "human" turned on this discussion.[35]

Since the Reformation, Protestant theologians have contended that Roman Catholic theology and all natural-law theories of human nature equated too much the normatively human with rationality. Much early Protestant theology also was shaped by a theological polemic about human sinfulness. The Roman Catholic tradition stressed that sin did not so sully the human capacity for reason as to render it untrustworthy. Protestants challenged this "confidence" in reason, and some also insisted that the corruption of sin could destroy the *imago dei*. Although modern Protestant neoorthodoxy eventually abandoned this polemical point against Roman theology, it continued to dissent from the equation of *imago dei* with reason. The refusal to equate divine action with a natural process remains a distinctive motif of Protestant neoorthodoxy and consequently Protestant theologians have been at pains to differentiate their views on what makes human life unique from any form of "naturalism." In the most creative Protestant neoorthodoxy, human life is distinctive not because of some natural quality inherent in biological existence per se but rather because of our capacity for free relationship with God. Karl Barth, for instance, increasingly placed the divine-human relationship at the center of his theological interest. Barth interpreted the *imago dei* as our capacity for relationship and, in his later work, as our capacity for responsible freedom in relationship.[36] So strong did this emphasis become for him that he transformed the notion of God's action as "divine decree" into one of "divine permission." In Barth's case, a Divine Command ethic was dramatically altered by the radical embrace of relationality, making the capacity for relationship the distinctive feature of genuinely human nature.

Barth's creative innovations notwithstanding, major questions have been raised in the last two decades about the Divine Command approach to Christian ethics characteristic of neoorthodoxy. Like all biblicist ethics, some Divine Command formulations imply that aspects of morality are not contestable in principle. Many Christian ethicists, however, have agreed with some moral philosophers that to give a priori assent to the idea that something is morally good because God commands it is to substitute theology for ethics. And yet such reasoned challenges to the more crassly deductive forms of Divine Command ethics have been far from definitive.[37] Some Protestant theologians have continued to argue, like anti-abortion warrior Paul Ramsey at an earlier stage, that abortion is wrong *not* because fetal life has intrinsic worth but because its value, like the value of all of human life, is the result of divine decree. Ramsey has shifted his position in more recent writings, but such theological ethics are still widely promulgated.[38] Ramsey's shift illustrates a trend away from Divine Command ethics, which assuredly is not in the ascendance among Protestant Christian ethicists today. Even as neoorthodox theological ethics have given way to new forms of relating theology and ethics, the lingering impact of "orders of creation" thinking about the family continues to leave an imprint on the work of many theologians who explicitly address the abortion dilemma. Some Protestant ethicists who support the availability of safe, legal abortion do so out of sympathy for women's situation, but without awareness of procreation and women's sexuality as theological problem areas requiring a new perspective. The integration of human sexuality, procreation, and intimacy structures into a historical world view is not yet consistently pursued.

Since World War II, Protestant neoorthodox theologians moved to endorse contraception and family planning. Roman Catholic theologians recently have joined their ranks, influenced by progressive currents in Catholic theology. As a result, Protestant neoorthodox and many Catholic moral theologians insist that, as far as procreation is concerned, use of contraception represents mature decision making, but, except where a mother's life is genuinely threatened, they find abortion utterly unacceptable morally. A not untypical example of this phenomenon is found in the work of German theologian Helmut Theilicke. In his influential *Ethics of Sex* he offers us, only pages apart, a romantic, even ecstatic celebration of family planning and an unqualified and total denunciation of abortion as "unthinkable."[39] The latent biblicism that made Protestant churches the major reactionary force in anti-family planning politics"[40] has been overcome. Likewise, earlier theological hand-wringing and predictions of the loss of "family values" accompanying the rise of contraception have been laid to rest. There still exists in neoorthodox theology, however, an unbridgeable gap between contraception as a permissible human freedom and abortion, a line now drawn by the most progressive Catholic theology as well.

The movement of neoorthodox Protestant thought and also of recent Roman Catholic theology to incorporate newer views of human freedom has been dramatic up to the issue of abortion. Once again, Karl Barth beautifully exemplified this movement and its limitations. In his early work, he stressed the radical objectivity and separateness of God's action vis-à-vis everything human, an emphasis aimed at forcing an acculturated and politically quiescent German Christianity to redirect its allegiance away from the rising tide of fascism. Barth began, then, by stressing *God's* freedom. As I indicated, however, in his later work the emphasis on God's radical freedom was increasingly counterbalanced by claims about the radicality of human freedom, grounded in divine freedom. Despite this ecstatic affirmation of the possibilities of human freedom under God, Barth toed a cautious and traditional line concerning women and procreation. His intention to break with natural orders thinking in ethics faltered under the heavy pressure of social convention. He is so equivocal and evasive in his treatment of abortion that he is frequently cited on *both* sides of the abortion question.[41] Consequently, those who cite his theology as support for the possible necessity of abortion under some circumstances need also to acknowledge the generally conservative tenor of his theology in matters related to women. Because of this conservatism, the most progressive neoorthodoxy has left us with few resources for revisioning an ethic of procreative choice and for making a fresh start on the question of the morality of abortion.

PROCREATIVE CHOICE AND
THEOLOGICAL LIBERALISM:
A CHECKERED HISTORY

The neoorthodox effort to revision the Christian tradition had some lasting impact on twentieth-century American Protestant Christianity. United States theology, however, never incorporated the strong revelational positivism (that is, the sharp distinction between the action of God and man [sic]) characteristic of European neoorthodoxy. Christianity in the United States more characteristically focused on human experience in its religious dimensions, an emphasis common to "liberal" theologies. Furthermore, the mainstream of Protestant theology was strongly affected by the social gospel movement, which challenged the dominant individualistic and even antisocial piety of the pervasive American biblicist tradition.[42] A distinctive aspect of American social gospel liberalism has been its tendency to bring theological reflection into direct dialogue with emergent social issues in our society. Whereas neoorthodox theologians ordinarily begin by examining past Christian tradition, many liberals purport to ground their theological reflection in social process.

Theological liberals also were committed to a nondefensive appropriation of newer scientific world views in the face of theological fear and resistance to new scientific knowledge. In the seventeenth and eighteenth centuries many entrenched theological conservatives insisted that biblical metaphors for creation were to be construed also as causal explanations about the origins of nature. The accommodation of Christian theology to newer, scientific modes of human self-understanding was no easy task. Theological liberalism attempted to respect the rapidly expanding power of human beings to interact with the rest of nature. Without the contributions of theological liberalism, Christianity would have become obscurantist with respect to modern modes of knowledge — that is, it either would have regressed into fundamentalism or would have become traditionalistic and culturally isolated as a form of modern Christian scholasticism. Liberal theologies, so much criticized by traditionalists, in fact opened the way for needed accommodation to scientific understanding and genuine historical thinking among Christians.

In recent decades, without question the best and most creative theological work in both Roman Catholic and Protestant circles has attempted to carry forward the agenda begun by earlier liberals. This has meant that the newer perspectives on human freedom have been integrated into theological self-understanding. Furthermore, by incorporating a scientific world view, theological liberalism was able to embrace the Genesis creation stories and the tales of Hebraic origin in a more spacious and cosmos-incorporating sense than earlier Christian theologies. Nothing is more characteristic of modern liberal Christian theological conviction than the generative idea that concrete world-historical human existence is the major expression of God's blessing on humanity. The basic metaphor of creation as the gift of God is perhaps the distinctive tenet of liberal theology. Theological liberalism, then, deserves more credit than it usually receives for again steering Christianity in a world-affirming direction uncharacteristic of dominant Christian spirituality over many centuries. Furthermore, it set a high standard for intellectual honesty among Christians in the encounter with secularism. Liberalism also embraced a positive recognition that the Christian story moves, grows, and deepens. Revelation, like everything living, changes, and human freedom is intrinsic to the direction creation takes. Theological liberalism strongly embraces responsible human freedom and affirms unqualifiedly the theological appropriateness of a world where human power shapes our destiny. This emphasis is at least as typical of modern Roman Catholic theology as it is of Protestant. A celebrated Roman Catholic philosophical theologian, Karl Rahner, has expressed the now-characteristic position that there be no equivocation as we face the new power gained by scientific research:

> Naturally the Church, along with individual Christians, must speak out with great determination against all abuses of man's [sic] self-creative power . . . But this danger does not warrant *any pre-condemnation of the coming age of self-creation.*
>
> Nothing is gained by retreating behind negative epithets of rhetoric about shameless barbarism and the destruction of "nature," and all this accompanied by dirges about the death of life in a technological culture. Nothing is accomplished by weeping over "pagan" insensibility to sickness, pain, death and poverty, nor by painting the future as an undifferentiated mass society where real history comes to an end among the static and faceless mass of zombies. Such an uncontrolled reaction comes from cowardice masking behind biblical ideals. (Italics mine)[43]

Neoconservative critics of theological liberalism charge that it has gone too far in accommodating modernity, emphasizing our human power to shape the world at the expense of "theological substance" and placing "man" too much at the center of things. Whatever the real or imagined faults of liberalism, it is doubtful that neoconservativism will match liberalism's intellectual honesty or will find an approach that successfully bypasses human experience. Liberalism also draws fire from the ranks of liberation theologians who object to liberal theology's individualism and its identification with power elites. The primary complaint of liberation theologians is that liberals too easily universalize, equating "humanity" with Anglo-European white male identity. This critique of liberalism's propensity for universalizing pinpoints its core inadequacy. But too often liberation theologians fail to make the connection between this propensity and liberalism's perpetuation of the dominant western interpretation of women's "nature" and human sexuality.

The fact remains that theological liberals, imbued with individualism and subjectivism, were markedly susceptible to romanticism and imbibed the myths of romantic love, including a "pedestalized" view of women, sooner than their more traditional counterparts.[44] Although less repressive toward and more affirmative of sexuality than most neoconservatives, liberals verged on deifying the family, albeit a companionate versus an eighteenth-century European patriarchal family. Liberals also finally embraced the "family-planning movement" with full force. Because of their deep investment in idealized family relations, however, too often their support of women foundered on sentimentality. When it came to a full, social justice feminism, male theological liberals made reluctant supporters. However much they celebrated women, theological liberals still considered the exemplary woman to be "truly" complementary to a man.

More recently, few theological liberals have recognized that radical insights about human freedom require a fresh approach to procreation and abortion as well as other matters relating to our human power to shape life and death. Over a decade ago, Daniel Callahan insisted that

> human experience together with reflection on freedom show that God does not directly enter into processes of nature and human life, at least not in the sense of immediately intervening in the biological processes of life and death . . .

man [sic] is responsible for everything to do with man [sic], including control over life and death. . . .[45]

Not all liberal theologians have come this far. Some continue to argue that nothing in a Christian theological approach makes abortion thinkable. In fact, by far the strongest and most damaging attacks on the pro-choice position by Christian writers in the last several years came from theological progressives, including some self-identified liberation theologians.

A recent issue of the pacifist and politically progressive evangelical journal *Sojourners* contained a symposium on abortion with a ferocious anti-choice bent unmatched even by the New Right. Though none of the contributors to the issue are professional ethicists, several are widely respected theologians, theorists, and activists for social justice causes. All, without exception, Protestant or Catholic, seemed to believe that "natural" or biological categories are fully equivalent to moral ones. Most appeared completely unaware that there are very good historical, philosophical, and logical reasons for not equating the biological category "fetus" with the moral category "human person" (a point I elaborate in Chapter 7). But this lack of conceptual sophistication aside, the articles deserve comment for their vitriolic innuendo, for their utter obliviousness to the cultural and historical diversity of Christian and other religious perspectives on abortion, and, with one exception, for a lack of historical-critical and structural understanding of women's situation. While innuendo and lack of pluralistic sensibility are not inveterate failings of liberalism, insensitivity to the latter issue is.

No effort was made in the *Sojourners* symposium to present a range of theological opinions about abortion, though one contributor offered a somewhat reluctant defense of women's right to make abortion decisions. The most characteristic anti-choice argument was voiced by Mary Meehan, Feminist for Life activist:

Good News: Somebody *is* consistent. There really are people who are pro-life in a consistent way. They think that *the child in the womb*, the prisoner on death row, the elderly, the poor, and everyone threatened by the bomb (which is to say all of us) have a right to life. They believe that life is sacred, or a great joy, a wondrous experience, an exciting adventure or all of those things. (Italics mine)[46]

The other pivotal theme in this broadside against a pro-choice position involved terminology about fetal life. The claim was made that because the Latin word *fetus* means "unborn child"[47] (a debatable point; Latin dictionaries are treasure troves of "traditionalist" theological opinion), those who use this term to mean anything other than "unborn children" or "aborted children" are simply trying to distance themselves from the murderous nature of abortion and to cover the moral problem of a pro-choice position. Even mainstream debates within Christianity about when the fetus really becomes animated were ignored. Throughout the essays, these moral purists conveyed the belief that they understood those of us who do not equate fetal life with full human life better than we understand ourselves.

The appeal to consistency in the *Sojourners* moral broadside illustrates another important problem with socially progressive liberal ethics. Theological progressives, including progressive evangelicals and liberals, are as likely to adopt a moral theory of single-principle, deontological monism as are neoconservative and neoorthodox Christians. As in the case of *Sojourners*, such single-principle ethical absolutism usually masquerades as rigorous "moral consistency." Apparently, all of the symposium participants are absolute pacifists — that is, they believe that the killing of a human person (or more vaguely, as in most of these articles, the "taking of human life") is *never* justified. Furthermore, for these writers the principle of "right to life" is not one among a number of basic moral principles to be respected; it is sole, singular, and sufficient. Failure to see this, they believe, results in moral turpitude. The espousal of such monistic absolutism as a moral theory in theological ethics invariably leads to vitriolic denunciation of everyone who does not agree. In this case, everyone must equate abortion with murder and repudiate it as an inexcusable violent act. I have deep sympathies for the ancient traditions of Christian pacifism, even though I do not fully share them. However, the *Sojourners* issue seems to me to illustrate why much Christian pacifism in this very modern, liberal, absolute-idealist formulation has made so little sense. The absolutizing of the prescription against killing makes it impossible to ascribe moral weight to the contingencies of life, which may sometimes justify the taking of human life.

The *Sojourners* articles also exemplify an imperviousness to women's lives, so typical of much progressive theology. From the period of the social gospel movement onward, liberal theological discourse has been permeated by that peculiarly antiwoman, feminine moral pedestalism that is, in my view, Christianity's last defense against mature social justice feminism. Even though many of the contributors to the *Sojourners* broadside were female, they obviously believed that "good women" do not experience ambivalence in child-bearing and that only wicked, sexually objectified, nonpious, "super-ficial" women really support pro-choice.

One could dismiss some of these articles as outgrowths of lingering cultural nature-romanticism, if *Sojourners* were not the voice of the new progressive evangelical Christian Left. I believe these articles disclose that much progressive theology in the United States remains wedded to the nineteenth century's moral pedestalizing of women and its theory of romantic love. The proponents of these views are enraged by any break with this presumed theological tradition. The "Christian feminism" this perspective generates is still only the celebration of the morally pure, good woman who exemplifies Christian sacrifice for life. Even James Douglas, the one, more perceptive male writer in the *Sojourners* symposium who acknowledged that misogyny bears on the abortion question, reflects this kind of romanticism.[48] As a Christian pacifist theorist of great sensibility, he offered a reluctant defense of legal abortion because "patriarchy and the Pentagon" make abortion inevitable:

> The point is that patriarchy (the systematic, institutionalized control of women by men) and its consequences, unwanted pregnancies, are the reason women get abortions.[49]

My sympathy with this point is obvious. Male control of women's lives frequently results in unwanted pregnancy. However, Douglas's perceptiveness to the extent of social injustice toward women remains entangled precisely with the form of nature and love-romanticism currently receiving strong endorsement from liberals. While acknowledging that he is "only beginning to understand, as a man, why women are *driven to desperate violence* in taking life in their wombs,"[50] he longs for the morally pure arena that he associates with "women's space." Douglas envisions the possibility of a day when each act of love between a man and a woman will represent such caring that both would welcome new life if it resulted from such love. I suspect Protestant liberal intimacy-romanticism has combined with Catholic liberal nature-romanticism to create a scenario of a perfect world where nature and human spontaneity would merge to end all moral dilemmas.

What this *Sojourners* issue demonstrates is that much liberal theology now goes even further than neoorthodoxy in unquestioningly embracing the romanticized view of the modern family, deeply sex-affirming but celebrating procreation intimacy as a spontaneous act outside the realm of history. Considering sexuality not merely as procreative but as more centrally "communicative" leads liberals to reinforce the ideal of companionate marriage and romantic love more strongly than ever. All of modern Christianity grants to companionate marriage a sanctity at least as great as it extends to doctrinal formulations. While not all feminists would agree, I believe that any such notion of a natural zone of love intimacy, totally benign and outside historical structures, is dangerous theological nonsense. As we will see in Chapter 6, the lives of countless numbers of highly fertile women have been thwarted by nature's supposed "bounty," while others desiring, but unable to conceive, children have been victimized by such natural piety. This sort of romantic "naturism" also exemplifies a patriarchal rejection of genuine embodied finitude, a finitude that respects the limits of action set by our relational context. We always have an ongoing need to avoid idealizing nature and to recognize genuine hard choices as intrinsic to our existence in nature, culture, and history. We may welcome any genuine sympathy for the complexity of the abortion issue on the part of male theologians, but many soft feminist nature-romantics need a stronger awareness that our ideals, including those concerning nature, are constructs of our moral imagination, always expressing both the positive values and the limits of our moral sensibility.

The new wave of assault on the pro-choice position by theological progressives shows that attitudes toward procreation really are a test of whether a Christian theology fully appropriates the radicality of human freedom in all its complexity and moral ambiguity. To appreciate the lingering inconsistency of liberal theology, it is necessary only to ponder again the extent to which such theology otherwise *takes for granted and affirms the awesomeness of human power and responsibility.*

Questions are rarely raised by progressives about our technical power to alter the conditions of human physical life in myriad ways. The contours of human life and society are viewed as malleable and fully within the province of our moral choice. Yet we now know that *all* manipulation of the environment has life-altering implications, often including implications for prenatal life. One recent study has shown that provisions for pregnant women in the workplace often betray the most minimal concerns for the safety of the woman and the fetus. Furthermore, few object when men are encouraged to work under conditions that threaten them with genetic defects that may be passed on to their offspring.[51] We rarely ask questions about the effects of most life-changing manipulations of our environment unless abortion is involved. Passion for the sacredness of human life in its earliest biological stages, untouched by realistic compassion for living women, continues to pass as Christian piety.

It is nevertheless disappointing that liberal theologies, in particular, have not broken more forthrightly with views of the family emergent in the nineteenth century, or the practice of interpreting procreation as largely outside the arena of legitimate freedom. The dominant theological ethical approaches to procreation still maintain a startling continuity with older Catholic natural law theories. And even though a large number of contemporary theologians have forcefully under-scored the inadequacy of much Christian theological reflection on marriage and sexuality, and a few have begun to reformulate the issues,[52] papal and hierarchical opposition on the Roman Catholic side and the biblicist trend in mainstream Protestantism threaten even these small gains. A few creative Protestant and Roman Catholic theologians have come to recognize the depth of the problem of misogyny in Christian tradition and have learned much from feminism, but the impact of this development on the procreation issue and abortion is so far very indirect. Evidently most of this group have chosen to secure the beachhead of support for artificial contra-ception won in the last generation while avoiding direct engagement with teaching on abortion. To cement this strategy, Catholics and Protestants alike insist that the distinction between artificial contraception and abortion is unbridgeable.

In addition, few Protestant ethicists or Catholic moral theologians will acknowledge publicly the connection between the abortion con-troversy and some churches, existing reactionary stances on sexuality, or their disavowal of women's theological, moral, and social equality in the churches. Nor do they appear to understand the vehemence of reaction within Christianity to women's call for gender equality, compared to modest, favorable responses to other social justice movements.[53] Few theological liberals have appreciated how deeply modern theories of the family and sexuality (including psycho-analytic theories) are ideologically defensive of male privilege. They hardly seem aware that when uncontrolled procreation is celebrated as a metaphor for God's blessing within the intimacy structures of a male-dominated society, it is the male's power that is enhanced by this "divine gift." Because there is so much evidence that Christianity evolved to legitimate male efforts at social control of procreation, it is time to acknowledge that church teaching on the subject of contraception and abortion is implicated in a system of control over women's power to reproduce the species. Only when this acknowledgment becomes a point of departure for theological discussion of abortion will fresh insights emerge.

RESOURCES FOR RE-VISIONING ABORTION IN MAINSTREAM THEOLOGY

Two trends in modern post-neoorthodox liberal theology, however, have contributed to a needed theological reassessment of abortion. One, noted before, emerged in Protestant neoorthodoxy earlier in the century and has now become important also to recent Roman Catholic theology. This is the theological emphasis on the relational and intrinsically social nature of human existence. Our capacity for relationship, community, and deep communication are coming to be recognized as distinctive and critical features of our humanness. Roman Catholic theology had never been as individualistic as Protestant theology because of the Roman Catholic stress on the intrinsically organic nature of human life. But until the rise of theological liberalism, a static view of society prevailed in Catholic theology, just as individualistic subjectivism held sway on the Protestant side. The merging of the relational motif with a thorough-going cultural-historical-social-psychological understanding of life, however, has slowly gained momentum in modern Christianity.

Several liberal theologians and ethicists, especially in the United States and Britain, aided this process by intentionally revisioning our social relationships as central to our self-understanding. H. Richard Niebuhr pursued this project self-consciously in his earlier work in the 1930s, and he was more aware than many of his contemporaries of the tremendous theological shift a genuinely social and historical perspective would require.[54] Scottish theologian and philosopher of religion John MacMurray developed the first thorough, systematic modern Protestant theological social theory of human action. MacMurray's most powerful insight, developed in a two-volume work, is that apart from our sociality there is, and can be, no such thing as genuine personal existence.[55] He laid the groundwork for an understanding of the human person that places our social relations at its center. John C. Bennett and James Luther Adams,[56] distinguished and underappreciated American social ethicists of the liberal theological tradition, began to integrate sociohistorical analyses with moral and theological discourse, a necessary step toward an ethical method that transcends the discrete-deed approach of so much Christian ethics criticized here. Analogous developments have taken place, especially since Vatican II in Roman Catholic theology, and, if anything, Catholic theologians have pressed the relational motif and developed it more centrally than Protestant theologians in the last decades. In France several Roman Catholic theologians have gone so far as to insist that Christian theology requires a relational criteria in its definition of a person.

The development of a sociohistorical perspective on culture and society in theology and moral theory is a necessary precondition for the deliverance of theological liberalism from its entanglement with absolute idealist moralism. As I have observed, much theological liberalism, lacking an integrated sociohistorical method and cross-cultural perspective, repeated the mistake of earlier neoconservative Christian ethics — it adopted a moral theory of absolute idealism or monistic-principle absolutism. The result was not a deepened morality but a moralism, brittle and self-righteous, incapable of adequate complexity. Men like Niebuhr, MacMurray, Bennett, and Adams were seeking a way around this moralism to develop a consistent and critical socio-ethical method.[57] I believe that now a liberation theological hermeneutic — that is, *the specific commitment to struggle against real, concrete, material suffering* — must be incorporated into the social vision of theological liberalism. Without such concrete praxis, modern Christian theological ethics revert back both to more scholastic and formalist interests and to a subjectivist individualism.

Another trend in twentieth-century liberal theology also has been helpful in grounding a more adequate theological perspective on procreation and abortion. A movement known as process theology has aimed to incorporate modern scientific-cosmological assumptions into a Christian theological understanding of nature, thereby breaking the hold of static notions of natural process implicit in older cosmological perspectives. Process theologians employ the philosophical cosmologies of Alfred North Whitehead and his followers, such as Charles Hartshorne, to clarify theological constructs.[58] These process philosophers used the relativity theory of modern physics to re-create a cosmology consistent with modern views of nature. An analogous development in Roman Catholic theology occurred through the anthropological speculations of Teilhard de Chardin, who pressed for an evolutionist approach that would enable Christians to see reality as a natural-social-cultural-historical continuum.[59] Many critical questions from a moral point of view can be asked of both theological movements, especially concerning Teilhard's evolutionist approach. Theological theories grounded in natural, scientific perspectives tend to project a teleology into nature such that progress or development comes to be understood as inevitable. Such assumptions sever the nerve of human moral responsibility. There is nothing "inevitable" about moral progress. Even so, all these newer cosmological theories have helped dislodge the previously unbroachable hiatus between "nature" and "history" in traditional Christian theology. They have served to reduce the conflict between theologies that claimed to be ontological or essentialist in method and those that were historical, rooted in event and story.

Process theologians envision reality as an integrated web of social relationships, which over time engenders a degree of subjectivity and self-directed freedom in the social process itself. Subjectivity and self-direction come to characterize the nature/history process through the relational complexity and subjective freedom of human beings. Humanity develops as the dimension of nature in which self-determination comes to fruition. Our multifaceted relationality, mediated through culture, enables us to make a subjective appropriation of our world and to gain some transcendence over predetermination. Our knowledge of our world, continuously changing and deepening, is conducive not only to ever greater freedom but also to genuine enhancement of value, provided that we use our freedom wisely. Freedom here is not total autonomy but differentiated relationality. Never mere liberty from relational entanglement, freedom enables the development of authentic human centeredness and mutual relations, such that we enhance value through our interaction. Community and freedom are here correlative, not inimical, possibilities. Furthermore, in process theology, movement, not stasis, is the source of all our knowledge. Our rationality is grounded not merely in cerebral function or cognitive structure but in a total bodily apprehension of the relational matrix of the world. A process perspective yields a rich understanding of human reason as wholistic apprehension and creative transmutation of the world. In this perspective, process is the only inexorable reality we know; all of human reality — our knowledge, our values — must be understood as embedded in temporal spatial movement. Only that which is dead does not change, and change may go on even beyond death. And, important to our topic, human intelligence is both conditioned by and conditions all change. The moral stakes of life are perpetually and irrevocably heightened by human freedom. All the interventions that we make collectively and individually in the world process become part of our natural-historical reality. To be human is to bear the burden of a genuine freedom grounded in God, but in which even God cannot arbitrarily intervene.[60]

Many female theologians have perceived the value of a process perspective for a theological revisioning that is adequate to their demands for a wholistic and experiential approach to theology.[61] Process theology can help overcome the sharp dualisms of matter and spirit, mind and body, nature and history so characteristic of mainstream Christian theology. Not surprisingly, process theology also has led some male theologians to appreciate that it really is simplistic to view early fetal life as full human life.[62] How a process perspective may contribute to our view of fetal life will be discussed in Chapter 7. It is also clear that the overall perspective enables a less static understanding of the web of relationships to which women must answer in making abortion decisions.

Recently, Jean Lambert, feminist process theologian, demonstrated the richness of a process viewpoint in interpreting the abortion experience. She rightly insists that the discussion rests in a biological-social-moral nexus that requires a complex assessment of many values relevant to the decision. Given the tragic nature of the choices women face in the abortion dilemma, she also emphasizes that a process theological perspective makes room for mistakes and conflicts and does not ascribe absolute uniqueness to the dilemma. Of the woman weighing an abortion decision, she says:

It is important for her to recognize . . . that her decisions are made in a world in which there is a call to do good, a call to be generous, a call to self-fulfillment. But it is also a world in which it is also certain that creation both recovers from wrong decisions and continues to be alive to the processes of creation. It is important for her to be open to the possibility that the way this "works" is not best understood by natural law, but by forgiveness. . . . In this perspective, she may recognize that God's purposes include her freedom to choose, and that God's resources of imagination and forgiveness are available to heal, direct, and enrich her life whatever she decides. Her life may be lived responsibly and creatively with or without a pregnancy to complete and the gains and losses involved, though real, are not the last word on anything.[63]

Such insight confirms the hope that the best resources of modern liberal theology can be enlisted in the service of a viewpoint on abortion that respects women's lives. A revisioned theological perspective on procreation and abortion should draw upon both the Protestant motif of our genuine historicity and the traditional emphasis of Catholic theology on the cosmic context of our lives. With the Roman Catholic tradition of moral theology, the revisioned theology affirms our ability as intelligent beings to wrestle with the circumstances of existence and to reach moral resolutions. At the same time, such a theological approach must accept, without equivocation or qualification, women's full and nondependent cohumanity with men and our full capacity as free, centered rational moral agents to make decisions that most deeply affect us.

One further step is also necessary. We need to begin to realize that there is almost nothing more urgent, in light of changing circumstances on our planet Earth, than to recognize that the entire natural-historical context of human procreative power has shifted. While the so-called issue of overpopulation is often approached with little sensitivity to the moral dimensions of the problem, it is childish to deny that the question of population growth is not a human moral issue overall.[64] Because survival of the species is no longer at issue, we desperately need to desacralize our biological power to reproduce the species. I am fully aware that both nonwhite and poor people legitimately fear the concerns that inform some white people's anxiety about the population question. Racial genocide *is* a real issue in our world.[65] Increasingly, however, it is masculinist Christians who hurl the accusation of genocide at pro-choice proponents. The perspective I advocate here is one that places abortion in the context of the appropriateness of procreative choice for each woman's life and insists that racial and ethnic women are at a special disadvantage, given white supremacy, in decisions about childbearing. Those who accuse the proponents of legal abortion of genocide do not care about the devastating effects of racism on women's procreative freedom. Furthermore, they imply that *any* concern for population growth is morally inappropriate. In this regard, they are not to be taken seriously. Population growth is a complex moral question.[66]

A basic theological issue is how we are to break the ancient unquestioned equation between divine blessing and procreative power while simultaneously increasing our sense of urgency about creating widespread conditions that foster genuine human dignity. This is, admittedly, a challenge and a complicated task, both morally and theologically. We are obligated, however, to make our ethical and religious traditions, like our own lives, responsive to the often new requirements of the human species and to personal well-being.

To desacralize procreation does not imply devaluing it or denying the great beauty of childbearing and its intrinsic or social value. Rather, it means that we need both to end the exclusivity and to reduce the intensity of our reverence for unshaped or undirected procreative process, while deepening our celebration of other valuable, community-shaping human activity. Human fertility, like other human capacities, is never untouched by human decision, and it requires, more than ever, our intelligence and moral discernment. We also need to rapidly move away from the idea that divine blessing of humanity is best expressed by metaphors rooted in biology. Social and relational values bear the image of the holy most adequately. Recently this point was made eloquently by a distinguished Roman Catholic feminist sociologist of religion, and she deserves to be quoted at length:

> As long as the central human need called for the continued motivation to propagate the race, it was essential that religious symbols idealize that process above all others. Given the vicissitudes of life in a hostile environment, women had to be encouraged to bear children and men to support them; child-bearing was central to the struggle for existence.

Today, however, the size of the base population, together with knowledge already accumulated about artificial insemination, sperm banking, cloning, make more certain a peopled world.

The more serious human problems now are who will live, who will die and who will decide . . .

Today father-right has been replaced by human rights as the ethical norm for international relations as well as for communal relations under the law.[67]

To appreciate, as Marie Augusta Neal does, that morals must shift as objective historical conditions shift is not *moral* relativism. In the past, it may have been right to legitimize the celebration of procreation among human beings unequivocally, but that is no longer so. Historical relativity in theology and ethics is not moral relativity, nor is it subjectivism. Our obligation to act, consistent with our considered moral judgment, is not denied. What a historically based perspective on change enables us to see is that our theological power to image and revision a world grounded in relations of justice and love can be a resource for directing that change to serve not only species well-being but cosmic community.

By contrast, those who believe that Christian theology, as the "queen" of sciences, requires a privileged position and that its "truth" can live untouched by change end up equating Christian theology with an ideology of the status quo. Worse, such Christians drive a wedge between Christian theology and any growing, living moral point of view. Many already believe that it is not possible to be both moral and Christian, which is mute testimony to how often Christians have voiced obscurantist theology. But an intrinsically moral Christian theology, one that actively supports the ongoing struggle for genuine human emancipation from oppression, is possible. The dominant misogyny and masculinist theological impulses of Christianity can be laid to rest and replaced with a spirituality both more life-affirming and more respectful of human finitude. The theological elements of such a spirituality need to be further developed so that we can place our understanding of procreation and abortion in a theological context that actually celebrates women's lives.

4

Toward a Liberating Theological Perspective on Procreative Choice and Abortion

A LIBERATION THEOLOGY PERSPECTIVE

The analysis in Chapter 3 of contemporary Christian theological attitudes and teachings pertinent to procreative choice reveals that theological assumptions infuse the moral debate on abortion not so much at the level of principle but at subtler levels that we may not recognize if we focus only on the specific moral arguments. This chapter identifies an alternative Christian theology that can inform an ethic of procreative choice, one that enables us to embrace our capacity to make decisions about childbearing in a humanly inclusive way. Although it is possible only to trace the main outlines of such a theological outlook here, even a preliminary sketch may help us recognize that there is no contradiction between deep religious sensibility and a morality that supports procreative choice as well as the option of abortion in some or many circumstances.

I agree with those liberation theologians, newly emergent in Christianity and admittedly a minority, who understand that any theological conception is rooted in and shaped by our way of acting in the world. In other words, a living theological tradition is one that actually is grounded in responsible moral choice.[1] When, through courageous moral action, we anticipate an alternative, historically liberating mode of being in the world, a new sense of God's living presence unfolds. Out of a moral struggle to embody deeper patterns of human community, freshly empowering visions of God are born. Of course, this does not imply that such moral efforts have always been easy or inevitably victorious. On the contrary, such efforts are rarely vindicated. The crucifixions of those who act boldly, in courage and love, are actually more the norm than the exception in our history. The Crucifixion remains a meaningful Christian motif not because, as fundamentalism teaches, God demands sacrifice or solely because Jesus was crucified but because such confrontation is costly, as is demonstrated in the lives of those, including Jesus, who powerfully challenge injustice. Theological vision, at its best, is intrinsic to our struggle against the moral evil so tenaciously present in life. While not the dominant and reigning understanding of Christian faith, this interpretation does have ancient roots in Hebraic and Christian tradition.

The prophetic writings of ancient Israel, the life of Jesus, and the most liberating theologies generated by Christians over the centuries articulate a call to serious immersion in real, concrete human suffering.[2] This tradition provides us with an "authoring past," an authority to courage which, through time, helps us ground ourselves in faithful action in the present. We stand within this tradition, but, as my previous discussion of biblicism made clear, such a tradition in no way substitutes for creative and intelligent moral action in the present. A morally accountable theology cannot consign the locus of all moral truth to the past. I have argued that moral struggle is the dimension of our lives that emerges, in the here and now, when new circumstances confront the norms of received tradition. The existence of newer means of birth control, including abortion, has resulted in this kind of confrontation. Such encounters engender conflict but also create intellectual ferment and fresh reflection on our present reality and received traditions. The connection between our theological vision and our moral sensibility, including our capacity for moral reasoning, is dialectical and reciprocal, not deductive. Moral reasoning proceeds inductively from real, given dilemmas. Simultaneously, our sense of the value of life and what it means to live humanly is shaped and informed by past pilgrimages, the accounts of those preceding us who share a passionate love of life and a desire for universal justice. Though the trajectory of human history is not one of simple moral progress, a humane theology perceives real moral gains in history and even in dismal times inspires the hope that our lives and our environment need not be relegated to inhumane forces.

From this theological perspective, faith is understood chiefly as the power (and it is a power, a shared or communal power) to live one's life fully, genuinely engaged in receiving and communicating a sense of life's joy and possibility. To live by faith means to accept one's own power, always partial and finite, always power-in-relation, but nonetheless real, to engage life with others and to tenderly shape the processes of nature/history for genuine human and cosmic fulfillment. Such faith, according to an ancient Christian theological formula, requires hope as its ground and love as its foundation. The opposite of such faith is not, as in rationalistic theology, intellectual doubt or disbelief in specific doctrines or theories. The opposite of faith is despair, hopelessness, acquiescence to one's powerlessness, and refusal to act as a responsible agent in moral struggle. Faithful persons and communities are those who find ways to "keep on keeping on."[3] Juan Luis Segundo is correct when he says that faith is the power of "learning how to learn"[4] in order to live in a faithful manner.

The agenda of placing such a moral vision at the center of Christian theology has always been advanced best by marginalized Christian groups who were, in one way or another, the victims of morally disordered authority and power. What liberation theologians refer to as "the epistemological privilege of the poor" is not a cliché.[5] Those on "the underside of history" best comprehend how arbitrary the historical structures of privilege are. Privileges — life advantages that give us usually unnoticed power over others — obscure moral perception. Those who live outside these structures of privilege often discern systemic moral evils ignored by the powerful, who mystify the world by equating status with virtue. Liberation theologies in Latin America, Africa, and Asia, and those in the United States articulated by blacks, Hispanics, Asians, indigenous Americans, and feminists (both women of color and white women), take it as axiomatic that this epistemological privilege is rooted not in race or gender as mere biological categories but in the concrete experience of living on the underside of history.[6] Whatever their differences, liberation theologians are united in saying an unequivocal no to the trends in human history that have elevated some as masters and rendered others as their slaves.

As I have indicated, a feminist liberation hermeneutic requires an understanding of social oppression expansive enough to incorporate all women's reality. Women are an underclass within every group and community, even though we are an absolute majority of the species. While specifically targeting the moral and theological assumptions that feed religious legitimations of the oppression of women, a feminist perspective also recognizes that the structures of race and class are not reducible to gender oppression.[7] At the same time, we know that all who are powerless, men and women alike, will be considered "feminized" or masculine-deficient people. A feminist liberation perspective cannot compromise the awareness that the idolatry of male supremacy is never absent when patterns of domination exist.

The insights of various liberation theologies about a theological praxis that challenges oppression are not without parallel in some Christian theological perspectives developed by white men.[8] In Chapter 3 I reviewed some of the contributions of liberal theology to acknowledge that the concern for locating the moral point of view at the center of Christian life and practice has precedents among Euro-American male theologians. To be sure, many of these theological liberals either have been too naive about the corruptions of power — any power that is not reciprocal power[9] — or have identified too closely with the affluence of "enlightened people" to grasp the depth of the problem of *human* evil or the social complexity of the moral task. Many have become so identified with the existing order that they block the emergence of crucially needed skepticism about power and privilege in our society. Few have permitted themselves to face the scope of social injustice. Nevertheless, a liberation hermeneutic is interested not in condemning white males but in calling all people to thoroughgoing moral accountability for our world, which we are in danger of passing on as an even greater moral disaster.

Because an emancipatory or liberation hermeneutic rejects the notion that theory (theological, moral, or social) stands in *deductive* relation (and therefore in a position of control) to actual experience, we stress that our knowledge itself is grounded in our agency or activity. We "see" the world through the interests embedded in our action, and our rational, cognitive reflections are moments internal to that ongoing activity. *Praxis* — a term that helps us bypass older, dualistic notions of a split between thought and practice — implies that all our activity, including our reflection, truly shapes our way of perceiving the world and, therefore, what we know of it. Philosophers as diverse as Karl Marx, John Dewey, and Alfred North Whitehead have stressed this understanding of intellectual activity over against the dominant idealist western tradition's division of thought and action, in which practical activity proceeds deductively from thought.[10] What we do influences what we perceive and therefore what we come to know, which means that our human projects fatefully determine our world view. This is why moral arguments always are as much about what *is* the case as about what ought to be the case. If the praxis of a person or group is devoted to maintaining the order of the world as it is, then the group's reading of the "facts" will always support the status quo. By contrast, if a person's or a group's praxis aims to overcome what thwarts their common life in the present, they will know the world in a different way, and "official truth" will appear as the distortions of the powerful who are in control.[11] Much of what the privileged take for solemn truth the dispossessed know as "lies, secrets, and silences"[12] through which the powerful interpret reality as benign.

The major polemic against Christian liberation theologies is that they lack "objectivity," that their proponents are caught up in advocacy and cannot make reasoned judgments like more "dispassionate" (often this means "uninvolved") people. Such claims obscure the differences between liberation perspectives and the idealist views of knowledge. Objectivity is a theoretical ideal, not the "possession" of anyone.[13] A liberationist viewpoint assumes that everyone has an "interest" — that is, that our energy is focused toward and invested in some configuration of social relations. To be objective, we must own these loyalties and commitments rather than profess to stand above them. Furthermore, objectivity is not the province of any group or class. Intellectuals, in particular, sometimes presume that objectivity is guaranteed either by a particular method of inquiry or by one's social location in academic institutions. That such institutions have specific allegiances and investments in society is obvious enough. In addition, every method of human inquiry is rooted in social interest. Therefore, knowledge is a form of power, with moral implications for how we use it. Idealist epistemologies fail to acknowledge this. An objectivist, detached understanding of knowledge obscures our accountability to those affected by the power of knowledge.

Rejecting "disinterestedness" as a sufficient notion of what constitutes objectivity does not preclude liberation theologians from embracing the criteria of clear reason-giving, careful documentation, and public accountability. Furthermore, a posture of open advocacy is in no way antithetical to or compromising of these criteria, whereas spurious claims to disinterestedness may undermine them. A feminist liberation commitment, in particular, is necessary precisely to assure the full integration of women's experience within theology as well as accountability to its dimensions, unacknowledged in the masculinist bias of established Christian truth. Without a fully feminist revisioning of Christianity, the misogyny deeply embedded in Christian tradition, yet prompted quickly to the surface when women's lives, procreation, and abortion are at issue, will not be laid to rest.

FEMINIST THEOLOGIES: EMERGING CONVERGENCES AND TENSIONS

Christian feminist liberation theology has emerged side by side with other powerful feminist theological perspectives generated by religious feminists in other traditions. Jewish feminism is a robust, creative force.[14] And many women, though raised in Christianity, no longer wish to be identified with efforts to transform Christian theology in the direction outlined here. Christian women may well be a minority in a broad-based feminist spirituality movement, many sectors of which consciously oppose Christianity and any other male-controlled religious system. Some of the most forceful and suggestive expressions of feminist theology come today from the pens of such women, who represent a serious and important dimension of female religious experience.[15] Women have always been a minority religious voice in Christian culture, and, as we will see, much that is feared as "pagan" in Christian history encompasses the silenced expression of women's experience and, perhaps, women's religious practice. Feminist Christian liberation theology, if it does forthright work, is bound to have as much or more in common with these other women's theologies than with the official established and dominant versions of Christianity. No Christian feminist need feel uneasy about this fact. By now it should be clear that far too much that passes today for Christian orthodoxy is but the account the victors give of those they have vanquished, to paraphrase Simone Weil's trenchant way of describing official history.[16] For this reason, Christian women cannot afford to renege on their own experience or be intimidated by charges of heresy.

What Christian liberation feminists embrace is *not* the dominant orthodox traditions but an "underground" tradition of Christianity, drawing from the stories that make up this tradition a word of courage and power for resistance to our own and others' subjugation. Feminist Christians share with post-christian feminists a grave suspicion of patriarchal or masculinist spirituality and a pledge to live in protest against it. Starhawk, a perceptive theologian of the new feminist spirituality, is correct in her insistence that

> it is with the future that any system of ethics and justice must be concerned, because the ethics of the unarguable, historical, well-documented and patriarchal religions and cultures have brought us to a point where our chances of destroying ourselves and poisoning the biosphere seem much greater than our chance of preserving life into the future. Never before have we as a species had the potential for causing such widespread social, biological and irreversible destruction, yet never before have we had such potential for the alleviation of poverty, hunger, disease, and social injustice and for the fostering of individual freedom, growth and creativity. The choices we must make, although they are rarely posed in these terms, are essentially ethical choices.
> The conceptions of justice in the Western, patriarchal religions are based on a worldview which locates deity outside the world. Of course, within each tradition there are exceptions, but in the broad view of Christianity, Judaism and Islam, God is transcendent, and his laws are absolutes, which can be considered in a context removed both from the reality of human needs and desires, and the reality of their actual effects. . . Because when we believe that what is sacred — and therefore, most highly valued — is *not* what we see and sense and experience, we maintain an inherent split in consciousness that allows us to quite comfortably cause pain and suffering in pursuit of an unmanifest good.[17]

A feminist Christian liberation theology joins post- and non-Christian feminists in placing the burden of proof on dominant patriarchal forms of religion to demonstrate their compatibility with what is concretely good for people and for creation.

Central to feminist religious theory is the notion that our lives are intrinsically culture-creating. For feminist spirituality, our human existence is distinctive by virtue of our shared creative power, our work as culture formers. All human expression is creative. Speech and listening, for example, are reciprocal acts such that we hear each other into speech[18] and become centered, self-determining selves by owning the power to name, shape, and express our world.[19] A feminist theological perspective acknowledges that a religious mode of expression is one among several ways by which we seek to situate ourselves and our world, to ground and mold our creative power. For a feminist theology, our spiritual power emerges as we begin to hear, speak, and name our own stories. The mutual appropriation of these stories fosters a basic bonding with others. Out of the reciprocal acts of hearing and speaking, the power of relationship is born.

Feminist theological discourse is not, as much masculinist discourse is, a privileged mode. Rather, it is both a valued and a conditional mode of understanding. Even in its most abstract forms, theological discourse is understood as a finite language of lived human experience, a way of naming for ourselves what is sacred or of consummate value. Nor does a feminist theology give precedence to analytic, abstract, or explanatory modes of theological discourse. Though feminists do not eschew these modes, they identify the primary mode of all theological reflection as *image, metaphor,* and *movement.*[20] Theological utterance becomes possible via every mode of human expression. Movement, as ritual and dance, poetry, the visual arts, and music, is perfectly suited to theological expression because it inspires human creativity to express the depth and richness of the life-world process and, in turn, to tap its power.

A Christian feminist liberation theology, then, embraces the power of creativity as foundational to human spirituality and to morality. Seen from this perspective, the aim of theological expression becomes one of making the world luminous, enabling us to apprehend, via our own creativity, the power of the creation that enfolds and sustains us and to responsibly shape that creation through our agency. There are, however, bipartite emphases to this feminist theological revisioning of the Christian story. On the one hand, we celebrate creation, receive it as a gift of God, and pass it on, transformed through our shared creative power. This cosmic-natural-world-historical process, whether envisioned as energy or as matter, is good and precious, the bearer of divine blessing. Reverence and celebration are appropriate responses to what is life-giving in this process. On the other hand, the lure of life, our longing for fulfillment, and our longing for connectedness to the whole is no transhistorical constant. Brokenness and evil are not mere flaws in an otherwise seamless web of life and cocreativity. They are real forces, active forms of misdirected power that crush, wound, and render us blind to our cosmic connections, our basic and irreducible cohumanity in relation to God, and to our power to act in mutual relationship and, therefore, our power to be.[21] As a feminist, I remain a Christian not because organized Christianity has any deeper perspective on or sensitivity to this cosmic-natural-cultural matrix than other religious world views but because my own struggle with injustice has been shaped by an understanding of love and justice mediated through a particular history that bears this Godly power of right relationship. Jesus of Nazareth and some of his followers have forged new bonds of cohumanity, incarnate evidence of God's power in our midst. In light of this history, I have learned that the world God yearns for through us, and that we long for in God, is a place free of brokenness and evil, a domain where, as Jules Girardi puts it, there are "no excluded ones."[22]

The task of feminist liberation theology is not merely a causal or explanatory one, confined to a linear form of thought. In one dimension, it works critically to identify and analyze the past and present order of things and to understand our contemporary situation and how it has been shaped by our social history. But the other fundamental dimension of its work is utopic envisagement. Feminist theology has joined other Christian liberation theologies in defending our very human need for utopic and ecstatic vision against an acute anti-utopian strain in much mainstream Christian theology.[23] Utopian thinking is important not merely because it is creative but, more significantly, because it breaks the hold of the here and now in all of its oppressive dimensions. It is an irreducible element in the empowering of human beings not only to resist what destroys life in the present order of things but to risk new steps toward a humane world. Without such vision, we could not strive for richer, more expansive, and inclusive modes of community; we simply would settle for our existing gods and loyalties. The image of utopian community, which many feminists term the "Commonwealth of God," is one in which genuine solidarity exists between all human beings and God. In feminist terms, God is not the One who stands remotely in control, but the One who binds us and bids us to deep relationality, resulting in a radical equality motivated by genuine mutuality and interdependence.[24] In a community transformed by this utopian vision, power would be experienced as *reciprocity in relation*. In other words, our individual power to act would be nourished and enhanced by mutual regard and cocreativity.

Freedom, when understood as the power of creativity, achieves its consummate expression in deepened community. The illusion that "freedom" signifies either invulnerability to others or freedom from the power of persons to affect us appears in feminist perspectives as a distortion of life's possibility. To be free means possessing the power to imaginatively interact with others, to give and to receive, to act upon and to suffer (that is, to be acted upon), to participate with others in cocreating a world. If the world we create turns out to be unfit for human habitation, it will be because our interpersonal relations have been dominated by the desire for control over, rather than collaboration with, each other. From a feminist theological perspective, radical human evil of such magnitude can be overcome only if we reshape our institutions and patterns of praxis to render our cohumanity realizable. Needless to say, such a theology does not look to an all-powerful deity to "save" or "redeem." Rather, it draws on a sustaining power, immanent in life, and a concrete history of forerunners whose acts of love and courage "held open a place for us" before we were ready to take our own place.[25] In a feminist Christian theology we dare not confuse such a vision, which is literally u-topia (no place), with the historical world we inhabit and in which we must live as moral agents. In the absence of real engagement with moral evil, utopian thinking breaks loose from its concrete moorings in human creativity and tends toward grandiosity and romanticism. Thus unmoored, we catapult from losing touch with the finite nature of human existence to underestimating or evading the extent of the entrenchment of moral evil in our world. Even if deep social-historical evil were not a reality in our lives, all of us are constrained by the limits set by our relatedness to others and to a manifold environment. Appreciation of the pluralism and complexity of the total, cosmic environment is central to any feminist vision, while the fundamental connectedness and the interweaving of all of life have emerged as a pivotal theme in Christian, Jewish, and post-christian women's theological reflection.

Once we acknowledge the interconnectedness of life, however, it is necessary that we overcome any vestiges of subject-object split in our modes of knowledge, along with any exclusionary categories in our world views. All feminist theologies have offered a compelling account of the relation between dualistic thinking and the rigid gender distinctions necessary to keep a patriarchal mythos in place. When theological categories are employed with an either/or logic — either divine *or* human; *either* strong *or* weak; *either* in nature *or* in history; *either* spirit *or* matter; *either* subject *or* object — we may hypothesize that inelastic gender constructs are at work. As Nancy Jay has observed,[26] conservative groups across a number of cultures, who inculcate rigid gender dichotomies, take male supremacy as the pattern for their religious outlook and also internalize an either/or perception of reality.[27] While a few feminist theologians appear to uphold gender dichotomy by reversing male and female supremacy[28] or by claiming the spiritual superiority of the "feminine" or of distinctively female experience,[29] the mainstream of feminist theology protests such exclusionary logic as counter to the intrinsic relationality of all life. In reaction to patriarchal, male-superiority themes in traditional theology, there has been an understandable tendency in some feminist theology to perpetuate reverse dualisms.

In reaction to the patriarchal notion that God is totally transcendent and therefore the sole possessor of uncorrupted spiritual power, for example, some feminist theologians have reverted to advocating the total immanence of deity. The goddess or god, in opposition to the objectified and alienated "wholly other" transcendence of patriarchal deities, is deemed wholly immanent. Instead of revisioning the issue, these feminists end up embracing the other side of a false dualism. I believe that transcendence and immanence in divine and human experience are reciprocally related; our experience and knowledge of God as transcendent come to us through both our own radical immanence *and* God's radical immanence in nature-history.[30] Furthermore, in our creative power we can be said to transcend God's present manifestations, just as, in differing ways, God transcends us.

Another dualism perpetuated by some feminist theology is the nature/history split, already so endemic to Protestant Christianity. Women's special connection to nature[31] has been proclaimed and women's spirituality interpreted exclusively as a form of natural piety that eschews historical consciousness. Occasionally, the theme of "receptivity" to life and nature has become strong enough to expunge the "dualism" of good and evil. To be sure, both good and evil are complexly interwoven in our lives, and moral discernment in history is difficult. Moreover, these realities are compounded by the fact that much evil is perpetrated by persons of great moral certitude. But a feminist spirituality that does not encompass our historicity can lead to a form of idealism in which the "proper" subjective attitude is considered sufficient to overcome evil. Such theology is doomed to lapse into abstract individualism in which "our" spirituality is realized apart from relationship. I have already protested as "romantic" any view that looks upon nature as a completely benign force or eschews freedom and self-determination as constituent aspects of the natural-historical-cultural process. Not only are nature and history inseparable but they coalesce in a unified, interactive process. Inexorably we dwell in nature-culture-history, and we function as subjects and objects simultaneously. A feminist analysis should attempt to dislodge an objectified view of nature, not to separate human intelligence and action from it. Masculinist theory aims to know and identify entities in nature as "objects," in and of themselves, but a feminist theological approach cannot pretend that we comprehend anything "in itself." When objectified, existing entities become mere abstractions. All that exists does so in relationship, and all relations are shaped by continuous cocreative action.

The centrality of relationality to a theology that respects women's experience is, as I have already noted, of utmost importance when we approach the abortion question. To recognize our relatedness-in-process to all things is to acknowledge that we are a part of nature in an implacable way, and, through human species-being, the natural cosmological process has become a creative world-shaping historical process as well. But we are also, through and through, natural-historical beings, shapers of nature through culture and history. Childbearing in its natural dimension is *sui generis;* it cannot be understood through social analogy, yet it cannot be understood apart from its systemic social context. It is at once a biological, cultural, social, and historical reality. If we do not see this clearly, our "reverence for nature" could lead to the romantic view that any exercise of moral choice about childbearing is a manipulation of otherwise spontaneous "natural" process. Affirming only one side of the nature/history dualism or insisting that women have a special relationship to nature by virtue of our procreative power sounds very reminiscent of an older, nonrelational biological determinism. By virtue of our agency, we are always cocreative participants in reproduction. Culture, society, and history shape the meaning of pregnancy. Therefore, the expression of the human power of procreation never has occurred outside a relational context of human cocreation.

Whether or not we choose to bear children, whether or not we choose to bear all the children we happen to conceive, our creative agency is an ingredient in what transpires. We cannot, and do not, leave any part of our world unchanged, whatever we choose. Whether we say yes or no to pregnancy, both may be creative historical actions. The former response does not lie outside of history, in nature, nor is the latter nonnatural. Both constitute human, historical choices. As creative respondents, we are making and being made constantly, in/by/with our world. The thoroughgoing sociality of all things is such that we coinhere in each other, and our decisions leave their mark. It has taken both scientists and theologians too long to learn that we inhabit only one environment, an intimately interacting web of life. Because we are constantly acting and being acted upon within a highly complex environment, we cannot shun our freedom or our responsibility for the way things are. This recognition should deepen our sense of awe and respect for the tender but formidable power we possess in relation to our own and each other's being-in-the-world.

Without such awareness, the consequences of our human activity often outstrip our knowledge or capacity to adjust and control our actions. We leave our touch, our mark, on the total environment throughout our lifetimes. Grounded in this understanding, we can adopt a form of "reverence for life" as a basic attitude of a feminist spirituality. But "reverence for life" is not, nor can it be, a sort of naturalistic mysticism that requires our passivity or quiescence in relation to each other or the rest of nature. It is that sort of "naturism" that dominant theological teaching predicates for women. By contrast, a feminist spirituality seeks to expand our capacity for receptivity and creative action simultaneously.

LIFE AS CREATIVE AGENCY: AFFIRMATIONS OF A FEMINIST CHRISTIAN SPIRITUALITY

A feminist spirituality, in sharp distinction from masculinist forms of Christian spirituality, does not permit us to accept a split between contemplation and activity or a division between receiving life as a gift and shaping life as an agent. The primacy of contemplation in patriarchal spirituality implicitly affirms passivity as *the* proper religious attitude. Furthermore, such spirituality makes "obedience" a central moral virtue.[32] By contrast, feminist spirituality esteems responsibility, as cocreativity in action, as fundamental to moral value. We are at our best, morally, when we find new ways to act, explore previously untried social strategies to meet our moral dilemmas, or discover fresh approaches to old problems. I have argued elsewhere that contrary to male-articulated theories of "women's nature," women have been the activists in various human communities;[33] the major exception may be the modern "feminized" or "passivized" woman, the bourgeois ideal of the nineteenth and twentieth centuries. Not merely procreation but all of women's work has been basic to communal survival. Usually women provide and maintain the wider primary life-support systems within their communities, which has meant not only childbearing and childrearing, but, just as frequently, coping with unwanted fertility when communal survival is at stake. No theology reflective of women's experience would equate spirituality with withdrawal from mundane, world-sustaining activities or neglect the spiritual power generated through them. Holiness in the form of world-withdrawal neither pertains to a woman's experience nor characterizes women's primary mode of religious experience.

Women, as the artists of communal survival, have never been strangers to hard choices. The mundane activity of life maintenance through which women's moral agency has been expressed is continuous and ongoing. In daily life, women have been actively involved not only in reproducing the species but also in constructing and transmitting a foundational cultural world. Living close to a material base; knowing what it means to need food, clothing, shelter; practicing the domestic arts so essential to survival have made most women realists. Rearing and raising children, caring for the sick and the aged have made women aware of what it means, and what it really takes, to build and sustain human community. Prior to the rise of the capitalist market system with its centralized mode of production, women and men, far more than now, shared in production *and* control of whatever material resources a family unit accumulated. The separation of the home as the arena of private domesticity from the economic world of production and public order is a fairly recent phenomenon, intrinsic to a centralized mode of production. The economic organization and development of capitalism, which created the mobile nuclear family, increased the isolation of individual women, sundering women from larger family networks as well as from traditional women's culture, which oversaw not only childbearing and nurturance but, often, material provisioning for the community. Male-generated theories have encouraged many modern women to perceive themselves as passive, acquiescent, and, above all, lacking in the real power of agency necessary for full personhood. Many women actually have believed themselves incapable of handling social power and responsibility, because "women's work" has come to seem so unworthy in men's eyes. The myth of the cult of true womanhood, stressing both woman's greater moral sensibility and her greater innocence in relation to power, gained so much force precisely because of women's increasing lack of access to power as societies became more differentiated structurally.

The contrast between women's historical activism and the ideal of agency in masculinist aspiration is especially striking. From the perspective of dominant ideals, "real agents" are those who can and should exercise a sort of Promethean power of contol. Both perfectionism — the ideal of perfect self-control — and messianism — the ideal of perfect deliverance through another's acts — are products of masculinist, nonrelational aspirations. In such a vision of moral agency, human reason is understood as that which furnishes us with a capacity for control as dominion over our world. Traditional Christian ethics, to be sure, is ambivalent about this scenario of human mastery. On the one hand, the Christian is one who speaks and acts for God and even pronounces God's will unambiguously. On the other hand, the Christian totally renounces the self to God's will. I have already noted that the radical self-renunciation pole of this ethic is usually relegated to women, while the power to proclaim the "Word" is earmarked for men.

A feminist Christian spirituality, by contrast, affirms the appropriateness of the power of being we possess, share, and express in reciprocity with others. Our freedom and power of agency does not mean that we have any presumed Promethean power as individuals who in isolation direct the world or other people. We need neither mastery over others nor total self-possession. But it is not surprising that theologically conservative abortion opponents perceive legal abortion as granting women the right to "play God." They see and invariably interpret the resort to abortion as women's possession of an utterly inappropriate power-of-control over society. Erected on the scaffold of a masculinist concept of power, this interpretation obfuscates the fact that a woman's procreative power is but one thread in a complex web of relationships. As often as not, a woman's decision to have an abortion is the result of her intricately balancing several values and responding to a multifaceted set of accountabilities.

In feminist theology, the new appreciation of women's sexuality referred to earlier is understood as critical to revisioning our power of procreation adequately and to appreciating that we are "our bodies ourselves."[34] A plethora of feminist scholarship has begun to revision women's understanding of our sexuality and its relation to procreation.[35] Because women are taught to live in relation to male expectations, many of us have come to realize that our sexuality has been enshrouded in a mythos gauged to keep us from knowing even our own needs and desires. Many women have been robbed of the appreciation of their own sensuality through repression in the service of being "good women" and the expectation that women's sexuality is mobilized and mediated only when we are in sexual relationships with men. Women have come to recognize and affirm the centrality and pervasiveness of sensuality in all aspects of our lives. We do not merely have bodies. The body-self is the integrated locus of our being in the world. We are related to everything through our body-selves; our bodies ground our connection to our world. Our bodies are the vehicles of relation that put us in touch with reality at every level.

Celebration of sensuality and of feeling as its medium, however, must go hand in hand with another dynamic stressed in women's discovery of what genuine liberation entails: the integrity of centered self-direction in expressing our power of relationship. Our dignity as persons depends upon that. Our bodies *are* ourselves, and they *should be* ours, unmediated by others' power to determine, control, manipulate, or seduce. Without this emphasis, "the sensuous woman" degenerates into another, better playmate for patriarchal fantasies of male as mediator of women's sexual experience. Women too long have been perceived only as bodies, objects for male ego enhancement, whose integrity, dignity, and power of self-direction may be ignored or denied by men. It is a rare — and privileged — woman who does not assimilate the generalized fear of body objectification through some man's presumed "right" to treat her body as an object. Widespread social patterns of spouse battering, rape, incest, and sexual harassment, to which women usually fall victim, testify loudly and clearly that we live in a culture that allows men to do what they will with women's body-selves. These forms of abuse demonstrate that our society does not understand sexuality as sensuality, but rather equates or confuses it with control over another, with manipulation, or even with violence — control by the power of physical force. Sexuality as the tender sensuality of mutual pleasuring apparently does not turn on many people.

This vision of the integrity of our body-self fuses with our understanding of the relationality of all things, to help us recognize that the integrity of self-directed body space is never an end in itself. Carter Heyward makes the point with characteristic feminist precision, when she says of the body:

> there is nothing higher, nothing more holy. It is nonsense, it is wrong, to contrast God as "spirit," with the body, be it the individual human body or the body of humanity or, indeed, the body of all that is created.
>
> My body is not a shell into and out of which God moves, leaving me either godly or ungodly. The body of humanity and of creation is not a network of bone and flesh and cells and particles that is either or not visited by God, leaving the world either holy or unholy. . .
>
> Granted, we encounter a puzzling confusion between the holy value of who each of us is as a body on the one hand, each of us needing badly to realize and celebrate the wonder that she or he is, and a preoccupation with the self on the other. Therapy, spirituality, charismatic religion, women's and gays' movements have heightened our capacities to claim our worth and power. This can be, and usually is, a very very good thing. Its positive role expectations replace other false expectations that prevent our knowledge of ourselves. We are meant and called to be more creative, I think, more honest, more joyful and more caring human beings when we do this, than when we see ourselves largely through the eyes of others — parents, employers, doctors, lovers, gurus, those to whom we give social and ecclesiastical authority. Yes, there is a moral imperative to love ourselves, to be tender with ourselves, to comfort and enjoy ourselves, our bodies. To grow in self-esteem, to take pleasure in who we are precisely because our bodies are members of God's body in the world. And in tending our own needs and yearnings, we are tending God's. But this same self-centeredness, this centeredness of self, which I believe is vital to our constructive faith, can, as all good things, be perverted, distorted. And this happens *in the very instant we forget the relation.* We forget that all bodies are holy and as important as our own. And that, therefore, you must be as holy to me as I am to myself. (Italics mine)[36]

The consequence of breaking through male-projected definitions of woman-as-body has been to enable women to step outside the "looking-glass effect" — that is, the practice of perceiving ourselves through a mirror, objectified.[37] The experience of beginning to live from the center of ourselves outward has invigorated women with a new sense of spiritual power. This process enhances our capacity for action and self-direction and augments our ability to face life in its full complexity and interconnectedness. It allows us to experience spirituality not as life denial, but as body animation, living passionately through our embodiment. Such a spirituality takes seriously the full range of conditions necessary for human well-being in the world.

The rediscovery of life as an act of relationship, mediated by sensuality, transforms our expectation and conception of God. God/Goddess[38] is no longer envisaged as an isolated, invulnerable, all-competent agent who rules and remains in control. God is not the "wholly other" projected by patriarchal piety; nor is God the "He" who remains unaffected by the world. God is the preceding one, a representing power present to us as companion, one who supports, encourages, lures us into activity-in-relation. We encounter God through relationship with all that nurtures and sustains life. It is not "God's will," understood as inscrutable fiat or abstract intention, that determines what occurs or is uniquely sacred. Rather, God-in-relation to and with us acts to ground, sustain, and bring forth concrete value.

In a feminist theory, questions such as "Who is God in Himself?" and "What was He doing before He created us?" are perceived as mere conceptual conundrums. The proper answer to such questions, however, is "We do not, and cannot, know." We may protest, with fairness, that such questions distract us from living in the here and now. Divine and human action coinhere and cocreate the world. *This much we do know*. We do not make affirmations about God-world relations or address theological questions for their own sake or for the purpose of arriving at "explanations" of the way things are. Our scientific methodologies provide answers to these sorts of "why" questions. And when there are no scientific answers to the questions, we wisely may abandon them. We do not *need* "answers" to questions that transport us beyond the finite and contingent character of our world; the longing to "be as Gods," in our knowledge and power of action, represents an effort to surmount our finitude, a way of attempting to flee our humanity.

We affirm our relationship to God, then, never as a substitute for an integrated, informed scientific world view, but as a spontaneous act of gratitude, an ecstatic acknowledgment of the depth and inclusiveness of our being-in-relation as agents. We reverence God not because, as in the patriarchal model, God encompasses all that we are not or because we are the source of all evil and God the source of all good. It makes sense, out of ecstatic spontaneity, to praise God for all good gifts, but not because reverence for God should replace reverence either for people or for the total environment of life itself. All love coinheres. "Worship" of God gives way to celebration, the praise of God and all good things in God. Reverence is not congruent with obeisance, but with deep respect and acknowledgment. Nor does it make sense, as in traditional theology, to discuss "God's action" in isolation from our own. What anything is, in itself, is unknown to us and quite irrelevant to our being-in-the-world. Any abstracting of God's acts from our own world reifies the subject/object split characteristic of the positivistic views of knowledge that govern patriarchal idealism. It has no place in a feminist relational theology.

THE IMPLICATIONS OF A FEMINIST CHRISTIAN THEOLOGY FOR ETHICS

Some may wonder why a vision that incorporates human cocreativity as radical freedom does not disavow a theological ethic altogether in favor of joining those existentialists or subjectivists in ethics who claim that nothing of value in the world exists but through human action. To move in such a direction, however, would belie the seriousness and depth of this moral theological vision. Mutuality, interdependence and relationality are not the capricious preferences of women; they are, rather, patterns of relation that enable us to experience the "really real," to discern the nature of things. The moral world, although the coconstruction of subjects, is never merely subjectivist. Given our powers of cocreation, divine-human interaction effects or brings genuine value to fruition; concrete good is actualized in interaction, not otherwise. Of course, we cannot actualize all of the potential value-in-relationship present in life — a point of utmost importance with regard to human fertility and procreative power — nor should we aspire to do so. In a body-self centered existence, morality no longer means acquiescence to "superior" authority, but rather the embracing of possibility and the recognition that we live within limits. There is no need to flee hard choices or to deny real grief and pain as part of a deeply lived life.

The moral life involves a process of selecting and integrating many potential values through strategic choices. Frequently we have to choose between courses of action, weighing several valid principles or choosing between values that are all positive. At other times, our human options represent only choices between lesser evils. There is no place in a feminist theological ethic for a type of moral idealism or moral theory that can be "applied" universally to, but floats free of, the world-historical context of the moral dilemmas we face. Perfectionism, for example, stems from the need to force every moral dilemma into a simplified schema, as if one supreme value or principle were adequate to all life situations. Perfectionism assumes that moral agents are capable of escaping the conditions of finitude. Moral dilemmas, more often than not, are the result of both our need to act within the limits of our finitude — that is, to choose among several genuine values — and to forge our way through evils in a structural context where nothing is "ideal."

In a feminist theological perspective, human responsibility for good *and* evil is much more far-reaching than in traditional theological models. In some patriarchal approaches, human agents are, unambiguously, responsible for moral evil, whereas God alone is the source of moral good. In feminist perspective, the cost of moral irresponsibility in human life is the destruction of good as well as the doing of evil. Furthermore, a radical view of freedom asks us to understand that human responsibility cannot be conceived of in a rationalistic way. Usually it is assumed that we are responsible only for those matters we influence directly in our face-to-face relations. Yet this individualistic assumption that we are responsible only *if and when* we ourselves, viewed as monads, act intentionally to affect another directly, misrepresents our actual condition as historical and social beings.

We are all born into a web of historical sociality in which our very existence is conditioned by the past. And, more important, our lives are conditioned by those structures of power that distribute privilege and disadvantage in ways that shape our lives long before we have embraced our own power of agency. It is no accident that most of us prefer to organize our lives so that we need only consider our responsibility to those closest to us or most like ourselves. Therefore, it is absurd to say that we bear no responsibility for this relationally patterned privilege or that we cannot surrender it over time. Privilege as a pattern of action that avoids reciprocity can be relinquished and replaced by mutuality.[39] Critical consciousness of our common cohumanity in spite of privilege is indeed a painful gift, born of a transcendence that comes with acting to resist evil. Yet it is crucial to a feminist theology and moral viewpoint to understand how structural patterns of power and privilege condition all moral life. An adequate theology determines moral responsibility relative to our access to social power, which means that the privileged are more responsible for the way the world process moves than are others. This also means that the responsibility of those who lack such privilege is rightly shaped by realistic awareness of the social constraints on their action. To imply, for example, that a poor or physically weak woman must bear as many children as she may "naturally" conceive bespeaks a moral theory devoid of socio-structural insight. Such a theory will also lead to a subjectivist misdiagnosis of social evil. It is not sufficient, for example, to attribute the immorality of racism simply to the fact that some whites feel disrespectful toward black people. A racist society such as our own is one in which a palpable structure of white privilege functions continuously. The actions of those who are white continually reinforce and perpetuate this structure, regardless of whether our personal attitudes toward black people are negative. An adequately relational moral theory helps me understand that the objective existence of racism shapes my actions whether I perceive it or not. When responsibility is construed in an individualistic, nonrelational mode, I thereby am excused morally from acknowledging my privilege as a structure of power. If I believe my responsibility ends with "changing my feelings" about black people, I will continue to bolster the social praxis of racism unawares. It is hardly surprising that men and women of color, as well as white women, often mistrust the "friendship" of liberals — that is, those who perceive moral responsibility chiefly as a matter of individual attitude apart from ongoing social relations.

Since our moral responsibility is determined by and differs in relation to the structures of power in which our lives as moral agents are set, it makes good moral sense to insist that women's moral need to control our procreative power is urgent, given women's lack of social power generally. Part of the aim of any ethics is to help us know what it means to augment and to equalize our responsibility for living as free women and men.

A further moral implication of our freedom and cocreative power is relevant to the issue of procreative choice and abortion. Our freedom and cocreativity constitute real value. We must not assume that "sacredness" or "the intrinsic value of things" exists apart from our valuations in relation. Intrinsic value and holiness exist through mutual acknowledgment. Therefore, our moral decisions also influence that which, over time, comes to be recognized as intrinsically good. This conception stands in sharp contrast to patriarchal thinking, in which God's action, understood in a mythic-causal way, *distinct from* and *superior to* human power, alone creates what has intrinsic value. In fact, power as the capacity to make things happen, and to realize the good, increases only when shared. God, without our coagency, suffers real loss of power to affect our lives for good. In a patriarchal schema, humans have value because God grants it, by virtue of willing people special status; furthermore, what God does is, by virtue of His doing it, holy or sacred. The reciprocity of relationship is denied. A theological approach that incorporates human relationality and embodiedness into the world process understands "sacredness" and intrinsic value as literally created by transactions of love that are integrations of divine and human action. Potential for value exists in all being, grounded in God, but that value reaches fruition only by the power of mutual interaction, the affirmative acknowledgment between free, centered beings. To speak of our participation in the creation of intrinsic value does not imply a subjectivist view of value. I do not create value through any individual act or merely by ascribing value to something. We realize potential good by our receptivity to potential good, embodying potential value in community, making a real, sensual reality of what before was only potential. We cannot trivialize our freedom by surmising that there is a givenness and externality to intrinsic value that operates apart from our relation to it. As we will see, the biological potential, emergent in fetal life, requires our receptive assent, and not only the receptive assent of a pregnant woman but of the wider community.

Conversely, the theological envisagement proposed here leads us to perceive our lives and actions as a "moral field," through and through, such that all our modes of relating and all our transactions either concretely embody what is valuable or block its realization. In any case, we choose what is sacred or has intrinsic value for us, and, in turn, those perceptions affect our mode of being in the world at every level. We can adopt modes of life and community that are destructive of genuine well-being, and we frequently do so. Analogously, whenever we acknowledge that something or someone has "intrinsic value," we are apprehending a centered power of being in that other and also recognizing the other's capacity to affect us or act upon us. A genuinely respectful attitude toward all of life is so vital morally because such reverence of other beings opens us to deeper bonding with all that exists.

Further Implications of Feminist-Theological Ethics

A feminist spiritual perspective harbors even further implications for our biological fertility, for procreative choice, and also for assessing the value of fetal life in relation to other life values. In masculinist theology, women must acquiesce to a static God-given definition of the meaning and value of fetal life that seals our fate as childbearers. This is why Christian masculinist discussions of abortion so often hinge on determining the one static moment when God "acts" to create intrinsic or sacred value. Once this principle holds sway, we human agents (always female in the case of pregnancy) are presumed to be relieved of decision making regarding the life process and its context of human interaction. Our lives, like that of Mary, the mother of Jesus, get misinterpreted as merely passive, lacking the power of creativity. "Behold I am the handmaiden of the Lord. Let it be unto me according to your Word."[40] There can be no answering back, no reasoning why or whether it is humanly wise to receive this "gift" at this particular moment. God is active, the female believer utterly passive, with respect to sacredness or intrinsic value. Every woman is familiar with the fiction involved here, but the pregnant woman in particular knows that pregnancy is an active process requiring positive assent and real engagement. The notion that human life "begins" at conception, at genetic implantation, or at some other specific, fixed biological point makes little sense in a dynamic perspective. The claim that some fixed starting point is necessary lest one's thinking become muddled, fuzzy, or imprecise — that is, "feminine" — makes little sense to those who know that gestation is a long, slow, and complex process of interaction between a woman's body and developing fetal life.[41]

The abundance of potential value in our natural environment is nowhere better exemplified than in the case of biological fertility. Because potential value is suffused throughout the natural environment, there is more potential value at the biological level than any agent can bring to fruition. Fertility is a problem for many species, and certainly for many human communities, even though of differing proportion under diverse social and cultural circumstances. The passivity attributed to women in static, traditionalist interpretations of procreation belies the continuous efforts of women to balance, as best they can, the value of procreation and other goods. Women recognize that decisions about childbearing are now, and always have been, dialectically related to existing material conditions for sustaining life at any given time. The modern sensibility to the intrinsic value of each individual human life is, in part, the result of shifts in material conditions that enable us to aspire to a world in which such recognition is securely grounded in our moral practice. Such an aspiration could not have arisen in the absence of certain historical conditions or without interaction between human creativity and the wider nonhuman environment. It is the fruit of the exercise of human intelligence in its widest and deepest sense. Furthermore, in light of recent developments in medical science, the question of the point at which we are *morally wise* to recognize the "intrinsic value" in fetal life is a new moral question. Earlier teaching on abortion did not focus on this issue, as we will see in Chapter 5.

In a feminist moral theology, this question of the value of fetal life, along with many others that must be tackled in relation to abortion, can be answered only by careful, moral reasoning. Feminists stress, as do most Catholic moral theologians, that even a *normative* theological vision does not preclude the need for ongoing participation in molding our human conduct through rational deliberation. The claims we make in defense of a woman's moral right to procreative choice and the availability of safe, legal abortion as the morally proper social policy are predicated on such reasoning. These claims exemplify in this time and place our best considered judgment about what human norms of justice should be. A feminist Christian theological vision, which I have only begun to sketch here, can play an informing role at the theological level as women face the abortion dilemma. What it does not permit us to do is to escape the burden of proximate moral judgment. And such a vision frees us from the illusion that childbearing is in any way exempt from our freedom or that it imparts a distinct, discrete spiritual value over against other valuable dimensions of our humanity. God's action as creator in no way precludes our actions as cocreators, in making decisions about these issues; they are ours to make, if we are to make and keep human life human.[42] This vision also delivers us from the vicious assumption that individual women must bear the burden of procreative power alone, without reference to how their community supports them in childbearing and childrearing. It permits no abstraction of the act of abortion from its social setting. It is also worth noting that a feminist theological ethic has more in common with a Roman Catholic moral approach than with Protestant biblicism.

What I have said so far about a feminist Christian liberation perspective does not clarify fully how Christian feminists re-vision the more specific and radical expectations of the Christian ethic itself. A feminist Christian moral theology stands in continuity with historic Christian ethics by stressing the centrality of radical love (traditionally called *agape* in much theological discussion).[43] But feminist Christians embrace this norm with a radical understanding of its meaning. Perhaps I need only observe that, for feminists, Christian love is not differentiated in any extreme way from "mere" human love or "mere" love of the human. On the contrary, to be loving is to be passionately related to people, to the creation, and to God. Love is a praxis of being actively engaged in mutual and respectful cocreation of community. Loving human beings and loving God are intermeshed, life-shaping commitments, not merely norms for individual choices or singular, unintegrated acts. Furthermore, love and justice are inextricably related norms that we learn in moral struggle. Christian life involves sustained engagement in the struggle for justice as making right relations or, in some situations, at least ending injustice.

An understanding of justice as making right relations incorporates the insight of the Hebraic tradition that "doing justice" entails not merely advocacy *for* those marginalized and excluded but solidarity *with* them in the form of mutual accountability. Justice in a liberation perspective is not a secondary and proximate norm, a mere social norm that poorly approximates a love that is personal. On the contrary, justice and the struggle for justice are *foundational to love itself*. It is naive to believe that genuine love can live and flourish where unjust social relations prevail. Because God becomes embodied in our midst through our mutually caring interaction, there can be no love of God apart from community. Our culture is indeed atheistic and irreligious, as many conservatives contend, but it is also filled with those who claim to love God more than anything mundane. There are few who truly love their neighbors in God. Precisely because we disvalue and disrespect each other, and imagine that so little is at stake in our interaction, we lack the depth and subtlety of people who have a firmly grounded social theistic vision. It is this that makes our culture "ungodly."

The current theological crusade against safe, legal abortion is predicated on a sometimes well-meaning, but disastrously misguided, conviction that the termination of freedom of choice in an area of human life that intricately and irrevocably affects women's experience will put our culture back on a "God-fearing" track. An adequate theological perspective helps us to see that, in fact, we would be taking a step backward both historically and morally. To return our society to a legal policy of prohibiting abortion is not to be confused with the quite different matter of ending the necessity of abortion. Enlisting the collective power of the state to make a woman bear a child each and every time she conceives one, regardless of the circumstances, would be no moral gain. From a feminist theological point of view, prohibition of legal abortion involves the effort to deny freedom or centered moral agency, and hence full humanity, to over half the population. That our masculinist theologies have successfully obscured this reality is no accident. In fact, they were designed, in part, to accomplish this task.

We need no longer confine our spiritual vision to a sort of theology that portrays God as power in alienation from ourselves. As co-creators, reverently related to One who is Holy yet closer than our hands and feet, we can root our spirituality in the recognition that we, together, have full, unqualified responsibility for the moral quality of the world we choose. This means, too, that we have responsibility for the well-being of every member of our species, whom we welcome into the potentially glorious web of social relations that is our common life. Our need to welcome them is no surface gesture; it is not extrinsic to the moral meaning of childbearing. Since it is within our power to create the most basic conditions for human well-being, together we have responsibility for whether our environment is life-giving or death-dealing to the newly born. That determination is *not* within an individual mother's power. It is not merely that we ought to assent to the life of every child who is born. The time has come when we must make it our responsibility to do so.

Nor can individuals any longer bear children frivolously, in the absence of an act of radical love, one that says "I chose you, I welcome you, I covenant to be with you through the long and not always easy passage into life, and through your growth into a wider community of relation." To view the birth of a member of our species this way, to recognize what it means to mother *and to father* a child, is to exemplify what several Christian theological traditions have meant by "making covenant." In the early Hebraic story, God is said to make a covenant to life with each of us from the foundation of the world. As we have seen, masculinist Christian theology often turns this beautiful poetic image into a rationalistic calculating doctrine of a God who has elected some (usually not all) to life or at least to a salvation better than life. In fact, God's covenant is a spontaneous and loving act of a free being who calls us forth in freedom, a loving invitation to enter into relationship with Godself to fully share the tending of creation.

It should be obvious by now that I believe there is nothing to be gained by pretending that a feminist theological viewpoint is consistent with what other theologians too often call "*the* Christian tradition." Historically, much Christian theology has claimed to be governed by the Vincentian Canon,[44] which declares that what we claim as Christian truth must be based on what has been taught among Christians everywhere, at all times; otherwise, it is not genuine. Such a formula is pretentious nonsense. Christian doctrine changes, and should do so, as the world changes and, with it, as human self-understanding changes. The lure and excitement of doing theology come from the call to revision the meaning of our faith. Theological affirmation is like a good poem — though it draws upon the language we know and recalls familiar elements of our story, each time we hear it we nevertheless experience it as a new word, one we have never quite heard before. It is precisely when the novelty, the creative act, transpires that new life is joined to the old.

It is my contention that living Christian theologies will assume new forms in every generation and that their dynamic fidelity to the past will cohere in their continuity with the ongoing struggle for justice and love, not in the mere repetition of dogma. Theologically, we must teach what we see from our struggle that deepens our relations in mutuality, even as we retell those stories that remind us that we have precursors and a living community in that struggle. Human freedom has deepened over time, along with our awareness of the meaning of that freedom. Now we must incorporate this reality fully into our comprehension of procreative power. Even though some developments in contemporary Christian theology have opened the way for such an appropriation, the mainstream of Christian reflection lags far behind.

Out of a critical liberating theological sensibility, fresh historical questions must be posed. How, for example, has Christian refusal to understand procreation as a social and historical reality shaped our understanding, as Christians, of abortion?

The all but universal belief is that on the specific issue of abortion Christians, over time, have been univocal in condemning it as not only morally wrong but tantamount to murder. If, as I have suggested, Christian theology has been implicated directly, and forcefully, in the effort to legitimate male control of the social power of procreation, we might well expect to uncover a history of condemnation of abortion. It is that history that I will now address. I will show that what we actually find in early Christian teaching is a minor and marginal tradition of moral condemnation related to the insistence that sexuality is solely for procreation. But we also find a surprisingly varied strain of severity in the way abortion was viewed. Furthermore, such condemnations of abortion as existed were yoked from the beginning to negative attitudes toward women, specifically those whose actions in relation to sexuality defied the "natural" destiny to which women purportedly were born. Surprisingly, in light of this, for centuries the issue was treated by most Christian theologians with an attitude best described as indifferent. The widespread social furor over safe, elective abortion is, as I have already suggested, a relatively new phenomenon. What we will see is that the negative attitudes Christians brought to the abortion question, when it became a public issue, had been shaped by moral reasons having little to do with the current concern for the "intrinsic value" of fetal life.

5

The History of Christian Teaching on Abortion Reconceived

FROM METHODOLOGY TO IDEOLOGY: THE DISTORTION OF THE CHRISTIAN LEGACY ON ABORTION

Christian ethicists aspire to place current ethical issues and moral dilemmas in historical perspective. I have also insisted, however, that each contemporary Christian theological vision — whether fundamentalist, conservative, liberal, or liberationist — carries within it a perspective on time and history and an attitude to change dictated by its particular ideological commitments. Not surprisingly, then, ideology molds our historical perceptions of any moral issue in basic ways. To some extent, we all see in the past what we want or need to find there, given our present value commitments." None of us is without predecessors, and we remember our forebears, in part, because they resonate with our own contemporary value orientations." Even when we "correct" for our own biases, as we all need to do in historical work, our interpretations of the past will depend on and differ according to our varying loyalties. Differing loyalties prompt us not only to look to divergent sources of data and types of evidence from the past but also to value the opinions of diverse persons, granting them varied degrees of historical authority. Given these obvious facts, it is surprising — and somewhat discouraging — that little work in the history of Christian ethics is informed by liberal-critical or liberationist principles of interpretation, especially those suspicious of the overwhelming pattern of male supremacy. Though I share the concern of many of my colleagues for a historical focus to our work, I do not share their enthusiasm for much that passes as the history of Christian ethics and, more especially, for what is credited as the history of Christian teaching on abortion.

There is a tendency, when the issues of ethics and morality become the center of historical interest, for Christian theologians and ethicists to assume that ethical writings, especially the prescriptions of a few famous theologians, genuinely represent the morals and ethical reflection of the majority of Christians and their churches in a given period. What social historian John Boswell found to be the methodological limitation of Christian histories of sexual ethics provides an exact analogy to the inadequacies I consider obvious in historical discussions of abortion:

> It is indeed too often overlooked that just as there was a pagan ascetic and antierotic tradition, so was there a Christian tradition of tolerant and positive attitudes toward love and eroticism . . . It is almost fatally tempting for the historian, like the moral theologian, to pick out those fathers and doctrines which eventually gained universal acceptance as orthodox and to point to these as crucial in the development of Christian attitudes on particular points. Because the modern Catholic church traces its doctrines back in an unbroken chain to specific opinions of early fathers, the historian is apt to accept the notion that a particular opinion triumphed because this or that influential thinker espoused it, disregarding the fact that many equally prominent theologians, some of whom the church regarded as worthy of sainthood, may have held contrary views or that the authority in question may have himself held other views of the same subject which are not incorporated as dogma. Teachings now central to Catholic doctrine were often no more than casual observations of those who first enunciated them, and opinions which seemed crucial to the fathers of the church must frequently be brushed aside by later Catholics as embarrassments.[1]

With respect to abortion, this sort of selective use of theological writings or the invocation of opinion uttered in passing is only one part of a broader methodological problem. Historians of the Christian ethics of abortion rely too exclusively on the methods of intellectual history as adequate to a basic understanding of this aspect of the Christian moral past. Those who pursue the history of Christian moral teaching are not always well versed in the newer methodologies of social and cultural history. Exclusive reliance on the textual evidence of a handful of theologians is insufficient to an understanding of moral practice when more sophisticated cultural, historical, and archeological evidence is available to help us grasp the actual practices and attitudes of whole cultures. This is especially true when the affected population is female, as in the abortion dilemma, because Christian theologians frequently understand little of women's culture and women's lives.

Not surprisingly, recent contributions more helpful to a moral revisioning of the Christian past have come from nontheological academic historians, frequently feminist or neo-Marxian, who provide a textured reinterpretation of the ethos, mores, and morals of various Christian cultures and movements.[2] Furthermore, the newer feminist historical scholarship is aiding our revisioning of this past by making visible the lives of the half of the species ignored by traditional historiography. This newer scholarship, however fragmentary, promotes skepticism about whether, as yet, we know anything about how most Christians, especially women, really understood the issue of abortion. A critical social history of abortion in Christian cultures that incorporates the actual practice, range of moral evaluations, and social location of women has yet to be written. In Chapter 6 I address some of the perspectives requisite for such a critical historical treatment of abortion in the Christian and human past. First, however, it is necessary to explore in some detail problems that arise in the present Christian historical interpretation of abortion.

Christian moral theologians discussing abortion proceed, as Boswell contends, by isolating fragments of teaching from a few Christian writers often not very influential in their own time. Theologians tend to forget that their "current" authorities were often minority or controversial voices when they arrived on the theological scene or were marginal to the mainstream Christianity of their day. Augustine of Hippo, for example, was a bishop of a minority sect of Christians, and Thomas Aquinas was an anathematized heretic for nearly a century after his death.[3] Though, as we shall see, these theologians really did not much influence their contemporary milieu, their views are cited as reflective of mainstream Christian opinion in their lifetimes. To identify a pastiche of literary texts as the definitive history of Christian moral teaching on a given point is always dubious, but it is especially so in an interpretation of the history of the Christian ethic on abortion.

A further reason why much historical research on abortion is misleading derives from another methodological assumption prevalent among those who have worked at the history of Christian ethics.

There is a tendency to "do" historical Christian ethics as "rule" or "code" ethics. Whenever we read the history of Christian ethics on a given topic — and here the abortion issue is exemplary — what we encounter are citations of prohibitions, prescriptions, rules, and codes. Often these prescriptive formulations are ripped out of their original social and cultural context yet presented as if they meant, in their time, precisely what they mean in ours. It is a truism of contemporary moral analysis that the meaning of an ethical injunction is discovered through the reasons given for its justification. Yet much history of Christian ethics not only fails to analyze the moral reasons offered for prescribing or interdicting abortion but also overlooks the moral ethos of the wider context in which a particular prescription was proffered. Rules and principles, by virtue of the abstractness that is one of their merits as action guides, summarize values and patterns of action. But taken out of context, rules and principles do not communicate the cultural information required for decoding their moral justifications. They, like literary texts whose setting is not yet understood, often give the impression of stasis and immutability at the moral level when in fact the meaning of the rule or principle in question varies greatly in differing cultural contexts. History is not external to some purported core of moral or theological meaning; a prescription's meaning lies in the moral valuations of a given cultural setting. Our failure to view principles or acts within their full historical and cultural context can result not only in our confusion but in a complete inversion of their ethical meaning.

The preoccupation with the prescriptive content of rules and codes in Christian ethics has produced another distortion in much male-generated history of abortion teaching. Ignoring historical change or the diversity of cultural settings that offer similar prescriptions, historians may miss shifts in the sorts of actions to which a prescription applies. By focusing only on the "rule pattern" of censure of abortion, for example, some interpreters obscure the changing definition over time of what constitutes an abortion, both in Christian teaching and in various cultures. Christianity did not start out with a unanimous or well-defined view of prenatal development. Some prohibitions against abortion were in place long before serious, elaborated discussion of when the fetus was "animated" or "ensouled" began. For this reason, many premodern Christians defined the act of abortion as interruption of pregnancy, not at conception but at a later point. This was Augustine's view.[4]

Because knowledge of embryology was very primitive, not much was known about the physiological processes of conception and early pregnancy until as late as the latter half of the nineteenth century. Furthermore, what was known by women about these matters often may not have been shared with men because of cultural taboo or women's self-protectiveness. Throughout most of history, women discovered their pregnancies through the commonsense criterion of menstrual interruption, which was passed along in women's culture. Needless to say, this criterion was not always a reliable indicator of pregnancy. Because women's general health was more precarious than it is today, making menstrual irregularity more common, women themselves may not always have known whether they were pregnant until "quickening." This may explain why, existing "science" notwithstanding, the experience of quickening became a common-sense criterion for ensoulment. It may well have been the indicator many Christian pastors employed in assessing abortion.

Among intellectuals in the period of Christianity's emergence, of course, there were other theories. For those who knew Aristotelian science, any interruption of pregnancy from a week after conception may have been deemed abortion, but animation or the achievement of full fetal rationality was thought to occur, at least for the male fetus, at forty days. For Aristotle, females never reached "full rationality," but rather they "vegetated" in slower fetal development.[5] Aristotle's views, however, had no direct impact on *early* Christianity. The distinction about when and whether the fetus was ensouled by God did emerge. Debates about ensoulment, as we shall see, were intimately related to the body/soul dualism pervasive in late imperial Roman culture. For those who believed ensoulment occurred during pregnancy, the condemnation of abortion frequently applied after ensoulment. Abortion was wrong only when a pregnancy was terminated some way into the process. It was only in the late nineteenth century that Pope Pius IX, intrigued by new discoveries about the embryo, moved to standardize official Roman Catholic teaching on abortion. By designating conception as the moment of full hominization, he presumed that Catholic teaching would arrive at definitive consonance with "modern science." A few Catholic scholars still appeal for recognition of the earlier diversity of opinion about when termination of prenatal life constituted an abortion,[6] but, as we have observed, direct dissent on abortion is limited.

Another dimension of historical change neglected by code-history approaches to the morality of abortion is also critical. Prior to the recent development of genuinely safe, surgical abortion techniques, the act of abortion frequently referred to something done to a woman, with or without her consent. Abortions were sometimes the result of an act of violence toward a woman or of real dangers posed by the primitiveness of methods used to induce voluntary abortion. Some abortions were the consequence of inadvertent side effects of other treatment. Today, of course, moralists assume that it is the woman and her doctor who commit the "wrongful" act. In the contemporary debate, few pause to observe that until recently any act of abortion *always endangered the life of the mother* every bit as much as it imperiled the prenatal life in her womb. Some earlier Christian reasons for opposing abortion offered by moral theologians incorporated the danger abortion presented to *a pregnant woman*. There was considerable tradition of pastoral concern for women, which is often suppressed in current debate.[7] Through historical change, this premodern moral reason for opposing abortion is now located on the side of those who support it. Ironically, then, improvements in medical techniques for abortion have laid to rest some moral objections to abortion on grounds of its dangerous and harmful effects on women. Much contemporary Christian anti-abortion teaching is, as a result, more misogynist and more disvaluing of women than much earlier Christian teaching. Because, statistically, abortion is safer than childbearing, the expression of genuine concern for a pregnant woman's well-being today clearly means supporting the option for procreative choice and legal abortion.

While concern for women's well-being was not normative or widespread among male Christian theologians, we should nevertheless not forget that at least some traditional opposition to the morality of abortion derived from rightful skepticism about the effect of abortion on women's well-being. It is not too much to say, therefore, that so-called pro-life advocates cannot really press the full sense of the earlier Christian moral tradition without weighing this concern.

PROBLEMS IN THE MASCULINIST INTERPRETATION

Most of what purports to be the historical reconstruction of past Christian teachings on abortion has been conducted by canon lawyers and moral theologians rather than professional church historians.

While not every Christian ethicist and moral theologian accepts canon lawyer John Noonan's statement that fetal life has been granted "an almost absolute value in Christian history,"[8] this claim has enjoyed a credibility which, in my view, it in no way deserves. It is easy enough to compile statements that anathematize abortion written by Christian theologians over the centuries. But it is quite another thing to suggest that the moral justification for these theologians' opposition to abortion stemmed from their deep concern for the value of fetal life.

Noonan's work on abortion, when first amassed as part of a vast compendium of Christian teaching on the history of contraception,[9] offered a tentative defense of contraception against the church's official position. His opposition to abortion has remained implacable,[10] however, and many other moral theologians have reinforced his general interpretation of the Christian ethics of abortion, which assumes that Christian anti-abortion teaching reflects an all but universal and consistent line of moral reasoning focusing on the fetus's full human value.[11] Furthermore, Noonan's book on contraception echoes the ideological tone characteristic of the views on women's nature, sexuality, and procreative vocation that I protested in Chapter 3. He consistently interprets the story of Christianity as an unequivocal triumph of Catholic teaching over "pagan" and heretical efforts to separate sexuality, marriage, and procreation.[12] Noonan has no doubt that Christian teaching corresponds to the "enlightened" view of the finest medical practitioners of ancient cultures. He celebrates the Hippocratic oath as testimony that the most distinguished physicians opposed the use of abortifacients.[13] He says nothing of the appalling primitiveness of the Hippocratic corpus of medical writings[14] or of their frequently contemptuous attitude toward women. Nor does he acknowledge that the oath, like much of the Hippocratic material, most probably reflects the medical opinion that abortion was a dubious procedure because women's safety could not be guaranteed.[15]

Noonan's entire argument is geared to demonstrate the central value of childbearing and children in Christian tradition and an unqualified affirmative attitude toward marriage and procreation in Hebraic and Christian scripture. He consistently uses scriptural data to demonstrate the rigorous and "high" moral quality of early Christian teaching on abortion. By piecing together passages from the synoptic gospels, especially the sections of Luke's story about the pregnancies of Mary, the mother of Jesus, and her cousin, Elizabeth, and Jesus' "Suffer little children and do not prevent them from coming to me" (Matt. 19:13-14), he attempts to link procreative functionalism with a deep feeling for children as characteristic of the primitive Christian community. While this tradition of Jesus' love of children retains venerable standing among Christians, as I have already observed, most modern New Testament scholars believe that Jesus' attitude toward marriage and family, like that of many of his followers, was shaped by his expectation of an imminent end to the world. In contrast to Noonan, Catholic moral theologian John Connery offers a more accurate characterization of the situation of early Christianity, acknowledging that, because of the expectation that the world might be coming to an end, Christians were not strongly pronatalist, much less concerned about such dilemmas of everyday life.[16] In any case, later mounting Christian support for procreative functionalism was not related, explicitly or implicitly, to great sensitivity to children. In what follows it will become clear that condemnations of the use of potions to inhibit conception and abortifacients to prevent birth were much more intimately tied to fear of women's presumed sexual "looseness" or to protests against "pagan" practices than to concern for the well-being of infants.

John Connery's study of the history of Roman Catholic teaching on abortion is substantively more accurate than Noonan's. He at least offers evidence that premodern Roman Catholic casuists were *more* sympathetic to women's well-being than, for example, Noonan or many other contemporary Roman Catholic and Protestant moralists. Yet Connery also is willing to endorse an unqualified picture of Christian teaching on abortion, rooted, by implication, in the high valuation of fetal life.[17] In fact, in the Christian literature on abortion one encounters little, if any, direct challenge to the idea that fetal life has possessed "an almost absolute value" in Christian history. Thus, the distinguished Roman Catholic moral theologian Bernard Häring, although displaying clear awareness that Noonan's historical claims are at best overstated, nevertheless refers to Noonan's historical work on abortion as "masterful."[18] Noonan remains the most frequently cited "authority" on the Christian history of abortion teaching.

My specific quarrel is with the judgment, passed on by Noonan and others, that Christian teaching about abortion has been unambiguous and almost unanimous, especially with regard to the value of fetal life as *the moral reason* for Christian opposition to abortion prior to the modern period. I find it far more accurate to say that the vast majority of Christian theologians, even male, celibate theologians, have remained relatively silent on the question of the morality of abortion until the modern era. Throughout most of Christian history, abortion was opposed in proportion to the degree to which definitions of normative sexuality were identified with the function of procreation and in relation to the strength of a theologian's view of the "good" woman's essential, God-given vocation to either procreation or celibacy. Christians originally were not pronatalist but became so over time, even while celibacy retained a more highly valued life status for some theologians.

If Noonan's claims are true, how are we to explain the relative paucity of developed moral reasoning on the question of abortion in Christian literature until the modern period? The anti-abortion traditions invariably cited by traditionalist historians consist of fragmentary statements, condemnations often not of abortion per se, but of contraception, abortion, and sexual activity without procreative purpose.[19] Abortion was typically anathematized in the same breath with contraception and "illicit" sexuality. Many of Christianity's most misogynist theologians considered it a murderous act if a married woman was *in any way* sexually active apart from procreative intent or resistant to childbearing as her vocation. And these theologians are overrepresented in anti-abortion historical surveys.

Noonan also insists that it is not difficult to differentiate Christian antisexual teaching from positive teaching about the value of life, but he nowhere documents this claim. Portraying the attitudes of Roman culture to fetal and infant existence as "strikingly callous" and "indifferent to life,"[20] Noonan simultaneously deems the children that Roman imperial procreative policy required women to bear (three in the case of freed women, four for slaves) as "moderate numbers."[21] Moreover, while arguing that Christianity everywhere had to battle against the undervaluing of procreation that was rampant at the time, he fails to explain why "the very loose law on abortion was never changed even in Christian times."[22] Actually, Noonan's work repeatedly asserts the intimate interconnection of sexual ethics and anti-abortion teaching. He counts *all* endorsements of procreative sex as necessarily implying positive valuation of fetal life, but this is a questionable assumption, to say the least.

Over time, Noonan has escalated his claim that, almost without exception in Christianity, a fetus has been viewed as a fully human person and abortion unequivocally denounced. In his most recent work, a diatribe against present social policy on abortion, he has even inveighed with special rancor against those, like myself, who claim that official Roman Catholic teaching on sexuality, especially its teaching against contraception, constitutes a reason why the Roman Catholic tradition is so adamantly opposed to abortion.[23] Noonan insists, even though in some of his work he has actually cited data to the contrary, that it always has been maintained among Christians that abortion is without exception the killing of human life.

In a recent monograph on the Roman Catholic abortion ethic widely praised by Christian ethicists, Susan Teft Nicholson argues that it is a moral necessity, for the credibility of a natural law killing ethic, to carefully differentiate it from a natural law antisexual ethic. Nicholson rightly contends that

> even if the fetus were not a human being, (orthodox) Catholics would still view abortion as evil. This explains why the condemnation of abortion did not falter during those periods when Church fathers rejected the notion that a human being was present from conception onward . . . One effect of this theological animus toward sexual pleasure was the elimination of any basis for a connection between sexual pleasure and the expression of love . . . This stunning impoverishment of life was imposed upon Catholics by exclusively male and predominantly celibate theologians for almost 19 centuries.[24]

Later Nicholson adds, "Hence it is misleading in the context of the public debate, to maintain that the Roman Catholic Church has *always* condemned abortion."[25] Even so, Nicholson furnishes us with only a modest correction of the Roman Catholic abortion teaching derived from its killing ethic. She observes, in passing, that no justifications are ever given in papal argument for considering the fetus a human being, but it seems not to occur to her why this is the case.[26] Her own study provides clear evidence, however, that denunciations of abortion as homicide and murder in Christian theological writings were often rhetorical flourishes, while the *moral reason* for opposition was condemnation of women's sexuality, aimed at censuring wicked, "wanton" women — that is, those who expressed their sexuality apart from procreative intent. In the texts she cites, abortion is a special evil because it signifies female wickedness and a refusal of women's divinely decreed lot.

Few have paused to notice, however, that Nicholson merely questions, but does not examine, whether any differentiation between a killing ethic and an antisexual ethic would leave intact a well-considered, morally compelling Christian antikilling ethic applying to abortion. Nicholson appears to accept, without challenge, Noonan's claim about the centrality to Christian teaching on abortion of the arguments on the value of fetal life.[27] She also seems to assume that the clear stream of condemnation of abortion based on anti-sexual teaching can be "peeled off," leaving an adequately justified "abortion is killing" ethic intact. I believe that this assumption is simply a historical mistake. No premodern, specific Christian anti-abortion teaching is unsullied by procreative functionalism and the antisexual bias Nicholson rightly acknowledges.

The ebb and flow of Christian anti-abortion teaching parallels too closely the periods of ascendancy and decline of sex-negative asceticism and the resurgence of negativism toward women to sustain the illusion that the chief element in Christian teaching against abortion was an exclusive or overriding concern for the value of fetal life. Yet Christian historians continue to claim that Christian motives for decrying abortion were morally clear, aimed only at thwarting "pagan" insensitivity to the value of human life. This self-congratulatory attitude would be dubious enough, given widespread Christian complicity in violence and killing, but it also happens to misrepresent the actual motives of the few but ardent anti-abortion warriors in the history of Christianity. Many of the latter feared not the loss of all fetal life but the destruction of male fetuses by evil and wanton women, or they feared women's sexuality, unfettered by an ahistorical divine destiny. The victims of this persistent misreading of rationales for opposing abortion, and of masculinist Christianity in general, are women, who must continue to cope as best they can with the ongoing problems of sexual fertility, whatever their life circumstances.

Obviously, I believe a feminist liberation ethic must result in an even more tough-minded intellectual honesty, requiring a recognition that, contrary to popular opinion and customary wisdom, patriarchal Christianity did not develop an abortion ethic fully because official attitudes toward women and procreation were so ideologically embedded in male supremacy that no differentiation between its sexual teaching and the question of abortion was possible. Many, even most, historians of Christian ethics have missed completely the relation between present intense debates and disagreements around issues of human sexuality in the churches and the subject of procreative choice for women. That traditional male supremacist assumptions about procreation play a part in the extreme rigidity of Christian abortion teaching must be acknowledged. However, just as a list of literary texts condemning adultery as wickedness may leave us with the impression of unbending absoluteness and rigor in the Christian sexual ethic, knowledge of the actual practice of penance in a medieval parish would provide a quite different notion of the sexual mores and morals of the time. So, too, a list of anathemas against abortion implies a different picture of Christian rigidity on abortion than concrete knowledge of the practices of Christian women would imply.

THE ANTI-ABORTION LOGIC OF THE FRAGMENTARY CHRISTIAN TEXTS

Abortion, when condemned, was usually one act in an anathematized continuum: illicit sex or adultery (genital sexual activity not aimed at procreation), contraception (because it facilitated sex for another purpose), and abortion. In the writings of some of the ascetic "fathers," prostitution was sometimes linked with contraception and abortion because all were equally onerous violations of woman's God-given vocation. Nearly all extant early Christian objections to abortion, when any moral reasons were enunciated, either directly condemn wanton women (those who seek to avoid pregnancy) or denounce the triad of adulterous, pleasure-oriented sex, contraception, and abortion. These were undifferentiated elements in a disparaging attitude to nonprocreative functional sexuality and a negativity to "promiscuous" women, grounded in what was, within Christianity, the antisensual spirituality of its most ascetic, frequently celibate theologians. The essentially virtuous and morally responsible woman was also to be celibate and could thereby become "manly." But if married, any woman who refused childbearing was thereby a murderer. This was the nexus of moral reasoning informing those theologians who make up the usual roster of early Christian anti-abortion citations.[28]

Yet these anti-abortion citations are also limited in number and fragmentary — too fragmentary to be taken as characteristic of the ethos, rule, or practice of all Christians at the time in which they were written. Importantly, the traditional hermeneutic on this issue also fails to explore the significance of the widespread silence about abortion that characterizes so much Christian theology of the same periods. What is surprising to the critical observer is that abortion received so little treatment among Christians or in certain geographical areas or epochs of the church. How can this be the case if Christianity were truly involved in the effort to foil morally inferior forces so cavalier toward human life? The answer, I believe, is that concern about abortion constitutes a minor, episodic matter in Christian discussion until the late nineteenth century. Furthermore, I find no evidence until the modern period that compassion for the presumed "child" in the womb was a generating source of Christian moral opposition to abortion. Rather, the intertwining of sexual mores and abortion teaching was so complete that there was always a definite correlation between extreme denunciations of abortion and a theologian's objections to sexual intercourse except within marriage for the purpose of procreation.

I have been unable to identify any examples of moral reasoning in premodern Christian history which exhibit clear-cut and direct support for the contemporary moral claim that *because the fetus is a human being* we are obligated to defend its life. The status of the fetus as "full human life" is not debated, *but assumed,* because all conception is "from God"; procreation remains a metaphor for direct, divine intervention. Nor did theologians who commented on abortion treat it in relation to their own theories about human ensoulment. Later interpreters conflated their predecessors' teachings on ensoulment with their anti-abortion utterances. Only after the equation of abortion and homicide was well established by rhetorical denunciation of all nonprocreative sex as murder, a connection made inevitable by treating procreation as *the* divinely ordained purpose of sex, did Christian theologians begin to theorize about *when* the prohibition against abortion should be applied, that is, before or after animation. Discussions of the moral value of fetal life, as such, are simply not present, because the shape of emerging teaching on sexuality never encouraged a focus on that question. Procreation, as the primary value, preempted consideration of the meaning either of fetal life *or* of women's lives apart from procreation.

Today, traditionalists celebrate Pius IX's insistence that humanity is fully present at conception. To traditionalists, his declaration served as further evidence that the church, in the wisdom of its magisterium, moved to extend, with ever greater consistency, its long-standing and adamant condemnation of abortion as homicide, especially evil because it involved the taking of *innocent* human life. Traditionalists forget, however, that this same anathema still informs papal teaching, not only in regard to abortion but also with respect to the use of artificial contraceptives in sexual intercourse within marriage.[29] A letter of sixth-century bishop Caesarius was, in the tenth and eleventh centuries, appropriated by the most ascetic groups. Caesarius's position was an altogether characteristic piece of reasoning on this point:

> If someone to satisfy his lust or in deliberate hatred does something to a man or a woman, so that no children be born of him or her, or gives them to drink, so that he cannot generate, or she conceive, let it be held as homicide.[30]

To be sure, current papal pronouncements omit contraception from the direct equation with homicide: "Therefore from the moment of its conception, life must be guarded with the greatest care, while abortion and infanticide are unspeakable crimes."[31] This represents a minor shift, however, not a reversal of the logic of papal argument. Abortion was considered homicide in earlier Christian teaching *because* nonprocreative sex was.

In this light, it should be clear why contemporary Christian discussions of the ethics of abortion concentrate only on argumentation for the purpose of strengthening anti-abortion teaching or for clarifying the distinction between direct and indirect abortion. From the point at which canon law was codified beginning in the tenth century, the prohibition of abortion as part of an antisexual perspective gradually became axiomatic in Christianity. However, even in the tenth century, it was not a major penitential offense. Furthermore, disputes about the point in pregnancy when the abortion prohibition was to apply continued into the twentieth century.

SELECTED EARLY CATHOLIC
TEACHING ON ABORTION

Our knowledge about post-New Testament Christian teaching on abortion is fragmentary at best. The earliest Christian post-canonical text invariably cited as condemning abortion is *The Didache* (The Teaching), and along with it *The Epistle of Barnabas*, a paraphrase of *The Didache*. *The Didache* receives some attention in the history of Christian ethics because it is one of the few early examples of Christian morals extant from the second century. The writer of *The Didache* addresses his treatise to a young man, one who, if he would aspire to the Christian way of life, must follow the commandments. The text instructs the faithful one:

> You shall not commit murder. You shall not commit adultery. You shall not corrupt boys. You shall not commit fornication. You shall not steal. You shall not produce magic. You shall not practice sorcery. You shall not kill an unborn child or murder a newborn infant.[32]

Precisely what context or act is implied in murdering an unborn child is not specified. We now know, however, that *The Didache* represents the teaching of an early Jewish-Christian writer or group. A number of historians believe that overall proscriptions in *The Didache* in fact are related to the intense conflict between Jewish Christians and their unconverted coreligionists. There was considerable rivalry, especially regarding moral rigorism, between some groups of early Jewish Christians and their non-Christian Jewish counterparts, and it is now recognized that the author of *The Didache* took over his moral formula from a rigorist Jewish sect. There were many such groups in the second century vying among themselves and with the newer Christian groups. The text tells us nothing about when in the course of pregnancy the writer may have assumed a "child" to be present or how this teaching relates to traditional rabbinic positions about the preeminence of a pregnant woman's well-being in childbearing.

Apart from this code, explicit denunciations of abortion, separate from views on the irreducible responsibility to procreation, are rare in early Christianity. Noonan's claim, typical of mainstream theological pronouncement, that "by 450 [C.E.] the teaching on abortion East and West had been set out for four centuries with clarity and consistency"[33] is doubtful at best, though the fragmentary evidence on the question makes dogmatism either way impossible. The silence in canonical New Testament writings and in most extant theology of the period is noteworthy, if only in light of traditionalist claims that Christian condemnation of abortion merely follows in a direct and logical fashion from the Christian command to love. If the contention is correct that abortion was an urgent question in the first century, because it was rampant in the decadent Roman imperial culture, then the widespread silence about abortion in early Christian writings is hardly explicable. The *ad hominem* implication of this argument — that empires which have "permissive" attitudes toward abortion risk collapse — is also spurious, though it appeals to current antifeminist sensibilities.

Ironically, after *The Didache*, the first elaborated denunciation of abortion in Christian theological writings appears to have been advanced to defend Christians from the pervasive charge that they were antisocial and immoral. In the first several centuries after Jesus, Christians composed, after all, a tiny social minority — looked upon as a band of people espousing a religious viewpoint, at best eccentric, at worst offensive to many "respectable" contemporaries in the Roman Empire. Christian religious practice was often belittled and caricatured. In fact, several early theologians defended Christians from rumors circulating to the effect that Christian rites were cannibalistic. No doubt the origin of such allegations lay in Christian liturgical practice. Christians were accused of "eating" the body and blood of their leader. Perhaps that is why Christians also met with charges of infanticide. In any case, Christians were frequently faulted for moral laxity, and many of them responded with rigorist defenses of Christian ethical conduct.

Tertullian, a strict, even moralistic, early-third-century theologian, protested such charges of immorality, citing Christian attitudes toward abortion as an example of the extent of Christian scrupulousness about killing. In this connection, he enunciated the opinion, later influential, that "the seed" is, because of its potential, already "man." "He is a human being [*homo*] who will be one; the whole fruit is actually in the seed."[34] His comments reflect assumptions current in the time that "the seed" — that is, the sperm — was the male's contribution to procreation. In this androcentric view, a woman contributed only a place for "the seed" to germinate. As is often pointed out, this portrayal ideologically correlates with the assumption that children are really the fruit, even the possession, of men. Furthermore, any "waste" of semen or seed was considered a homicidal act in some Christian tradition, though not by Tertullian.

For Tertullian personally, as for many later rigorist theologians, abortion may have been appropriate to save a woman's life;[35] as such it was a necessary evil. Nevertheless, Tertullian was to become an important figure in the development of Christian doctrine, not chiefly owing to his rigorism on abortion in defense of Christian morals but because of his focal involvement in another controversy. One of his great theological interests was clarifying the correct view of the spiritual "animation" of man vis-à-vis his contemporaries' more secular scientific-philosophical views about human nature. Tertullian elaborated a position, called in technical theological language *traducianism* — the teaching that "body" and "soul" coexist from the moment of conception.[36] It cannot be stressed too strongly that Tertullian did not formulate this doctrine in answer to the modern question "When does human life begin?" Rather, he accepted the widespread dualistic religious assumption of his day that spirit merged with matter to form human life. He attempted to clarify how body/spirit unity was accomplished in order to interpret what Christians believed about salvation. While traducianism influenced some later Christian thinking on abortion, Tertullian himself never related it to his fragmentary comments on abortion. Nor did traducianism, as a theory of body/spirit unity at conception, have much influence among early Christian theologians. At the time of the Reformation, debates about how body/soul unity occurred were still under way.

Some other early Christian theologians, all celibates — namely, Justin Martyr, Origen, and Clement of Alexandria[37] — were vitriolic toward women. By contrast, Tertullian's views on women were "moderate," but, particularly in his later years, he was markedly, even phobically, antisexual. In light of this, his attitude toward abortion was less harsh than might be expected. Yet he is invariably cited as an early author of an ardent Christian anti-abortionist tradition.

Speculations about the relation between matter and spirit were standard in the writings of all learned men during the first four centuries of the Christian era. Intellectuals already held considerably divergent views, which in turn were reformulated by various Christian theologians. The Stoics, among the most sophisticated of the philosophical elites who were to influence Christianity, believed that human life truly began only at birth. Their view was shared by many ancient groups, including several strands of Jewish culture that did not envision reality in terms of a body/spirit or matter/spirit dualism characteristic of wider late Hellenistic culture. It is clear, however, that most early Christian thinkers were influenced less by the Stoics or by Hebraic traditions than by the sharp dualisms of other late Hellenistic religion.

So dualistic was the Hellenistic world, in fact, that even some Jewish thinkers, like their Christian counterparts, assimilated a clear body/spirit dualism. For example, when the Pentateuch was translated into Greek by Alexandrian Jews in the second century, this Septuagint translation of Exodus 21:22ff. (discussed in Chapter 3) introduced a distinction between an unformed and formed fetus uncharacteristic of the original Hebrew text. As a result, the original proscription against causing the death of a pregnant woman was transformed by translation into a command to exact the same penalty if a "formed" fetus died. Roman Catholic historian John Connery acknowledges that it was this mistranslation that motivated the Jewish thinker Philo Judaeus's rigorous tract *Two Ways* that was adapted by the Christian writer of *The Didache*. The result, which Connery also grants, was that this mistranslation of the Septuagint influenced Christians far more than Jews. As Connery observes, "Rabbinical Judaism, after the destruction of the temple, reverted to its own traditional interpretations of life in the womb as . . . a part of the mother's body."[38]

Much subsequent speculation among Christian theologians about when the full animation of body by spirit transpired was no more aimed at clarifying the meaning of abortion than were Tertullian's reflections. Rather, the discussion was carried on to determine when and how human responsibility for sin and evil emerged and to grapple with the disparity between divine ensoulment and "the fall of man." For the great fourth-century polemicist Augustine, these theological speculations took on great urgency, not because abortion posed the need for a clear-cut answer but because, by then, the Christian community was fractured with controversy over how human sinfulness related to divine salvation. Augustine adamantly opposed Tertullian's traducianist view, because he thought it unspiritual.[39] For Augustine, the infusion of rational soul, which was truly spiritual, could not be coterminous with the mere biological process of conception. At the same time, he was firmly opposed to the abortion of a "formed" fetus. Examination of his moral justifications for condemning abortion makes it clear that Augustine, who, especially in his later years, must stand fairly high on any list of antisexual phobists in Christian history, opposed it collaterally, not only with contraception but with any absence of procreative intent in sexuality.

His was a litany growing more common in fourth- and fifth-century Christian theology — that sex, except for the purpose of procreation within marriage, was murderous.

> This . . . cruel lust comes to this, that they even procure poisons of sterility and if these do not work, extinguish and destroy the fetus in some way in the womb, preferring that their offspring die before it lives, or *if it was already alive in the womb* to kill it before it is born. Assuredly, if both husband and wife are alike in this, they are not married, and if they were like this from the beginning they came together not joined in matrimony but in seduction. If both are not like this, I dare to say that either the wife is in a fashion the harlot of her husband or he is an adulterer of his own wife. (Italics mine)[40]

Scholars such as Nicholson cite this text, noting that it carried over into canon law, through the *Decretum* of Gratian, and was incorporated into Peter Lombard's *Sentences,* as a basic Christian theological text of the medieval period.[41]

Augustine's position that, from conception, original sin mars our existence implied that sexuality itself is the source of sin, a theory not surprising from one so racked with ambivalence about sexuality. On the point of the sinfulness of human nature, however, Augustine did not sway western Catholic orthodoxy. The universal "fall" of "mankind" envisaged by Augustine reemerged emphatically in Christian theology only at the time of the Reformation. It was the Protestant Reformers, especially Luther and Calvin, who, following Augustine, believed that sin had entered the world in such a drastic way that human innocence was no longer a possibility. By contrast, Roman Catholic theology continued to stress the innocence of "natural" existence as a polemical point over against these passionate Protestants' ideas. Here again, polemics within Christianity shaped abortion teaching, but insistence on the "innocence" of the "unborn child" figured strongly in abortion debates only much later.

Augustine, like Tertullian and most other men of the educated classes, continued to perpetuate what historian George Williams rather quaintly coined the "sire-centered" view of embryology referred to earlier[42] — that in procreation the male provided "the seed," the woman merely the generative space for fetal development. A variant understanding was that a woman supplied some of her menstrual blood as "matter" for fetal development.[43] In this theory, the spirit, or rational soul, was the male contribution. In any case, Augustine employed the distinction between formed and unformed fetal life, applying a prohibition of abortion only to a "formed" fetus. In fact, several times he opined that the death of an unformed fetus was *not* homicide. Furthermore, on at least one occasion, this rigorist bishop subscribed to what may have been an uncharacteristic sympathy for the life of the pregnant woman, insisting that an embryotomy to save the life of the mother would not impair a fetus's prospects for participating in the resurrection of the dead. The absolute prohibition against abortion at the risk of killing a pregnant woman has never been the dominant Christian view. Such a position would have seemed heartless even to some of the more militant misogynists of early Christendom.

Theologians like Augustine's older contemporary Jerome (c. 340-420) always figure prominently into citations of Christians who anathematize abortion. But scrutiny of Jerome's views hardly provides evidence of great moral sensibility. A man of virulent ascetic rigidity, sex-phobic in the extreme, he railed against "loose" women, castigating those who in any way hid their "unrighteousness" or lack of chastity. He believed the truly spiritual Christian would live free of marriage, but he condoned marriage as a necessary evil "to prevent the death of offspring out of fear."[44] Whether he meant abortion or infanticide is not clear from the text. With Jerome, the Christian misogynist tradition of affirming only the virginal, ascetic woman crystallized dramatically.[45] Nevertheless, he remained extremely controversial among Christians in his own time. Jerome's ardent asceticism hardly commended him to his Christian contemporaries. More significantly, his elitism and identification with the wealthy made his contemporaries suspicious of his early life and ascetic integrity.

Evidence for the development of anti-abortion teaching in the ongoing theology and penitential practice of the Christian community, as noted, cannot be traced simply through the writings of a few prominent theologians. Augustine's influence on later church doctrine belies his status as bishop of a minority Christian community. Likewise, Jerome's stature on the abortion question conceals the fact that his contemporaries considered his theological teachings excessively harsh and moralistic. The pervasiveness of Augustine's denunciations of heretics, particularly the Pelagians and others he suspected of lacking sufficient Christian ascetic rigor, suggests that his views on these matters were by no means normative for many in the Christian community of his day.[46] Some groups of Christians were, in fact, even more sex-negative than Augustine and his followers,[47] but others were "permissive" and, by his standards, "licentious." It is not unlikely that some of those denounced by Augustine were more permissive regarding procreative sexuality.

If the "evils" of abortion were as universally recognized among Christians as anti-abortion proponents suggest, it is difficult to understand the minor part given to discussion of abortion not only in theological writings but also in the developing church discipline spelled out in deliberations of church councils adjudicating controverted issues of faith. Invariably, in the attempt to demonstrate the unanimity and intensity of Christian anti-abortion teaching, anti-abortion scholars point to the teaching of two fourth-century councils, but always without full notation of what those councils specifically addressed in terms of abortion. Around the year 309 C.E., a small gathering of priests and bishops at the Council of Elvira held in Granada, a remote province of what is now Spain, attempted to codify disciplinary canons for their churches. The Council of Elvira is important precisely because it provides evidence for the early development of a specific penitential system within Christianity. The canons of Elvira introduced penances for numerous offenses, clarifying the severity of the various sins of Christians. More recently, however, this council has been identified as problematic in Christian theological development because it represents the first attempt by Christian bishops to regulate sexual offenses. Historian Samuel Laeuchli has assessed the Council of Elvira for the way in which control of sexuality and the growing hierarchical structure of the church were interrelated.[48] With an honesty uncharacteristic of much patristic scholarship, he observes the utter preoccupation with sexual sin on the part of the bishops and clerics in Granada. He suggests that the loss of identity following Roman imperial persecutions may have led some church leaders to shape Christian identity in terms of sexual conformity. This minor council was, in fact, a generating source of increasing Christian sex-negativity.

It is startling, given claims in mainstream anti-abortion interpretations of Christian teaching, that the Council of Elvira, far from "proving" that early Christianity deemed abortion a heinous sin, demonstrates the intimate connection between abortion and the condemnation of "sexual sin." It is not abortion per se that is condemned, but abortion undertaken by a baptized Christian woman to conceal adultery.[49] Infanticide was a lesser crime if performed by a catechumen,[50] who could be baptized "in the end." Until the twentieth century, many church historians discussed the significance of the council without mentioning abortion. Now it serves to substantiate the "great anti-abortion tradition" of Christendom. For the bishops and clerics at Elvira, abortion signified a "crime of killing" only because such sexual sin was considered murderous.

Just as the Council of Elvira is cited as evidence of the triumph of anti-abortion teaching in the then western church, the Council of Ancrya in 314 C.E. is cited as confirmation of the victory of anti-abortion teaching in early eastern Christianity. A council of eighteen bishops of the eastern church, more than attended at Elvira, convened to establish penances for those who had lapsed from Christianity during the Roman imperial persecutions of Christians under Maximus. Many church historians have reported on the significance of this council or summarized its actions on penance without mentioning abortion.[51] The textual evidence is oblique as to whether the council's actions referred to abortion at all. If, however, abortion was deliberated, it was treated under the rubrics of adultery, use of soothsaying, and resort to "customs of the Gentiles." The penances prescribed for adultery and abortion to conceal adultery were more moderate than those established at Elvira.[52]

Anti-abortion historians of Christianity explain the discrepancy between the supposed massive and unanimous theological condemnation of abortion and the erratic penitential treatment of abortion by church councils and, much later, in canon law, by making a sharp distinction between Christianity's "normative" moral position condemning abortion and its penitential tradition. They claim that the latter was necessarily less rigorist because of pastoral compassion and the more flexible requirements necessary to cope with the actual moral weakness of people.[53] By contrast, I believe that the early penitential treatments of abortion and the later canonical penalties established for those who performed or sought abortions reflect both the extension of control of sexual conduct by an emerging hierarchy and the disinterestedness of the church in the question of abortion except as sexual sin.

It is not easy to trace the slow historical process that transmuted scattered condemnations of abortion into the widespread, axiomatic taboo that abortion was homicide, a process that took well over a millennium. What remains incontestable is that in the early centuries of Christianity, the most severe denunciations of abortion came from those who also severely denounced any sort of "sexual permissiveness" — that is, sex for nonprocreative purposes. The letters of the third-century Bishop of Rome, Hippolytus, which are often cited as a source of authoritative anti-abortion teaching, provide a clear example of this connection. Hippolytus's comments on abortion emerged as he inveighed against his papal predecessor, Callistus, whom he specifically denounced for moral laxity. Callistus, a popular pope, is charged by Hippolytus with agreeing to ordain priests who had been more than once married and also with tolerating abortion. Hippolytus's diatribe against his predecessor links the popularity of Callistus with this "permissiveness." Callistus, he argued, like the biblical Noah, was guilty of "tolerating creatures of all sorts in the church."[54] Yet this same text can be read as evidence that the bishops who were more rigorist on sexual matters were not highly regarded by their fellow Christians. That Hippolytus's view was more "normatively moral" than Callistus's is true only if one presumes sex-negativism as more normative for Christian ethics.

I have already observed that around 1140 C.E. when the distinguished canon lawyer Gratian compiled the diverse traditions of canon law into his *Decretum*, which became the authoritative source of canon law for Roman Catholics until the modern period, he took over the passage from Augustine linking the condemnation of abortion and contraception as sexual sins. Gratian's compilation of existing canons, however, was not enthusiastically championed in his own day. He drew his teaching on abortion from the letters and texts of other church fathers, not from existing conciliar opinion. Although there are some inconsistencies among his sources, Gratian himself appeared to take for granted the distinction between the formed and unformed fetus. He also did not incorporate penances for the "sin" of abortion. Connery believes Gratian decided to drop the penances because it was "certainly simpler to do this than to attempt to reconcile the confusing mass of prescriptions from the past confronting him."[55]

A number of other texts in this period, including at least one other canon law compendium, also explicitly connect condemnations of abortion with denunciations of nonprocreative sex. The high medieval period of Christian history was characterized by major and racking controversy over sexuality, clerical celibacy, and sexual mores. It needs to be remembered that several centuries later the most sex-negative group achieved victory, and the canons and theology most vociferously condemning abortion carried the day. It took several centuries for clerical celibacy actually to become the norm, of course, and Christian sexual practice rarely followed canonical prescriptions, but it was ultimately the sex-negative trends among the most powerful theologians that cemented the equation of contraception and abortion with "homicide."[56] Although canonists such as Gregory IX reintroduced the term *homicide* into their condemnations of abortion, most of the canonists, such as Magister Rufinus, applied this same term to contraception and sterilization. It strains credulity to argue that the rhetorical equation of abortion with homicide actually represented in early medieval Christian thought a clarified moral evaluation of fetal life.

Furthermore, there is much evidence that, over most of these centuries, those who reiterated Christian prohibitions of abortion more often than not accepted the distinction between a formed and an unformed fetus. Theologians offered differing stipulations as to when a fetus could be considered "formed," but, as the most careful Roman Catholic scholars observe, there was little consensus on the matter. It was only after Thomas Aquinas became the "master" theologian of the Christian tradition, nearly a century after his death in 1274, that Aristotelian biology came to play a direct role in Christian thinking about sexuality. Aristotle had hypothesized that humans were a threefold integration of vegetative or nutritive, animal or sensitive, and intellectual or rational structure. Full "hominization" occurred only when the highest level of integration of these stages was reached. Aristotle held that the male fetus's "rational" soul was vital at forty days after conception but that the development of the female fetus was slower because females did not fully integrate the third phase, the rational soul. These Aristotelian distinctions, reintroduced by Aquinas, influenced later discussions. It should be emphasized, however, that Aquinas did not relate Aristotelian biology to the question of abortion. He said little on the subject except to condemn abortion of a formed fetus. Viewing abortion as an act *done to* a woman, he considered it homicide.[57]

Few pause to wonder why if medieval Christianity really had so thorough a moral grounding in anti-abortion, pro-fetal life considerations as modern spokespersons claim, the master theologian of medieval theology could have all but ignored the topic and dealt with it so marginally. That Aquinas is frequently associated in contemporary perspectives with strong and vivid teaching condemning abortion probably results from his close identification with the view that all sexual activity not aimed at procreation is sin. It has often been noted that, given Thomas Aquinas's understanding of "natural" sexuality, rape was a "natural" sexual act, whereas masturbation and anal or oral intercourse between a married couple were perverse and unnatural evil acts.[58] No matter how inadequate his view of sexuality, however, Aquinas was all but silent about the morality of abortion.

Aristotelian formulas on the "formation" of the fetus were really of little value in a world in which neither the process of conception nor the embryological process of fetal development was correctly understood. More often than not, as I have stated, "quickening" — the point when the fetus becomes active in the mother's womb — probably served as a rule of thumb for presuming ensoulment, or the formation of the fetus, especially in pastoral contexts. It was only in the fourteenth century, with the distinction between the formed and unformed fetus already well established, that medieval Catholic theologians began to clarify more directly the meaning of the now widely accepted condemnations of abortion. By this time, the focus of the question was set by the prevailing assumption that abortion was an unqualified wrong. Discussions continued to center on whether the prohibition of abortion applied to the formed or unformed fetus, but eventually, at least by the sixteenth century, controversy erupted around the question of the circumstances under which a therapeutic abortion could be justified.[59] The arguments of a number of prominent theologians that therapeutic abortions were justified to save a mother's life provided a "tradition" often invoked today by those Roman Catholic moral theologians who interpret Catholic teaching as legitimating therapeutic abortions in many instances.

The slow development of Roman Catholic debates regarding abortion from the thirteenth century onward have been well recounted by John Connery, and I will not rehearse them in detail.[60] Clearly, the trend after the thirteenth century was to reinforce anti-abortion teaching while delineating circumstances that might permit exceptions. Yet what is noteworthy to the critical reader of Christian teaching is the extent to which these debates, even well after the thirteenth century, were episodic. Frequently they broke out in relation to "reforming" efforts to stamp out "pagan" practices, those that feminists now associate with remnants of women's resistance to patriarchal religion. Sixtus V, one such "reforming" pope who was adamant about eradicating pagan practices, in 1588 formally decreed excommunication as the normative penalty for a woman having an abortion and anyone who assisted her. Sixtus even ceased to honor the distinction between the formed and unformed fetus and put sterilization on equal footing with abortion. That his views did not go unchallenged is obvious from the fact that his successor reinstated the distinction between the formed and unformed fetus and required excommunication only for abortion of the animated fetus.[61]

Nearly a century elapsed before any further serious discussion of the abortion question ensued, but when it did arise, the debate finally began to focus on circumstances that might justify an abortion. At this point criteria drawn from the just-war "killing ethic" discussions were related to abortion. Clearly, the question of whether such criteria *ought to* apply to abortion was not raised. Abortion was already widely anathematized and classified as homicide, along with all other practices facilitating escape from the procreative functionality of sex. It is interesting to note, given the well-established distinction between the formed and unformed fetus, the diversity of opinion then operative about whether the prohibition of abortion applied to the formed or unformed fetus. During this period the distinction between a direct abortion (one aimed to take the life of the fetus) and an indirect abortion (one performed to save the life of the mother and consequently requiring the death of the fetus) began to be elaborated, a distinction to be called upon in modern Roman Catholic moral reasoning on the issue.[62]

A REVIEW OF REFORMATION AND POST-REFORMATION TEACHING ON ABORTION

That premodern Christian theology marked the beginning of distinctively human life at the point of rational "formation" is evident from the fact that, at the time of the Reformation, Martin Luther understood himself to be breaking with this tradition by reinstating a traducian view that body and soul merge at conception. As with earlier theologians, Luther's interest was not to clarify the abortion question but to voice objection to the major Reformation polemic against Catholic teaching regarding sin and salvation. The Reformation had little impact on the abortion question, and, as I have stressed in Chapter 3, the reformers strongly reinforced and extended theological emphasis on the centrality of marriage and the role of procreation in sexuality.

An ingenious explanation of how Christian teaching moved away from the view that abortion applied to terminating the life of a "formed" fetus toward the present "orthodox" papal view that the fetus is, at the moment of conception or implantation, a fully existent human being has been offered by a Protestant historian totally sympathetic to present Roman Catholic teaching. George H. Williams, believing that modern science vindicates the post-Reformation Roman Catholic understanding that fetuses are, in fact, fully human persons, celebrates the conquest of Protestantism by Catholic teaching. For him, fetuses are "the unwitting and diminutive denizens *of that universal and mysterious realm of maternal darkness* from whence we all emerge!" (italics mine).[63] Williams acknowledges that most pre-Reformation Christian theologians did in fact observe the distinction between "formed" and "unformed" fetal life characteristic of the day. Even so, he contends that it was the teaching of the major Protestant reformers, Martin Luther and John Calvin, that forced the Christian tradition to shift to identifying the fetus or zygote as a full human being.

Williams contends that Luther contributed to this change, in spite of the fact that when discussing abortion he assumed a distinction between the formed and unformed fetus. In his discussion of salvation, Luther argued for Tertullian's traducian view that body and soul merge at conception, though he mistakenly credited Augustine with traducian doctrine. Williams does acknowledge, very much in passing, that Luther's "vindication" of the full humanity of the fetus from conception

> was prompted by a concern to involve the mind and spirit as much as the flesh in the guilt and consequences of original sin, . . . and not in any awareness of the correlation of this view with the problem of abortion.[64]

Williams argues that later Catholic moral theology responded to Luther's teaching and applied it to abortion. He contends that Calvin's "rigor" on this matter also encouraged greater Catholic movement toward viewing fetal life as human from conception onward. To be sure, Calvin interpreted Exodus 21:22 to mean that abortion should be a capital offense if either a pregnant woman or the fetus in her womb were killed. But Williams's suggestion — that post-Reformation Roman Catholic theologians, confronted with Luther's and Calvin's firm opinions, adopted similar views in order to match their theological rigor — is questionable. He goes so far as to claim that "Lutheran traducianism induced a change in Catholic creationism *and by the nineteenth century* had eliminated in Catholic moral theology an *un*ensouled stage in the development of the fetus" (italics mine).[65] One should treat with considerable skepticism this thesis that Protestant teaching "improved" Roman Catholic opinion on the matter. Such reasoning about historical causation is intellectualistic in the extreme. Most Counter-Reformation Roman Catholic theologians did not possess a thorough grasp of either Luther's or Calvin's work, and their later discussions of abortion seem unrelated to wider points of Reformation theological debate.

The theological issue that made the question of the precise moment of the humanization of life urgent to the Protestant reformers was *not* the question of abortion but the issue of "original sin" and the way in which human beings were implicated in that sin through "the fall." The doctrine of salvation, not the morality of abortion, was at issue. Roman Catholics rejected Reformation claims that sin enters human experience irrevocably, such that at no point is human life genuinely innocent or free from responsibility for sin, but this dispute had little bearing on interpretations of the evaluation of abortion. While there is a trend in eighteenth- and nineteenth-century Catholic theology toward abandoning the "formed" and "unformed" distinction, there is no textual evidence to support Williams's argument that Reformation polemics "positively" effected this shift in Roman Catholic teaching. The Catholic moral discussions of the time focused on clarifying the distinction between direct (illicit) and indirect (possibly licit) abortion.

It also would be more accurate, historically, to observe that Luther and Calvin displayed little interest in the question of abortion and that neither reasoned about the issue directly. Both assumed the then traditional condemnation of the act. Luther knew the antisexual condemnations of contraception and abortion because he had studied *The Sentences* of Peter Lombard, which incorporated Gratian's *Decretum* condemnation. Furthermore, Lutheran teaching was not uniform on ensoulment. Melanchthon, another early Lutheran theologian, insisted, contrary to Luther, on the previously "traditional" view that the soul is infused into the body not at conception but at some later point. He strongly rejected the traducianist doctrine, insisting that God's grace cannot be equated with the "simple quickening of beasts."[66] In this view, Melanchthon anticipated what later became a widely held Protestant differentiation between "nature" and God's "grace," a trend that made it more difficult for Protestants to conflate biological and theological categories, except, as noted earlier, where women and sexuality were concerned.

Calvin, who clearly classified abortion as killing, was also not particularly concerned to elaborate pertinent moral issues or to formulate legal sanctions against abortion. Calvin vented his sexual prudery, more severe than Luther's, in expressing rigorist objections to adultery and related sexual sins, including, in fragmentary references, abortion. Even granting his exegesis of Exodus 21:22ff., however, it is something of an overstatement to portray him as a strong anti-abortionist. The intellectualistic fallacy of isolating fragmentary passages to produce a normative moral reading of the anti-abortion tradition is nowhere clearer than at this point. The abortion question was totally marginal to Calvin's moral concerns. If Calvin, so influential in determining not only the theology but the legal structure of the city of Geneva, had in fact raged militantly on the abortion question, we would expect to uncover legal sanctions against abortion in Geneva, where civil magistrates followed his lead. Yet civil law was mute on abortion, all the while championing the pro-marital enthusiasms of Calvin and his political supporters. Parents, for example, were expected as a duty to arrange the proper marriages of their offspring, and sexual sins were punished. One of these sexual sins was infanticide, redefined to include any *concealed* pregnancy that produced a stillborn infant.[67] Abortion per se went unmentioned. Reformation teaching on abortion, then, was at best fragmentary, and, like their predecessors, the reformers in no way elaborated their denunciations in moral terms related to the value of fetal life. As in earlier Catholic theology, the moral wrong of abortion was assumed. By custom, or more accurately, by established taboo, it was construed as human killing, but the valuation of fetal life was not the pivotal moral reason for equating abortion and homicide. The divinely sanctioned procreative intent of sexuality and divine animation of the soul, not the nature of fetal development, grounded the view of the fetus as fully human.

On the Catholic side, the convergence of an antikilling ethic with the anti-abortion ethic that had evolved from procreative functionalism was strengthened in Counter-Reformation moral theology, in part because more precise pastoral distinctions and clarifications were necessary. Although the anti-abortion ethic was already in place, some abortions seemed justified *in spite of the prohibitory trend.* Hence, the reasonings about when the killing of a fetus might be justified were elaborated to clarify possible exceptions to the rule. Furthermore, the emergence of the earliest anti-Aristotelian biology, which challenged the philosopher's ensoulment views, eventually exerted more direct influence on Catholic discussions. It took well over a century, however, before Catholic theological discussion was directly impacted by this opposition to Aristotelian teaching, which began when several seventeenth-century physicians in Rome declared that the "rational soul" was infused not after but on the third day of conception.[68]

In spite of his own dramatic identification with current Roman Catholic tradition, George H. Williams correctly summarizes the subsequent history of abortion within Protestant Christianity as disruptive of the anti-abortion tradition. According to Williams, the modern Protestant toleration of abortion, which he deplores, was the consequence of Protestant return to scripture as the sole authority in normative Christian theology. Protestants, he argues, were cut off from

> patristic texts against abortion in the Greco-Roman environment. . . . As Protestants and then particularly Calvinists lost touch with *the body of traditional materials on the moral issues relating to conception and intra-uterine life,* they began to forget what even Luther and Calvin *had said quite clearly but inconspicuously* on abortion; and they would by the nineteenth century, as evangelical biblical literalists, assimilate directly from the Scriptures the pre-Hellenistic "Jewish" view or they would, as liberals, join forces with the proponents of the latest genetic and embryological theories. (Italics mine)[69]

Williams is correct that Protestants did not develop so forceful an anti-abortion teaching as Roman Catholic theologians, though as my discussion of biblicism in Chapter 3 pointed out, the shift to a biblical norm did not usually alter the anti-abortion stance among Protestants. One exception to the post-Reformation neglect of the question occurred in the Church of England. The Anglicans retained Roman Catholic canonical prohibitions against abortion and incorporated them into post-Reformation English ecclesiastical rules. The Church of England went through several periods when it encouraged relaxation of sexual rigor, but some official harshness on the issue is evident from scrutiny of the English common law tradition. Judges often supported women, over against the church, protesting existing ecclesiastical standards as insensitive to women.[70] And there is scattered testimony that many Anglicans, including Anglican clergy, ignored the canonical condemnations out of sympathy for women's plight.[71] In light of the rigidity of English church teaching, English common law evolved to prescribing that the state make the welfare of a mother its proper legal consideration in adjudicating claims about abortion.

Ironically, U.S. Supreme Court Justice Blackmun's opinion in the 1973 *Roe v. Wade* decision, which established women's personal freedom of choice in the first trimester of pregnancy, cited this common law tradition as a precedent for the majority ruling. Many Christian anti-abortionists, including Noonan, have caricatured this element of Blackmun's argument.[72] On the basis of a single English jurist, William Blackstone, whose work, he contends, "was the bible of American lawyers," Noonan places the entire British common-law tradition on the anti-abortion side of the argument.[73] The fact is, however, that Justice Blackmun had done his homework on common law precedents, whatever other criticisms might be raised about his arguments in *Roe v. Wade*.

It was in the United States that Protestant Christian understanding of abortion came to truly exemplify the freedom from the patristic and canon law traditions of which George H. Williams complains. Unfortunately, however, Protestant Christianity hardly exhibited the characteristics Williams imputes to it — an "extreme feminism," characterized by "a self-righteous indifference about the destiny of the fetus in [its] overriding preoccupation with 'the dignity of the woman' as a sovereign individual who should not be socially enthralled by motherhood."[74] Women, and fair-minded men, who know the history of women's struggle for full standing in Protestant Christianity in the United States can only express astonishment at

Williams's objection. Those who have scrutinized even the most liberal mainstream Protestant social gospel views on women, sexuality, and marriage must take special umbrage at Williams's insistence that social gospel Christianity promoted "extreme feminism."

The loosening of U.S. Protestant Christianity's ties to the anti-abortion tradition are far better explained by two other factors.[75] One is that many U.S. Protestant groups were rooted historically in the left wing of the Reformation and hold a more antagonistic and skeptical attitude toward dominant theological tradition than do Lutherans or Calvinists. The other factor pertains to shifts in later Calvinist Puritan theology, which rendered the question of ensoulment moot in its theological anthropology. Divine election was, in the Puritan tradition, rooted in God's foreordination quite apart from the biological processes of conception. As a result of these factors, U.S. Protestantism was, until recently, more silent on the issue of abortion than were earlier Christians.

If the history of Christian teaching on abortion had not been so astonishingly misrepresented in discussion of the history of Christian ethics, however, the conclusions reached by historian James Mohr, in his celebrated study *Abortion in America*,[76] would not have come as a surprise to so many people. What Mohr discovered was that no clergyman or theologian gave early support to proposed laws banning abortion in nineteenth-century America. Mohr demonstrates that abortion became illegal in the United States because of a political crusade mounted by the medical profession, which demanded, and eventually got, stringent laws in most states. Medical journals in the latter decades of the century were replete with articles condemning clergy for their insensitivity and lack of moral concern on the question of abortion.

Though Mohr does not speculate on the matter, it is my impression that nineteenth-century Protestant clergy, usually married and often poor, were aware that romanticizing "nature's bounty" with respect to procreation ushered in a great deal of human suffering. When some Protestant clergy finally joined the anti-abortion crusade, they did so for explicitly racist and classist reasons. As evidence cited by Mohr demonstrates, it was a group of conservative white clergy, fearing that America's strength was threatened by the lower birth rate among white, middle-class, "respectable" women compared to that of black and ethnic immigrant women, who finally led some

Protestant clerics and churches to enter abortion politics on the side of the medical profession.

Contrary to Williams's unique thesis, mainstream Protestant clergy in the United States were divided on the issue of justice for women. In fact, as we have seen, the churches eventually joined the later movement "sacralizing motherhood," identifying with conservative political trends and groups. What I have elsewhere termed "soft feminism" — that is, an ideology that casts women, by virtue of their "femininity" and/or biological power of childbearing, as morally superior to and religiously more sensitive than men — was a reactive stance on the part of many late-nineteenth- and early-twentieth-century churches.[77] As a result of this backlash against the women's movement, and also because of the persistent force of misogyny in biblicist Protestantism, the mainstream Protestant churches aligned themselves with rising opposition to the birth control movement *more readily* than they have recently united with the crusade to prohibit legal abortion. Needless to say, opposition to birth control is hardly evidence of a purported "extreme feminism" on the part of Protestant churches.[78] In fact, it is better understood as a reassertion of fears of changes in society that would ensue from sundering procreation and sexuality so sharply. Even in "liberal" Protestantism, the connection between "acceptable sexuality" and marital procreative intent remained vivid enough to mobilize opposition to birth control. The current sentimental pieties of the biblicist U.S. Protestant backlash against justice for women, discussed before, parallel the earlier conservative responses of liberals, threatening to reverse once again a fragile liberating trend in Protestant sensibilities to women.

Enough has been said here to clarify why it is questionable to portray *the* Christian tradition on abortion as concise, well developed, or monolithic. It may be a long time before we have a genuinely critical, adequate historical review of abortion in its full Christian socio-moral context. Meanwhile, a "hermeneutic of suspicion" about prevailing interpretations is very much in order. My contention is that anti-abortion proponents in their "historical research" chiefly have tapped the sometimes hysterical antisexual bias leveled especially against any woman who did not confine her sexuality to procreative functionalism. Even so, the Holy Crusade quality of much contemporary masculinist Christian teaching on abortion is quite new in Christian history. Abortion was a matter of relative indifference in Christianity until its widespread existence, together with its safety, could no longer be ignored. The current intensity of the debate is related to contemporary cultural shifts that place pressure on the various Christian churches to choose sides in a turbulent ideological arena and that demand reconsideration of basic Christian attitudes toward sexuality and women.

Now, however, many Christians would make the state the instrument of Christian moral enforcement. Through much of Christian history, no such merging of Christian morality and state power was envisioned. Even those who strongly oppose the morality of abortion acknowledge that normative moral teaching was not enforced rigorously by either the church or the state. Now some abortion opponents would condone state imposition of the view that abortion is homicide. At the very least, all participants in the abortion conflict need to actively renounce the dubious assumptions holding sway about women and a procreative functionalist view of women's sexuality. To value and respect human life in relation to the abortion issue must mean, at the very least, that one recognizes the possibility of genuine conflict between the life and well-being of a pregnant woman and the fetus she carries. If one cannot even envision such potential conflict, it will surely be because for that individual, women do not yet count as full, valuable persons *in their own right*, apart from their social utility as procreative beings.

What this brief review of the history of Christian teaching on abortion should clarify is the power of current ideological interests in the abortion controversy in shaping our perceptions of Christian history. Ideological blinders lead Christians interpreting this history, at best, to scrutinize this past without any careful weighing of the moral reasoning involved and, at worst, to portray a "triumphant" tradition of moral sensitivity that credits Christians with a moral clarity on the issue of abortion that, in all truth, our tradition has never possessed.

Before we turn to the urgent question of making a moral evaluation of the specific act of abortion, we need to ask ourselves what the "history of the morality of abortion" might look like if women's lives were respectfully taken into account. Given the limits of our knowledge, we can address this question only fragmentarily. But we already understand enough to recognize that, though masculinist Christians never mention it, the story of women's struggle to gain control over their power of procreation is where the real history of the abortion issue resides, just as it is within this concrete context that its morality must be assessed.

6

Notes Toward a Feminist Perspective on the History of Abortion

BEYOND MASCULINIST HISTORIOGRAPHY

In contrast to the historiographic approach of dominant Christianity, a liberation interpretation of the history of Christian ethics must assume that whenever Christianity has functioned structurally or institutionally as part of the social system of male supremacy, white racism, or class ideology, its ethics also bear the ideological marks of those structures of domination. This nonliberating dimension must be faced, acknowledged, and transcended in Christian practice. If those who currently perceive themselves as the "defenders of fetal rights" were more candid about the substance and context of the moral reasoning concerning abortion in the Christian past, they would have to acknowledge that the picture they present is romanticized and distorted. Neither a recognition of the intrinsic value of fetal life, children, or women nor a concrete concern for improving the lot of women and children has been a major hallmark of Christianity over the centuries. Dominant Christian groups have been concerned more with control of sexuality and the social order and the preservation of male prerogatives.

In a masculinist scenario, as discussed in Chapter 3, Christian teaching on abortion is said to intervene as a noble effort to affirm life-enhancing values in the face of a colossal and growing moral insensitivity and capricious disregard for human life characteristic of hedonistic and self-indulgent cultures. The problem with this sort of argument is that it already presupposes a functionalist perspective on human sexuality. To persons who hold this viewpoint, any effort to separate women's sexual activity and procreative fertility is evidence of moral decadence. The Christian ascetic tradition is replete with claims that any attitudes and practices that separate sexuality and procreation are a sign of moral laxity. That the true intent of the church was to cement these claims is evident in the ruse it devised to counter oppositions. As Samuel Laeuchli has acknowledged, "The Christian church. . . always tried to discredit its rivals as sexually inferior, an apologetic slander technique which has worked to this day."[1]

Even a more honest, more critical, and therefore less pretentious picture of where masculinist Christian thought has moved on the abortion issue would not yet enable us to place it in its proper historical context. From the patristic period onward, the selective perceptions operative in the historical judgments of Christian teaching on abortion are skewed, because women's well-being is not perceived as a central moral issue and women's experience and reality are not understood as relevant to a moral analysis of abortion. Laeuchli, whose work on early Christianity I have already affirmed for its atypical honesty about the role of sex-negativism in the formation of Christian teaching, has observed:

> We do not really know much about the women of the church. Patristic texts, through which we find access to the hopes and fears of ancient man, were written with extremely few exceptions by men, and of those, by clerics or believers strongly advocating the ascetic life. What these texts. . . show is a crisis of male identity. In the image of manhood [presupposed]. . . the woman as sexual being was excluded. Where such sexual dualism was predicated, man no longer defined himself in relation to woman. . . instead he defined himself in separation from woman.[2]

None of the Christian historical treatments of abortion has addressed, much less attempted to begin reconstructing, the real historical perspective in which the contemporary discussion belongs: the historically universal struggle by women to cope with and gain some proximate control over their fertility and the dilemmas it poses.

No woman has ever lived untouched at the deepest level by the interaction of her presumed biological power to bear children and her society and culture's expectations for her life. Even under the most adverse conditions, women as a group have attempted to develop some controls in relation to their fertility — in every culture, without exception, regardless of existing morality or religion. But women's lack of social power, in all recorded history, has made this effort to control fertility difficult for a great many, probably most. Many women have managed to do whatever seemed possible, given available knowledge, to avoid too-numerous pregnancies. For a number of women, nature's sometimes vicious profligacy often has presented a life-threatening situation.[3] And when a woman was unable to bear children, her life was irrevocably marked and frequently scarred by her atypical relation to procreative power. The "barren woman" is one of history's fated figures in cultures where procreation is a woman's only deeply valued social function. Women who elect to avoid sexual relations with males, either through celibacy or lesbian love, are not exempt from these problems and pressures. With very few exceptions, they are forced to bear a heavy social stigma for their refusal of heterosexual relations and the traditional female role of procreation. It is quite likely that the considerable attraction of ascetic religion and celibacy to women in the past was related to their limited number of life options apart from childbearing.[4]

There can be no doubt that many women coped with their childbearing capacities with grace and that others resigned themselves to whatever "fate" held in store for them, but in any case "women's lot" was shaped by biological fertility and cultural patterns developed around their procreative power.[5] Not to recognize this, and therefore to make these realities a presupposition of one's "historical perspective" on abortion, leads to claims about the past that are grossly insensitive to the lives of the moral agents who, without exception, bear the direct consequences of the outcome of any debate about abortion.

Historian Gerda Lerner has observed:

> Slowly . . . historians of women's history have become dissatisfied with old questions and old methods, and have come up with new ways of approaching historical material. They have, for example, begun to ask about the actual *experience* of women in the past. This is obviously different from a description of the condition of women written from male sources . . . What kind of periodization might be substituted for the periodization of traditional history, in order for it to be applicable to women? . . . The important fact which distinguished the past of women from that of men is precisely that until very recently sexuality and reproduction were

inevitably linked for women, while they were not so linked for men. Similarly, child-bearing and child-rearing were inevitably linked for women and still are so linked. Women's freedom depends on breaking those links . . . we can and should ask of each historical period: What happened to the link between sexuality and reproduction? . . . The next step is to face, once and for all and with all its complex consequences, that women are the majority of mankind and have been essential to the making of history. Thus, all history as we now know it, is merely prehistory. Only a new history firmly based on this recognition and equally concerned with men, women, the establishment and the passing away of patriarchy, can lay claim to being a truly universal history.[6]

We are, of course, a long way from an adequate alternative understanding of women's collective struggle to acquire a semblance of control over biological reproduction. Feminist historical reconstruction is in its early phases and remains invisible in much of the official and literary histories that pass for our "remembered" past.[7] The historical reconstructive task that must focus the history of the problem of abortion in terms of women's actual lives is massive and has not yet been undertaken in a systematic way.

Yet even now some fragmentary notes about women's struggle with biological fertility can be gleaned from the new feminist historiography. Feminist historians and anthropologists are beginning to attend to women's culture as an important, perdurable, and neglected dimension of the true story of all human culture. Women's way of meeting the challenges of fertility, pregnancy, and childbearing is a most basic dimension of the human story, even though it has been invisible in the tales the dominant histories tell. The new feminist historiography has begun to explore intimacy and gender relations, taking seriously the culture of reproduction as the earliest and most primal dimension of human culture. Very gradually, a picture is emerging that upsets the most entrenched assumption of masculinist historiography — that women's lives have been static, unchanging, and "ahistorical." In contrast to the portrait of the past conjured up by patriarchal consciousness, the new historiography presents a world in which there has been great diversity and continuous change in gender relations, sexual mores, family life, and patterns of intimacy. The official patriarchal version of western culture's family life — that it constitutes an intractable, unbroken line in which women's lives were ruled by "nature" and in which moral conventions regarding sexuality (including abortion) and women's roles were homogeneous and static — collapses in the light of a more critical, informed approach. For serious critical scholars, the notion that there once was an ahistorical pattern of constant male-female intimacy and universal child-care structures and sex-role expectations is a thing of the past. In our time, the family has come to be viewed as a cultural institution, buffeted by the wider socio-economic and political structures of society. Those who would save the family (read "mid-twentieth-century nuclear family") are in fact the same people who give uncritical allegiance to the very socioeconomic system that is rendering the family dysfunctional, even perhaps obsolete.

In an earlier phase of the development of our modern economic system, centralized modes of production drew many people from the land into the cities, separating nuclear families from the matrix of the extended rural family. Over time, the urban nuclear family unit became the statistical norm, especially during the post-World War II period. In the late decades of our century, we are living through another structural shift in our political economy, one that creates a statistical norm that lower- and middle-income families must rely on two paychecks to cope with the escalating costs of housing, food, education, and health care. The massive numbers of women entering the paid work force out of economic necessity, albeit usually in the lower-paying "pink collar" jobs,[8] attest to the magnitude of these changes. Given such pressures, childbearing must be carefully planned and controlled, and many families experience the decision to have a child (or a second or third one) as a trade-off with, for example, buying a home. As we will see in Chapter 7, moralists frequently interpret such decisions as frivolous, "mere" lifestyle choices, severing the issue of achieving even modest economic security in a society such as ours from "moral" considerations related to childbearing.

But if the pace of change in gender relations and family life is accelerating now because of the dynamics of our neoconservative political economy,[9] change in that dimension of our social relations actually has always been ongoing. Most important, perhaps, in relation to the abortion question is our recognition of changes wrought by the social relations that are distinctive to capitalist economic and political development historically. Our modern division of society into public and private spheres, which accords economic functions to the former and domestic life to the latter, leaving women socially and economically disempowered in quite new ways, is of prime importance when we discuss procreative choice.[10]

Prior to the rise of a centralized, factory-centered mode of production, the family unit was the center of both reproductive culture and economic production. With respect to economic life, women and men shared in producing goods for consumption and also for exchange. Now, except on the family farm, the "domestic" sphere of family life has little direct productive function. And even where "the household economy"[11] still operates, for example where families work as artisans or craftspersons, these families are economically vulnerable. Health care, retirement income programs, and other noncash "work" benefits taken for granted in industry are unavailable to them. Everywhere wage labor or money income has replaced family labor, barter, and service exchange as the medium for obtaining food, shelter, health care, and security in old age. It is difficult for some women to realize that the modern, middle-strata homemaker is probably *more* economically vulnerable than her grandmother was. The growing plight of "displaced homemakers" in the United States — that is, homemakers divorced or widowed without adequate financial resources to meet their daily needs and bereft of "saleable skills" — testifies that changes in our political economy are increasingly disadvantageous to large groups of women. So does the increasing number of single-parent, female heads of households, women who struggle daily as the sole providers for growing children. None of these trends in people's life situations will be altered in the near future, given current directions in national policy.

The rapidly changing function of the family in our political economy has been paralleled by equally important alterations in what I call "the culture of reproduction." In rural extended families, women bear children surrounded by female relatives and friends who ease the pressures of coping with newborns and share the incessant demands of the dependent young. In an urban context, women are more isolated from the remnants of women's reproductive culture and its support system. Urban women must have money available to assure adequate prenatal care and to feed the newborn.

At best, we have only fragmentary data prior to the modern period concerning women's culture and women's experience of childbearing to help us understand what the burdens of pregnancy and childbearing really meant to the women involved. From the late nineteenth century onward, however, testimonies from women about these matters have been documented. In 1913 and 1914, experiential reports were gathered from 160 women in London, among them a few factory workers, the others dependent on their husbands' wage-labor. Their stories articulate the relentless pressure and considerable suffering they endured owing to their fertility, as well as the realism and self-respect they gained from their struggles to cope with reproduction. Although abortion and attempted abortions were rare among this group of women, miscarriages and stillbirths were frequent, as were the early deaths of their young children.[12] Few portrayed themselves as helpless victims. Many bore witness to their own greater fortune compared with the dreadful suffering of other women they knew. What they sought for themselves and other women were things many of us take for granted today — greater knowledge of their bodies, sex and health education, better nutrition for themselves and their children, affordable medical care, a less stressful life, and fairer wages for their husbands. Every aspect of their lives had been determined fundamentally by their childbearing, and these women longed for conditions that would make childbearing a happier, easier lot.

Nothing is more striking than that most of these women bore their children without help and support, except that which their overworked husbands could extend. Parents, relatives, and friends were conspicuously absent in their accounts. And many found the most unendurable aspect of pregnancy to be the necessity of leaving their beds immediately after delivery to resume full-time housework and care of other children. It is not unreasonable to wonder whether an urban industrial society is not, unenviably, a distinctly more difficult social setting in which to bear and rear children than the contexts earlier cultures and societies provided.

As the new historiography begins to make inroads into women's invisible past and assumptions that cause many people to project the modern (extended or nuclear) family backward in time throughout western history, it becomes apparent that ahistorical appeals to the "traditional values" of "family life" function ideologically to serve dominant social interests. As I have observed, for example, it is now widely recognized that the modern child-centered family is a recent consequence of increasing economic affluence in Europe and the United States. The conception that women are "by nature" suited to "private" domestic roles as homemakers is also the result of the recent division of labor between home and workplace. Our ideas about femininity are far from the cross-cultural constant that the ideological interpretations of patriarchy suggest. It is not just women's roles that have shifted. In society, sex roles are reciprocal.[13] Changes in the typical patterns of women's lives have necessitated changes in the typical patterns of men's lives. What the new historiography enables us to see is that such changes are part of an ongoing and shifting reality and that our sexual ethics, including our mores of gender relations and "ethics of marriage" so pivotal in patriarchal formulations, also have been neither inflexible nor characterized by a simple uniformity.

If we cannot yet place the abortion controversy squarely in the history of the social relations of reproduction, we can now anticipate the day when we will have some secure and textured sense of the strength, courage, and capacity of women to cope with diverse and difficult circumstances. In the meantime, we can begin to isolate, in a preliminary and provisional way, a few parameters of the changing world of women vis-à-vis reproduction. Even this sort of sketch can assist us in seeing why the crusade to deny women procreative control has both a negative moral meaning and a deleterious social consequence that its historical agents resist acknowledging.

In this chapter, I will take a brief look at how the new sociocultural history is beginning to inform our understanding of the way procreative control has functioned, historically. I will also review some of what we know about women's fertility and abortion practice in the contemporary world. As fragmentary as this story is, it at least helps place our discussion of the morality of the act of abortion (Chapter 7) in the proper concrete setting — a world in which women must cope with, and frequently make choices about, their fertility, a world in which women's social power is limited and the range of life choices open to them are, more often than not, severely constrained.[14]

THE ANCIENT PROBLEM OF
FERTILITY AND ITS CONTROL

As we turn now to ask how the history of abortion ethics appears in light of women's historical experience, we must begin by reconnecting what recent defenders of orthodox Christian teaching on abortion insistently separate — contraception, or efforts at fertility control, and abortion. As much as male moralists separate them, I have insisted that in women's lives the two issues are never, ever separable. The major reformist strategy in mainstream Christian ethics — to separate fertility control, or contraception,[15] from abortion[16] — is the worst sort of casuistry. Abortion is and always has been a means of birth control, as its all but universal practice attests.[17] And I believe we must continue to assert that, given the limits of birth control technology, it will remain the birth control method of last resort for many women, whether or not it is legal and/or safe. In fact, for many women it is the most reliable, and, at least when used infrequently, it is safe.[18]

In maintaining that the vast majority of women do not live out their lives in an ethos of genuine choice with respect to their procreative power, I have attempted to do justice to the diversity of life situations in which women must cope with fertility. The magnitude of the problem of fertility control that women have faced in human history has varied, of course. Just as an individual woman may, by biological "accident," find herself unable to conceive, many others are all but unable to avoid pregnancy if they are sexually active with men.[19] As we appropriate the fact that childbirth, parenting, and mothering are not in any sense ahistorical constants, we can also come to recognize that fertility itself is no ahistorical constant either. Fertility varies with levels of nutrition and general levels of health and well-being. It is shaped by varying cultural expectations about the proper age of marriage and the rites of matrimony. Efforts to control human fertility have sometimes been shared by males in some cultural contexts, but this sort of mutual accountability has been, to say the least, rare. The relationship between male and female attitudes toward family size and the appropriateness of procreative restraint also differs greatly within a given culture. Males in non-patriarchal cultures sometimes have joined women in recognizing that it was wise to limit the number of children in a family unit, and many contemporary men are eager to restrict family size for complex and diverse reasons.

Not surprisingly, there appears to be a correlation between patriarchal-masculinist religion and male refusal to share responsibility for fertility control, probably because in cultures where women and children are property, fertility is a manifestation of power, virility, and wealth. I also believe that, the otherworldliness of masculinist religious systems notwithstanding, the dominant male role breeds a lack of acceptance of finitude in men and an uneasiness about their mortality, which in turn creates a psychic need for the "immortality" and "omnipotence" progeny are felt to assure. Men in patriarchal religious systems, large sectors not only of Christianity but of Islam, Hinduism, and Judaism,[20] are notoriously resistant to their own or, if married, their wives' participation in fertility control. This same resistance characterizes adherents of more recent patriarchal religions. Mormons, for example, often bear this patriarchal hostility to fertility control. Moreover, the most powerfully patriarchal groups in existing religious systems have perpetuated the gap between male moral perception and female experience in relation to fertility, procreation, and abortion. Women in most of the cultures dominated by masculinist forms of religion, now and in the past, frequently resort to abortion regardless of its anathematization by theologians and religious moralists. It is not too much to say that social outrage functions here to reinforce the chasm between what men and male-identified women perceive and what many women do, when faced with the lived-world struggle of coping with fertility. Masculinist moral outrage, voiced by the powerful and reinforced by legal sanction, creates a secretiveness on the part of women, denies women the possibility of dealing openly with the real dilemmas they face, and robs them of the self-respect that comes from courageous coping with concrete problems.

To recognize this, however, is not to suggest that contemporary men have no self-interest in fertility control. If, as demographer Judith Blake argues, much of the current support for abortion comes from men who value women's greater sexual availability when abortion is legal,[21] this shift represents an adjustment not in religion, but at the cultural level of men's expectations regarding sexuality and their social relations with women. Male expectations have altered because women in modern societies are no longer the legal possessions of men and because both genders have developed companionate expectations for male-female relations.[22] Contemporary men expect forms of sexual and emotional support from women in quite different ways than premodern men did. The evidence mounts that modern attitudes toward birth control are shaped less and less by religious ideology or traditional culture than by the total socioeconomic matrix of a given society.[23]

Even so, efforts to control fertility are hardly new; they are probably more ancient than recorded history. Prior to the domestication of agriculture, fertility may well have been a crisis issue for ancient human communities. Hunter-gatherer societies often existed in precarious dependence on the immediacies of the natural environment. We have observed the dialectical relationship that exists between theology and morality on the one hand and the material conditions necessary for the realization of human value on the other. The celebratory attitude toward procreation that we encounter in the ancient Israelite "generative stories" and in the religious literature of many other premodern societies, which was appropriated totally by later theologies, could not have emerged under most ancient preagricultural conditions. Given the limited options available in ancient societies, it is not surprising that infanticide was evidently not uncommon.[24] A wandering community probably was unable to accommodate all of the offspring it was capable of birthing. The survival of the entire group might depend on not permitting reproduction to exceed the limits set by a relatively inflexible and unreliable food supply. This is still true today in places like Irian Jaya in Indonesia, where the tribal peoples inhabiting the remote mountainous interior strictly regulate sexual activity because of their severely limited food supply.

The domestication of agriculture was, of course, a great leap forward in the development of the human species, enabling groups and communities to provide more stable conditions for survival. Furthermore, the domestication of agriculture did much to enhance the need for and value of new members to the community. Those born into a community could, under the best environmental circumstances, not only share but expand the common labor available to provide for the community. The development of moral strictures against fertility control evidently began to make their appearance in agricultural societies.

Obviously, our understanding of how fertility was controlled in ancient times is limited. No doubt, many communities controlled fertility by carefully ritualizing sexual relations between men and women, at times patterning such behavior rigidly. The origins of marriage as a legal institution, and the myriad patterns of male control of women's fertility must be seen, at least in part, as an aspect of this control over human fertility. While we must always be mindful that such institutions were *not* the cross-cultural constants that some feminists have implied,[25] the diverse institutional forms of male dominance bespeak the ongoing connection between female reproductive power and male supremacy.

Until the latest generation of feminist scholarship, anthropologi-cal and archeological data were usually gathered by men who were frequently not much interested in these sorts of questions. And even when literary records existed in a society, those dealing with fertility, gestation, birth, contraception, and abortion were usually written by men, frequently those who functioned as part of a "medical" class. I have observed that a dimension of the current dominant historical bias in Christian ethics is expressed in the high regard many male moralists have for this very early "medical" history, in spite of its primitiveness. By contrast, we must not assume that when men con-trolled health and "medical" practice in a given society, the society thereby was more "advanced" or "scientific" or "higher" than those societies in which women's culture oversaw procreative practice apart from such presumed "science." It is naive to conclude that the best source for whatever knowledge a society possessed regarding fertility control, pregnancy, and childbirth is to be found in texts writ-ten by male elites, including medical practitioners. Those who make this assumption simply have not read such texts critically.

Furthermore, we know, at least with respect to European and Anglo-American culture, that the male "doctor" had little prestige until the nineteenth century. As we saw in the previous chapter, male medical practitioners in the United States had to mount a crusade against abortion, unsupported at first by the clergy, to dislodge women's control of reproductive culture. Even so, full control of the birth process by the medical establishment did not occur until the twentieth century.[26] In addition, our understanding of women's cultural control of reproduction is influenced by criticisms of mid-wifery extracted from the writings of male health-care and medical practitioners who often perceived midwives as competitors.[27] We need to recall that in most societies, including much of western culture, women were the healers and health-care practitioners in everyday life. In other societies, even when men controlled the treatment of illness, women oversaw fertility control, pregnancy, prenatal care, and the birth process, and the transmission of pro-creative wisdom was integral to women's culture. As I have observed, some feminist historians have gone so far as to suggest that male medical practitioners' control of prenatal care and childbirth was itself a symptom of a repatriarchalization process in reaction to early feminism. Regardless of whether this thesis can be sustained, we must remember that as a consequence of a new and unprecedented medical monopoly on procreative knowledge, women's culture was displaced from what had been its point of greatest influence and social power.

It is no longer possible simply to dismiss charges of conspiracy in the medical crusade against abortion and midwifery as the mutterings of biased and enraged feminists; no less than a half dozen recent historical studies have confirmed how massive and organized the medical profession's efforts were to take over prenatal care and the birth process in the United States. The nineteenth-century crusade organized by the medical profession to make abortion illegal was, in fact, integrally interwoven into the campaign to "upgrade" (as doctors claimed) prenatal and birth care by ending the widespread practice of midwifery among women. Until very recently, doctors exerted a powerful political influence on the status quo in relation to procreation, whether this meant restraining midwifery and fighting nonmedical interpretations of pregnancy, opposing government proposals to educate women about maternity health care, or, at times, resisting the spread of contraceptive information. Clearly, if the birth control movement had not made its peace with medical control of contraception, such opposition might have continued. Without a well-developed and powerful male medical profession, pregnancy and childbirth probably would never have come to be seen as analogous to "illness." Pregnancy, after all, is not a disease. Certainly today, no area in the world matches the United States, Canada, and northern Europe in treating pregnancy and birth as a medical matter. In their history of childbirth in the United States, Dorothy and Richard Wertz note that "the central and unique aspect of American birth is its being viewed as a potentially diseased condition that *routinely* requires the acts of medicine to overcome the processes of nature."[28]

Even though we remain far from being able to adequately reconstruct the history of women's experience of fertility control, it has become obvious that in every society women, sometimes in concert with men, sometimes in conflict with them, have sought to shape their power of procreation to the overall possibilities and constraints of their communities and their lives. Numerous primitive "birth control" techniques, including some rather effective ones, have existed for a long time. Pessaries, potions, and douches of various sorts, some very effective, others extremely dangerous, have been employed in nearly all societies of which we have any knowledge.

It has long been recognized that either coitus interruptus or one or another "barrier" method is helpful in preventing conception. The primitive lore of ancient "medical" texts attests to the range of instruments and medications used to prevent conception, including many that were acknowledged as abortifacients.[29] Fragmentary anthropological data suggest that in some parts of the contemporary world, women continue to use ancient abortifacient formulas that are surprisingly effective.

Most of the "medicines" and formulas available throughout history, however, were neither very effective nor genuinely safe. Fortunately, nature itself provides needed abortions in many instances. A conservative estimate is that less than half of all ova actually fertilized result in successful pregnancy.[30] Those who invoke a special sacredness about the moment of fertilization, adopting what they believe is a biologically dictated perspective on conception, rarely explain the frequency of spontaneous abortions as a "typical" phenomenon of nature. Luckily, women have sometimes been able to take advantage of this same natural proclivity to lessen the capriciousness of fertility. We also cannot evade a sober awareness of how often the actions women have taken to induce abortions resulted in their deaths or maiming. Abortion is a major cause of female death across large sections of the world today, and in some areas, such as parts of Latin America, the death rate of young, impoverished women from abortion is high.[31] Nor are extremely desperate measures — such as women resorting to ground-glass douches to cope with unwanted pregnancy — a rarity in some areas of the world.[32]

In the past, even when moderately effective methods of abortion were available, they involved a risk both to the pregnant woman and to the fetus, who might be born damaged if the abortion attempt failed. Abortion as a surgical technique was, of course, rare. The uterus is extremely sensitive tissue, and a pregnant woman's uterus is especially susceptible to hemorrhage. When ruptured, the capillaries of the uterus emit blood at four times the rate of other parts of the body. The ancient practices of embryotomy — destruction of the fetus in the uterus — or craniotomy — destruction of the fetal head — were appallingly painful and dangerous and probably were undertaken only in extreme situations to save a woman's life. It was not until the invention of both antiseptics and anesthesia that surgery could be used for abortions except as a desperate measure of last resort. The dramatic improvement in surgical technique, not merely the new knowledge of embryology, finally made abortion both safe and reliable. Even so, tirades against those of us who stress the greater medical safety of abortion continue. John Noonan's latest diatribe is predicated on the assumption that birth is always a surgical procedure:

> There is not a whit of evidence in the nineteenth century that abortion carried out in a hospital was any more dangerous than childbirth. *The surgery required to deliver a baby* [sic] *was just as unsanitary as the surgery required to perform an abortion.* (Italics mine)[33]

Because surgical advances paralleled new knowledge of embryology, only a few decades were required to bring about the changes that have precipitated — for the first time — a deep, culture-wide debate on abortion, because safe, effective surgical techniques are new. I have already insisted that, little as medical scientists may have intended it, abortion as a safe surgical procedure does create a great watershed in the history of women's lives. The intensity of the abortion struggle is not unrelated to the fact that the abortion controversy merges into and taps the still-virulent, lingering opposition to contraception and family planning.

Although improvement in older barrier methods of contraception and invention of new methods (the pill and the IUD, among others) were forthcoming, lack of genuine concern to extend aid to women in controlling their fertility was instrumental in making abortion a preferred means of birth control for many women. Though the birth control pill is the most broadly used means of artificial contraception, the current uncertainty about its long-term safety has been a factor in a contemporary shift from women's long-standing reliance on the pill to contraceptive strategies of abortion alone or barrier methods with abortion as a backup. The unreliability of barrier methods, legitimate questions about the chemical control of fertility, and the alarming increase in unnecessary cesarean sections and other hazards related to delivery in the United States make comprehensible many women's reliance on abortion when all else fails. Much medical opinion supports the wisdom, from the perspective of women's health, of relying on barrier methods with abortion as a backup. This, many insist, is the safest means of birth control.[34]

The development in the last decade of the suction methods of uterine extraction represents a particular breakthrough. With increasingly effective means of detecting pregnancies early, suction techniques make effective early abortion both safe and relatively simple. It is a great gain that a decision regarding a particular pregnancy can be made at an early stage when abortion is safer than childbearing and when fetal tissue is in the early stages of development. That many women and teenagers still do not confront the possibility that they are pregnant soon enough to terminate their pregnancies early, if they are disposed to do so, is the consequence of many interlocking social factors. The intensity of cultural pressures against contemplating an abortion, sometimes coupled with religious scruples against either abortion or women's expression of sexuality, encourages women to not use contraception and to procrastinate when faced with pregnancy. Other factors such as ignorance or real lack of access to affordable gynecological services also contribute. But even where women have access to the technology that can provide early rather than late abortion, acute life pressures and the force of social disapproval continue to impact powerfully on women's decision making about pregnancy.

The medical facilities available for abortions are invariably safest when legal, but many women, even in the United States, do not have access to adequate medical care, much less access to legal abortion. And lest we become too romantic about surgery in relation to women's reproductive systems, we also need to remind ourselves that the same surgical advances that provide safe abortions have opened the way to new methods of sterilization and, therefore, to an increase in sterilization abuse, including excessive use of surgery on women's reproductive systems. Even so, modern medical science, for all of its unacceptable misogyny, has replaced some rather ghastly, dangerous abortion practices still used where surgical abortion is unavailable. Modern medical science, as opposed to institutionalized health care and the social practice of medicine, has changed our understanding of reproduction and fertility, extending our control over — and therefore our responsibility for — human fertility. While such new knowledge can be abused in severing the technology it engenders from moral constraints, we must recognize that natural-scientific breakthroughs represent genuine gains in human self-understanding. The widespread social irresponsibility in medical practice, exacerbated by a male monopoly of the medical profession that is only now changing, must not be confused with the value of authentic scientific discoveries.

In light of these gains, we privileged western women must not lose our ability to imagine the real-life pressures that lead others to submit to injurious abortion practices, such as inserting reeds into the uterus. In fact, we need to speak more frankly of these matters so that all of us may understand the real, historical character of our struggle. Because millions of women do not yet have access to any but the most primitive modes of contraception, much less to wider conditions of choice, the resort to abortion, even under terribly dangerous conditions, will continue. I have argued that fewer and fewer women alive today remain ignorant of the fact that their fertility or capacity for childbearing need not, any longer, fatefully control their lives. Passivity about childbearing is decreasing, and more and more women, cross-culturally, aspire to placing the power of procreation within moral control.

The emergence of more adequate (still not fully adequate) contraception and the existence of safe, surgical, elective abortion have represented a genuine, positive historical advance for women toward full human freedom and dignity. No one concerned for women's well-being should forget that in the United States it took a generation-long struggle even to make contraception legal and widely accessible. The "birth control movement," as feminist scholarship has reminded us, encountered opposition from its inception in the late nineteenth century, and opposition still lingers. The predictions about the negative social consequences of widespread legal contraception were no less dire than the predictions now made by opponents of abortion about the chaos that will ensue with legalization of abortion.

Those early feminists in the nineteenth century who began to envisage the need for women to control their own procreative power could hardly have imagined the depth of social ostracism that awaited them and their heirs in struggle. Every demand the organized women's movement has made in the course of two centuries, from suffrage to full social equality, has been met with derision and its proponents branded as "perverts," "radicals," or "unfeminine, failed women." But nothing caused greater derision than the birth control movement. Linda Gordon has documented in her excellent historical study *Woman's Body, Woman's Right: A Social History of Birth Control in America*[35] that this movement finally gained respectability by repudiating the radical feminist claim for full liberation of women and by instead promoting birth control strictly as a means of family planning within marriage. The ideology of "planned parenthood" was aimed at avoiding arousing fears among "respectable" people that birth control could be an element in a broader sexual liberation of women. On the contrary, the planned parenthood movement affirmed women's traditional roles as full-time homemakers and professional mothers. This same ideology, Gordon demonstrates, was bound up with a subtle white supremacy doctrine and an anti-working-class bias.

The truth is that ever since white women began to articulate our claims to equality in an organized and collective way, we have been urged by dominant males to accommodate to racism, class elitism, and nativism. The fate of the birth control movement is no exception to this general rule. Although Margaret Sanger, who courageously led the fight for legal birth control for a long time, ended by catering to conventional morality and although organizations like Planned Parenthood eventually accommodated to the ideology of the feminine mystique, the birth control movement did secure the family-planning option. The struggle for safe, legal contraception created conditions that could deliver women from the caprices of nature or what many leaders of reform, and even the macho Ernest Hemingway, have characterized as "women's battleground" — the agonies of too-frequent childbirth.[36]

Originally, Sanger was willing to risk a felony conviction, was branded a common criminal, and endured incredible vilification to help many poor women escape from the continuous and frequent pregnancies that robbed them of energy and even their lives. At the time, the United States did not have an enviable record either with respect to infant mortality (the picture has improved with legalized abortion) or in deaths of mothers in childbirth (legal abortion has also reduced maternal mortality). In the United States in 1913, fifteen thousand women died in childbirth, and the infant mortality rate was the highest of all nations in which modern medicine was practiced.[37] Things have improved somewhat since then, though many believe that conditions of maternal health care for the very poor in this nation are even less adequate now than prior to the efforts of progressives in earlier decades to improve maternal and child health care.

Furthermore, anti-abortion and anti-birth control groups in the progressive era also opposed strong governmental initiatives for maternal and child health care, as such groups do today. The fate of the highly effective Sheppard-Towner Act, a progressive bill that supported maternal and infant health care for nearly a decade, until its repeal in the right-wing politics of 1929, makes this clear. From 1918, when the first female member of Congress, Jeannette Rankin of Montana, introduced maternity-care legislation, until the Sheppard-Towner Act in 1921, political opposition was highly vocal and well organized, perhaps because supporters of the legislation assumed that "health care should be the right of every citizen regardless of background."[38] In any case, even though funds channeled for maternal and infant health care through the Sheppard-Towner Act were never large, the program reached up to four million people in the final year of its existence, and while it was in effect the national infant mortality rate dropped 11 percent. Even the American Medical Association (AMA), the most implacable foe of the Sheppard-Towner Act, acknowledged that maternal death from eclampsia (toxic convulsions) had been dramatically reduced because of it.

Some attitudes linger into the present from the attacks made on the Sheppard-Towner Act by, among others, Senator James Reed, Democrat of Missouri, who derided feminists who supported the act as "female celibates too refined to have a husband." The continuous assault on this legislation, led by the AMA, was ultimately successful. The *Illinois Medical Journal* described the bill as "a piece of destructive legislation sponsored by *endocrine perverts, derailed menopausics,* and a lot of other men and women working overtime to devise means to destroy the country."[39] Both its congressional opponents and its AMA enemies recognized that the Sheppard-Towner Act was the first major, successful public-health-care legislation that was predicated on the public's right — in this case the female and child public's right — to adequate health care. It was, as might be expected, scorned as "socialized medicine." Since its repeal, there have been no comparable leaps forward in legislation aimed to improve the quality of prenatal and infant care in the United States, and many believe that the momentum gained in improved health care for poor women has since been lost.

In spite of this checkered history, as the medical profession was gradually won over to the cause of family planning, doctors also shifted to active support for women having fewer and more widely spaced births. Even though advances in medical knowledge that make abortion safe and guarantee a considerable degree of fertility control also open the way to sterilization abuse, few of us — whatever our positions on the morality of abortion — would choose to return to a premodern state. There has been an objective gain in the quality of women's lives for those fortunate enough to possess choice. For the first time in history, large numbers of women are free from the total conditioning of our lives by a power we do not control. That millions and millions of women do not yet possess even the rudimentary conditions for such choice should be recognized as a moral challenge. Actively increasing procreative choice should be our moral goal. The crusade against legal abortion should give way to a struggle against the *real* barriers to humane procreation — poverty, racism, and cultural oppression — which prevent authentic choice from being a reality for every woman.

Women have had to understand what patriarchal men cannot seem to grasp or choose to ignore — that the birth of an infant requires some person or persons prepared to care continuously for the child, providing tangible material resources over time, energy-draining attention, and physical and emotional support. Men, perhaps especially celibate men, often romanticize infants and children, at the same time ignoring or minimizing the total and uncompromising dependence of the newly born infant and, later, the child on the existing human community. Such dependence is even greater in a fragmented, centralized, urban-industrial culture than in rural cultures where the child provides another pair of hands that can increase an extended family's productive power. Given the historical myths of the existence of an invariant "family life," most of us are conditioned to forget that not many centuries ago a peasant rural child in Europe reached functional adulthood at about age seven. In such circumstances, childbearing and mothering had quite different implications than they do now. In a society like ours, where children are often dependent on their parents through adolescence and sometimes even into young adulthood, the physical, emotional, and financial demands of bearing children are exacting. Women have never occupied the "privileged" position that makes it possible to ignore such demands. We must insist that only those who are deeply realistic about what it takes to nourish human life *from birth onward* have the wisdom to evaluate procreative choice.

As I began intensive research for this book several years ago, a major New York newspaper reported that the cost to a middle-income family of having a baby in our nation's largest city was well over six thousand dollars. This estimate incorporated the costs from conception to the time the newborn left the hospital for a home moderately well equipped for its early care, including optimal prenatal medical costs for the mother, standard gynecological and hospital fees, diapers, preliminary supplies for feeding, and household effects required for a baby's first year of life. Meanwhile, however, medical costs have continued to escalate disproportionately to an otherwise distressing rate of inflation. Under the circumstances, it is hardly surprising that responsible parents — those who anticipate the implications of raising children in this society — are choosing not to have large families. Those who suggest that such modifications in procreative aspirations are the result of immoral, secular forces invariably ignore the objectively different circumstances of childbearing and childrearing in the modern world. Those who are careful and realistic about childbearing are not the selfish and morally insensitive among us, as anti-abortionists imply, but the most responsible.

CONTEMPORARY BASEPOINTS IN WOMEN'S STRUGGLE FOR PROCREATIVE CHOICE

Another dimension of the history of reproduction neglected in dominant tradition is the effect of general health on women's ability to control their fertility throughout history. Ironically, it was almost certainly easier for women to control fertility under social and environmental circumstances that were (and in some cases still are) less favorable to physical survival than it is under modern technologically and scientifically advanced conditions. One reason is that life expectancy has increased dramatically in the west over the last century and a half. In fact, it has doubled. Significantly, a major factor contributing to our increased longevity is the lower birth rate among women and the dramatically fewer number of fatalities in childbearing. Along with a lengthening lifespan has come longer periods of human fertility and more regular reproductive cycles. Many of us forget that the onset of puberty in females and males has occurred earlier and earlier in modern societies. The shifts here have been rapid and significant, with the typical age of menarche having dropped to twelve, whereas two centuries ago it was not unusual for menstruation to begin at sixteen.[40]

But the fact that modern women are capable of childbearing for many more years than their grandmothers or great-grandmothers is only half the story. Better nutrition and health in the population generally mean that larger numbers of women experience regular fertility cycles. Poor nutrition and health contribute to irregularity in menstruation, to more frequent, noninduced miscarriages, and to higher maternal and infant mortality. It is not possible to generalize accurately about the historical differences that have existed in "typical" female patterns of fertility through time or across cultures. But there appear to be dramatic differences today between the regularity of fertility cycles among women in modernized, affluent, and technologically complex societies and the regularity of women who live in poverty, especially rural poverty. One study of fertility rates compared a statistically typical poor, rural African woman who used prolonged lactation to prevent the resumption of ovulation after pregnancy and a statistically typical woman in the urban United States. The results demonstrated that the African woman experienced only about 48 menstrual cycles during her childbearing years, whereas the urban, more affluent U.S. woman, although less frequently pregnant, had 420 cycles to control.[41] While little can be generalized from just one study, we need to be aware of the growing scope of the problem of fertility control in a modern context.

Another dimension of procreation in women's lives that has altered tremendously and affected the reality of childbearing is the rate of infant mortality. Not surprisingly, there appears to be a connection between the rate of infant mortality and the attitude of childbearing women and of the larger society toward the value of pregnancy. Cultures in which many infants die in the early years seem to resist procreative control, and family planning seems inevitably to fail. This does not mean that the rate of induced abortions is necessarily lower where prenatal attitudes are positive, but we know that where infant mortality is reduced, as it has been overwhelmingly in large sectors of the globe, women begin to experience a proportionately greater need for procreative control.

As more children survive, and women's health and life expectancy improve, the need for effective methods of fertility control becomes more urgent. It is often overlooked that the most frequent "natural" means of birth control, perhaps the most widely practiced historically apart from sexual abstinence or coitus interruptus, is prolonged lactation after childbirth. While it is an immensely unpredictable method that works for some women but not at all for others, a standard claim in the population literature is that as many as one hundred million women each year use prolonged breast-feeding as a mode of birth control.[42] This "home-remedy" method of contraception has been widely encouraged and practiced in numerous cultures. Medical scientists do yot yet know fully how or why prolonged lactation works as a contraceptive for some women. It may be that a menorrhea is induced by hormonal changes or that a malnutrition factor is involved. Unfortunately, most contemporary women who practice prolonged lactation are also severely malnourished and may more readily abort spontaneously. We must never forget that women and their children, as a group, are disproportionately represented among the hungriest people within every society across the earth.[43] Women's poverty and ill health may well be the most "effective" means of contraception in the world today. Certainly no analysis can claim to be feminist that does not stress this dismal reality.

In spite of many uncertainties, it is now widely recognized and agreed that the conditions for the practice of most "natural" birth control, including prolonged lactation, are completely undermined by modern urbanized, industrial living. Even if the sexual prudery and misogyny that discourages most western women from breast-feeding in public could be overcome, the modern urban woman cannot keep her infant at her side, or on her breast, with the ongoing regularity that is required to make this mode of birth control effective. Not surprisingly, the African community in which the study cited earlier was conducted has experienced a great leap in population growth with the onset of urbanization. There is some evidence that wherever rural-to-urban migrations occur, women's fertility increases. In most discussions of the morality of abortion all of these shifting realities are neglected. Women hardly can ignore them, and most evidence suggests that women's attitudes toward birth control change in populations where infant mortality drops and where industrial, urbanized patterns of social life prevail.

There has been some quite appropriate resistance to liberal, westernized family-planning and population-control ideologies among third-world populations. This is so particularly among groups, such as Puerto Rican women, who have been the victims of socially inspired experimentation with that nonreversible and cruel means of birth control — sterilization. Furthermore, in some nonwestern poor countries, U.S. aid programs have dumped birth control technologies that are inappropriate or dangerous.[44] Little wonder that the suspicion exists that genocidal motives toward nonwhite and nonwestern peoples inform the population control enthusiasms of some western proponents. Elsewhere I have argued that affluent and rich groups who are the "high consumers" of goods and energy have a far greater moral obligation to practice birth control than do poor and third-world people.[45] The outrage many westerners voice at the larger families characteristic of nonindustrialized societies, in particular, is totally inappropriate given the much greater per capita rate of consumption in the richer nations. There is no fixed relationship between population size and exploitation of the earth and its resources, but there is a connection between exploitation of the world's resources and the overwhelming affluence of wealthier nations. In any case, there is some evidence that the aspiration for large families diminishes when a nation's affluence increases, urbanization occurs, and infant mortality is reduced, so that those who bewail rising birth rates elsewhere may better direct their energies to securing a more just international economic order.

Even so, third-world nations must cope with the pressure of booming population growth that can result from the intersection of "traditional" pronatalist values and rapid industrialization and urbanization. In nations such as Mexico, where the religious and ideological constraints against family planning are massive, the government has been forced to actively support family planning. China, whose official formal position during its most decisive revolutionary period reflected traditional Confucian opposition to population control, nevertheless adopted social policies that encouraged a dramatic drop in population growth. While acknowledging the sensitivity required to evaluate population growth in poorer societies, we must also recognize that rate of population growth is relevant to the moral evaluation of family planning and procreative choice within a society.[46]

Appreciating the structural inequities of our global economy does not diminish the importance of procreative choice in women's lives, for, as I have insisted, poor women often need procreative options more than the affluent. And it is important to reiterate that in many areas of the world abortion is the method of birth control used by the poorest and most marginalized sectors of the female population. Illegal abortion is endemic across the poorest regions of Latin America and Africa.[47] Whatever demographic claims may be made about the United States, many population experts assume or believe they can demonstrate that in the poorer, economically dependent countries today, abortion is typically the birth control technique of the poor. In most parts of the world, either the more reliable means of artificial birth control are unavailable except to the affluent or, in some countries, the highest-risk methods are being imposed sternly on poorer women in particular. And even where abortion is legal, its practice is often institutionalized in brutalizing ways. In the Soviet Union, for example, women voice angry complaints that adequate contraception is not provided, that abortion facilities are dirty and substandard, and that they endure rude and contemptuous treatment when they seek abortions.[48]

Many women who have resorted to abortion in the face of the mores and social pressures of their communities are unwilling to acknowledge that they have had or favor the availability of abortion.[49] Black women in the United States, for example, report a high incidence of reliance on abortion as a birth control method of last resort,[50] but many of them also report unwillingness to endure vitriolic disapproval by publicly acknowledging this fact. The black community, like any severely oppressed group, exhibits strong pronatalist sentiments; historically, the black slave community in the United States made an effort to welcome every baby born into it. No black child was viewed as illegitimate or as an outsider to the community.[51] Even so, black women have had to endure the pressures of a one-generation shift from a rural to an urban environment, where black men are marginalized and humiliated economically and socially and where black women are often left isolated to function as working single parents dependent on a dehumanizing welfare system. Similarly, orthodox and conservative Jewish women often have to confront the abortion option in the face of growing hostility in their community, born not of traditional Jewish attitudes but rather of a pronatalism engendered by fear for Jewish survival in the modern world, given twentieth-century Christian genocide of the Jews. While racism and anti-Semitism remain virulent sources of and motives for some whites' enthusiasm for "family planning," charges of genocide must not prevent us from recognizing that the poor and more oppressed women in this society need legal abortion the most.

As surgical abortion has become safer, it is obvious why it has become one of the most widespread means of birth control to which women resort.[52] Even when abortion is illegal or is performed under less than optimal medical conditions, new medical knowledge permits illicit practitioners to perform abortions with far less risk than in the past. The truth is that in many cultures, especially those where patriarchal religions exert powerful influence, abortion is *more* accessible than other means of birth control. Women in such cultures need the cooperation of their spouses or mates to use barrier methods of artificial contraception successfully. By contrast, legal abortion is something women often can elect free of male subversion. In spite of the degree of ideological ingenuity devoted to arguing that only "affluent, modern, liberated" women are concerned about abortion and that poor and less technologically aware women approach motherhood, whenever it occurs, in a celebratory way, the number of abortions appears to be on the increase globally. Claims that only affluent, elite women care about access to legal abortion are belied by a wide range of data.

It is well, however, to exercise some caution in any effort to estimate the number of abortions that occur in the world today. Some responsible medical experts insist that 8 percent of the world's fertile women have abortions every year,[53] which indicates how widespread the use of abortion is as a birth control means of last resort. It is also clear, however, that in different cultures different populations of women have access to abortion. In the United States, very young or unmarried women have nearly as many abortions as married women with children, and the percentage is rising.[54] In some regions of the world married women with several children are the major users of abortion.[55] In the United States, where accurate records are kept, we know that, in 1981, 1,400,000 abortions were performed, a considerable increase from the previous year. Such statistics, however, include abortions performed on non-U.S. citizens. Because U.S. law is now more permissive and health-care facilities for abortions are more accessible than in Mexico, Canada, and other nearby nations, some women from those areas choose to have their abortions in the United States.

The rising rate of abortion is one source of outrage among anti-abortionists, who portray us as caught up in massively escalating genocide. In fact, however, while these figures represent a considerable increase in abortion over prelegalization years, we cannot be certain how large the increase actually has been. One can find estimates of the number of illegal abortions performed in the United States prior to legalized abortion that range from two hundred thousand to two million per year.[56] Six hundred and fifty thousand would be a safe, probably conservative estimate of the number of illegal abortions done in the United States, which means that the number of abortions has slightly more than doubled since legalization.

Several other factors have changed in the meantime, however. Undoubtedly, children in this culture become sexually active earlier than they did in previous generations. Another dramatic source of increasing numbers of abortions has been the growing anxiety about the safety of oral contraceptives, and hence a decline in their use, along with the even earlier typical age for the onset of puberty. We need also to recognize that a source of increase in the number of abortions has been the growing and now widespread view, supported by much reputable medical opinion, that from the standpoint of a woman's health, the *safest* long-term means of fertility control are the barrier methods, combined with abortion as a backup. Clearly we are in a period when controversy about the safety of chemical contraceptives will increase, precisely because medical evidence about their carcinogenic implications will remain ambiguous for some time to come.

Furthermore, there is apparently little or no prospect of imminent breakthroughs to new, safer methods of contraception.[57] If anything, increasingly stringent scrutiny of testing procedures relating to chemical control of conception is in order, in light of the irresponsible procedures that made Puerto Rican women the victims of experiments for the original development of oral contraceptives. Adequate testing of new contraceptives has become a slow process, and prospects for highly effective male or female contraceptives are not bright. In addition, it appears unlikely that the major political forces militantly opposed to abortion as well as to federal funding of birth control research will modify their positions or lose influence in the immediate future. Neither the National Conference of (Roman) Catholic Bishops in the United States[58] nor some of the right-wing politicians who currently lead the crusade against legalized abortion[59] are likely to withdraw their opposition to government's support of fertility control. Funding for birth control research has dropped significantly in recent years,[60] and the same groups who oppose legal abortion also reject governmental social policy in support of research on procreative control.

We need to be aware, then, that both the current political climate and conditions for scientific research are most unfavorable to the development of new, safer means of birth control for women. Nor are we, in the present patriarchal climate, likely to see a great increase in men's willingness to assume responsibility for fertility control, although there is a positive trend toward sterilization among some younger men, including liberal practicing Catholics. Because the strongest pressures against women's right to control our fertility — which at this point in human history must include access to legal abortion — come precisely from masculinist groups who seek to block new research on fertility control, no feminist should allow herself or himself to dream of a quick technological breakthrough that may deliver us from long-term involvement in the difficult and controversial politics of abortion.

Only a sober historical recognition that our present struggle seeks to overturn centuries of institutionalized strictures aimed at control of women's procreative power will be adequate to ground us in the long and intense conflict over abortion. Ancient patterns of male supremacy are being called into question when women demand the right to control procreation, and the powerful do not yield without struggle. Only a few men have been willing as yet to see the moral centrality of this issue to the deeper question of women's authentic liberation. Only a few understand that pregnancy is a life-shaping experience, such that no woman can be free if she must live her life under pressures to bear children against her will or in spite of her rational deliberation.[61] Florynce Kennedy's well-known aphorism "If men became pregnant, abortion would be a sacrament"[62] is more than mere hyperbole, given the cumulative social resistance to this major historical shift in the power relations between men and women.

Given the dramatic change in opinion about contraception within the last generation, we are also likely to forget the intensity of social conflict that has characterized every step in women's recent collective struggle for procreative choice. What James Reed has called the rapid move from "private vice to public virtue" did not occur without vitriolic opposition.[63] Nor does the abortion struggle. Resistance to enhancing women's prenatal health care as well as infants' and women's postnatal care, especially in the United States, also underscores much hypocrisy in the political opposition's reputed "concern for human life."

Liberal theorists still have difficulty accepting the depth of the opposition to women's control of procreative choice, precisely because liberals tend to deny conflict, the realities of power, and the depths of misogyny. They also underestimate the far-reaching changes that have occurred, and will continue to occur, in women's lives as more and more women gain some power over their fertility. Conservatives sometimes have a more candid sense of what is at stake. It is critical to recognize now how far-reaching these changes are and how probable their extension, if only because the ancient assumptions that women's lives are (and ought to be) continuous with nature, limited by the inexorable hand of nature's bounty or lack of it, are collapsing. Use of abortion as a birth control means of last resort may be, as I have already argued, the result of social and economic pressures against genuine procreative choice rather than the result of positive conditions for such choice. Given the reality of the world of women, the availability of abortion is a critical necessity. It will become less so only in a world where effective and safer alternative means of birth control are readily available.

Meanwhile, millions of abortions will continue to occur each year, replacing the earlier widespread practice of infanticide. Some may protest that acknowledging a historical connection between the reduction of infanticide and the increase of abortion verifies the presumed moral insensitivity of women. Feminists, however, have recognized and insisted upon emphasizing two social dimensions of the practice of infanticide. On the one hand, girl babies have always been the most likely victims of the practice, because of the deep disvaluation of females and the economic burden female babies represented, compared to the social wealth projected for male infants. On the other hand, women frequently have resorted to infanticide in grim, dehumanizing situations and have been viciously punished as a result.[64] Only those who cannot recognize the concrete pressures of women's lives, including the meaning of their fertility, will imagine that resort to infanticide was always motivated by callous indifference. To the contrary, women frequently have been faced with the choice of terminating the lives of newborn infants or condemning their infants to lives of unspeakable misery. That the availability of safe surgical abortion enables women who have access to it to avoid this dilemma should be a cause of celebration. Abortion is *not* infanticide, but in the absence of choice even infanticide was not always a morally despicable act.

This point — that infanticide is an institutional practice that abortion displaces in women's history — will always offend those who insist on romanticizing women's lives. It is wiser to recognize infanticide as an index of the desperation that has characterized many women's lives in the face of unwanted pregnancy. That many, from time immemorial, have chosen to let newborn infants die is not evidence of women's immorality. Some cultures have chosen to mark the date of "birth" as falling well after the fetus emerged from the womb, perhaps because those cultures recognized the social complexity of communal survival over against simple biological reproductive process.

Anthropologist Laila Williamson, in a cross-cultural review of available data regarding infanticide, puts the matter bluntly:

> We tend to think of [infanticide] as an exceptional practice, to be found only among . . . peoples . . . far removed in both culture and geographical distance from us and from our civilized ancestors. The truth is quite different. Infanticide has been practiced on every continent and by people on every level of cultural complexity . . . including our own ancestors. Rather than being the exception, it is the rule.[65]

As Williamson notes, infanticide has been difficult to detect. A gynocentric perspective makes us aware, however, of its prevalence. We may never know how many "infant mortalities," crib deaths, asphyxiations, and early illnesses were the result of a mother's desperation to cope with the sometimes unbearable problem of fertility. Infants are vulnerable to accident and to disease, and during certain premodern periods infant mortality was so high that survival of babies was as much the exception as the rule. Nor was the line between abortion and infanticide always as clear as it is today. In some cultures the fetus was killed in the womb in late stages of gestation to induce stillbirth.[66]

In many situations, infanticide has been recognized as a caring act, necessary that some may survive. The familiar pronatalist patriarchal ideologies have not always carried the day. Certainly, there is every reason to acknowledge that the reduction in the frequency of infanticide represents a moral gain in the quality of human life. To grant this, however, is also to see that early abortion is morally preferable to infanticide as a means of fertility control. The power of procreation is an unqualified blessing under some circumstances, but a dreaded curse under others. Those who are realistically sensitive appreciate this fact, which accounts for many women's support of legal abortion even when they doubt that they themselves could ever choose to have one.

Magda Denes, whose powerful work on abortion examined the "culture of abortion" within an actual abortion-hospital setting, helps us appreciate the depth of realism and the nuances of reasoning that lead women to choose abortion. By exposing in an unsentimental way the complexity and ambivalence of abortion decisions, Denes defends women's right to choose abortion without denying the life-and-death issues at stake. What she says of the abortion predicament, however, might better be said of the predicament that women's procreative potential often creates:

> My rage . . . is at the human predicament. At the finitude of our lives, at our nakedness, at the absurdity of our perpetual ambivalence toward the terror of life and toward the horror of death.
> Abortions, I think, should be legal throughout the world. They should be at the mother's will, on demand, safe, dignified, provided free by the state, supported with mercy by the church . . . If we remove abortions from the realm of defiance to authority, remove them from the category of forbidden acts whose commission is the embodiment of risk and the embodiment of self-assertion in the face of coercive forces, if we permit them to be acts of freedom as they should be, their meaning, private and collective, will inescapably emerge in the consciousness of every person.
> I think it is a far, far lighter task to regard oneself as a martyr than to know the private sorrows of unique commitments and the heartache of self-chosen destiny.[67]

My only quarrel with Denes's analysis is that she fails to say, and perhaps to recognize, that the power of re-creating the species has always required these "unique commitments" that women have had to bear, sometimes as a lonely burden, throughout history.

As we turn now to examine the question of the morality of the specific act of abortion in greater detail, we need to bear in mind that all these matters affecting women's lives constitute the genuine historical setting of the abortion dilemma. Our moral schizophrenia about abortion is exhibited by many people who believe that women have a *moral responsibility to practice contraception* and that family planning is a great moral good but who rule abortion out of the moral arena altogether, even when they know contraception is often a precarious matter. Such a split consciousness ignores the fact that there is no inexorable biological line between prevention of conception and abortion.[68] Even more important, such consciousness obscures the genuine risks involved in female contraceptive methods and diffuses the harsh reality that we do not have more concern for contraceptive research into safer and more adequate methods of contraception for women (and for men), because matters relating to women's health and well-being are *never* urgent in this society. Only if we keep these facts in view as the genuine historical dimension of the problem will we recognize the depth of moral hypocrisy involved in a so-called pro-life movement that proclaims that even a zygote, at the moment of conception, is a "person" and should be viewed as a citizen but still denies full social and political rights to women.

Those who deny that women deserve to control their own pro-creative power proclaim that they do so out of "moral sensibility," in the name of "the sanctity of human life." We have a very long way to go, in this society and in this world, before "the sanctity of *human* life" will include genuine regard and concern for *every concrete, existent female person,* and no social policy which obscures that fact deserves to be called moral. Hopefully, the day will come when it will not be called Christian either.

Only when the history of abortion is understood, as it must be, in terms of the real lives of millions and millions of women can we approach the discussion of the morality of abortion in a way that clearly dissociates a moral position from that ancient and long-standing misogyny of the dominant Christian patriarchal tradition. Women have a serious charge to bring against male-articulated traditional attitudes to abortion, and those of us who are feminists understand that we are making a serious moral claim when we support legal abortion. If this is not understood, it is because the methods of professional moralists make it difficult for them to gain a textured and realistic perspective about the moral dilemma abortion poses in women's lives. This is the context that is needed to locate the contemporary moral claims of feminism and to appreciate the fundamental rightness of Ellen Willis's argument:

> To oppose legal abortion is to define women as child-bearers rather than autonomous human beings, and to endorse a sexually repressive morality enforced by the state. Often at a particular historical moment an issue emerges that illuminates the nature of the larger struggle. It is the sort of issue that precludes neutrality, that despite its ambiguities

and complexities (and there always are some), poses that
most basic of political questions — which side are you on?[69]

Willis's claim is bound to sound excessive, even irrational, to those
who have not grasped the centrality of procreative choice to women's
well-being and the importance of procreative choice as a foundational
element in a good society that includes women. But the time will
come when moral opinion must shift and her point come to be
understood.

With this insistence, it is possible to turn to the question of the
morality of abortion as an act, and more particularly to the moral
evaluation of fetal life. Here, where most discussions of the morality
of abortion begin, we find a tangled web of philosophical considerations that condition the contemporary debate. To ask how we should
view fetal life from the moral point of view involves not only a review
of differing opinions but a probing of presuppositions too infrequently
examined.

7

Evaluating the
Act of Abortion:
The Debate About Fetal Life

THE CONTEMPORARY MORAL DILEMMA

The overwhelming majority of discussions of the morality of abortion focus on the question "What is the moral significance of a singular act of abortion?" Most moral assessments of abortion begin with the act of abortion itself, assuming that its morality can be considered in abstraction from the total life plan of the pregnant woman, that the intrinsic moral value of the act can be determined without reference to any question save one: "What is the moral value of fetal life?"

I have insisted that this line of ethical analysis is a modern development. Ironically, those who believe they are appealing to venerable moral traditions about the intrinsic value of human life also often adamantly argue that it is modern embryology and biology that require or corroborate the view that the fetus in early development is actually an individual human life. Moral traditions concerning the distinctive moral value of human life are indeed venerable; it is the explicit and elaborate application of these traditions to the fetus, appealing to data about fetal biological development, that is new. Those of us who disagree with the conclusion that the fetus is properly understood as "a" human being or as a "person" now almost invariably are accused of being "utterly oblivious to biology"[1] or insensitive to biological criteria for assessing the question of when human life begins.[2]

The new biomedical developments in embryology and genetics are impressive indeed. But so influential have they become among ethicists that most of the technical discussions of the morality of abortion focus narrowly on biomedical developments. Given the complexity and sophistication of the knowledge about embryological development now available to us, some people presume that mastery of these newer scientific perspectives somehow will provide the key to the identification of biological criteria that will justify our moral evaluation of when full human life exists.

At the outset, however, we need to recognize that a growing and heightened consciousness about fetal life and a strong cultural trend toward equating it with full human life have been catalyzed by the rhetoric and ideology of the "pro-life" movement and by the new biology and developments in medical technology. Now that the knowledge and the technology exist to therapeutically treat fetuses *in utero*, a certain "fetus as patient" mentality is rapidly emerging.[3] The potential for correcting fetal abnormalities *in utero* and the prospects for replacing the woman's body as "reproducer" invite our imaginations to abstract the fetus from the pregnant woman and to view the fetus as "existent" in a manner analogous to the way we perceive the newborn infant. What Robert Veatch has protested and dubbed, in a quite different context, as "medicalizations" of moral choice[4] now operate powerfully in discussions of the moral value of fetal life. Ruth Hubbard, a professor of biology at Harvard, has identified the consequences of this dynamic for pregnant women:

> It is clear that at this point pregnancy has become a disease with *two* potential patients — the pregnant woman and her fetus — and of those, the fetus is medically and technically by far the more interesting one. Already a recent article in the *Journal of the American Medical Association* refers to the pregnant woman as though she were merely the container in which the real patient — the fetus — gets moved about.
>
> These medical innovations raise an entirely new set of problems for women. A pregnant woman can decide that she doesn't want to be a patient: she can refuse diagnostic tests and can birth her baby at home. But can she make that choice for her fetus? If she cannot say no for the fetus, then she, too, becomes a patient.
>
> At this time, there is still considerable disagreement among physicians about whether and when to initiate fetal therapy, and about what forms it should take. But once the procedures become established and are practiced more widely, the situation may become similar to what has begun to happen with cesarean sections. In the last year or so, several women have been mandated by court decrees to

undergo cesarean sections for which they had denied permission, because physicians testified that a vaginal delivery would endanger the fetus. In one instance, a hearing was convened in the hospital while the woman was in labor. *Two lawyers were appointed — one to represent her; the other, the fetus.*[5]

Before proceeding to an assessment of fetal life from a moral point of view, it is important to identify precisely what a *moral* analysis involves and then to clarify the way in which a range of philosophical considerations determines the current debate, especially with regard to fetal life. In the process, I also will review my moral arguments for the right to procreative choice.

A moral analysis of abortion differs, of course, from a social-scientific analysis. Some social scientists interested in the abortion question have been concerned to *describe*, not to evaluate, the values that engender the expressed attitudes and actions persons take vis-à-vis abortion. Thus, some social scientists have claimed that "concern for human life" actually does account for people's expressed attitudes and evaluations in opposing abortion, while others believe there is reason to doubt that this value operates strongly on either side of the debate. One pollster, John Fenton, asserts that there is a consistent "pro-life" profile among abortion opponents.[6] Using a set of questions that scale and interrelate attitudes toward suicide, euthanasia, and abortion, he concludes that there is a high correlation between negative attitudes toward these realities. By contrast, studies of the voting records of public officials, based on their legislative actions not merely on their expressed attitudes, suggest that those opposed to legal abortion are far more likely to support capital punishment, increased military spending, and a highly aggressive U.S. foreign policy.[7]

A third type of study, which presumed possible discrepancies between expressed attitudes toward abortion and actual judgments made about it in concrete settings, was designed to test for this disparity and to isolate the "cues" that lead people to approve or disapprove of abortion in specific cases. The researchers who designed these studies conducted a number of experiments with college students over a period of years, using sophisticated social-judgment theory to ascertain what circumstances actually were taken into account in decision making about abortion. Thus far, these experiments have documented a strong tendency among student subjects to make specific decisions about cases involving abortion on the basis of the social acceptability of a woman's sexual behavior that led to the pregnancy. In this study, the fictional women whose decisions to seek abortions met with approval were generally those who had taken contraceptive precautions. This pattern held sway regardless of the moral attitudes about abortion the student subjects professed to hold. As the social scientists conducting these studies have increased the lived-world complexity of their experiments by replicating actual decision situations more reliably, the pattern of judgment they have observed has remained stable throughout numerous experiments.[8] Perhaps this confirms the thesis I elaborated earlier — that evaluations of abortion are, in fact, intimately interrelated with perceptions of a woman's "sexual purity" and that, therefore, sexual attitudes play a powerful motivating role in people's moral assessments of abortion.

Such empirical studies are useful, and they enter into the debate regarding the morality of abortion in significant ways. Fenton's work is frequently cited by those whose moral position leads them to favor more restrictive legislation on abortion,[9] whereas the surveys of the legislative records and value consistency of those opposing legal abortion figure strongly into the analysis of people who advocate legal abortion.[10] The decision-situation studies, newer and more methodologically sophisticated, seek to help us uncover the gap between our expressed moral attitudes and our actual decisions and are therefore useful in moral self-assessment. Even so, none of these studies, and no data about abortion accumulated through social-scientific methodology, can foreclose the need for what ethicists call "normative moral analysis," that is, the attempt to arrive at a reflective, publicly expressed justification[11] for our convictions about what "ought" to be the case. In such a normative analysis, we are concerned neither with social-scientific description of how people act nor with the explanatory mode of accounting for why they act as they do, but with ethical evaluation and, more particularly, with normative ethics — the effort to justify the moral appropriateness of acts, policies, and institutions. As my argument in Chapter 2 makes clear, normative ethical argument aims to assess the rightness or wrongness, the moral goodness or badness, of a given act, policy, or institution, quite apart from whether people actually act in a morally optimal way. At the very least, then, a normative ethical approach acknowledges that there are some obligations and some values that thoughtful people ought to take into account in their actions.

As I pointed out in Chapter 1, there are several "theories of morality" or hypotheses about how best to identify and to reason about "the moral point of view." As a mixed theorist, I believe there are justifiable claims that some acts are morally dubious, consequences aside, because they violate intrinsic value — that which we ought to acknowledge as worthy apart from any functional or use relation to us. And within our human moral field, the human person most clearly and unambiguously may claim "intrinsic value." This does not mean to suggest that only human beings have "intrinsic value." I believe that all of nature possesses value, though not necessarily equivalent to the intrinsic value of persons. There are some uses to which we humans may put other dimensions of nature that are palpably moral. I also believe that God has intrinsic moral value and is, in one dimension, the "center of value,"[12] grounding the valuation of all things. But one need not be a theist to posit that it is "reasonable" to hold some things and some acts as intrinsically valuable or right-making. In fact, most ethicists hold that to enter at all into "the moral point of view" means that we should recognize that persons are to be acknowledged as having intrinsic value,[13] possessing worth in and of themselves, not merely in terms of some functional value they may hold for us. I argue that the lack of such an assumption makes a mockery of morality. Nothing in the moral defense of abortion that I offer here denies the supposition that persons have intrinsic value or that such an assumption is constitutive of the moral point of view. In acknowledging that human beings are, appropriately, to be viewed as ends, not means, I incorporate into my moral theory a duty-oriented deontological dimension presented in Chapter 2.

As a mixed theorist, however, I believe that an equally critical dimension of justifying moral judgments must rest with the teleological pole of our capacity as human moral reason-givers. This means that if our personal acts, social policies, and social institutions are to be weighed from the moral point of view, they must also answer to consequences of two sorts: (1) What will they mean concretely, over time, to those most deeply affected by them? and (2) How do they stand in relation to our best creative envisagement of the considerations that make for a good society? The former criterion calls for, roughly, utilitarian moral justifications, the latter, rationally or religiously generated teleological arguments related to what we believe constitutes a good society. We cannot do without teleological reason-giving in our ethics, even when there is broad consensus about intrinsic value, as there is among morally sensitive persons regarding the intrinsic value of human life, because many of our choices and our moral dilemmas gain their poignancy and moral force from conflicts between intrinsic values. Teleological reasoning is necessary to adjudicate these conflicts.

The widespread consensus that human beings are to be treated as having intrinsic value grounds a further moral consensus — that killing human beings, without moral justification, is wrong. Homicide can be justified but, differences in moral theory aside, it is doubtful whether any who take morality seriously can confidently eschew what some call "the killing ethic." The widespread moral and religious consensus that homicide, or the taking of human life, at the very least demands extremely weighty moral justification — as, for example, in the case of killing one human being to save others — is indisputable among morally serious people and is not at issue in the moral debate over abortion. The reason, then, that the debate about fetal life is so salient in the abortion discussion is that it is really a debate about *when* the notion of "the intrinsic value of human life" should apply to developing fetal life; hence, the debate about whether or when "the antikilling ethic" should apply.

To be sure, in a society so pervasively violent as the United States, it may appear strange to speak of such a widespread moral consensus. The rising enthusiasm for capital punishment, presumably as a means of deterring crime, and the massive militarization of our culture seem to attest to gross disrespect for, or dissent from, such consensus. Yet a moral consensus is not the same as a public opinion poll. To insist that such a consensus exists means only that those willing to deliberate and reflect on our obligations to others, on conditions and consequences of acts, and on values that make for a good society concur that unjustified homicide is wrong. Certainly, many in our society express no genuine concern for morality, and many equate morals with questions of taste or subjective preference. By contrast, I believe that concern for the moral point of view is coterminous with human concern for the conditions of our life together, including, as indicated, our life in relation to the rest of nature and to God. Nevertheless, because morality itself presumes some human capacity for reasonable judgment and stands in some tension with nonreflective, "authoritative" solutions to the dilemmas posed by our actions, it follows that there is no way to force anyone to adopt a moral point of view. Likewise, if those who support capital punishment or high military spending purport to do so "from the moral point of view," we must suppose that they have satisfied themselves that there are justifying moral reasons for supporting these things. So while there are many possible lines of justification for a "killing ethic" or, better, an "antikilling ethic," claiming a moral consensus for it means only that, on the whole, morally reflective people endorse it.[14]

The question "When does human life begin?" or (as we will see) the more precise moral question "When shall we predicate full human value to developing fetal life?" has become pivotal to the debate about the morality of abortion for reasons having to do with moral consensus. The moral status of fetal life simply is not the obvious fact that many "pro-life" proponents contend. Even though a moral consensus does exist about the intrinsic value of human life and the evil of unjustified killing, the evaluation of fetal life is complex. To conclude that fetal life, admittedly a *form* of human life, is already full human life does not follow from the premises of the moral consensus I have identified. Because predicating the intrinsic value of human life and opposing killing are the *least* controversial aspects of the moral debate, the question of the value of fetal life has become the core issue on which everything else appears to hinge.

DEFINING ABORTION: THERAPEUTIC OR ELECTIVE

I have not yet commented on definitions of abortion operative in the debate, although I have observed the changing meaning of the term *abortion*, given shifting social contexts. Sometimes abortion was presumed to be an act done to a woman that endangered the life in her womb (Exodus 22). In other contexts, as we have also seen, where theories of the formed and unformed fetus prevailed, the term *abortion* applied only to termination of a pregnancy after "formation" had occurred. Furthermore, even in contemporary discussion where the "medicalization" of the issue has occurred, the meaning of the term alters from one discipline to the next and from one socio-historical setting to another. As Potts, Diggory, and Peel observe, "In the case of the extraordinary subject of abortion even the use of the term is revealing of societal attitudes; definitions are confused, slow to change, and paradoxical."[15]

Though much is made of what medical science teaches on this issue, even medical practice regarding the term *abortion* varies from nation to nation and always is related to social assumptions embedded in a particular culture. In 1950, the World Health Organization (WHO), seeking to address the imprecision of the classification of medical data, urged that technical medical usage be standardized to employ the term *fetal death* as a general category and that *abortion* and *stillbirth* be used as restricted technical terms. *Abortion,* WHO proposed, should apply to all fetal deaths in the early period (up to nineteen weeks) and intermediate period (up to twenty-eight weeks) of gestation, whereas the term *stillbirth* should apply to the latest period. Even in medical circles, however, this proposed uniformity was never achieved.[16] Meanwhile, legal definitions of what constitutes abortion vary markedly from country to country. And in ethics, many have observed that the English term *abortion* is itself value-laden, connoting a negative moral valence, rooted in the taboo character of abortion in western Christian discourse. Even so, since the recent development of safe surgical techniques for terminating pregnancy, current debates regarding abortion prevalently construe it as an act undertaken by the pregnant woman, with medical assistance, to terminate an unwanted pregnancy at any stage in the process of gestation prior to birth.

In current ethical discussion, however, it is important to acknowledge that there is real ambiguity in defining *abortion*, because most existing legal frameworks create a distinction between *elective* and *therapeutic* abortion. Where there is considerable legal discretion accorded a woman to make her own determination about when abortion is appropriate, as in the United States, the abortion debate tends to focus on *elective* abortion. By contrast, in societies where the state or the medical profession completely controls the decision-making process regarding abortion, the operative assumption is that abortions should be undertaken for *therapeutic* purposes.[17]

Failure to distinguish between therapeutic and elective abortion engenders misunderstanding and enables some ethicists to ignore concerns I find central to the moral debate. While some ethicists seem to deny the moral validity of all, or nearly all, abortions,[18] most acknowledge that some therapeutic abortions can be justified morally. Among Roman Catholic moral theologians, for example, where only therapeutic abortion is acknowledged as being possibly legitimate, discussion focuses on cases where the termination of fetal life as an indirect consequence of the positive therapeutic act of saving a mother's life may be permissible. Many ethicists outside the Roman Catholic tradition also implicitly or explicitly adopt a therapeutic stance on abortion. When this is the case, the only "good moral reasons" for abortion hinge on whether the withholding of abortion will be "life-threatening" to a pregnant woman. In discussions that presume the legitimacy only of therapeutic abortion, the definition of "life-threatening conditions" varies. Sometimes they are construed in a narrow, biologically reductionist manner, such that only the actual physical survival of the woman justifies abortion. In other analyses, a more inclusive understanding is observed that incorporates, for example, extreme economic hardship and physical and psychological suffering.

Those who believe that fetal life, in all or most of its phases of development, is already a human being are, by virtue of that belief, drawn to a stance in which only therapeutic abortion is justifiable. At the very least, however, all opponents of elective abortion must recognize the moral implications and consequences of adopting such a stance. To argue, as I do here, that women are properly *the* moral agents of accountability in the decision about abortion is to claim that *elective* abortion is the proper context for assessing the morality of abortion. It does not follow from this recognition that every elective abortion is morally justified,[19] but apart from the existence of elective abortion, women have no standing as moral agents with regard to pregnancy.

The question of *who* is the responsible moral agent in this decision is worthy of moral evaluation. Although all answers to this question are already heavily freighted with value judgments about women and about women's competence as moral agents, when the entire discussion of the morality of abortion pivots on the question of fetal life, such moral considerations never enter the discussion at all. As I have argued throughout, considering the act of abortion without critically assessing its social context forces a defense of the morality of elective abortion into a pejorative, "forced-field" framework that occludes the full range of moral dimensions of the question. To foreclose the issue by accepting a therapeutic stance is to assume that agency in these matters should rest with someone other than the pregnant woman. This is why I make my strong and well-considered objection to isolating the normative question of the morality of abortion from the lived-world history of persons, especially women, in which the abortion dilemma arises.

THE WIDER MORAL FRAMEWORK FOR
THE ACT OF ABORTION

Women's capacity for full moral agency is only one of several foundational moral presumptions that require recognition prior to an evaluation of the act of abortion itself. We need also to acknowledge the bodily integrity of any moral agent as a foundational condition of human well-being and dignity.[20] Freedom from bodily invasion, a right increasingly recognized as having some precedents in our common law traditions, at least when coercion in medical treatment is at issue, is no minor or marginal issue morally; rather, it is central to our conception of the dignity of the person. Mental patients and the critically ill who wish to decline medical treatment are understood, rightly, as having claims to freedom from bodily invasion. Yet when the issue is abortion, the relevance of this acknowledged legal right usually goes unmentioned,[21] evidence, I believe, of the lingering misogyny in legal tradition that adheres to the ahistorical view of women as childbearers. Irrespective of how the fragile legal traditions are applied, respect for bodily integrity, or "body-right," must be understood as a foundational *moral* claim. To address human rights from the moral point of view is not to address only, as in discussions of legal rights, existing positive law, but to attempt to ascertain the minimal conditions that ought to exist in society to ground personal human well-being.

Some theorists evidently presume that human rights discourse is not primary moral discourse because, for them, "rights" arise only in selected dimensions of our lives that are "political." The person or moral agent is not understood as intrinsically social, but rather as a separate and discrete entity for whom social questions emerge only in specialized political activity, construed as a limited, singular aspect of life. Hence, human rights language is held to be political language, with at best secondary standing in moral discourse. In some cases, refusal to hear the moral basis of an appeal to procreative rights is rooted in this philosophy. But in most instances, ethicists and moral theologians do recognize the moral viability of human rights claims.[22] And some acknowledge that it is neither preposterous nor nonsensical to speak of having moral obligations to ourselves[23] or to insist that we have a moral responsibility to affirm and to realize the circumstances that are conditional to our basic well-being in society. Even so, few ethicists have gone so far as to maintain, as I do here, that bodily integrity, or the power of self-direction as an embodied human being, is even more substantively conditional of human worth and dignity than most of the political rights reputed to be basic in a liberal society. I reiterate the point at some length because I believe this is always the most neglected moral consideration in ethical discussions that touch the lives of women and because until it is understood, not only discussions of the ethics of abortion but all socio-ethical discussions will be morally off the mark.

"Rights" in a moral sense, then, are shares in the basic conditions of human well-being and, therefore, reciprocal accountabilities that are binding for all persons. I cannot claim as a "right" any condition of social existence that, at the same time, I will not agree to grant or extend to other persons. If I claim something as a "mere" liberty, in effect I am asserting that no one should interfere with me. If I claim a "right," I am not only seeking to constrain the other person's action, but I consent to constrain my own in recognition of our common accountabilities. "Rights," then, is a moral category pertaining to the mutually obligatory character of our social relations, whereas "liberty," per se, has no particular moral standing. No doubt, as many liberal theorists have argued, a good society will maximize liberty,[24] but it will do so only from a moral point of view. As much *liberty* is morally permissible as is consistent with either the human rights of others or basic conditions of human well-being. In other words, from a moral point of view, rights take precedence over liberties.

I have also insisted that rights are, properly, conditions that make for social justice and that these are always *more* basic to morality than individual appeals to "liberty." Although important, individual appeals to liberty should never be considered a moral end in themselves. The moral validity of individual acts can never be justified completely apart from a consideration of the sort of society these acts will create in the long run. Therefore, I argue that a society which would deny the conditions of procreative choice to women, or which treats women merely or chiefly as reproductive means to some purported end of that society's own self-perpetuation, is one that mandates women's inferior status as less than full, rational beings, denying women full claim to intrinsic value in the process. Likewise, a society that incorporates a perdurable structure of coercion, even violence, against women as morally appropriate to its functioning, but claims that it upholds the sanctity of or respect for human life is deluded.

Insofar as assessing the right of bodily integrity is concerned, however, I have also stressed the extreme weakness of our liberal political and moral traditions. Despite the liberal legal precedents of "bodily integrity" in our common law traditions,[25] discussions of basic political rights — those rights germane to standing in civil society and most highly valued because they were critical to the successful accomplishment of the revolutions in our European and American past — do not usually incorporate this concern. I have argued that the most powerful agents of those revolutions were male members of the rising middle classes, who had already gained a base of societal power in relation to the aristocracy through a new, emergent economic order. They had long since escaped the social conditions of serfdom and peonage and they were, at least in the United States, owners of slaves and unconscious of the rising demands from women for justice. As a result, the most basic, foundational consideration of human freedom and dignity, the integrity of one's body space — the right not to have one's person treated merely as a use-value or function of another's purposes or will — was largely overlooked. I also suggested, in Chapter 4, in stressing the centrality of embodied existence to a feminist liberation theological perspective, that there are forceful theological as well as moral reasons for objecting to such insensitivity.

It is little wonder, then, that feminist efforts to articulate a moral argument about bodily integrity and its relevance to procreation are met with almost incredulous disbelief, derision, or trivialization in the ethical literature on abortion.[26] To be sure, when fetal life is adjudged full, existent human life, appeals to body-right will not have automatic, overriding force because where two existent human beings are involved there will be a conflict of rights. (Such conflicts occur all the time in our social world.) But this recognition of *possible* conflict of rights is not usually what is assumed in discussions of the morality of abortion. Rather, appeals women make to their right to bodily self-control and self-direction are treated, at best, as nonmoral, morally irrelevant, or ethically confused and, at worst, as selfish, whimsical, or positive evidence of the immorality of women who choose to have or to defend legal abortions.

I claim that the fact of women's biological fertility and capacity for childbearing in no way overrides our moral claim to the "right" of bodily integrity, because this moral claim is inherent to human well-being. Furthermore, if the full implications of women's history were comprehended, including the morally onerous attitudes and violent practices toward women, then reproductive self-determination would be understood to reinforce the substantive social justice claim about bodily integrity. Reproductive choice for women is requisite to any adequate notion of what constitutes a good society. Transformed social conditions of reproduction are absolutely critical to all women's well-being. No society that coerces women at the level of reproduction may lay claim to moral adequacy.

I agree strongly with those who have argued that the notion of "rights" is intrinsically social; it pertains to conditions of relationship between existent beings. I would insist one ought not to impute the existence of "rights" in a social relation unless all parties fall within some justifiable definition of "existents" vis-à-vis our human relations. In discussing the moral meaning of fetal life, we cannot afford to overlook the social character of "rights." When anyone invokes the claim that a fetus has "a right to life," we are justified in being wary, unless or until a plausible account is given of the criteria grounding the contention that a fetus is properly a full member of the class of human beings.

I have also stressed a more utilitarian or "concrete consequentialist" argument for procreative choice that correlates with but is logically discrete from the foregoing one: namely, that given women's overall, continuing, disadvantaged socioeconomic situation, together with the de facto reality of childbearing, women should have procreative choice. Women most frequently must provide the life energy, physical and emotional support, and, increasingly, the economic wherewithal for infant survival, growth, and development. Under such circumstances, optimal conditions of procreative choice for women are mandatory.

I have constructed my case to put both good society or rights arguments and utilitarian teleological arguments in the forefront, not only because of my own methodological convictions but, even more important, because so much contemporary philosophical and religio-ethical analysis approaches the morality of abortion with such a weak sense of the relevance of these considerations. No moralist would be considered reputable if he or she argued the morality of economic life either by abdicating reflection on the meaning of a good society or by ignoring the concrete effects of economic policy and practice on people's lives. But, indeed, it *is* acceptable to discuss the morality of abortion without examining the implications of our moral judgments on what a "good society" should be and without taking into account the actual condition of women in society. Hence my ongoing contention is that, given the present climate of opinion among ethicists, it is necessary to insist that the positive principle of justice and the issue of social welfare, or social utility, are both at stake in procreative choice, or noncoercion in childbearing.

If one approaches the question of the morality of abortion without an acute sense of the viability of all these moral claims, then the question of the moral valuation of fetal life inevitably appears to be the only relevant question and the moral problematic of abortion seems to pose a fairly simple moral quandary. If, however, one recognizes the moral dubiousness of a society that treats women as less than full persons with an appropriate and serious moral claim to well-being, self-respect, self-direction, and noncoercion in childbearing, and if one also recognizes the disadvantaged state of most women's lives, one's approach to the morality of abortion must shift. Even if one holds, as I do *not*, that fetal life is, from conception or at the point when the genetic code is implanted, essentially a *full, existent* human life, it is necessary to comprehend that we are dealing with a genuine moral dilemma, a conflict of "rights," not a moral chimera in which the "innocent party" — the fetal "person" — is, *by definition*, the "wronged" party in the moral equation.

To address the question "When does human life begin?" or to ask more precisely "What is the moral status of fetal life?" is something we are bound to do, given our modern scientific understanding of embryological development. Yet the questions are a far more intricate matter than they may appear at face value. Biological science itself is a complex, cultural construct, and biological scientists themselves differ over the moral implications of their paradigm. None of us nontechnical interpreters of these scientific data proceed untouched by our own operating cultural and social understandings. In fact, beneath the diverse judgments moralists make about the meaning of fetal life lie differing philosophies of nature and of science, including quite disparate views of biological theory, as well as conflicting methodological assumptions about how scientific "fact" and moral valuation interrelate.[27] As my discussion of the relation of religion and morality in Chapter 1 implied, these differences are substantive and, in some cases, related to thought patterns conditioned by theological tradition.

HOW DIFFERING PHILOSOPHIES OF NATURE AFFECT THE DISCUSSION OF FETAL LIFE

In Chapters 3 and 5, I elaborated the strong trend in Christian theological ethics toward classifying sexuality, particularly women's sexuality, and our reproductive function as "natural" phenomena, unaffected by cultural and historical change. This trend, I suggested, is discernible even in some of the most sophisticated Protestant and Roman Catholic theology. Progressive theologians do not characteristically approach questions involving the rest of "nature" with the same static or nonprocess assumptions they bring to the subject of women's lives. No matter how sophisticated their guise, discussions of fetal life continue to be informed by strains of older theological "theories of nature."

A few Roman Catholic moralists, for example, still operate within a natural law framework conditioned by their appropriation of Aristotelian biology. The "potentiality" of the fetus is presumed to bear the full weight of "actuality,"[28] because the logic of older natural law thinking, especially where the legacy of Thomas Aquinas prevails, applied Aristotelian biology in a specific way. Under this rubric, it was assumed that the "organic" structure of things not only shaped but predetermined actuality, an assumption that still shapes some Thomism.[29] Movement in nature is from "lower" to "higher" organic forms of life, and it is presumed that the lower organic form delimits the higher one. This sort of premodern natural law perspective understands nature as relatively fixed at "origin" such that "potentiality" is an inexorable unfolding of the already given character of things. Where this conception of "nature" prevails, lower organic forms are presumed to set limits to appropriate development. It frequently has been observed that any such theory of nature also carries the moral assumption that one can predetermine, by virtue of the organic structure of a thing, what the morally permissible limits of its development are. Given the primacy of the organic limits set by a "static" nature, "potentiality" is, in a real sense, already actuality. Many moralists who bring this sort of theoretical framework to the analysis of nature may recognize that culture, society, and history play a formative role in some human acts and policies. But these theorists have a greater overriding tendency to exempt sexuality, and especially reproduction, which readily "appear" to be "purely natural," from any cultural-historical analysis than do moral theologians who have made a theoretical break with such a theory of nature. At least one modern reinterpreter of Catholic natural law ethics has conceded that issues concerning sexuality have been a most egregious example of inappropriate appeals to nature precisely because of this dynamic.[30]

The philosophy of nature implicit in this perspective involves an important moral assumption about human freedom too frequently obscured in moral discourse; namely, that freedom *ought not* to be expressed where "natural" potentiality is directly operative. It is not an overstatement to say that this "organic" theory presupposes that properly functioning human rationality is bound to acceptance, not transcendence, of the limits that "nature" supposedly "dictates." Such a "theory of organism" suggests that morally permissible change is delimited by organic structure.[31] The radicality and distinctiveness of human moral freedom and creativity, with all of the moral responsibility this freedom entails, is not only minimized but condemned by this theory. Because this assumption operates most clearly when gender relations are at issue, "freedom" in "biological reproduction" is understood as particularly inappropriate. Neither, then, is it an overstatement to say that this theory is permeated by misogyny.

Natural law theory also is sometimes manifest in the reasoning of biological scientists. Like the rest of us, scientists are shaped by their religio-cultural heritage. The uncritical articulation of natural law theory by scientists, however, carries the added weight of the "authority of science" so compelling now in western culture. Professor E. Blechschmidt, director of the Institute of Anatomy at the University of Göttingen, whose scientific views are often cited to support the thesis that the fetus is a human being, suggests that the distinctiveness and continuity of human life, in contradistinction to other life forms, obviates the meaningfulness of the moral question of the status of human life:

> Outsiders often maintain that a young human embryo is not yet a real human being. They do not know that this assumption is false. Only in about the last 20 years have the early stages of human development been more precisely

investigated, and on the basis of these investigations, the specificity of the human being from the moment of fertilization is authenticated today.

As long as the first embryonal stages of man had not yet been discovered, it was believed legitimate to infer the development of man from the early development of animals. Similarly, it was assumed that the embryos of all animals resemble each other in their early stages and therefore do not importantly differ from each other, even though it was known, for example, what differences exist between a chicken egg and a frog egg. . . .

Today, the question regarding the point in the course of prenatal development at which it is licit to speak of a human being can be clearly answered, because today we know that each developmental stage of the human being is demonstrably a characteristically human one. Already, on the basis of the well-known chromosomes of human ova, the specificity of a human germ can no longer be doubted. Therefore, this principle applies today: a human being does not become a human being but rather is such from the instant of its fertilization. During the entire ontogenesis, no single break can be demonstrated, either in the sense of a leap from the lifeless to the live, or of a transition from the vegetative to the instinctive or to characteristically human behavior. It may be considered today a fundamental law of human ontogenesis that not only human specificity but also the individual specificity of each human being remains preserved from fertilization to death, and that only the appearance of the individual being changes in the course of ontogenesis.[32]

Blechschmidt obviously assumes that the only relevant question at issue in the moral debate is whether fetal development is, in fact, human species development, as opposed to the development of another life form. When that can be established, with the information provided by "modern science," he presumes the matter is settled. Clearly, Blechschmidt recognizes that the earlier Aristotelian biology, using vegetative, animal, and human-rational distinctions for fetal development, left open the question of whether fetal life was fully *human* species life from conception. Now, because that question is closed, he presumes that the moral question about the meaning of fetal life is settled as well. What he does not recognize is the continuing impact of earlier organic thinking on his own position.

The developmentalist logic underpinning his argument assumes that "potentiality" incorporates the value of actual human existence. Unaware that such an assumption bespeaks human moral valuation, Blechschmidt's argument implicitly condemns those of us who have a different understanding of natural process and, for that matter, a quite different theory of science and of the relation between fact and value. We are condemned not for having a differing theory or moral judgment but for "ignoring" the "truth" of science.

By contrast to these older organic theories of nature, alternative philosophies interpret nature as inclusive of novelty and creativity and posit human freedom as substantively constitutive of nature. They recognize that human interactions intrinsically shape the natural life process and that actualization of potential in nature is always, to some degree, the result of valuation and choice. In Chapter 3 I acknowledged the usefulness of the movement known as process theology and philosophy, influenced by Alfred North Whitehead's metaphysical speculations, for a revisioning of our understanding of nature and the character of fetal life. Such process understanding of nature stresses novelty and spontaneity as intrinsic to the natural process at all levels. Therefore, nature is not a constricting category; it does not prescribe how potentiality is to be actualized. The realization of "actual entities" and "actual occasions," technical terms for existent reality, involves novelty and, in the case of human beings, freedom to select potential values that will influence the way things come to be.

While not all process thinkers find in this philosophy of nature the same implications for the question of abortion, a process view of nature automatically rejects the conclusion that all potentiality in nature must be realized. In fact, it is impossible to actualize all natural potential from a process perspective because, according to this theory, the natural-social process presumes selection, spontaneity, novelty, and, at the human level of natural existence, rational freedom as constitutive of reality.

My purpose is not to attempt to exhaust all the theoretical options that inform the ethics of abortion debate. Rather, in presenting the older, "natural law" theory and the more contemporary Whiteheadian framework for interpreting nature, I wish to illustrate that these and other theoretical assumptions always underlie discussions of the moral value of fetal life. More important, they either go unacknowledged or even seem to be intentionally obscured in both the factual claims and moral judgments of participants in the debate.

DIFFERING PHILOSOPHIES OF
SCIENCE AND THE RELATIONSHIP
BETWEEN FACT AND VALUE

I have maintained that descriptive, scientifically grounded statements, purporting to make factual claims, are not to be confused with evaluative statements, which make ethical claims. To observe this distinction does not deny a close connection between "fact" and "value." Recognizing that there are differing kinds of rational justifications required to sustain factual and moral claims, however, does involve a provisional fact/value distinction. At least in principle, factual or descriptive claims are falsifiable, either by appeal to additional data that contest the original factual conclusion or by appeal to an alternative theory or scheme of interpretation that makes "better sense" of the purported facts. Scientific theories are not, nor should they be, value-free, but they are constrained by a logic which demands that their justification be worked out in the interplay between empirical claims and the viability of the scheme in which these claims are set.

In addition, the temporal frame of reference that characterizes the logic of science moves from the present — What is the case? — to the past — Why is this the case? The explanatory mode of science heightens awareness of continuities and strives to adequately account for what *has come to be*. Moral justifications, on the other hand, concerned as they are with what *ought* to happen and how we *should* act as moral agents, move from the present to the future.[33] It is crucial to recognize that ethics presume a certain range for creativity, freedom, and novelty, together with an openness to the future, apart from which morality makes no sense.[34] To be sure, moral claims may be informed by perceptions of value derivable from the past. And support for action guides often appeals to already established moral consensus, whether that consensus is culturally or religiously specific or general. Distinctly moral justifications, however, require that we test, by reason-giving, both past value perceptions and venerable action guides from the standpoint of the present. Simultaneously, we must consider values and action guides in terms of a hypothetical future, whether as imaginative constructions of the good society or as assessments of the future consequences of their effects.

Therefore, to presume that "facts" constitute adequate reasons for moral convictions is to commit a rather gross form of what in ethical theory is called "the naturalistic fallacy."[35] While there are many perspectives on the ways in which "the reality of things" shape normative moral judgments as well as a number of permissible theories about the relation between fact and value, the overwhelming consensus among moralists is that positions which assume that scientific judgment obviates moral judgment are simply mistaken. Happily, most scientists are sufficiently sophisticated to avoid subsuming morals to the logic of any given scientific methodology, even more so when dealing with human sociocultural reality, which is infinitely less predictable than the behavior of atoms or chemicals. It was recently reported that Nobel geneticist Joshua Lederberg, in addressing a group of philosophers and theologians, asserted that scientists could help answer the question "When does human life begin?" only after some plausible philosophical or theological definition of "human" was proffered.[36] It behooves everyone, then, to recognize that scientific knowledge, per se, does not foreclose the need for moral judgment.

Debates around the question of fetal life, however, are replete with examples of the naturalistic fallacy. A particularly crass, journalistic example of such reasoning appeared recently in an article by Mary Meehan published in *Commonweal*:

> Yet it is biology, not faith, that tells us that a fertilized ovum is the earliest form of human life. *Biology does not deal with the theological concept of "ensoulment"; but it need not deal with that concept in order to reach conclusions about when human life begins.* This point is basic to the entire debate over abortion. . .Juli Loesch, founder of an anti-nuclear weapons and anti-abortion group called Prolifers for Survival, says that *it is the pro-choice people who make metaphysical statements about "potential life" and "meaningful life" and "personhood," while pro-lifers stick to "grubby little facts."* Such facts include the time when the embryonic heart starts beating (two to four weeks of age), the time when the fetus has a clearly human form (seven to eight weeks), and the fact that abortion usually tears apart the body of a tiny embryo and fetus. *If more liberals were to study embryology books, they would understand that the debate can be resolved without reference to theology.* (Italics mine)[37]

Meehan is right that theological justification is irrelevant, but her smug assurance that there can be only one side to the moral issue bespeaks the confusion that obtains whenever moral evaluation is suppressed by a refusal to distinguish between factual and moral claims. One can sympathize with the frustration of persons like Meehan and Loesch who believe that "facts" are so grubbily prosaic that they foreclose moral questions, but the result of this position is that the moral ground is cut out from under anyone who disputes their claims. Those of us who disagree are simply written off as "metaphysical speculators" who also, by implication, are both "unscientific" and resistant to confronting brute facts.

This sort of move to cut off serious moral debate is by no means limited to nonprofessionals. In the literature on abortion written by moral theologians and ethicists, one frequently encounters a similar refusal to grant the existence of an autonomous dimension of moral justification on this question. That human life begins before birth is said to be neither "an ethical judgment, nor one upon which biologists quarrel as do divines."[38] Obviously, biological scientists agree that life begins before birth. As a matter of fact, the biological point of view, as a heuristic of human inquiry, takes the continuity in the chain of life as a theoretical presumption rather than as a factual claim. Once genera and species classification of life forms are identified, continuity of those forms is presupposed. No one who did not adopt this hypothesis would be "doing" biology.

What is at issue in the moral debate about fetal life is the question of when, within an admittedly continuous biological process, we are wise to predicate a fetus's standing as a human being, or as a person, morally and legally. It is inconceivable to me that anyone affected by modern embryology would deny that a developing zygote, conceptus, embryo, or fetus, *considered in abstraction from the mother,* is *a form* of human life. But to imply that no conscientious person could entertain distinctions between "a form of human life," "a human life," "an individual human life," and a "person" simply flies in the face of our whole philosophical and theological heritage. Such distinctions have been elaborated extensively in modern philosophical and theological reflections on human nature in contexts unrelated to the abortion debate.[39] Nor will it do to suggest that in making such distinctions, ethicists are guilty of moral callousness or intellectual evasion. Yet such charges are daily fare in the moral debate over abortion.[40]

Some quite reputable and sensitive philosophers have insisted that, given the total range of what we know about human reality, it is philosophically inappropriate to equate the categories of "a form of human life" and "a person."[41] I happen to agree with this contention, but prior to developing my own position on the nature of fetal life I would maintain only that the moral debate requires at least the acknowledgment that such distinctions are meaningful. Those who insist on the equivalence of the terms "a form of human life," "a human being," "an individual human being," and "a person," or who deal with the issue merely by casting moral aspersions on those of us who observe these distinctions, deserve no credit for clarifying the moral issues involved. The moral questions about fetal life are complex, not by virtue of a smokescreen laid down by those of us who dissent from the view that the question is self-evident but because there are defensible differences in our interpretations of the matters involved.

HOW SHALL WE VALUE FETAL LIFE
FROM A MORAL POINT OF VIEW?

Because many Christian ethicists assume their tradition endorses "full hominization" from the earliest "justifiable" point onward, they bypass altogether the need for elaborated reason-giving with regard to fetal life. Rather, they embrace scientific species-continuity assumptions without requisite awareness that those who differ do not disagree with scientific data about the process of embryological development but remain unpersuaded that the presumption of species continuity warrants a moral valuation of a fetus either as individuated or as full human life, with the attendant implication that abortion is homicide. No one can speak meaningfully of the death of fetal life as *a human death* unless we have articulated reasons for believing that the fetus is a human life. Increasingly, the philosophers have prodded the abortion debate into a more nuanced assessment of the moral reasons for and against viewing prenatal life as morally continuous or discontinuous with existent humanity.

The judgment that we who disagree with the moral valuation of the fetus as a full human life are playing God must be ruled out on both moral and theological grounds.[42] Even the decision to treat a pregnancy as "direct divine action" with which human beings ought not to tamper *is a human interpretive choice*. When we ask not "When does human life begin?" but the more precise question "At what point is it morally wise to assess fetal life as a human life?" we are seeking developmental criteria for stipulating the degree of similarity to existing human beings required for counting fetal life as a human life. In putting the issue this way, we also avoid confusing ourselves about the inherent character of the moral choice involved in any formula we develop for this judgment. It is easy to mystify our moral freedom by the way we put moral questions to ourselves, often entertaining them in a fashion that leaves our own moral agency out of the picture. This practice, which social theorists call "reification,"[43] masks the fact that our own interpretive power is at work in any judgment we make on the issue.

A related form of reification can occur in the way we characterize alternative positions about fetal life. Sometimes writers portray positions as invoking either "social" or "biological" criteria, as though the decision to employ biological criteria was not also a social judgment, or as though social criteria did not imply biological assessments. For example, those who invoke the currently most sophisticated form of the argument that human life is existent in early embryological development insist that when the genetic code is fully implanted in the fertilized ovum an individual human life is present.[44] Such a judgment appeals to biological criteria directly, but the unspoken assumption in this argument is a social value judgment to the effect that the genetic information carried in DNA is the "real" triggering mechanism of the individual human life form. Such a judgment is a thoroughly social value judgment. In fact, it is suffused with the enthusiasm and, among theologians, even the awe and wonder that recent genetic discoveries have evoked. Conversely, people who believe that biological birth — the point at which a society recognizes that a new life has entered it — is when we may wisely and assuredly posit the beginning of a human life are not only appealing to a recognized social reality. They also are identifying a point in the biological process of fetal development when a full human life form is existent. The issue to notice here is that *neither* position "neglects biology"[45] or proffers definition apart from "the social construction of reality."[46]

The analysis of fetal life is further complicated by the reluctance of some to "rationalize" or to clarify stages of fetal development at all. The sensibilities, feelings, and intuitive reactions that cluster around our experiences of pregnancy and birth vary greatly, but the expectation of and birth of a child often engender a sense that mystery and awe are more appropriate human responses to prenatal development than philosophical analyses, which always require categories of differentiation. I share the awareness that, given their social meaning, pregnancy and birth properly resist philosophical analysis. Yet it is important to recognize that our new knowledge and technology, along with the new dilemmas they pose for our choice, pressure us toward previously unexplored levels of rational reflection about fetal life. Intuitive moral sensibility is, frequently, a good guide for personal decision making, but value conflict and differences about how to apply moral principle invariably push us to develop our own assumptions and to give a shared or public account of why we make our particular judgments. Without such elaborated reasoning, we can neither clarify our own convictions nor become aware of how the values of those with whom we disagree are informed by differing assumptions. Moral reasoning must move us beyond even our best intuitions to moral justification, not because reality is either inherently "rationalistic" or susceptible to fixed intellectual categorization but because refusal to publicly justify our assumptions and actions makes more probable the rule of "unreason."

The continuity of the human species life form is not at issue in the debate about abortion. Rather, the question at issue is when we are wisest to predicate the existence of a human being within a continuous process of life development. It is also important to observe that, given a clear scientific presumption of continuity of developing form, *all* possible *moral* positions on the status of fetal life are contestable and require moral justification, a point that at least one philosopher has upheld:

> There is no single problem of "the status of the unborn." The unborn entity changes and grows continuously, assuming new and dramatically different characteristics along the way, some of which could have crucial moral significance . . .
>
> The philosopher will be especially concerned with the *reasons* given for any judgment that draws a line between permissible and impermissible killings, for, like the legislator and the judge, he cannot be satisfied with anything less than *principled* solutions to practical questions. Moral principles, being in their essential nature *general*, are likely to embarrass one when applied to cases other than those they were initially designed to fit. For purposes of moral judg-

ment wherever one draws the line between stages in the development of a human being, one must be prepared, as Michael Tooley puts it, "to point to a *morally relevant* difference" between the stage during which killing is no longer permissible and the earlier stages during which it is not wrong. The problem of "drawing the line" in a nonarbitrary or principled fashion bedevils the liberal and the moderate in obvious ways, but it causes subtle problems for the inflexible conservative too . . .

The extreme conservative may seem at first sight to have escaped the problem, for he refuses to draw any line at all between conception and birth, holding that there is no nonarbitrary place to draw it. Still, this stance causes him at least two kinds of problems. To assert that a single-cell zygote, or a tiny cluster of cells, as such, is a complete human being already possessed of all the rights of a developed person seems at least as counter-intuitive as the position into which some liberals are forced, that newly born infants have no right to continue living. The conservative must find further convincing arguments that the *potentiality* of human personhood is itself sufficient ground for the possession of the rights of *actual* human personhood, a difficult task indeed. Second, the principled conservative must explain why he grants the right to life to the zygote but not to the ovum or the spermatozoon, which are also, in some intelligible sense, "potential human beings." (Italics mine)[47]

If we discount Feinberg's evident assumption that all philosophers are male, his point is well taken. The logic and constraints of criteria used in any "classification" of fetal life will have a certain arbitrariness, precisely because we are dealing with a continuum in the life processes of reproduction. All criteria will appear, in some degree, arbitrary, because they involve evaluation of the meaning of reality in process.

Furthermore, typologies used descriptively in philosophical discussions to classify the range of positions on fetal life are also always value-laden. The one employed in the preceding quote from Feinberg invokes the familiar political continuum — "conservative," "moderate," and "liberal," presumably apt because of the political positions on abortion that they represent. It is still well to observe, however, that there is not a necessary correlation between a given

philosophical view of fetal life and one's social policy stance in relation to abortion. Philosophers can too easily overlook the complexities that inhere when moral judgment has to be translated into
social practice; there is no necessary logical connection between a
given position on fetal life and a specific public policy position. When
used in nonnormative argument to describe a range of positions, such
typologies invariably betray a great deal about the *range* of
sympathies of the writer who employs them. Feinberg, for example,
designates as "moderate" all analysts along the spectrum from those
who recognize implantation of the ovum in the uterus to those who
deem quickening or the "viability" of the fetus as the criterion for
full hominization.[48] Not surprisingly, when this typology is employed,
anyone who attempts to defend the view that full life begins at birth
is inevitably characterized as "an extreme liberal."[49] Invocation of
"extremism" in our moral and political discourse has an automatically pejorative connotation. Yet is one who insists that full human
life *begins* at birth an "extremist"?

More important than the problem of typologies is the neglect of
a major differential in the philosophical debate about fetal life, the
observation of which is crucial to any feminist analysis. We need to
notice whether an analyst, in appealing to presumed biological data,
describes the level of fetal development as if fetal tissue already
exists as "an entity" apart from the woman's body. Is fetal development described, as it should be if biological science is invoked,
as an *interaction* between a fetal life form and a woman's body, which
far from a "mere" passive host, is *the* life system that enables
continuous fetal development from its simple to its complex form?
In discussing fetal life form, the point is to ascertain when the fetus
is analogically enough "like us" to warrant not species inclusion but
categorization as "a human life." But when the fetus is prejudged
as "an entity" from the beginning, we are invited to view fetal tissue
as directly analogous to us, in abstraction from and without reference
to the decisive role a woman's body plays in the process of fetal
development.

Although any judgment about the fetus is a judgment by analogy,
those who seek evidence for early "full hominization" often fail to
make their analogies explicit. For example, "pro-life" literature on
fetal life assumes that the full humanity of the fetus should be
predicated on its early morphological (structural) development. This
literature is replete with visual cues that invite us to draw analogies

between a fetus and a newborn infant. Those who understand fetal development are aware that these illustrated appeals to morphological similarity are misleading in the extreme, given the fact that gross structural formation precedes the slower and more subtle development of internal organs and the human neurological system.

But such pressure to understand the fetus as "an entity" or "existing agent" from the beginning is not exerted only by those who lack detailed knowledge of embryological development. The truth is that most descriptions of fetal development in philosophical and theological literature abstract it from the woman's body, ascribing a subtle "agency of self-development" to cells and tissue, as if the process of fetal formation were *not* biologically dependent on the pregnant woman's life system. This literature imputes agency to all prenatal life forms from the moment of conception onward. Even the fertilized ovum, a single-cell zygote, is sometimes described as if it were "an agent."[50] Likewise, the conceptus, a mass resulting from the cell division of the zygote implanted in the uterine wall, is frequently spoken of as if it were "one who acts." Similarly depicted is the embryo — a term pertinent to fetal tissue up to seven weeks after conception. In all such purported "descriptions of fetal life," one senses that something akin to conscious self-direction is presumed to exist at the outset.

The unexpressed intent of this literature is to ascertain the earliest point at which embryological data "permit" the designation of "an existent" human life. Hence, from a logical standpoint, the attraction to philosophers and theologians of the startling new understandings of the workings of DNA. Given the predisposition of traditional Christian moral theologians, in particular, to confirm early hominization, the discovery that even simple cells contain "information" for development offers a seductive analogy to human self-determination. For some theologians, genetic information attests to "an inner teleology" which, from that point onward, is equivalent to human self-direction.[51] Hence, more and more male theologians find it entirely plausible to predicate humanness to a fertilized ovum with its genetic code implanted. This is what they are calling *truly* human life!

It has startled some geneticists with whom I have discussed the matter to learn of this widespread "sacralization" of the genetic code among Christian teachers of ethics. Yet such reasoning permits an apparently more sophisticated invocation of "scientific data" than does the position of those arguing for full hominization from conception onward.[52] It avoids the difficulties of explaining the high percentage of "spontaneous abortions" that occur to fertilized ova prior to secure implantation in the uterine wall.[53] It also avoids the "difficulty" of having to "disapprove" contraceptive devices like the pill and intrauterine loops, which do not prevent fertilization of the ovum but obstruct uterine implantation. What the "genetic-code" position equally obscures, however, is that the woman's body is the full, living life system not only sustaining but totally nourishing this as yet very *simple biological form.* We may call it *"the* fetus," but it is not yet in any sense *an actually alive organism* with human complexity. The applied logic of potentiality often goes unnoticed here, as does the degree of the imputation of the concept "human" to the fetus. The analogy to an existent human life is very forced indeed; for, by anticipation, both autonomy and self-direction are projected back onto the fetus in its early development.

At the very least, we ought not to speak of the "existence" of a human life in the process of gestation until the fetal organism approaches a degree of actual complexity that can sustain the human analogies we employ to characterize it. "Self-direction" or "agency" are high-level human functions that make no sense when imputed to a form that lacks a fully developed brain structure and functioning neurological system. And I, for one, doubt the wisdom of imputing human agency to fetal life at all, although this does not mean that the fetus is "merely" a piece of tissue. (At least one well-meaning, and basically correct, writer got himself into largely undeserved trouble by making this rather dubious analogy.)[54] Nor is the fetus an organ, but a developing life system, and one of far greater complexity than a single organ.

Even so, I believe it is inadmissible to predicate to a fetus at any given point in its development existent human functions that its actual degree of structural complexity cannot sustain. Analogies to us, I believe, are inappropriate if they attribute to a fetus autonomous and existent human life functions that its structural development could not support. Hence, to call a conceptus or an early differentiated fetus "a human being," or even "a person" is, in my view, genuinely absurd, because the actualized biological structure existent in early fetal development cannot conceivably manifest the qualities we impute to "a human being," much less to "a person." Such analogies limp because they leap a biological chasm that only rhetorical force can bridge.

A well-known and much maligned philosophical argument in defense of women's "right" to abortion in some situations, proposed by Judith Jarvis Thompson, went awry, in my view, precisely because she embraced, rather than challenged, such analogies.[55] Thompson began by acknowledging "that the prospects for 'drawing a line' in the development of the fetus look dim"; so for purposes of argument she granted (though she did not personally accept) the assumption that from conception onward, the fetus is a human being, even a person. In her elaborate analysis, to which I cannot do justice here, she claimed that, given the source of at least some unwanted pregnancies, the fetus could be viewed as "an unjust aggressor" and the woman's choice of an abortion justified under the right of self-defense. Numerous objections to her argument,[56] not to mention satirizations of it,[57] have been formulated. Few have observed, however, that in accepting the ascription of agency to the fetus — for anyone characterized as an unjust aggressor must be an agent — she assented to the projection of human function onto fetal life, which its early level of biological complexity far from warrants. The import of this point, in terms of any morally normative view of fetal life, is that predicating *any criteria derived from analogies to autonomous human beings* is dubious until fetal development approximates the necessary biological conditions for discrete human existence.

Those in the philosophical literature who propose criteria for viewing the fetus as sufficiently "like us" at the point when the cerebral cortex is formed, when brain waves are detectable, or when "feeling" or "sentience" exists[58] join the genetic-code proponents in suppressing both the necessity to invoke biological criteria that are apt in terms of equivalence to human functionality[59] and the interrelational dynamic between the woman's life system and fetal development. They still operate in terms of the analogical similarity between the gross anatomical structure of the fetus and the gross body structure of human beings, not in terms of the capacity of fetal structures to perform the function human bodies perform. I agree with Charles Hartshorne, who assesses biological structure in terms of its functionality, in his implicit rejection of all such "potentiality approaches":

> From the gene-determined chemistry to a human person is a long, long step. As soon as the nervous system forming in the embryo begins to function as a whole — and not

before — the cell colony begins to turn into a genuinely individual animal. One may reasonably suppose that this change is accompanied by some extremely primitive individual animal feelings. They cannot be recognizably human feelings, much less human thoughts, and cannot compare with the feelings of a porpoise or chimpanzee in level of consciousness. That much seems as certain as anything about the fetus except its origin and possible destiny. The nervous system of a very premature baby has been compared by an expert to that of a pig. And we know, if we know anything about this matter, that it is the nervous system that counts where individuality is concerned.[60]

Some have found Hartshorne's use of a scientist's analogy between fetal tissue and a pig morally appalling. But in drawing this comparison, Hartshorne is calling for a *functional* link between fetal life form and human bodily form, the seminal issue that his critics' way of assessing fetal life ignores.[61]

It is precisely at the point where the functions of fetal structure begin to differentiate from the life system of the woman that has sustained it that genuinely relevant criteria should be sought. The "boundary" we require, if we wish to posit a moral boundary for when a human life as an individuated member of our species exists, is one that in some concise way respects the functional requisites of human bodily existence. Anything else hypostasizes admittedly complex but nevertheless primitive human biological structures and asks us to accord full human standing to an entity that is not yet a human body in any meaningful sense. Therefore, I hold that the most plausible early biological criteria for justifiably imputing to a fetus the status of an individuated human life form comes with the development of fetal viability. The major objections to "viability" as a criterion in the philosophical literature have chiefly to do with its "vagueness."[62] While it is true that rapidly accelerating medical advances reduce the period of time necessary for viability to occur, and also that machines now exist to replicate uterine conditions for sustaining life, the vagueness of viability criteria actually applies, as we have seen, to any "point" in biological development. Viability criteria are surely no more arbitrary than others, given the reality of a continuous gestational process. My own view is that those who find prebirth criteria relevant should focus on clarifying the range of options within the notion of viability, precisely because all earlier criteria are biologically reductionist. These criteria do not account for the fact that the woman's life system is the source of fetal survival until a very high level of differentiation has been achieved.

Viewed from my perspective, it is at best misleading to speak of the existence of a human life when fetal human life form has not developed functional biological complexity commensurate with the degree of functionality required for discrete biological existence. There is room for debate as to what constitutes a relevant degree of complexity. I do not myself believe that any position is implausible that designates as criteria for individuated biological existence fetal development from the end of the fourth month, when the lobes of the brain are biologically, though not functionally, mature, to the eighth month, when pulmonary maturation is sufficiently advanced to make "natural breathing" a possibility. Human biological brain function is, in my view, a minimum condition for defining fetal life as a human life, and any positing of "the inner teleology" requisite for inclusion in the human species is inappropriate before that time. We have every reasonable right to challenge any developmental approach that gives higher-order standing to an organism that does not yet have the minimal biological prerequisites for higher-order functioning.

It is also true that fetal life cannot "survive" if the pulmonary system is not functional. The capacity to breathe, to "take in," in a self-initiated way, the elements of the environment that sustain life, has long been appealed to in religious and moral tradition as "the act" that inaugurates a human life. Therefore, it is not morally unserious to suggest that the biological capacity to breathe is a meaningful criterion for asserting that now a human life exists. Admittedly, life-support machines often "stand in" for the mother's body in mediating oxygen to the premature neonate. Given the high incidence of pulmonary complications that threaten a prematurely born baby, we have reason to welcome this fact. But it is hardly "irrational" to insist that the existence of a human being as bodily organism requires a degree of pulmonary maturation.

Furthermore, in making an assessment of the moral meaning of fetal life, many philosophers have argued that *birth* is the clearest and most decisive watershed in the developmental process, uncontrovertibly marking the emergence of a human life. This does not mean that fetal life in the late stages of gestation is not worthy of respect. Rather, it means that birth is the critical developmental mark for conferring full human standing. The process philosopher William Hamrick, even though he appears to favor an earlier point for designating the individual human existence of the fetus, suggests that Whitehead could well have endorsed this view

> because of the tremendous importance of birth for the living personality of the human body. That is, in terms of morphological development and structural growth, there is a basic continuum between the late-stage fetus, the mature infant before birth, and the neonate. But we are not just personally ordered societies. We are also living personalities, and in terms of life, birth continues a historic route of occasions which will open us a frame of reference of staggering richness and complexity once physical maturation prepares us to appreciate it. Thus, with regard to life and the qualitative differences in experience that a high degree of life makes possible, birth is not a stage of continuous development, but rather a discontinuous, quantum leap forward. It is, of course, true that first experiences approximate James' "blooming, buzzing world of confusion," at least until the eyes are able to focus. But as the infant learns to adapt to, and grow in, his or her environment, [s]he is pushing outward the bounds of possible novelty which marks the presence of life and which gives us the qualitative differences of experience which are distinguishably human.[63]

Speculation regarding Whitehead's views aside, when biological criteria are analyzed in relation to the foundational bodily functional requisites for what we mean by "a human person," only late-stage gestational biological criteria are apt.

My reasons for eschewing the equivalent use of "a form of human species life" or "a human life" should by now be clear. From successful uterine implantation onward, a conceptus is a form of human life, developing toward differentiation into a human life form. Apart from morphological and functional maturation, however, the imputation of individuated human life to the fetus actually invites us to ignore concrete bodily complexity as a condition for specifying what it means to be a human being. Those who invoke early gestational criteria sometimes imply that they are taking bodily, physical existence seriously. However, because the achievement of physical embodiment involves a process, the imputation of "humanness" to highly undifferentiated organic life forms overrides the conditions of human body structure by anticipating qualities that do not yet inhere in the developing organism. The logic of "potentiality is actuality" operates vividly in this portrayal of fetal life, which, as I have stressed repeatedly, leaves the woman's mature, embodied life system out of the picture altogether. "Individuality" is, to say the least, a human category inappropriately applied to early developing fetal life.

Even though there are reasonable grounds for positing the existence of a genetically developed individuated human body form from sometime after the midpoint of pregnancy onward, it does not follow that we should consider a fetus to be "a person" from this earliest possible point of species differentiation.[64] Many have argued that the term *person* should be reserved to designate those who *actually belong* to the moral community by virtue of criteria derived from our understanding of living human beings. In a notable defense of this position, philosopher Mary Anne Warren has proposed the following criteria for "personhood":

> I suggest that the traits which are most central to the concept of personhood, or humanity in the moral sense, are, very roughly, the following:
> 1. consciousness (of objects and events external and/or internal to the being), and in particular the capacity to feel pain;
> 2. reasoning (the developed capacity to solve new and relatively complex problems);
> 3. self-motivated activity (activity which is relatively independent of either genetic or direct external control);
> 4. the capacity to communicate, by whatever means, messages of an indefinite variety of types, that is, not just with an indefinite number of possible contents, but on indefinitely many possible topics;
> 5. the presence of self-concepts, and self-awareness, either individual or social, or both.[65]

Warren does not suppose that any of these criteria are indisputable, but what she does maintain, correctly I believe, is that a fetus possesses *none* of the criteria that come to mind when we think normatively of a "person." While Warren's criteria are far too rationalistically proscribed to fully satisfy my own conception of normative personal qualities, I concur with her insistence that fetal life, even if sufficiently developed to count biologically as a human life, is not yet a "person" from the standpoint of any normative notion of personhood.

The moral philosophical reaction to Warren's position has been largely one of distress, on the grounds that her severing the genetic category of "a human being" from the notion of "personhood" opens the way for the moral legitimization of infanticide.[66] Then, too, it has been argued that her criteria exclude many living human beings — those, for example, having severely impaired brain functions.[67] In an addendum to her original essay, Warren countered the charge that her argument sanctioned infanticide. She supplemented her earlier formulation with an explanation of how "rights," understood as moral social relations, operate to preclude infanticide. I believe her to be correct on this point. Even so, her original argument could be strengthened by a more inclusive set of criteria for characterizing the normatively human. Warren's original criteria were too narrowly drawn and focus too exclusively on intellectual qualities. Obviously, from my perspective, one criterion that must be included as a foundational requirement of "personhood" is the discrete bodily existence achieved through birth. This criterion rules out, even more directly than Warren's addendum to her argument, *any* presumption that infanticide is no more morally dubious than abortion.[68]

Several contentions in Warren's argument that her critics have seemed to ignore, however, are those I find critical for an adequate moral theory. It is not that the fetus is without value; for, as Warren recognizes, a late-gestating fetus is approaching the condition of personhood. But she is right in claiming that fetuses, even when they have individuated human bodily forms, do not yet possess distinctly human qualities. Even more strongly than Warren, I would argue that fetuses in late stages of development should be extended respect, not because they are persons but because they have arrived at the threshold of discrete biological existence as a human life form — the point where it makes the most sense to posit the existence of foundational requirements of personhood.

Central to her argument that the fetus is not yet fully a person is her contention that "person" is a moral category implying participation in a "moral community." From a moral point of view, there are very basic reasons for accepting this theory of personhood. Morality presupposes social relations between centered beings. This is why birth is a critical juncture. A newborn, although not yet a person in any developmental sense of the term, has "joined" our society, and from that moment onward the quality of its moral relations sets constraints for the person the infant may become. If we reduce the category "person" to brute biological criteria, speaking even of a human life in the womb as "a person," we constrict the term, dissipate its moral force, and estrange ourselves from the normatively moral understanding of persons. By refusing to understand "personhood" as a reality that does not exist apart from moral relations between people, we obscure the moral foundations of society.

"Person" is a moral category, because in order to achieve full personhood we must intelligently reflect on our obligations to others, our values, and decisions. In the absence of this understanding of the morality of personhood, neonates would be born into a world devoid of moral relations, in which the evolution of their personhood would be determined by the accident of their birth rather than by a community's collective striving to include them as beings like us. In ethics, "person" is a normative moral category not because philosophers arbitrarily wish to exclude the unborn but because they realize that our existing social relations must come under the sway of our intentionality and capacity to reason. If we reduce the category of "person" to sheer biological criteria or correlate it with highly complex organic forms, we suppress the moral dimension of existence as constitutive of humanity. It is precisely because, as moral agents, we have the moral capacity to give respect to prenatal forms of life in the womb that we can probe and ponder our attitudes toward the unborn. To treat "person" as a gross biological category endangers our awareness of the meaning of our freedom as constitutive not only of morality but of society itself.

In the debate over the morality of abortion, those who correlate "personhood" with any level of gestational maturation seem to me to obscure, or to fail to appreciate, the integrity of arguments formulated by pro-choice supporters about the importance of "quality of life" questions regarding procreation and birth. Whether or not we wish to acknowledge it, the constitutive foundations of personality are bound up not with biological maturation of the human species life form but with the quality of our social relations. For centuries, even millennia, we human beings have permitted ourselves the luxury of imagining that our personal life follows inexorably from our existence as a natural or species life form, ignoring the now growing evidence that it is our human social relations, the quality of our interaction with each other, that conditions all that we become after birth. Ours is a world in which there is "a crisis of the personal"[69] — that is, a loss of the very conditions that make it possible for individuals who share human species being to live, grow, and thrive as genuinely personal beings having deeply centered personal relations to others. A biologically reductionist understanding of our species, which fully conflates the biologically human and the "person," threatens to intensify this crisis in our human moral relations. Ironically, the "fetishizing of fetuses" in the abortion debate may well exacerbate our already overdeveloped tendency to consider ourselves "normatively human" quite apart from the world of social relations our moral action creates. The birth of an infant, understood from the standpoint of organic embryological development, is an event. Birth is an inexorable watershed in organic process, however, because the care and nurturance of a newborn inaugurates an infinitely complex series of actions. Events happen; actions are born of our freedom, of our capacity to create moral relations.

Several decades ago, John MacMurray, in a quite different context, warned of the consequences of our failing to understand that personal life itself is rooted in our freedom:

> Contemporary thought, under the dominant influence of science, does, at least implicitly, conceive the world as a single process; either biologically as an evolutionary process, or mathematically as a material process of events obeying physical laws. But we are in a position to reject this alternative decisively. For we have seen that the conception of a unity of events, whether conceived physically or organically, is the conception of the continuant, and that the continuant is an ideal abstraction from our experience as agents. It is constituted by the exclusion of action. This concept of process cannot therefore include action as an element in the unity it seeks to express. If the world is a unitary process, it must be a world in which nothing is ever done; in which everything is a matter of fact and nothing is ever intended. We should have to assert, in that case, that there are no actions; that what seem such are really events. It will not be sufficient to say that all our actions are determined; for this is a contradiction in terms. The capacity to act is freedom; what has to be denied, if the world is one event, is that anything is ever intended. But in that case the assertion itself must be unintentional, and therefore mean-

ingless. In rejecting this alternative, we are merely using the criterion that we established earlier, that since the "I do" is the primary certainty, any theory which explicitly or implicitly denies it must be false.[70]

In a subsequent volume, MacMurray offered a powerful analysis of the way in which personhood becomes grounded in the life of an infant. He argues, rightly, that the human infant, being without instinct, is more helpless than any other newborn creature: "All purposive human behavior has to be learned."[71] What MacMurray recognized, an insight confirmed more and more by the newer developmental psychologies, is that it is "a covenant of caring" that *creates* personal existence:

> The baby must be fitted by nature at birth to the conditions into which he is born; for otherwise he could not survive. He is, in fact, "adapted," to speak paradoxically, to being unadapted, "adapted" to a complete dependence upon an adult human being. He is made to be cared for. He is born into a love-relationship which is inherently personal. Not merely his personal development, but his very survival depends upon the maintaining of this relation; he depends for his existence, that is to say, upon intelligent understanding, upon rational foresight. He cannot think for himself, yet he cannot do without thinking; so someone else must think for him. He cannot foresee his own needs and provide for them; so he must be provided for by another's foresight. He cannot do himself what is necessary to his own survival and development. It must be done for him by another who can, or he will die . . .
>
> His expression of satisfaction is closely associated with being cared for, with being nursed, with the physical presence of the mother, and particularly with physical contact. It would seem to be, from a biological point of view, unnecessary. There is no obvious utilitarian purpose in it; for the cessation of his cries would be enough to tell the mother that her efforts had succeeded in removing his distress. It seems impossible to account for it except as an expression of satisfaction in the relation itself; in being touched caressingly, attended to and cared for by the mother. This is evidence that the infant has a need which is not simply biological but personal, a need to be in touch with the mother and in conscious perceptual relation with her . . .

If we insist on interpreting the facts through biological categories, we shall be committed to talking puerilities about maternal instinct. There is no such thing, of course; if there were, it would have to include some very curious instinctive components, such as a shopping instinct and a dressmaking instinct. Even the term "mother" in this connection is not a biological term. It means simply the adult who cares for the baby. . . A man can do all the mothering that is necessary, if he is provided with a feeding-bottle, and learns how to do it in precisely the same fashion that a woman must learn.

From all this it follows that the baby is not an animal organism, but a person, or in traditional terms, a rational being. The reason is that his life, and even his bodily survival, depends upon intentional activity, and therefore upon knowledge. If nobody intends his survival and acts with intention to secure it, he cannot survive . . . He is not merely an animal organism; [however], if [he were] he could live by the satisfaction of organic impulse, by reaction to stimulus, by instinctive adaptation to his natural environment. But this is totally untrue. He cannot live at all by any initiative, whether personal or organic, of his own. He can live only through other people and in dynamic relation with them.[72]

With respect to the abortion controversy, it is worth remembering that *any* definition of "a human life" or "person" that neglects the moral reality required to nurture and sustain life after birth is very dangerous to our self-understanding. A "pro-life" movement that invites us to "respect" fetal rights from conception or genetic implantation onward actually undermines us by tempting us to imagine that personal rights inhere in natural processes, apart from any genuine covenant of caring, including the human resolve to create viable conditions of life for all who are born among us. Human rights are qualities that ought to inhere in our social relations. Any use of the concept that neglects this fact invites us to take with less than full seriousness the sort of claim we ought to be making when we say that human beings have "a right to life." Early fetal life does *not* yet possess even the minimal organic requirements for participation in the sphere of human rights. And like Mary Anne Warren, I do not believe that even the highly developed fetus can yet be said to have "an intrinsic right to life." Even so, I recognize that it is morally wise to extend such respect, de facto, to fetuses in late stages of gestation. But to do so is also and simultaneously to insist that rights are moral relations, born of our freedom as mature, other-regarding persons. In extending "a right to life" to fetuses in late stages of development, we are attesting that it is a good use of our freedom as agents, from a moral point of view, to do so.

. To argue that we may appropriately predicate to fetuses, in the late stages of gestation, "a right to life" does not mean, however, that the life of the pregnant woman should be overridden in decisions about late-stage pregnancies. Rather, it means that abortions, at least in the second half of gestation, are not to be undertaken without serious justifications. My own belief is that the physical and emotional well-being of the pregnant woman, as a valuable existent person, still outweighs the incremental value of the fetus her life sustains. Of course, it is true that in the later stages of pregnancy, abortions are matters of high risk for pregnant women. But doctors, who under most existing law have discretion as to whether an abortion is advisable at this stage, are themselves not likely to be "frivolous" about the decisions that confront them given the danger of late abortions.

A more difficult question than the issue of moral "imputation" of rights to late-gestating fetuses is the question of whether such fetuses should be deemed to have *de jure* or legal rights. As I have already observed, moral standards and legal standards are never to be identified. I have also referred to the growing number of cases in which courts, usually at a doctor's behest, have intervened on behalf of the "rights" of the fetus to force pregnant women to submit to cesarean sections when they preferred to deliver their babies by natural childbirth.[73] This type of imputation of "rights" under the law to late-gestating fetuses is new. To be sure, the Anglo-American common law tradition and some legal statutes in the United States confer legal rights on "unborn children," but these are usually "contingent rights,"[74] predicated on eventual birth. To legally invoke "the rights of the fetus" before birth as claims restraining a mother's right to elect the manner in which she wishes to bear her child is a quite different and troubling matter. It is particularly so in light of a growing and, as some believe, a massive legal trend toward ruling against women when any of their rights in relation to childbearing and childrearing are disputed. As one deeply mindful that misogyny is alive and well as a socio-structural reality, I believe it morally unwise to permit extensions of existing laws in the direction of granting *de jure* rights to fetuses, when women's well-being still matters so little before the law and when women's de facto rights are so poorly observed. In legal settings, someone must always "stand in" for the fetus to claim "its" rights. Invariably that person will be the husband, doctor, or lawyer, most frequently powerful men in this society whose judgment will be sustained against the pregnant woman's. One can recognize the great moral ambiguity in such cases and still maintain a principled defense of an existing woman's right, as the most affected party, to be the moral decision maker.

"Hard cases" aside, however, the greater moral respect we are wise to accord fetuses in late stages of gestation has very little bearing on the present abortion controversy. What few people recognize is that the overwhelming number of legal abortions in the United States — very conservatively, over 80 percent — are performed during the first trimester of pregnancy. Equally important is the trend in the United States and elsewhere toward early abortion *wherever abortion is legal*. In Sweden, where there is strong social support for encouraging women to detect, and where need be to terminate, pregnancy early, a norm of very early abortion — well before the third month of pregnancy — has been achieved.[75] In New York State, where numerous outpatient clinics perform legal abortions, the downward trend in the period of gestation during which abortions are performed has been marked since 1973. Furthermore, the availability of safe early abortion in New York has accounted for the large numbers of out-of-state residents seeking abortion there.[76] Women are obviously eager to have abortions as early as possible.

Second-trimester abortions sometimes are elected because it is at this stage of pregnancy that severe physical and mental defects can be detected in the fetus. More and more high-risk pregnancies are being monitored and tested for the presence of fetal abnormalities. Happily, 95 percent of tests conducted for this purpose reveal a healthy, properly developing fetus. The results of 5 percent of these tests, however, confront pregnant women with difficult choices, in which abortion may be the outcome. Nevertheless, abortions after the first three months of pregnancy are most often performed because the pregnant woman or girl is very poor and/or very young. That poverty militates against choosing abortion early is obvious enough, but in the United States it is the very young who have all but a tiny fraction of abortions performed after the fourth month:

> The strong inverse association of period of gestation and woman's age probably reflects the inexperience of the very young in recognizing the symptoms of pregnancy, their unwillingness to accept the reality of their situation, their ignorance about where to seek advice and help, and their hesitation to confide in adults. Economic considerations and, in many places, regulations prohibiting surgery on minors without parental consent also contribute to delays.[77]

Yet few pause to notice these data, while charges of genocide increase without reference to the considerable and mounting evidence that women are, responsibly, seeking early abortions when they have the social supports necessary to make such choices. The "hard cases" involving resort to abortion in the third trimester of pregnancy are, to say the least, rare. The increase in the total number of abortions in the United States can be used, as all data so frequently are used, to mystify the reality of what is going on in women's lives.

As I indicated earlier, abortions will continue to be available whether or not they are legal. Ironically, then, those persons insisting that a human life begins at conception or at an early stage of genetic human development may help to create a situation in which abortions, though they will not cease, will occur at a later stage of gestation. If we are forced to "honor" the sort of reasoning that predicates full humanity to early fetal life, we can safely predict that the trend toward early abortion will be reversed and that women who want to terminate their pregnancies early will find it more difficult to do so. A "life begins at conception" mentality constructs a social reality that requires us to accept not merely moral judgments about fetal life with which we disagree but life conditions that decrease the possibility of our terminating developing fetal life when it ought to be terminated — in the early stage of gestation. For any of us to celebrate the potentiality of a life we do not intend to care for concretely, as free moral agents, signifies not moral maturity but childish moral irresponsibility. To maintain that "society" (an abstract, not a concrete term) should welcome every conceptus simply because it has been conceived is to play fast and loose with the real character of our moral relations as persons.

Women, as childbearers, and all men as well need to understand that the quality of all our lives depends not on blindly embracing an automatic organic process but on the texture of concern and our very human, very moral readiness to provide for the children we choose to bring into the world. That the availability of safe surgical abortion in the early period of gestation, as a means of birth control, enhances our ability to make childbearing a moral choice is, I believe, an incontrovertible fact. If we turn back the clock, in the interest of early fetal "rights to life," we simultaneously will obstruct women in making the moral choices many of them have resolved to make in any case. We will undermine women who want to approach motherhood in a responsible way, aware of what they are undertaking and determining when they are prepared to provide the moral environment of caring imperative for the development of genuine personal existence. The "principled righteousness" of those who are determined to champion "the rights" of the embryo or fetus, treating women who have early abortions as criminals guilty of infanticide, is taking a heavy toll on the very social group that has made the greatest progress in recent decades toward assuming their full standing as moral persons — that is, women who have come to perceive that motherhood is no "natural condition" but, rather, a creative moral action to be undertaken in freedom, intelligently and with forethought.

Those who recognize that the processes of fetal development should be terminated early, precisely to avoid the "hard cases" where a woman's rights as a moral agent come to loggerheads with the value she imputes to the individuated human life form in her womb, need also recognize that only social conditions that make early abortions feasible are those that also make it *both* legal and, at least in the early stages of abortion, elective. To guarantee the feasibility of early abortion in any society, abortion must be decriminalized and pregnant women granted early discretion to choose it, medical reasons aside. When safe, legal, elective abortion is available, women experience strong social pressure for detecting an unwanted pregnancy early and terminating it with dispatch. Where abortion is illegal or discretion in the early stages of pregnancy is restricted to the medical profession, even before medical complications are detectable, social pressure operates in a different fashion. When the authority to make fundamental moral choices over one's own life is denied and placed at someone else's discretion, procrastination in confronting one's own reality, particularly if it means confronting another's power over you, is bound to ensue. Elective abortion is a precondition for early abortion.

The moral meaning of the act of abortion shifts, then, depending on the extent of the actual development of fetal life. Until the complexity of the fetal organism enables at least clear-cut potential, differentiated survival as a human body, recognizing the fetus as a human life should be viewed as an arbitrary classification. As the gestating fetus matures biologically, moving toward the point of functional maturation, the pregnant woman has good reason to impute claims to the fetus, grounded in intrinsic value, that weigh against her own. But from a moral point of view, there can be no "demand" that she take her own moral claim to life and well-being less seriously or as something readily to be discarded. What she — and the rest of us — need to understand is that it is best, when possible, to avoid living into situation where such conflicting claims arise. If a pregnancy is unwanted, a woman's moral obligation is best expressed by early recognition and termination of fetal life. That many women have yet to deliberate these matters seriously or to recognize that there is an obligation to intentionality in childbearing has much to do with female socialization and the objective disadvantage females incur in any society. The condemnatory ethos prevailing around the abortion debate in the United States is itself a force in delaying this "coming of age"[78] for many women. A society that does not extend genuine respect to women is also one that fails to recognize the moral issue at stake in whether women are helped or hindered in integrating decisions about abortion into their life plans. Without social support for women in making decisions about pregnancy and abortion, childbearing cannot be a humane and life-enhancing option.

If those who condemn all acts of abortion are successful, women's lives will be drastically altered for the worse. However, as I indicated much earlier, there are reasons for wishing that women were not forced to elect abortions, particularly second-trimester abortions, so often. It is incumbent that we, not our opponents, take seriously the question of how resort to abortion could be minimized. From a moral point of view, the proper way to frame this question is to ask what sort of society we would have to be in order to reduce resort to abortion, especially late abortion, *and* simultaneously enhance the quality and range of choice in most women's lives. I have already inferred what is to be my basic point in the concluding chapter — that only when we put the question this way can we approach the matter of compromise in the political arena without endangering the best moral wisdom we possess. And, until the question is framed this way, we are on firm moral ground in suspecting appeals to "political compromise" on the issue. Furthermore, we need to ask, "What is it that the proposers of compromise actually seek?"

8

Conclusion:
Beyond Abortion Politics

ROE V. WADE
AND THE CALL TO COMPROMISE

The calls for political compromise in the abortion controversy are accelerating. These calls converge on two groups who, though diametrically opposed morally, have been lumped together as "extremists." One group charged with "extremism" includes those who would make all, or nearly all, abortions illegal. The other includes persons like myself, feminists deeply committed to women's well-being in society, who insist that procreative choice is a substantive moral issue and elective abortion is morally appropriate. I am familiar with only one writer proposing compromise who so much as acknowledges that women's well-being is a concrete moral value that no attempt to resolve the debate can afford to summarily "compromise."[1]

Apparently there are a considerable number of people who, perceiving themselves as "moderates," view the political conflict over abortion as far too intense, hopelessly "emotional," and generally unseemly.[2] Those who portray themselves as moderates believe that both camps of "extremists" should tone down their "rhetoric" and proceed with greater dispassion and more "flexibility." The fundamental problem, however, is that the term *moderate* is usually embraced by either of the following two groups: (1) all those who believe that an individuated human being may be said to exist from any point between the implantation of the genetic code up to four months of gestation,[3] and (2) those who approve some or most therapeutic abortions but who do *not* support elective abortion or any discretion for women in the face of problem pregnancies. Unfortunately, such "moderates" rarely identify precisely what they think our social policy ought to be on abortion. What they express, rather, is general disapproval of those who believe clear-cut moral issues are at stake in the controversy, equating as morally "extreme" both the "life begins at conception" stance and the "women have rights against bodily invasion" position. Ironically, only a few Christian ethicists any longer support the former, so by these definitions of "moderate," even those who support very restrictive therapeutic abortion policies may count themselves "moderate."

It is important to recognize that nearly every "moderate" call to compromise already presupposes that something like "abortion on demand" is now the law of the land. Perhaps the greatest single "political coup" of the so-called pro-life movement has been its success in conveying to the public the assumption that "abortion on demand" is an accomplished fact of life in the United States. The scenario they invite us to adopt is that, in 1973, the Supreme Court, for inexorable reasons, suddenly and without provocation, struck down most existing laws against abortion as unconstitutional, thereby "creating" a divisive political issue where none had previously existed. Furthermore, according to this line of historical interpretation, the Supreme Court's decision in *Roe v. Wade* was a "winner-take-all affair," which tied the hands of legislators from that time forward and prevented elected officials from enacting "the will of the people" with respect to abortion. The scope of the problem of political compromise is often suppressed in just such unexpressed assumptions that this is the existing state of affairs with respect to abortion.

Two dynamics since the Supreme Court's 1973 *Roe v. Wade* decision lend plausibility to this story line and serve to reinforce its apparent truthfulness. One is the growing number of abortions, albeit early abortions, performed in the United States since 1973. The other concerns the relative lack of visibility of the politics surrounding abortion law reform prior to *Roe v. Wade*.[4] Before that decision, media focus on abortion was minimal and public awareness of the scope of illegal abortions muted. After legalization, the public became increasingly aware that abortion was widely practiced.

It is easy to overlook the fact that U.S. abortion laws, placed on the books in the nineteenth century at the behest of the medical profession, were more restrictive than those of most major non-Catholic nations.[5] From the late 1950s onward, groups, including some prestigious legal organizations,[6] organized for reform of these laws. The abortion law reform movement accelerated in the 1960s aided by the outcry surrounding the refusal of abortions to many of the 82,000 pregnant women who contracted German measles during the 1962-65 epidemic. Reliable estimates are that fifteen thousand deformed babies were born as a result. In that decade, doctors came to be prosecuted more often for performing abortions under existing laws, a fact that drew some medical professionals into reform efforts. The emergence of the women's movement was, however, the major watershed in abortion reform politics. Prior proposals for change had focused on legalizing abortion by "medicalizing" it — making abortion legal on a narrow range of medically approved grounds. Women's groups, who increasingly understood abortion reform as a women's rights issue, identified legal abortion as a basic condition of women's historical struggle for liberation.

Although some reforms were achieved in eighteen states, most notably in New York, where in 1970 a law was passed permitting medical discretion in abortion up to twenty-four weeks of gestation, for the most part legislators resisted reforms or accepted only the most restrictive ones.[7] As their reform efforts were rebuffed, women's groups, now the leaders of the reform movement, began to change their strategies. In ever-accelerating numbers, women turned to the courts to challenge the legality of restrictive abortion laws. Legal historian Eva R. Rubin has documented the flood of cases that appeared on lower-court dockets prior to *Roe v. Wade*. Though apparently no enthusiast for effecting social reforms through judicial litigation,[8] Rubin nevertheless acknowledges the problem women faced in appealing to state legislatures for change:

> Abortion, because of its position at the intersection of cross-pressures of so many kinds, was, in fact, a subject on which the state legislatures have had a particularly difficult time doing a careful and objective job of weighing and balancing values. Full of emotional dynamite and closely tied to religious beliefs, abortion was the kind of "bullet" issue that legislators have avoided when possible. Their decisions, when unavoidable, may be a response to the most vocal and politically potent organized interests, often well-financed minorities, rather than a reflection of judgement and balance.[9]

One might add that state legislatures have been slow throughout our history to redress discrimination or to protect citizens' rights, as their records on black people's civil rights and more recently on the Equal Rights Amendment attest.

As the appeals of lower-court rulings moved upward to the Supreme Court, it was simply no longer possible for the Court to side-step the question of the legality of abortion laws. The Court that agreed to hear the *Roe v. Wade* case was no longer a Warren Court, which had been noted for its activist sympathies in support of citizens' claims to "rights." Four of the members in 1973 had been appointed by President Nixon. In fact, speculation is widespread[10] that the *Roe-Wade* decision was delayed to avoid jeopardizing President Nixon's 1972 reelection campaign; in the end, all but one of the Nixon Court appointees voted with the 7-2 majority in the *Roe-Wade* decision.[11] Tremendous vilification of the Supreme Court followed *Roe v. Wade*, and Justice Harry Blackmun, author of the majority opinion, became a special target of those offended by the decision.[12]

Amid widespread discussion of the *Roe-Wade* decision, many legal scholars raised questions about whether the grounds on which the decision was made were optimal from a legal perspective.[13] Some, sympathetic to the substance of the decision, wished for a sharper appeal to legal principle in its framing.[14] Clearly, enough is known about the processes of negotiation among the majority concurring in the decision to help us understand why the constitutional claims invoked were not more explicitly drawn.[15] Like most Supreme Court decisions, in this respect *Roe v. Wade* was a compromise. What is startling, however, is the pervasive misperception about the actual substance of the decision and the attendant confusion as to its effects. Many ethicists, who should know better, speak as though abortion on demand became the law of the land after *Roe v. Wade*. They presume that everywhere in this country abortions may be secured, without legal constraint, throughout most of pregnancy. This is a palpably false interpretation of what has transpired. To be sure, well over half of the states had at the time massively con-stricting laws regarding abortion. After the *Roe-Wade* decision formulated the acceptable limits of legislation, all laws, save New York State's, fell outside these provisions. But it is libelous to imply, as many do, that *Roe v. Wade* "legitimated" abortion on demand. The majority opinion "balanced" clear-cut and conflicting claims in a manner, it must be added, that left few of the protagonists in the legal battle satisfied.

In the interests of representing the "extremes" in the abortion con-troversy as falling between those who consider each and every act of abortion "homicide" and those who support the "permissive"

Roe-Wade decision, "moderates" usually fail to remark that many women, in particular, were every bit as distressed by the *Roe-Wade* decision as were the "abortion is homicide" proponents, although for different reasons.[16] What the present politics of abortion ignore is that *Roe v. Wade* gave very provisional and extremely limited support for a woman's reproductive rights and explicitly denied any absolute right to control one's own body. Under the concepts of "liberty" and "rights to privacy" held to be implicit in the Constitution, the Court ruled that a woman may not be unduly constrained from exercising discretion to choose abortion in the first trimester of pregnancy; that abortion may be regulated for reasons of health until viability; and that after viability abortion may be proscribed in the interest of protecting fetal life.[17] In other words, while the Court found that the Constitution protected a woman's choice in the first trimester of pregnancy, after that time other competing interests, including the state's right to regulate health care and to protect fetal life, could be balanced against a woman's right to liberty and privacy. Regulations that restrict abortions for health reasons are permissible in the second trimester of pregnancy, a ruling that implied that doctors deserve discretion in this period, and protection of fetal rights is germane in the third trimester.[18]

The majority in *Roe v. Wade* did agree that there was no precedent in constitutional law for holding that the fetus is a person, a finding that has occasioned little dissent among legal scholars. But *Roe v. Wade* expressly permitted regulation of abortion, though not absolute prohibition, during the second trimester and was vague as to what might constitute undue interference in the first. Under *Roe v. Wade*, legislatures clearly are free to insist that the interests of the fetus completely override the woman's in the third trimester of pregnancy. The framework established by *Roe v. Wade* was, in no sense, "abortion on demand."

Many women remain adamantly opposed to the *Roe-Wade* decision, recognizing in its arguments a relegitimation of the ancient and expected logic so familiar to those who know women's history. Once again, when women's role as childbearer is at stake, reasons of state strongly prevail. Rubin aptly summarizes the response of many women's groups to the Court's determination:

> The women's groups and some others declared that governmental manipulation of the individual's reproductive life was

totally reprehensible, and that both "compulsory pregnancy" and compulsory sterilization laws involved state interference in what should be completely a matter for private decision. Since they saw no justification for state regulation of any kind, Justice Blackmun's division of the pregnancy into trimesters, with the state's interest becoming significant when the fetus became viable, was unacceptable. Among other things, they charged that Blackmun's distinction involved a doctrine of contingent constitutionality, making the woman's right dependent on the state of her pregnancy. The woman is free to choose until a certain point in time; after that "the woman and her fetus revert to state ownership." The viability distinction, they complained, also has the objectionable result of tying the woman's rights to the current state of science and medicine; the woman's right to choose will disappear when scientists are able to keep all fetuses alive in the laboratory. Indeed, they maintain, with the breathtaking advances in medical technique that now allow test-tube fertilization, the removal of a fertilized egg from one woman to another (perhaps even to a man), fetal surgery, ovary and testes transplants, and the possibilities of cloning and genetic manipulation, rights cannot be made dependent on the latest developments in bioengineering. A whole new jurisprudence may be needed to deal with man's [sic] ability to alter the human reproductive process at will, but until it is developed and accepted, human rights should attach, as they always have, only to those persons already born. Birth is a clear, recognizable fact; "all else is mystique and conjecture."[19]

Meanwhile, many women's organizations have consented to support the *Roe-Wade* decision, mindful that the time is not ripe to secure more adequate recognition of women's legal and moral standing and aware that the *Roe v. Wade* framework represents a political compromise significantly more just than the previously existing state of affairs. However, those who broach political compromise without reference to the fact that, for many, *Roe v. Wade* is already a dramatic compromise mislead us by portraying all *Roe v. Wade* defenders as "extremist."

At one end of the political spectrum in the abortion controversy are those who endorse state prohibition of all abortion. The granting of exceptions in the case of rape or to preserve a pregnant woman's life is already a "compromise" from the standpoint of this group. At the other political "extreme" are those who believe that there are *no* reasons of state sufficient to override a woman's procreative choice under any circumstances. Adherents to this view are, in fact, a diverse group, consisting of political libertarians who distrust state regulation in all or nearly all circumstances; religious anarchists (including a sizable number of Catholics)[20] who believe that deeply personal matters involving claims of conscience, such as marriage and childbearing, should remain outside the province of the state; those for whom the idea "life begins at birth" is as self-evident as "life begins at conception" is for others; and, with some overlap from the preceding categories, feminists who regard control of procreation as the institutional linchpin in women's historical subjugation[21] and any "compromise" with respect to procreative choice a tactic to forestall women's liberation.

It is difficult to know how many genuinely noncompromising "extremists" there actually are at either end of the political spectrum, but it goes without saying that within this existing political spectrum, supporters of *Roe v. Wade* deserve to be counted as political "moderates." An article in *Commonweal* attempting to counter the image of "pro-life" activists as zealots who condemn all abortions[22] portrayed many of the "pro-life" proponents interviewed as sympathetic to therapeutic abortion under certain circumstances. Yet such persons remain active in a movement that seeks, uncompromisingly, to foreclose access to all but a few legal abortions. When we fail to recognize that pro-choice activists have already compromised, we skew the actual political situation. Women like myself who believe that the feminist "extreme" is correct, being soberly realistic about the efforts of male-dominated institutions to control procreation historically, already have consented to a genuine balancing of legitimate interests. From our perspective, *Roe v. Wade* is such a decision. Many of us have been willing to accept it, however, not merely for politically pragmatic reasons, but because we grant the salience of the moral debate about the value of fetuses in the later stages of gestation. We await some sign that those who would foreclose nearly all legal abortion are prepared to extend the same concrete recognition of moral claims regarding women's well-being. This, we insist, is a requirement of "compromise."

Given the reigning mood of disapproval toward the Supreme Court for "getting us into politics" on this issue, it should be stressed that the *Roe-Wade* decision, fueled by a growing avalanche of lower-court litigations on the question, did not activate the "politics of abortion" but shifted the political balance. Until the legal battles began, anti-abortionists had controlled the field, reinforced by the lethargy of the legislatures that hitherto resisted calls for change. After *Roe v. Wade*, the tables were turned, and political opponents of legal abortion were forced to organize to reassert their interests. It is small wonder that those who excoriate the Court for "politicizing" the abortion issue are invariably those whose sympathies resided with the pre-1973 status quo. Women and members of the medical and legal professions who had been working for abortion reform for two decades were well aware, as we all should be, that the charge of "politicizing" is always hurled at those who seek or mandate change, while those who deny the need for change consistently appeal to some presumed pristine "nonpolitical" state of affairs.[23]

In the wake of *Roe v. Wade*, anti-abortionists were forced to become *overtly* political, a fact they deeply resented. Pro-choice political organizations were already in place, although their ranks swelled in response to the ensuing successes of the anti-abortion movement. Two specific developments were to shape "pro-life" politics in fundamental ways: the response of the Catholic hierarchy to the *Roe-Wade* decision and the active mobilization of Protestant fundamentalists into abortion politics.

In 1973, the Roman Catholic bishops, for the first time in modern U.S. history, explicitly called for civil disobedience to resist laws legalizing abortion.[24] And their rhetoric in this regard did not quickly abate.[25] Although long active in the effort to shape public policy, the National Conference of Catholic Bishops took the unprecedented stand in response to *Roe v. Wade* that obedience to law could be suspended on moral grounds. A further unprecedented step was taken in 1975, when the bishops sponsored a "Pastoral Plan for Pro-Life Activities," authorizing comprehensive grass-roots mobilization against abortion and openly endorsing a "single-issue" approach to abortion politics. The plan specifically encouraged Catholics to oppose each and every political candidate who supported the legalization of abortion.[26]

Those of us who have criticized publicly the National Conference of Bishops' actions on abortion have been accused of virulent anti-Catholicism,[27] without reference to the particularities of our objections to their activities. My own view, as should be clear, is not that the Catholic bishops, or any other group of Christians, should stay "out of politics" or refrain from being political about morality. I do object, and strenuously, however, to single-issue politics because, given the U.S. political process, the net result is inevitably the punishing of politicians in abstraction from their total contribution to a broad-based social justice agenda. This, of course, has been the effect of "pro-life" politics, insofar as it has had an effect — the replacement of moderates and liberals committed to a fairly broad social justice agenda with conservatives who have no such vision.[28] Furthermore, it was out of fear of just such consequences that many conscientious Roman Catholics became troubled by the bishops' actions.[29] But the primary reason for my opposition to the bishops' initiatives in "pro-life" politics concerns their professed moral position, which is from many perspectives debatable and, in my considered opinion, palpably wrong. Many have ducked the normative issue in criticizing the bishops' stance, but I have no desire to do so. They, along with leaders of other Christian groups, have tried to foist upon society as "rationally justified" a position about abortion whose "traditional" roots do not rest in concern for the unborn and whose contemporary rationales for deciding when a human life begins are simply not adequate. Not to say this is to abrogate the normative role incumbent on the Christian ethicist.

A second fateful development that has shaped "pro-life" politics in the meanwhile was discussed in the early chapters of this book: the unprecedented liaison in Protestant circles between the previously apolitical or antipolitical fundamentalist Christian groups and conservative, New Right political organizations.[30] From 1978 onward, newly affluent, media-sophisticated fundamentalist preachers have attempted to mobilize their followers, previously almost exclusively among the poor, to identify with the hard-core political Right. This effort has succeeded in eroding long-standing fundamentalist inhibitions about direct involvement in "worldly" affairs. Although, as I have noted, a wedge has been driven between the Reagan administration and many New Right religious adherents because the so-called social issues have been given back-burner priority by Washington because of economic problems, the affinity between Reagan and the New Right is not dead, and the liaison probably will be revived as the 1984 presidential election approaches. The ethos generated by the New Right, charged with the most flagrant and vicious hostility to all but compliant women, pervades "pro-life" politics, in spite of the efforts of some Catholics within the movement to formulate a program more sympathetic to the "unfortunate" woman facing a difficult pregnancy.

The so-called pro-life groups continue to reinforce the impression that *Roe v. Wade* was a "winner-take-all" decision. Much of their energy has been devoted to reversing this decision at the national level through congressional legislation and efforts to unseat "unsympathetic" senators and congressional representatives. While denouncing the Supreme Court for undermining the power of state judiciaries and undercutting the "will of the people" in *Roe v. Wade*, many "pro-life" groups nevertheless united in launching the ultimate bypass of state legislatures by proposing various constitutional amendments.

One set of amendments — the "Human Life Amendments" — would grant fetuses from conception full standing as citizens under the Constitution. The adamant and all but unanimous opposition of the legal profession to this staggeringly novel, ill-conceived proposal led to its (at least) temporary demise in Senate committee. Apart from the unprecedented departure from our legal traditions that designating a conceptus, an embryo, or a fetus as a person would represent, some versions of the "Human Life Amendments" also guaranteed "a right to life." Legal scholars were quick to observe that "the right to life" is not a constitutional guarantee for anyone in this society. Rather, the Constitution restricts government from depriving anyone of his or her life without "due process" or "equal protection" under the law. As Rubin notes, making the "right to life" a constitutional guarantee would amount to a "revolutionary change" in our philosophy of government, mandating "support for life not only from the cradle to the grave, but from the moment of conception to the moment of death — 'from womb to tomb.'"[31] Another proposed constitutional amendment, the Hatch Amendment, which has a better chance of passage, returns complete freedom to state legislatures to restrict abortions in any way.[32] In essence, it totally undercuts *Roe v. Wade* by vitiating the policy parameters staked out in that decision.

If so-called pro-life groups did not remain passive in the face of *Roe v. Wade*, neither did the state legislatures. In the two months following the decision, no less than eighty bills relating to abortion were introduced in state legislatures. By 1981, the number was over two hundred.[33] As I have noted, the *Roe-Wade* decision was somewhat vague, both as to what sorts of constraints would "unduly burden" a woman's discretion in the first trimester of pregnancy and in terms of when "viability" could be said to have occurred. Legislatures were quick to establish prerequisite conditions for the performance of abortions in the first trimester:

> These conditions included reporting and record-keeping procedures, requirements of written consent by the woman, consent of husband or parents, waiting periods, counselling, and similar provisions. Nebraska required notification of the grandparents! Many laws contained provisions protecting persons and institutions with religious scruples from being forced to perform abortions.[34]

Requiring a husband's consent to an abortion was overruled by the Supreme Court on the grounds that it violated *Roe v. Wade*.[35] Less-clear determinations have been made by the Court, however, on the issue of parental consent. The issue remains clouded, and the requirement has been continued or reinstated in many places.[36] Given the increasing number of teenage pregnancies, such continuing requirements, contrary to *Roe v. Wade*, have served to limit the option of abortion for the young. The Reagan administration has also established administrative restrictions on minors' receiving contraceptives without parental consent, though this is being contested in the courts.[37] Forty states have passed legislation exempting medical personnel from having to perform an abortion if they oppose it on moral or religious grounds. The Supreme Court has ruled, in *Poelker v. Doe*, that public hospitals receiving government funding may refuse to perform abortions. Furthermore, the trend of the Court's decisions since *Roe v. Wade* has been to make it more difficult for women to elect early abortion. Federal Medicaid funding of all but a few therapeutic abortions has been cut off, and with the *Poelker-Doe* decision, medical facilities for abortion are now not available at all in some areas. The *Roe-Wade* decision, then, has not prevented states from regulating abortion. Furthermore, the view Justice Blackmun expressed in *Roe v. Wade* concerning women's health and well-being has been, to say the least, muted in subsequent Supreme Court decisions aimed at clarifying the *Roe-Wade* decision. Justice Lewis Powell, writing for the majority in decisions that enable government not to use public funds for abortion, went so far as to insist that "the State has a valid and important interest in encouraging normal childbirth," which "exists throughout the course of a woman's pregnancy."[38]

Since 1977, the growing strength of the new "right to life" movement has been felt even more powerfully at the level of state legislatures. All but sixteen states have cut off public funding for abortions, and many have also terminated funding for family planning groups and organizations involved in abortion referral. Indirect efforts to pressure doctors have been used. In Minnesota, for example, a law was proposed requiring doctors to make public the number of abortions they performed and the fees they charged for them.[39] In many states, doctors are now subject to criminal prosecution if they fail to take every conceivable step to keep alive any fetus surviving an abortion. As Rubin noted, medical pregnancy tests, waiting periods, counseling sessions, and consent forms are now standard requirements in many states before an abortion may be secured.

City and county governments also have been mobilized in the crusade to circumvent the *Roe-Wade* decision. A complex law passed by the Akron, Ohio, city council, the most thwarting of the Supreme Court's intent to date, will be reviewed by the Court this term, now that the district court in Ohio has struck down four (only four!) of its fifteen provisions. Furthermore, the Akron ordinance already has become the model for laws in eleven states. Rubin details its provisions:

> The so-called Akron Ordinance went beyond regulation of facilities and equipment and provided a complex arrangement of conditions designed to discourage those considering abortions. It required a burdensome waiting period, notice to the supposed father or the woman's parents or guardian, parental consent for minors, and written consent by the woman herself. In addition, the ordinance required that the physician give the woman a lecture on the physical development of the fetus, explain to her that "the unborn child is a human being from the moment of conception," and describe things such as its "appearance, mobility, tactile sensitivity, including pain perception or response, brain and heart functions," and the presence of internal and external organs. In addition, the woman must be told that the fetus may be

viable if twenty-two weeks have elapsed and that she would have no parental rights in a live fetus [sic]. The ordinance also placed various restrictions on abortion clinics and prohibited the use of saline abortions after the first trimester, requiring the doctor to use the technique most likely to save the life of the fetus if the possibility of viability exists.[40]

This summary of the political maneuverings in response to *Roe v. Wade* should clarify that the heart of anti-abortion politics has been, and will continue to be, the effort to reverse the one aspect of *Roe v. Wade* that opened the way to genuine, if limited, procreative choice for women, namely, the acknowledgment that elective abortion in the first trimester of pregnancy is legally legitimate. Although the majority opinion in *Roe v. Wade* identified the medical profession as the proper locus of decision making throughout the greater part of pregnancy, and in tone and nuance made pregnancy a medical issue, the majority nevertheless granted limited discretion to women during early pregnancy under legal provisions of privacy and liberty. The clear aim of so-called right-to-life politics, then, *is to revoke this limited discretion*. We are being called upon to "compromise" on this already restricted provision.

Few "moderates" in the abortion controversy, who appeal for "less zeal" on all sides, display that they understand the actual state of affairs in abortion politics. As long as the parameters set down by *Roe v. Wade* are perceived as representing an "extremist" position, there will be little room for rational discourse around the options that face us. The truth is that in large sections of this nation, women can secure abortions only by passing through a process of legally legitimated harassment, which also ensnares medical personnel who perform abortions. In some states, abortions are not easy to secure at all. At present, actions to obstruct legal abortions do not, in most instances, prevail, but such efforts often delay the point in pregnancy at which women, especially poor women and young girls, may secure abortions. When women who seek abortions — and their number is increasing — confront unwanted pregnancy early, the social and legal pressure generated by right-to-life politics most likely will forestall their efforts to secure early abortion. Those states that genuinely have attempted to comply with the Supreme Court's provisions by not unduly encumbering women's decisions in early pregnancy are few in number, and efforts to devise novel encumbrances are not likely to cease soon. The so-called pro-life movement is powerful, resourceful, and well funded — by most testimonies, far better funded and organized than pro-choice groups.[41]

In light of this situation, what are those of us to do who support a definite, if not unlimited, right of women to procreative choice and who disagree with claims that early-gestating fetal life is fully individuated human life? Along with proponents of fetal "rights to life," we are portrayed as "uncompromising" and, not infrequently, as "zealots." I do not believe that appeals to compromise get far, precisely because the politics of abortion are dramatically obscured by these charges. Nor am I of a mind to hear suggestions, such as a recent one by a thoughtful Catholic, that because the human status of early fetal life is a somewhat "complex" question, a "compromise" might be struck permitting abortions up to two months of pregnancy.[42] Such a proposal already implicitly assumes the position I have protested here — that the full human status of early fetal life is the sole, relevant moral issue in arriving at compromise.

Until women's well-being, concretely and uncompromisingly, becomes a positive concern of purported "compromisers," we are, I believe, wise to demur. But what if we approach the question another way, a way that, I submit, has strong legitimation from a moral point of view? What could those who support both procreative choice for women and respect for fetal life *do together* to simultaneously reduce the necessity of frequent resort to abortion and to enhance women's well-being in society? Until both commitments are forthrightly expressed in "the call to compromise," we will, I believe, continue to find ourselves at war with each other over abortion.

RESPECT FOR WOMEN;
RESPECT FOR THE SOON-TO-BE-BORN:
INTERRELATED POSSIBILITIES

The new social reality in the abortion controversy is public knowledge of the frequency with which women resort to abortion. I have argued that abortions have never been rare throughout history and across societies, but they have become frequent in the last century, even in the United States prior to legal abortion. With a degree of elective discretion now legalized, the absolute number of abortions has increased, although there is a marked trend toward earlier termination of pregnancies. Both public awareness of abortion and a rising-rate of abortion among U.S. women of childbearing age have astonished and frightened many people.

It is in the ambience of this reaction that so-called right-to-life politics move. The unspoken accusations forming in the minds of many people, it seems to me, go something like this: "Aren't women becoming too 'uppity' and too particular about timing their pregnancies? Are not women becoming too sexually active, experimenting too much, casually jumping into and out of bed with too many men? Can the 'sexually liberated' woman really be the 'good and pure' mother most of us believe we had? Are not abortions evidence of women's loss of caring or their reluctance to be self-giving?" Such unarticulated judgments, I believe, shape the ethos of discussions about abortion, and it does no good to pretend that they do not operate in the abortion debate.

I have identified two developments that contribute to the increased number of abortions in the United States — the growing anxiety about the safety of long-term use of oral contraceptives and the accelerating rise in teenage pregnancies. While ever-larger numbers of teenage children are themselves bearing children, probably many more are seeking abortions when they are in a position to secure them. We know also, from both cross-cultural and U.S. domestic studies, that socioeconomic factors increasingly influence the demography of abortion in vital ways. I have argued that economic pressures are not, in a late-capitalist, industrial, urban setting, mere "externals" that can be shunted aside when women ponder the meaning of childbearing. To be able to provide for a child in our world requires a genuine margin of economic security. I believe that the escalating economic crisis, severely curtailing most women's life options, is a major source of the accelerating rate of abortion.

If we are ever to become genuinely serious about reducing the need for abortions in the United States, we must cut through the miasma of fear and suspicion about women's sexuality[43] and confront, by concrete analysis of women's lives, the conditions that lead women to resort to frequent abortion. It should be clear that I do not imagine that all abortions can or should be eliminated. The availability of safe surgical, elective abortion in the early stages of pregnancy is considered an abomination only by those who value *potential* human life more than they value existing women's lives. But if those intent on reducing the number of abortions are serious, they will have to take with full and nonjudgmental seriousness the conditions of women's lives and women's social reality.

Much earlier in this book, I identified four groups of females most likely to face unwanted pregnancies. Putting aside those tragic cases where a pregnant woman, desiring a child, discovers that the fetus gestating in her body is deformed or harboring genetic disease,[44] women or girls now confront the abortion question (1) when, as is the case with many young girls, they become sexually active without an adequate grasp of contraceptive measures or the possible consequences of sexual involvement; (2) when they engage in sexual activity without contraception out of carelessness, resistance from their partners, or fear that taking contraceptive precautions would make them "loose women"; (3) when either their own or their partner's contraceptives fail; and (4) when they are the victims of sexual violence. Probably the largest number of abortions occur in the third category, and here foundational economic pressures often determine the outcome. We can make very little progress in reducing the number of abortions in this category without greatly strengthening the degree of economic opportunity and overall social security for the vast majority of females in this society. Many women, we may be sure, might elect to bear an additional child if they could be certain that doing so would not threaten their families' access to better health care, food, and housing. It should be obvious, however, that to reduce the number of abortions resulting from contraceptive failure also requires breakthroughs in female and male contraception, changed male attitudes toward contraception, and new patterns of institutional life that would place equal emphasis on male responsibility for procreation and long-term care and nurturance of children. These developments, I insist, are not imminent, the more so because many "right-to-life" advocates are obdurate opponents of efforts to improve available contraception or to change sex-role patterns in the family.

Almost as often, girls and women become pregnant for the reasons summarized in categories one and two above. Abortion clinic personnel and agencies providing contraceptive information and abortion referral report that a considerable number of patients who have frequent "repeat abortions" fall into the second category — those who seem unable or unwilling to take contraceptive precautions. This group of "repeaters," victims of the "passive female syndrome" intrinsic to female socialization in a patriarchal ethos,[45] are hardly positive candidates for motherhood, any more than are the many young girls who find themselves becoming mothers in our society. What we are to do about changing this pattern of female socialization in a society that despises the strong, self-directed, "responsible" woman is a problem usually only feminists address. Yet we must not allow ourselves to be silenced by those who perpetuate the disvaluation of women, including many religious groups who work in the anti-abortion arena and ignore the connection between their daily actions and rhetoric and the abortion scene they deplore. Certainly the woman-child who resists acting on her own behalf to prevent pregnancy is the "successful" product of a society that not only tolerates but advocates institutional sexism, including its manifestation in female passivity. But such "successful" psychological entrapment can be addressed only by a deeper appropriation of a feminist social agenda that challenges such female socialization at its root. This agenda, including the broadest interpretations of what social justice for women entails, is the key to eradicating much of the self-destructive behavior that leads many to repeat abortions.

Because I presume, perhaps optimistically, that most people in the United States endorse legal abortion for women and girls who are victims of rape and incest,[46] we can put aside this category when asking how the need for abortion might be minimized. However, we cannot afford to overlook rape and incest altogether if we wish to examine the issue of "compromise" regarding abortion. Ethicists frequently dismiss any mention by feminists of the accelerating rate of sexual violence in the United States as irrelevant to the abortion question, because victims of rape and incest, they contend, make up only the smallest fraction of women seeking abortions.[47] Many point out that last year, under the Hyde Amendment provisions that allow Medicaid funding of abortions for rape and incest victims, less than one hundred abortions were performed. Admittedly, the number of abortions sought because of rape and incest is small compared with other categories, but it is naive in the extreme to imagine that the number of victims willing to submit to the cumbersome and humiliating procedures needed to secure government funding for such abortions tells the story accurately. In many states prior to legalization, and under the Hyde Amendment, any rape or incident of incest must be reported at the time it occurs if a woman would have a subsequent claim on Medicaid funds for a legal abortion. Given this fact, it is astonishing that *any* poor woman qualified under Hyde in the past year!

What remains important with respect to social policy on abortion is the escalating rate of sexual violence against women in the United States.[48] If it were ever the case, it is no longer the statistically rare woman who has been the victim of rape or incest. The combined number of wife batterings, rapes, and incidents of incest annually in this country is staggering. I believe there are far more of these occurrences each year than there are women who have abortions. Nor do rape estimates reflect the magnitude of the problem. Marital rape is not even considered a crime in many states, although a recent study suggests that 19 percent of all women have experienced rape in marriage.[49] The scope of family violence, which is chiefly violence against women or girls and not infrequently sexual violence against them, is one of our best-kept, dirty little secrets as a nation, in spite of widespread pioneering efforts in the last decade to "tell the story." It is my conviction that the tenor of so-called right-to-life politics is exacerbating the hostility toward women on which the reality of social violence against women feeds. It does not matter, in my opinion, that many, probably most, individuals who are anti-abortion activists themselves deplore such violence. The rhetoric and implicit assumptions in right-to-fetal-life politics about the "moral iniquity" of women who seek abortions, now so many in number, fuel the legitimation of this pervasive and growing reality. But even putting aside this legitimation of abuse toward women, every proponent of restrictive legislation for abortion (for therapeutic purposes only) needs to recognize that the de facto consequences of such policy is to mandate a highly bureaucratic, inhumane procedure for every prospective victim of rape or incest. Already, by FBI estimates, only 10 percent of rapes are reported each year.[50] Mandating more harassing procedures for abortion will only make it more likely that women will not seek assistance after rape.

Even though most female victims of sexual abuse escape pregnancy, only a blindfolded observer of the U.S. scene can ignore the strong connection between women's actual social experience of sexual abuse and many women's burgeoning sense of what is at stake when elective abortion is denied. And no one serious about actually reducing the need for abortion can address that issue without also addressing the escalating problem of sexual violence. Not to do so bespeaks a moral idealism unencumbered by compassion for the real nature of our moral problems. I know of no way to hazard an accurate guess regarding the number of abortions related to sexual abuse, though I am certain that if sexual abuse by spouses or regular mates is included, the number is not insignificant. However, the salient point here is not to establish some hypothetical ratio of the unwanted pregnancies caused by such abuse. Rather, it is to insist that concern to reduce the resort to abortion must be coupled with concern to actively oppose the growing incidence of sexual violence against women.[51]

I have stressed my conviction that only uncompromising, extensive support for a feminist agenda of social justice for women can hold out any hope of reducing the need for abortions in this society. Yet, in discussions of political "compromise" on abortion, a feminist analysis of the way in which our social institutions reinforce the problematic of women's historical subjugation is usually sacrificed. If necessary, we must risk being accused of obduracy, excessive zeal, and moral rigidity in order to press this analysis. Tomorrow, if by the wave of a wand, every child, woman, and man were to become passionately concerned about the well-being of every fertilized ovum but still no change was forthcoming in our practices and attitudes toward female persons, the discernible effect would *not* be enhanced concern for the value of human life but continuing depreciation of women as functional, procreative appendages to the rest of (male) society. Failure to grasp this is a good index of the scope of misogyny in our society and in our ethics. If we do not grasp the reality of women's status as full and valued members of our species, we dare not speak of "compromise" in abortion politics.

From a serious, historically informed feminist perspective, the reasoning of the *Roe-Wade* decision is, at best, a partial expression of a feminist vision of respect for women. The reality of elective abortion during the first trimester of pregnancy, where states have respected *Roe v. Wade*, has established the *minimum* condition for procreative choice. Nevertheless, few would claim that abortion is an optimally desirable means of birth control. Its legal availability and safety have given women a measure of definite negative control over pregnancy, which has released many from a fatalistic connection to "natural process." But, as yet, our society pays next to no attention to establishing positive conditions and supports that would enable women to embrace the procreative option of motherhood. Witness the fate of day-care funding and earlier efforts to improve pre- and postnatal health care. Under the circumstance, legal abortion functions as a barrier not only to protect women from untimely pregnancies but equally to shield them from our massive social irresponsibility toward living children. Again, anyone serious about reducing the need for abortion must confront the lack of social support for childbearing that women experience daily. Otherwise, restrictive abortion will continue to mean what it has always meant — a social trade-off between women's well-being and society's expressed, but unenacted, and therefore abstract, moral concern for the value of infant life.

Many have claimed that the ongoing, frequent practice of abortion, institutionalized over time, will foster and feed growing disrespect for human life. Once abortion as a social practice gains wide-ranging acceptance, so this argument goes, society either will cease to revere human life or will treat it more cheaply. It is difficult to counter this "slippery slope" argument,[52] a name given by ethicists to any appeals to conditions presumed inevitable once the "precipice" of a given policy line has been crossed. Yet it is surely not self-evident that a nation such as Japan, with the most permissive abortion legislation in the world since 1948, has, as a result, become a less humane society.[53] In fact, we may argue that Japan, whose abortion policies were permissive when ours were most restrictive, has exemplified greater concern for its peoples' welfare than has the United States. But regardless of how one perceives the "slippery slope" contention regarding abortion, I believe that my point is indisputable: that early elective abortions can be proscribed only at the cost of worsening women's social conditions and reinforcing attitudes of human disrespect for women. How a society could conceivably "enhance respect for human life" while simultaneously actively undercutting the conditions of well-being and respect for women is the issue that anti-abortionists need to face, but don't.

I have argued that fetuses are not yet agents — neither "innocent persons" nor "unjust aggressors." A conceptus, an embryo, or an early-gestating fetus are *potential* forms of what will become individuated human life. When a woman says no to that potentiality, she already has weighed a broad range of values, relational realities, and specific life circumstance. If she is inclined to say no, she will be eager to terminate that potential life as quickly as possible, unless, of course, she is caught in bureaucratic procedures that slow her access to abortion or is trapped in the evasions and denials that society imbues in its female children. If we know anything about these matters, we know that encouraging women to seek early abortions succeeds only where *a strong social ethos of acceptance of procreative choice prevails.*[54]

Our goal, and the goal of all persons of irenic spirit, should be to support those policies that actually will minimize the need for abortion by furthering genuine procreative choice. Some "right-to-life" proponents, arguing that anti-abortion politics incorporate active concern for the well-being of women, have reached out to already pregnant women with offers of support and counsel during the processes of childbearing. But far more than this is necessary if the number of abortions is to be reduced. Helping the pregnant woman to embrace her pregnancy, rather than experiencing it as something "unwanted," does not address women's well-being as a caste. Given the reality of most women's lives in this nation, such "help" smacks of the dubious connotation "charity" has come to impart whenever persons respond to others as isolated individuals apart from the social reality that creates their dilemmas. Most pregnant women have evaded, and will continue to evade, such "charity" when faced with painful choices about pregnancy. I believe they are right to do so; for the attitudes conveyed bespeak "forgiveness" for the "fallen woman" rather than tough-minded understanding of the realities with which women have to cope.

Much, of course, can be done to support girls and women who want to carry their pregnancies to term. I believe most pro-choice proponents join me in advocating support services for women and girls who choose to give birth. But "right-to-life" efforts to "support" women in this process fall short of providing actual support in that they so readily adhere to a functionalist view of female procreation in which pro-creative *choice* has no place. This notion of women as functional, pro-creative members of society must give way to respect for women as fully autonomous, unconditionally valuable members of our moral community. Women have every right to be treated as intelligent, competent decision makers, capable of weighing the values and principles relevant to pregnancy in the context of the full range of their relationships, responsibilities, and obligations. And women have as much right as men to embrace their own well-being as a positive moral good and to be taken seriously in their process of decision making. So much "right-to-life" rhetoric implies that servility is a moral virtue in women. Servility is never a moral virtue, either in men or in women.[55] Nor are our responses to childbearing exempt from this rule. Women, like men, may indeed elect self-sacrifice, but self-giving is no virtue apart from free choice. Furthermore, those who lack self-respect also lack the capacity for genuine self-giving.

So-called pro-life politics, intent as it is on eliminating all elective abortion, is so suffused with the implicit judgment that women are *not* responsible decision makers that it is difficult to visualize how a common social agenda between antagonists in the abortion debate could emerge. On the one side we have those who claim that they or, on a more abstract level, society should "stand in" for the "rights" of the fetus from conception, or from some very early point when pregnancy is not yet even unequivocally verifiable. On the other side we have the most affected party, namely, women who are pregnant and wish not to be. The distinctive nature of the biological experience of pregnancy is such that neither group can "win" without adversely affecting the "interests" of the other. This fact gives abortion politics its nonnegotiable reality. Unless those who are eager to "stand in" for the fetus exercise some restraint in what they deem as their "good work," the lives of women facing unwanted pregnancies must, necessarily and unequivocally, fall hostage to their "righteousness." Until we become aware that trade-offs between the protection of early fetal life and women's well-being are inevitable, little progress can be made.

Serious negotiations, if there ever are any, in a political process begin only when the tangible interests of both sides have been conceded. To date, in all talk of compromises and moderation around abortion policy, the legitimacy of women's interests have been treated with disdain. Nor has it been acknowledged that in supporting the *Roe-Wade* decision many women actually have assented to the legitimacy of legal restrictions on abortion, including restrictions that subscribe that a fetal life deserves, in late gestation, to be counted as one of us. My question to those who counsel compromise is this: To what extent have your proposals addressed these facts and moral concerns? If they have not, proposals for compromise will lack the evenhandedness that serious, not rhetorical, negotiations require.

We may hope to move beyond abortion politics, but that will happen only when "pro-life" advocates among us link their concern for fetal life with an ethically adequate concern for the well-being of women and the children they bear. The focus of our moral concern must shift to the overall conditions of childbearing in this society. It must entail not merely a patronizing concern for women already facing "problem pregnancies," but a strong and realistic commitment to social support for those women who wish to bear children as well as genuine respect for those who choose not to do so. When the conditions for "the quality of life" (certainly no mere slogan) of women and children deteriorate, as is certainly the case at present, "pro-life" passion for saving fetuses has the actual consequence of further impoverishing the conditions of human existence. The human cost of women bearing unwanted children is high — for them, for their children, and for the community.[56] Our society detests and punishes "the failed mother" as ruthlessly as it punishes any other "fallen woman."

Many women, I believe, share my wish that new lines be drawn and fresh and more creative initiatives be undertaken in the politics of abortion. By frequent repetition, the rhetoric and arguments on all sides indeed grow stale. I have met many women who profess themselves "burned out" by their engagement in the politics of procreative choice. Certainly there is considerable evidence that the anti-abortion forces may defeat us or so thwart our deeper agenda that some will give up. The psychology of weariness has overtaken many who support the feminist agenda just now, fueled by massive efforts to return women to "our place." There is some evidence, however, that while attacks on a formal feminist political agenda succeed, the rate of change in women's *personal* lives does not abate.[57] This dynamic is an historical one: hence, my prediction that even the reversal of the legality of early elective abortion will not greatly reduce the number of abortions in this society. Abortions in the early stages of pregnancy are simple and, under reasonable conditions, safe procedures. Someone will provide them, albeit at considerably greater cost, and numerous women will obtain them, whatever happens. If abortion is thoroughly recriminalized, many will feel that "respect for life" has been secured. But no moralist could endorse with impunity the widespread illegal social practice that would ensue. Of course, there is plenty of precedent for blinking at illegal practices in our nation's history. Women themselves were seldom prosecuted for resorting to illegal abortions prior to *Roe v. Wade;* the person who performed the abortion was prosecuted when, in rare instances, prosecution occurred. If nearly all abortions become illegal again, no doubt women will be punished this time, although the probability is high that poor and nonwhite women will be represented disproportionately among those whom authorities will "catch." Just as white-collar crime goes largely unpunished in the United States, white-collar abortions will probably escape prosecution as well.

In the face of these realities, it is, I believe, time to reconsider the wisdom of "the balance of interests" Justice Blackmun addressed in *Roe v. Wade*. If, as I have argued here, women's claims to bodily integrity have compelling moral force, every bit as serious as the rightful legal claims to freedom from bodily invasion that psychiatric and medical patients possess, can the event of pregnancy automatically override a woman's bodily integrity? How can "rights" imputed to early fetal life so easily outweigh a woman's indisputable claims as a moral agent? Why are those who insist that fetal rights overshadow a woman's rights so readily given credence when compromise is called for, but those who disagree are dismissed as moral zealots?

Relevant to creating an ethos of compromise is the need for greater acknowledgment among anti-abortionists that pro-choice adherents, now so readily labeled "extremists," also hold a principled moral stance. The preemption of the "right-to-life" slogan by those opposing legal abortion was, admittedly, a political coup, but it certainly has not encouraged less acrimonious abortion politics. The implication, reinforced by the attitude of many "pro-lifers," that their "side" is the unambiguously "moral" one in the dispute, places a heavy burden on pro-choice proponents. Civility is hard to maintain in the face of innuendo regarding one's standing as a moral agent. I have observed frequently the way in which anti-abortion proponents define their opponents as existing outside the moral argument altogether.[58] The so-called pro-life position seeks support by invoking the general principle of respect for human life as foundational to its morality in a way that suggests that pro-choice advocates are unprincipled. Such maneuvers may be perceived as "good politics," but they are not morally wise. I have already insisted that pro-choice advocates appeal to the same moral principle and that this debate, like most that are morally acrimonious, is in no sense a debate about basic moral principles. I do not believe there is any clear-cut conflict of principle in this very deep, very bitter controversy.

I have emphasized that we all have an absolute obligation to honor any moral principle that seems, after rational deliberation, to be sound. This is the one absolutism appropriate to ethics. There are often several moral principles relevant to a decision and many ways to relate a given principle to a decision-making context. Most who favor the "right-to-life" position acknowledge only one principle as relevant; hence, a single principle is absolutized. Admitting only one principle to one's process of moral reasoning always means that a range of other moral values is slighted. Obviously, anti-abortionists are also moral absolutists in the questionable sense that they admit only one possible meaning or application of the single principle they espouse. Both these types of absolutism obscure moral debate and lead to less, not more, rational deliberation. No morally serious person disputes that the principle of respect for human life is one we should honor. But it also should apply to women who face unwanted pregnancy. Adequately understood, this principle means that we should treat all that falls under a defensible definition of human life as worthy of respect. But the principle of respect for human life per se offers little help in choosing between two intrinsic values, in this case between late-gestating prenatal life and the life of the pregnant woman. Nor does it exempt us from respecting the principles of justice, particularly as they relate to women.

One further proviso on this issue of principles in moral reasoning: there are several distinct theories among religious ethicists and moral philosophers as to what the function of principles ought to be. One group believes moral principles simply should be "obeyed," thereby terminating the process of moral reasoning. Hence, if this sort of moralist tells you always to honor the principle of respect for human life, he or she means that you stop reflection and act in a certain way, in this case accept pregnancy regardless of consequences. By contrast, others of us believe that principles (broad, generalized action guides) or rules (narrower, specific moral prescriptions) need to function always to stimulate our reasoning processes, not to close them off. The principle of respect for life, on this reading, is not invoked merely to prescribe action, but to help locate and weigh values, to illuminate a range of moral factors that always impinge on significant human decisions. A major difference in the moral debate on abortion, then, is that some believe that to invoke the principle of respect for human life settles the matter, stops debate, and precludes the single, simple act of abortion. By contrast, many of us have found that the breadth of this principle requires thoroughgoing reconsideration of how the essential moral quality of human life can be sustained. This, among other things, means increased moral seriousness about choosing whether or when to bear children.

Persons of authentic theological sensibility must continue to insist that every child who is born among us deserves to be embraced in a covenant of love and affirmation that includes not merely the love of a mother, or a father, but the active concern and respect of the wider community. We must never imagine that the conditions for such deeply humane covenant exist. I noted at the outset that if women did not have to deliberate the questions relating to our procreative power in an atmosphere of taboo, we would be able to turn our attention to the positive moral task I have commended: what it means for us to use our procreative power responsibly. In the present condemnatory atmosphere, such moral reasoning will go largely undeveloped.

Even so, the deepest reappropriation of the theological theme of the covenant that women can make requires our perception of procreation as a moral act, one we must enter into with maximum awareness of what it means to bear a child. We are still a long way from a historical situation in which women really will have the conditions that make such a genuine covenant and choice an easy matter. Safe surgical abortion has created only the negative conditions for procreative choice. We often now live in situations where it is easier to say no than to say yes to this prospective covenant. The current circumstances in which women choose abortions are often dominated by desperation. And yet it is now possible to begin to anticipate what it would mean to incorporate this covenantal image into the total process of species reproduction. When such a covenant of life is embodied in the birth of every child, an incredible reduction in human suffering will have been accomplished.

Any of us who have experienced human joy in the knowledge of our birth at some level have heard God's call to life through the "yes" of our parents. Without that yes, life is immeasurably impoverished. In fact, it is necessary to put the point more strongly. Those who are born in the absence of such an act of human covenant by already living persons (of course, not merely by our biological parents) frequently do not really live at all. Our acknowledgment of each other in relation is not an optional addition to life, an afterthought; it is constitutive of life itself. For a vital human life to be born, a woman must say yes in a strong and active way and enter positively into a life-bearing, demanding, and, at times, extremely painful process. Freedom to say yes, which, of course, also means the freedom to say no, is constitutive of the sacred covenant of life itself. Failure to see this is also failure to see how good, how strong and real, embodied existence is in this world we are making together.

POSTSCRIPT

For years, as I have lectured on this topic, I have been asked whether I would have wanted abortion to be legal at the time I was born and whether I have ever really contemplated how it would have been if my mother had chosen abortion instead of bearing me. The truth is that each of us, as self-reflective persons, can ask this question and, in the process, presumably get in touch with the inexorable value of the life we have lived. But such reflection is the fruit not of our existence as biological members of our species but of our lives as socially related beings who have been nurtured and valued and, for that reason, have come to value ourselves and to rejoice in our birth. The question, when it has been pressed on me, has always caused me to smile; for I almost was a medically dictated abortion, and I have lived much of my life with that knowledge. But I also know, as anyone who comprehends the development of self-awareness will understand, that if I *had* been aborted, there would have been no "I" to experience it. Like the philosopher Charles Hartshorne, I can say that I am glad to be alive, but concur with him that

> this expression does not constitute a claim to having already had a "right" against which no other right could prevail, to the life I have enjoyed. I feel no indignation or horror at contemplating the idea that the world might have had to do without me. The world would have managed, and as for what I could have missed, there would have been no such "I" to miss it.[59]

Furthermore, the "I" who was born into the world exists, in large part, out of the freely given, active caring of a woman who was willing both to take a genuine risk in bearing me and my siblings and to struggle to provide for us after the premature death of our father. My mother's love and courage, like all women's, were no mere biologically induced responses but the expressions of her moral commitment to us. In the absence of such tenderness and care, born not of instinct but of moral freedom, it would have been better for me, or for anyone else, not to have been born.

All things considered, it is this reality, so basic to every living person's sense of well-being, that we endanger when we insist that women should bear all the children they conceive, merely because they have conceived them. And it is the capacity of women to undertake, in freedom, the consummately moral action of childrearing that is threatened when the politics of abortion play fast and loose with the particularity of women's lives. It is this particularity that I have insisted remains invisible, as the far more abstract concern for early fetal life escalates in this society.

Whatever the permutations of abortion politics, all who are morally serious must learn to see, hear, and name the truth of women's lives. For many women poets, "abortion" stands as an image and metaphor for the lost promise of women's lives, thwarted by oppression. So Pauli Murray characterizes black women's reality:

> Ours is a tale of charred and
> blackened fruit,
> Aborted harvest dropped from
> blazing bough,
> A tale of eagles exiled from the nest,
> Brooding and hovering on the edge
> of sky —
> A somber shadow on this native
> earth,
> Yet no faint tremor of her breast
> Eludes the circle of our
> hungered eye.[60]

Another feminist poet, Adrienne Rich, seeking to make language answerable to women's particularity, has warned us that only the most concrete language can succeed in rendering women's lives visible. Use of terms like *humanity*, which never actually incorporate women, she suggests, will only further victimize women. In the argument that I have constructed here, I have not always heeded Rich's warning.[61] What I have argued here is that in the modern world, women face all the same struggles for survival and dignity which men of their nation, culture, race, and class engage. In addition, they bare most of the concrete burdens of human reproduction. We must not neglect Rich's warning to respect the particularity of women's lives, most especially when we address reproduction and its control, including the question of abortion. Any expressed moral concern for human well-being in relation to abortion which fails to do this remains empty rhetoric, the hypocrisy of those whose moral ideals do not engage reality.

This reality, as it takes form in most women's lives, is not merely struggle but courage and strength in adversity. Whatever the outcome of debates about the morality and politics of abortion, the well-being of all of us continues to be dependent on women's resource-

fulness. Poet-theologian Dorothee Soelle reminds us to take our hope
and shape our songs from this awareness:

> . . . sing about women
> just looking at them makes me stronger
> makes me laugh . . .
>
> I'm tired of all the whining
> play me a song about anna and the two rosas
> play about real people
> about women strong and vulnerable
> caring for others and independent
> fighting for you too
> in your teller's cage at the bank
> for all our sisters
> play about bread and roses
> play about the price of meat and a free labor union
> play against steel helmets and what's inside them
> play against atomic missiles and what's behind them
>
> you can't arrest the sun
>   it shines
> you can't censor the roses
>   they flower
> you can't keep women down
>   they laugh . . .

Notes

Index

Notes

1: The Abortion Controversy

1. The three-year period from 1977 to 1979 saw a tremendous upsurge in incidents of vandalism, arson, and assaults directed at abortion clinics and their personnel. Fortunately we have witnessed the decline of such violent episodes around the country. Even so, in August 1982, the operator of an abortion clinic and his wife were kidnapped by a radical anti-abortion group protesting government failure to denounce abortion. The couple was released unharmed. Nathaniel Sheppard, Jr., "Abortion Doctor and Wife Are Freed," *New York Times*, August 21, 1982, p. A7. See also Andrew H. Merton, *Enemies of Choice: The Right-to-Life Movement and Its Threat to Abortion* (Boston: Beacon Press, 1981). Anti-abortion tactics are monitored by the Religious Coalition for Abortion Rights in its newsletter *Options*. See also Roz Kramer, "The Great Abortion Battle of 1981," *Village Voice*, 26:1 (1981), pp. 1, 14-15.
2. See Sarah R. Bentley, "Becoming the Subjects of Our Lives: The Implications of Objectification for Women's Ethical Consciousness," unpublished M.Div. thesis, Union Theological Seminary, New York, 1975. See also Sheila Rowbotham, *Woman's Consciousness, Man's World* (Middlesex, England: Penguin Books, 1979).
3. In much ethical discussion, "the moral point of view" is a technical term used to designate whatever set of characteristics or criteria is considered essential to acquire moral perspective on a given matter. Obviously, there are many theories about what constitutes the moral point of view, and a spirited debate revolves around these positions. For an excellent summary of moral theory, see Roziel Abelson and Kai Nielsen, "Ethics, History of," and Kai Nielsen, "Ethics, Problems of," in *The Encyclopedia of Philosophy*, ed. Paul Edwards (New York: Free Press, 1967), pp. 81-134.
4. Stanley Hauerwas, "Abortion: Why the Arguments Fail," in James T. Burtchaell, ed., *Abortion Parley* (Kansas City: Andrews and McMeel, 1980), pp. 325-352, especially pp. 325-326..
5. Many professional Christian ethicists who take a "pox on both your houses" view of abortion politics imply that both sides have "played equally rough" in the process. I flatly deny that pro-choice supporters have matched in any way the dubious coercive tactics of anti-abortionists. Much was made in the press of the expulsion of a group of young women from a U.S. Senate hearing for shouting while senators discussed abortion legislation. An acquaintance of mine present on that occasion — a middle-aged Roman Catholic woman — reported that she was ashamed of herself for failing to join the shouting. "The comments and innuendo concerning women in that hearing were unspeakable. I admired the courage of these young women. They were right to protest."

6. For example, see John T. Noonan, Jr., ed., *The Morality of Abortion: Legal and Historical Perspectives* (Cambridge: Harvard University Press, 1970), and a number of essays in Edward Batchelor, Jr., *Abortion: The Moral Issues* (New York: Pilgrim Press, 1982). An older work, Daniel Callahan's *Abortion: Law, Choice, and Morality* (New York: Macmillan, 1970), is in many respects an exception to this criticism. It appeals to cross-cultural and social-scientific data to raise questions about many traditional assumptions concerning abortion. Nevertheless, Callahan does not speak to the central concern about the moral impact of misogyny on our understanding of abortion.

7. I believe the reason Christian theology has been so resistant to feminism is related to the depth of the institutionalization of misogyny in Christianity. See Beverly W. Harrison, "Homophobia and Misogyny: The Unexplored Connections," *Integrity Forum*, 7:2 (1981), pp. 7-13.

8. Beverly W. Harrison, "The New Consciousness of Women: A Socio-Political Resource," *Cross Currents*, 24:4 (Winter 1975), pp. 445-462. The methodological point of stressing feminism as a moral commitment is to remind us that it is not a set of opinions (though a theory develops in its wake) but a commitment to advocacy for women's well-being and to social change.

9. In 1979 numerous theologians and ethicists signed "A Call to Concern," a statement supportive of legal abortion and the need of poor women to receive Medicaid funding for abortions. The Call criticized aspects of the "pro-life" movement's arguments and the Conference of Roman Catholic Bishops at several points. Publication of the document signaled a movement among Christian ethicists on the issue but brought forth a storm of controversy in the field. See *Christianity and Crisis*, October 3, 31, and November 14, 1977. Fortunately some recent discussions of abortion by writers in religious ethics have shown greater sensitivity to women's lives. See, for example, Ronald Green, "Conferred Rights and the Fetus," *Journal of Religious Ethics*, vol. 2 (Spring 1974), pp. 55-73. Green formulates a positive argument for women's choice analogous to my own approach. James Nelson has incorporated the concern for women's well-being in interpreting Protestant positions on abortion. See James Nelson, "Abortion: Protestant Perspectives," *Encyclopedia of Bioethics*, ed. Warren T. Reich, vol. 1 (New York: Free Press, 1978), pp. 13-17. Some theorists have helpfully stressed that sound policy needs to incorporate awareness of who is most at risk in the abortion debate, namely, women. See Thomas Shannon, "Abortion: A Review of Ethical Aspects of Public Policy," in *The Annual Selected Papers* (Society of Christian Ethics, 1983). Another religious ethicist who has been sympathetic to women's concerns in the Roman Catholic tradition is James F. Bresnahan. See his "Social Ethics and Public Policy on Abortion in a Catholic Perspective," *Probe* (Publication of the National Assembly of Women Religious), 7:7 (April/May 1978), pp. 3-7. Bresnahan is uncharacteristically careful to represent the legal and ethical issues precisely. Neither Bresnahan nor Shannon dissent from the mainstream Catholic teaching on fetal life, but they do recognize the possibility of internal disagreement on the public policy question.

10. This qualification is necessary because of the tragic fact that the abortion dilemma can and frequently does arise, given modern prenatal technology, in cases where it is known that a fetus is genetically diseased. This can pose an agonizing dilemma for a woman or a couple who has actively sought pregnancy and desires a child.

11. A strong objection to "discrete-deed" approaches to Christian ethics was formulated by Richard Niebuhr, who recognized that human action is often falsified when we treat a single deed as meaningful in itself rather than as an aspect of a strategy, project, or life plan. See H. Richard Niebuhr, "The Christian Church and the World's Crisis," *Christianity and Society*, vol. 6 (1941), pp. 1-7. Niebuhr, of course, did not apply this critique to abortion.

12. The results of this bias are beginning to be recognized in the literature. For a critique of the ideological bias of biomedical experts, and of much religious ethics developed in this context, see Lon Weldon Palmer, "New in Every Dimension: Religious Ethics and the Biological Revolution," unpublished manuscript, Union Theological Seminary, New York, 1983.

13. The term is from Mary O'Brien's work *The Politics of Reproduction* (London: Routledge & Kegan Paul, 1981), pp. 5ff.

14. This position that women should not rely on any male intellectual traditions has been forcefully advanced by many feminist theorists, notably by Mary Daly in *Gyn/Ecology: The Metaethics of Radical Feminism* (Boston: Beacon Press, 1978). I concur with Daly that the problem of patriarchy is pervasive, but I do not share her sharp distinction between male and female nature. See Beverly W. Harrison, "Feminism and Process Thought," *Signs*, 7:3 (Spring 1982), pp. 704-710.

15. O'Brien, pp. 16-17.

16. Some of these issues are usefully discussed by James Gustafson in "Contextualism: A Misplaced Debate," *New Theology No. 3*, ed. Dean G. Peerman and Martin Marty (New York: Macmillan, 1966), pp. 69-102.

17. H. Richard Niebuhr, *The Responsible Self: An Essay in Christian Moral Philosophy* (New York: Harper & Row, 1963), pp. 127-145. The particular term *commonwealth* is not used by Niebuhr. I prefer this Puritan term as a theological symbol for our shared humanity under God over its more customary counterpart, *Kingdom*.

18. Dorothy Emmet, *The Moral Prism* (New York: St. Martin's Press, 1979). See especially Chapter 2, pp. 22ff. Most philosophical literature ignores theological teleology. This may be because it is possible to recast theological teleology into a more concrete utilitarian argument.

19. For a well-known debate about utilitarian theory, see J. J. C. Smart and Bernard Williams, *Utilitarianism For and Against* (London: Cambridge University Press, 1973). Suggestive defenses of utilitarian theory are contained in Tom L. Beauchamp's discussion of suicide in *Matters of Life and Death: New Introductory Essays in Moral Philosophy*, ed. Tom Regan (New York: Random House, 1980), pp. 67-108, and in R. F. Harrod, "Utilitarianism Revised," in *Lying: Moral Choice in Public and Private Life*, ed. Sissela Bok (New York: Vintage, 1979), pp. 293-301.

20. By moral intuitions, I mean those deeply felt reactions — empathy or revulsion — which catapult us into ethical reflection. I affirm the

importance of intuition as a ground for moral reasoning, but I am not an intuitionist when it comes to moral theory. Often our moral intuitions function well in registering things morally amiss in a given situation. Sensitive people with a well-developed conscience are deeply attuned to their moral intuitions and do well to trust them. Our intuitions per se, however, are not infallible. Moral reasoning serves to test our intuitions, provided of course that conditions of openness and mutual respect prevail. In political debate, however, the necessary condition of genuine openness is rare. Given this rarity, it is understandable that many women are drawn to moral intuitionism. Certain in the knowledge that their feelings are a good moral guide, they are reluctant to trust, and some even distrust, their power of reason-giving. To a great extent, their embrace of intuitionism is a defense against the abstract character of much moral theory. I believe we are right when we value feeling as the point of departure for our reasoning, but unwise when we endorse complete reliance on it as a full and sufficient theory.

21. Proponents of the two positions often collaborate. See Tom L. Beauchamp and James F. Childress, *Principles of Biomedical Ethics* (New York and London: Oxford University Press, 1979). Much of the traditional hostility among theorists is dissipating, perhaps because recent analytical methods have encouraged professionals to focus their attention on the ways in which people in the course of their daily lives actually argue morally. Early-twentieth-century British moral theory noticeably lacked grounding in such reality.

22. The impact on moral development of the differences in male and female socialization is explored by Carol Gilligan most recently in her book *In a Different Voice: Psychological Theory and Women's Development* (Cambridge: Harvard University Press, 1982). Gilligan wisely uses abortion as a focal point for understanding the nature of women's moral decision-making processes amid crises. Her data suggest that women — and, no doubt, many men — employ a different theory of justice and reason about moral dilemmas in a way at variance from subjects studied by psychologist Lawrence Kohlberg.

23. The data on attitudes toward abortion most frequently cited are from Gallup opinion polls. Conservatives often use the analyses of these polls developed by demographer Judith Blake, herself a feminist and a supporter of legal abortion. It is her thesis that the strongest support for legal abortion in the 1960s and early 1970s was found among affluent white men, a thesis often cited by opponents of legal abortion to imply that women oppose legal abortion. For example, see Judith Blake, "Abortion and Public Opinion: The 1960-1970 Decade," *Science*, vol. 171 (February 12, 1971), pp. 540-549, and "The Supreme Court's Abortion Decisions and Public Opinion in the United States," *Population and Development Review*, vol. III, no. 1-2, 1977, pp. 45-62. It is difficult to understand how the data about women reviewed in Blake's studies relate to more recent data from a Yankelovich poll conducted for *Life* magazine, which reveals both women's strong reservations about the morality of the *act* of abortion (56% believe it is morally wrong) and stronger support for the legality of abortion (67%). Even higher

percentages of women in this poll supported the legality of abortion when a woman's health is at risk (92%), when a woman has been raped (88%), when genetic disease is involved (87%), or when incest is the cause of pregnancy (86%). Perhaps the recent politics of abortion have shifted women's views dramatically. Alternatively, this study may reflect both women's general reluctance about abortion and their capacity for empathy for those confronting concrete circumstances beyond their control. See *Life*, 4:11 (November 1981), pp. 45-54.

Several women who have devoted years to abortion counseling have suggested that Gallup Poll data may lack sufficient subtlety to detect women's deep ambivalence about abortion. Having been encouraged to think of the abortion dilemma in a personalistic (not personal) way, some women remain dangerously innocent of what public policy is or has been all about. I encounter many women who hold negative opinions of abortion as a personal option. When exposed to the broader social policy dimensions, however, their views change. This is especially true as women listen carefully for the first time to what actually is being said *about them* in the abortion debate.

24. L. W. Sumner, *Abortion and Moral Theory* (Princeton: Princeton University Press, 1981), pp. 73-81, 88.

25. See James Burtchaell, "Continuing the Discussion: How to Argue About Abortion: II," *Christianity and Crisis*, 37:21 (December 26, 1977), pp. 313-316. Also see John T. Noonan, Jr., *A Private Choice: Abortion in America in the Seventies* (New York: Free Press, 1979). Noonan offers not one word of justification for viewing the fetus as "a child" or a human being. Throughout, the pregnant woman is referred to exclusively as "the gravida" (a Latin term meaning "pregnant one") or "the carrier," never merely "the woman." No clear moral argument is presented in the entire book. See also several articles in *Catholic Perspectives*, ed. John Garvey and Frank Morriss (Chicago: Thomas More Press, 1979).

26. *Cora McRae, et al. v. Joseph A. Califano, Jr.*, 76 Civ. 1804, United States District Court Eastern District of New York (1978). The U.S. Supreme Court brief (1980) *Harris v. McRae* is contained in Thomas A. Shannon and Jo Ann Manfra, eds., *Law and Bioethics: Texts with Commentary on Major U.S. Court Decisions* (New York: Paulist Press, 1982), pp. 121-138.

27. See "Abortion, Religion and Political Life," an editorial in *Commonweal*, 106:2 (February 1979), pp. 35-38. Also see *Hastings Center Report*, August 1978, and "C & C Symposium on *McRae v. Califano*," *Christianity and Crisis*, 39:3 (March 5, 1979).

28. See David M. Feldman, *Marital Relations, Birth Control, and Abortion in Jewish Law* (New York: Schocken, 1975). An excellent review of the current spectrum of Jewish opinion is contained in Annette Daum, "The Jewish Stake in Abortion Rights," *Lilith*, no. 8 (1982). See also Daum, *Assault on the Bill of Rights: The Jewish Stake* (New York: Union of American Hebrew Congregations, 1982), pp. 112-139.

29. This was H. Richard Niebuhr's conclusion. In his early work he made

the analysis of social movements a central ingredient in his method of theological ethics. In his *Radical Monotheism and Western Culture* (New York: Harper & Row, 1956), he went so far as to suggest that social movements are the locus of divine revelation, pp. 38-44, 56-63.

30. The Bible contains two versions of the Decalogue: Exodus 20:2-17 and Deuteronomy 5:6-21.

31. My thinking about this process has been informed by Robert Bellah's speculations of the evolution of society, social structure, and self. See especially Chapters 2 and 13 of his *Beyond Belief: Essays on Religion in a Post-Traditional World* (New York: Harper & Row, 1970). I also assume here that because the theological differences are always rooted in conflicts about action guides, theology has its origins historically in moral conflict. On this point, see Tom F. Driver, *Christ in a Changing World: Toward an Ethical Christology* (New York: Crossroads, 1981).

32. Parker Palmer, *The Company of Strangers* (New York: Pilgrim Press, 1982). Palmer rightly insists that Christians have an obligation precisely to public life, that is, the place where "strangers" meet.

33. Particularly pertinent is Daniel C. Maguire's "Moral Absolutes and the Magisterium," in *Absolutes in Moral Theology?* ed. Charles Curran (Washington, D.C.: Corpus Books, 1968), pp. 154-185. On dissent possible within Catholicism regarding abortion, see Charles Curran, "Abortion: Its Moral Aspects," in Batchelor, pp. 115-128.

34. For the political strategy of the Roman Catholic bishops see Chapter 8, n. 27. The Catholic bishops' conference has also pledged to make termination of government support for birth control a continuing high priority. Catholic theologians have recognized the danger that this single-issue approach presents to the broader Roman Catholic political goals. See George C. Higgins, "The Pro-Life and the New Right," *America*, 143:6 (September 13, 1980), pp. 107-110.

35. The National Leadership Conference of Women Religious, beginning in 1977, has issued several statements proposing an alternative to the bishops' public policy stance and insisting that a "pro-life" stance must also be a pro-woman stance. See "Choose Life: Promoting the Value and Quality of Life," LCWR Task Force Report, *Origins*, NC Documentary Service, 7:11 (September 1, 1977). Most recently this group took explicit exception to the bishops' support of the Hyde Amendment. Catholics for a Free Choice (CFC) is another locus of dissent. Some 5,000 members of this organization have developed an articulate and theologically informed strategy of resistance to official teaching. Although several priests have been involved energetically in CFC, the able leadership of laywomen has been especially noteworthy. A number of Catholic women theologians also signed the pro-choice theological statement "A Call to Concern," discussed in Chapter 3.

36. The quotation is from a familiar hymn of the liberal theological tradition by James Russell Lowell, "Once to Every Man and Nation."

37. My examination of Christian theological approaches to abortion aims to identify the subtle, de facto impact theology has on Christian attitudes to abortion. Even when groups of Christians differentiate

the logic of morals from the logic of theology, certain theological dispositions continue to have existential impact. The continuing refusal of moral philosophies to distinguish between the logical autonomy of morals and such ongoing existential impact of theology greatly obfuscates social policy discussion. See, for example, Lisa Newton, "The Irrelevance of Religion in the Abortion Debate," and Baruch Barody, "Religious, Moral and Sociological Issues: Some Basic Distinctions," *Hastings Center Report*, August 1978; Eunice Kennedy Shriver, "Abortion Is, Above All, a Moral Issue," Newspaper Enterprise Association, September 1, 1977, tape no. 5. Newton's essay is reprinted in Batchelor, pp. 3-6.

Chapter 2: The Morality of Procreative Choice

1. See, for example, Richard A. Viguerie, *The New Right: We're Ready to Lead* (Falls Church, Va.: Viguerie, 1980). Viguerie edits *The Conservative Digest*, the theoretical voice of the New Right. For an analysis of the impact of legalized abortion on the New Right, see Allen Hunter, "In the Wings: New Right Ideology and Organization," in *The New Right: Fundamentalists and Financiers*, press profile no. 4 (Oakland, Calif.: The Data Center, 1981), pp. 6-23. See also Rosalind Pollack Petchesky, "Antiabortion, Antifeminism, and the Rise of the New Right," *Feminist Studies*, 7:2 (Summer 1981), pp. 206-246.
2. Judith Blake, "Abortion and Public Opinion: The 1960-1970 Decade," *Science*, vol. 171 (February 12, 1971), pp. 540-549. See Chapter 1, n. 23, above.
3. See Paul Seabury, "Trendier Than Thou: Manners and Morals in the Episcopal Church," *Harper's*, October 1978, pp. 39ff. See also Veronica Geng, "Requiem for the Women's Movement," *Harper's*, November 1976, pp. 49ff. Seabury's hostility to women is palpable and his insensitivity to social justice for women transparent. Geng's assessment of the "failures" of feminism is predicated on contracts and interviews with a few radical feminist groups, but her "requiem" was widely read as justification for the "decline" of feminism.
4. This thesis separates some liberal feminism from more radical feminist theory. According to the latter, a liberating agenda for women requires the transformation of the social exploitation of women in both the so-called private or domestic sphere, where nearly all women toil perpetually, and the public workplace, where some women earn (small) wages. Liberal feminism often stresses equal pay for equal work or identifies "separate" issues for reform but has no analysis of the full range of structural constraints on women. See Zillah R. Eisenstein, ed., *Capitalist Patriarchy and the Case for Socialist Feminism* (New York: Monthly Review Press, 1979). See also Ann Oakley, *The Sociology of Housework* (New York: Pantheon, 1974); Sheila Rowbotham, *Woman's Consciousness, Man's World* (Middlesex, England: Penguin Books, 1979), and *Women, Resistance, and Revolution: A History of Women and Revolution in the Modern World* (New York: Vintage, 1974); Barbara

Mayer Wertheimer, *We Were There: The Story of Working Women in America* (New York: Pantheon, 1977); and Eli Zaretsky, *Capitalism, The Family and Personal Life* (San Francisco: Agenda Publications, 1973).

5. For an analysis of the relationship between religious belief and voting behavior in Congress, see Peter L. Benson, "God is Alive in the U.S. Congress, but Not Always Voting Against Civil Liberties and for Military Spending," *Psychology Today*, 15:12 (December 1981), pp. 47-57. Benson finds a close connection not between denominational affiliation and voting patterns on such issues as military spending, pro- or anti-civil liberties stances, and so on, but between "types" of religious belief and political position. Using a multifaceted factor analysis to classify types of "religious belief," he shows that when "religion" is dealt with more subtly than in the past, high correlations of religion with political behavior appear. See also Chapter 7, n. 7.

6. See, for example, Nancy Jay, *Throughout Your Generations Forever: A Sociology of Blood Sacrifice*, unpublished Ph.D. dissertation, Brandeis University, 1981. See also Nancy Chodorow, *The Reproduction of Mothering: Psychoanalysis and the Sociology of Gender* (Berkeley: University of California Press, 1978); Dorothy Dinnerstein, *The Mermaid and the Minotaur: Sexual Arrangements and Human Malaise* (New York: Harper & Row, 1977); and Adrienne Rich, *Of Woman Born: Motherhood as Experience and Institution* (New York: Norton, 1976). An excellent survey of available anthropological data on gender is contained in Ernestine Friedl, *Women and Men: An Anthropologist's View* (New York: Holt, Rinehart and Winston, 1975). See also Rayna R. Reiter, ed., *Toward an Anthropology of Women* (New York: Monthly Review Press, 1975), and M. Z. Rosaldo and Louis Lamphere, eds., *Women, Culture, and Society* (Stanford: Stanford University Press, 1974), especially Sherry Ortner, "Is Female to Male as Nature is to Culture?" pp. 67-88.

7. This thesis is developed further in Chapter 6.

8. The effects of the destruction of women's culture on childbearing are widely discussed in feminist literature. See Jane B. Donegan, *Women and Men Midwives: Medicine, Morality, and Misogyny in Early America* (Westport, Conn.: Greenwood Press, 1978); Barbara Ehrenreich and Deirdre English, *Witches, Midwives, and Nurses: A History of Women Healers*, Glass Mountain Pamphlet no. 1 (Old Westbury, N.Y.: Feminist Press, 1973); essays in John Ehrenreich, ed., *The Cultural Crisis of Modern Medicine* (New York: Monthly Review Press, 1978), pp. 144-226; Ellen Frankfort, *Vaginal Politics* (New York: Quadrangle, 1972); Robert S. Mendelsohn, *Male Practice: How Doctors Manipulate Women* (Chicago: Contemporary Books, 1981); Richard W. and Dorothy C. Wertz, *Lying In: A History of Childbirth in America* (New York: Schocken, 1977). A helpful review essay covering the full range of new American historiography is Nancy Schrom Dye, "History of Childbirth in America: Review Essay," *Signs*, 6:1 (1980), pp. 97-108.

9. For an analysis of the implications of the possible negative effects of "reproductive engineering" on women, see Jolna Hammer and Pat

Allen, "Reproductive Engineering: The Final Solution?" *Feminist Studies*, 2:1 (Spring 1982), pp. 53-74. A decade ago, a few feminists were highly receptive to the development of technology designed to relieve women of the necessity of childbearing. See Shulamith Firestone, *The Dialectic of Sex: The Case for Feminist Revolution* (New York: Bantam, 1971). Such optimism has dissipated almost entirely for reasons Hammer and Allen make clear. A further concern is that when parents can choose the gender of their offspring, the bias toward males may adversely affect the female birth rate. See Roberta Steinbacker, "Preselection of Sex: Social Consequences of Choice," *The Sciences*, New York Academy of Science, April 1980. Steinbacker documents serious discussions among scientists to the effect that the birth of fewer females would be an efficacious means of controlling population size.

10. See Betty Rollins, "Motherhood: Who Needs It?" *Look*, (September 1970). pp. 15-17. For a profound analysis of the dilemmas of women's consciousness about mothering, see Sara Ruddick, "Maternal Thinking," *Feminist Studies*, 6:2 (Summer 1980), pp. 342-367.

11. Scattered testimony to this fact is found in books dealing with the abortion experience. See especially Magda Denes, *In Necessity and Sorrow* (Middlesex, England: Penguin Books, 1977), and Linda Bird Francke, *The Ambivalence of Abortion* (New York: Dell, 1978).

12. The effects of powerlessness on women's socialization have been widely researched and analyzed. The phenomenon of the use of pregnancy to avoid threatening alternatives is also widely discussed. See Judith M. Bardwick, *The Psychology of Women: A Study of Biocultural Conflicts* (New York: Harper & Row, 1971). A popular treatment of this issue is contained in Colette Dowling, *The Cinderella Complex: Women's Hidden Fear of Independence* (New York: Pocket Books, 1981). One limitation of these and other psychological analyses is that they come close to "blaming the victim" through failure to analyze the total range of sociological pressures that affect women's lives. The assumption that powerlessness is chiefly a psychological "problem" misrepresents the reality of most women's lives. For a more adequate social perspective, see Alice G. Sargent, ed., *Beyond Sex Roles* (St. Paul: West Publishing, 1977), especially the section "Social Change," pp. 353-469. See also John L. Hodge, Donald K. Struckmann, and Lynn Dorland Trost, *Cultural Bases of Racism and Group Oppression: An Examination of Traditional Western Concepts, Values and Structures Which Support Racism, Sexism, and Elitism* (Berkeley: Two Riders Press, 1975).

13. According to the November 1981 *Life* magazine poll, 33% of women do not consider abortion a moral issue. Based on my experience, I doubt that this group is much represented among pro-choice political activists.

14. Richard A. Wasserstrom, *Philosophy and Social Issues: Five Studies* (Notre Dame: University of Notre Dame Press, 1980), p. 22.

15. Matthew Fox, *On Becoming a Musical Mystical Bear* (New York: Paulist Press, 1972). See especially the introduction to James B. Nelson, *Embodiment: An Approach to Sexuality and Christian Theology* (Minneapolis: Augsburg Publishing House, 1978).

16. This statement may surprise those who have read Susan Teft Nicholson's *Abortion and the Roman Catholic Church*, JRE Studies in Religious Ethics/II, ed. James Childress (Knoxville: Religious Ethics, 1978). This artful study assumes (it does not demonstrate) that the Catholic "anti-killing ethic" can be differentiated from its "anti-sexual ethic." In order to do so, I believe it would be minimally necessary to acknowledge that their intimate connection is precisely what makes any full reconsideration of the status of fetal life so unlikely. See Chapter 5.
17. See, for example, Kai Nielsen, *Ethics Without God* (Buffalo: Prometheus Books, 1973).
18. That abortion is being used as a means of birth control is often hurled at women as a "charge." See Germain C. Grisez, *Abortion: The Myth, the Realities and the Arguments* (Washington, D.C.: Corpus Books, 1969).
19. The American Medical Association has acknowledged the widespread resort to unnecessary hysterectomies as a problem. Community health organizations have protested that poor women are subject to hysterectomies in training hospitals in order that residents may gain surgical experience. According to Jane Brody's "AMA Report on Incompetent Doctors" (*New York Times*, vol. 125, no. 43102, January 27, 1976, pp. 1, 24), some 260,000 women undergo needless hysterectomies each year.
20. The problem of sterilization abuse is widespread and takes many forms, among them using tubal ligations or hysterectomies to prevent further conceptions and requiring sterilization to prevent conception among welfare recipients or emotionally retarded women. Sterilization abuse of welfare recipients has been documented in several states. See Rosalind Pollack Petchesky, "Reproduction, Ethics, and Public Policy: The Federal Sterilization Regulations," *Hastings Center Report 9* (1979), pp. 29-42. See also *Women Under Attack: Abortion, Sterilization Abuse and Reproductive Freedom* (New York: Committee for Abortion Rights and Against Sterilization Abuse (CARASA), 1979). The American College of Obstetricians and Gynecologists has relaxed various professional constraints on the use of sterilization in recent years. See "Sterilization: Women Fit to Be Tied" in *Health Policy, Advisory Center Bulletin* no. 62 (January/February 1975), p. 4. See also Karen Lebacqz, "Sterilization: Ethical Aspects," and Jane Friedman, "Sterilization: Legal Aspects," in *Encyclopedia of Bioethics*, vol. 4 (Washington, D.C.: Georgetown University Press, 1978), pp. 1606-1617.
21. The contrast between Christian theological reasoning in relation to participation in war and reasoning on the morality of abortion requires further exploration. The surface distinctions are striking, however. The entire tradition of just-war reflection after Augustine turned to elaborating criteria to *justify* Christian participation in war. See Frederick R. Russell, *The Just War in the Middle Ages* (London: Cambridge University Press, 1975). By contrast, discussion of abortion riveted on the question of when in the course of pregnancy the prohibition of abortion was to apply.

22. There is an important technical issue at stake in contending that abortion is a *sui generis* biological experience. In ethics, an evaluation of an act frequently hinges on its analogous relationship to other approved or disapproved acts. With respect to abortion, the *sui generis* claim means that most analogies are rendered ineffective. See Chapter 7.

23. Rosemary Radford Ruether, "Italy's 'Third Way' on Abortion Faces a Test," *Christianity and Crisis*, 41:8 (May 11, 1981), pp. 130, 141-143.

24. The importance to personal development of "taking the role of the other" was explored initially by sociologists Charles H. Cooley and George Herbert Mead. Both sensed its importance for moral development. Charles H. Cooley, *Human Nature and Social Order* (New York: Schocken, 1902); George Herbert Mead, *Mind, Self, and Society* (Chicago: University of Chicago Press, 1934).

25. Ronald Green, "Conferred Rights and the Fetus," *Journal of Religious Ethics*, vol. 2 (Spring 1974), pp. 55-74.

26. John Rawls, *A Theory of Justice* (Cambridge: Belknap Press, Harvard University Press, 1971).

27. For a critique of this view of moral reason, see Daniel Maguire, *The Moral Choice* (New York: Doubleday, 1978).

28. The phrase reverses Deborah S. David and Robert Brannon, eds., *The Forty-Nine Percent Majority: The Male Sex Role* (Reading, Mass.: Addison-Wesley, 1976).

29. In Puerto Rico, owing to a variety of factors, sterilization came to be used widely in public health facilities and in Protestant mission hospitals. No one disputes that by now at least 30 percent of Puerto Rican women of childbearing age have been sterilized. Naturally, this situation has engendered pervasive resentment among Puerto Rican people. See especially Dr. Helen Rodriguez, "Population Control: The U.S. and Puerto Rico," in *Theology in the Americas*, Detroit II Conference Papers, ed. Cornel West, Caridad Guidote, and Margaret Coakley (Maryknoll, N.Y.: Orbis Books, Probe Edition, 1982), pp. 34-39. Puerto Rican and other third-world women have been used also as "guinea pigs" in experiments involving other means of contraception. See Mary Forell Davis, "Contraceptive Research: U.S. Policies and the Third World,"unpublished manuscript, Union Theological Seminary, 1976. See also Dr. Helen Rodriguez, "The Social Politics of Technology," *Women's Rights Law Reporter*, 7:5 (1983).

30. A sociology of knowledge perspective attends to the total configuration of social interests in which ideas are embedded. The sociology of knowledge is not, as some have claimed, a discrete methodology or discipline. Rather, it is a conceptual sensibility relevant to any mode of inquiry. See James E. Curtis and John W. Petras, eds., *The Sociology of Knowledge: A Reader* (New York: Praeger, 1970).

31. Christopher Lasch, *The Culture of Narcissism: American Life in an Age of Diminishing Expectations* (New York: Warner Books, 1979). For an analysis of Lasch's assumptions about women, see Berenice M. Fisher, "The Wise Old Men and the New Women: Christopher Lasch Besieged," in *History of Education Quarterly*, 19:1 (1978), pp. 125-141.

32. Frances M. Beal, "Double Jeopardy: To Be Black and Female," in Robin Morgan, ed., *Sisterhood Is Powerful* (New York: Vintage, 1970), pp. 340-353.

33. John R. Wikse, *About Possession: The Self as Private Property* (University Park: Pennsylvania State University Press, 1977), pp. 13ff. To reject liberty as a key category for conceptualizing rights is to break with dominant liberal political theory. In my view, "rights" are basic shares of the conditions of well-being a society can provide its members.

34. Zillah Eisenstein, *The Radical Future of Liberal Feminism* (New York: Longman, 1981). See also Susan Moller Okin's excellent *Women in Western Political Thought* (Princeton: Princeton University Press, 1979).

35. For a discussion of some of the "exemptions" of women under the equal protection clauses of the Constitution, see Jeanne Mager Stellman, *Women's Work, Women's Health: Myths and Realities* (New York: Pantheon, 1977), pp. 188ff. Recent Supreme Court decisions on abortion have rejected the view that indigency is relevant to the issue of equal protection. Hence the decision that the Hyde Amendment, prohibiting the use of public monies to finance abortions, does not violate the principles established in *Roe v. Wade.*

36. For the text and legal interpretations that have developed, see Thomas James Norton, *The Constitution of the United States: Its Sources and Its Application* (New York: Committee for Constitutional Government, November 1962 edition).

37. For a compelling analysis of the problems of individualism in feminist reflection on abortion, and a fine statement of what is at issue in terms of women's control of their reproductive capacity, see Rosalind Pollack Petchesky, "Reproductive Freedom: Beyond a Woman's Right to Choose," *Signs,* 5:4 (Summer 1980), pp. 661-685. Petchesky's work in this area has led her to a conclusion very similar to my own.

38. See Kristen Booth Glen, "Abortion in the Courts: A Laywoman's Historical Guide to the New Disaster Area," *Feminist Studies* (February 1978), pp. 1-26.

39. The term is Michael Lewis's. See *The Culture of Inequality* (Amherst: University of Massachusetts Press, 1978), part 1.

40. This maxim is most often associated with the moral theory of Immanuel Kant. In interpretations of Kant's ethics, his "teleology of ends" is often ignored. See Jeffrie G. Murphy, *Kant: The Philosophy of Right* (London: Macmillan, 1970).

41. The phrase is Juliet Mitchell's, "The Longest Revolution," *The New Left Review,* vol. 40 (November-December 1966), pp. 11-37.

3: The Theologies Behind the Moral Debate on Abortion

1. See especially Mary Daly, *Beyond God the Father* (Boston: Beacon Press, 1973), and *Gyn/Ecology: The Metaethics of Radical Feminism* (Boston: Beacon Press, 1978).

2. See Elizabeth Cady Stanton, Susan B. Anthony, and Matilda Joslyn Gage, *The History of Women's Suffrage*, vol. I (New York: Fowler and Weeks, 1881), passim; Beverly W. Harrison, "The Early Feminists and the Clergy: A Case Study in the Dynamics of Secularization," *Review and Expositor*, 72:1 (Winter 1975); Matilda Joslyn Gage, *Woman, Church, and State: The Original Exposé of Male Collaboration Against the Female Sex* (Watertown, Mass.: Persephone Press, 1980). Nancy F. Cott details the response of the evangelical clergy in New England to the changing social pressures generated by the women's movement in *The Bonds of Womanhood: "Woman's Sphere" in New England, 1780-1835* (New Haven: Yale University Press, 1977). If fundamentalism was a response to early feminism in the United States, many historians of the New Right believe that legal abortion was a major catalyst for its politics. See Allen Hunter, "In the Wings: New Right, Ideology and Organization," in *The New Right: Fundamentalists and Financiers* (Falls Church, Va: Viguerie, 1980) pp. 6-23, especially pp. 19ff.
3. A further surprising source of documentation for this merging of political Right structure with fundamentalist religion is an informative essay by Johnny Greene, "The Astonishing Wrongs of the New Moral Right," *Playboy* (January 1981), pp. 117-118; 248-260. Richard Viguerie, *The New Right: We're Ready to Lead*, contains justification for the legislation they seek. He contends that women and blacks who are clear-headed politically will support it. See also Alan Crawford, *Thunder on the Right: The "New Right" and the Politics of Resentment* (New York: Pantheon, 1980), and Daniel Maguire, *The New American Subversives: Anti-Americanism of the Religious Right* (New York: Crossroads, 1982).
4. Gary Potter, president of Catholics for Political Action, as quoted in Greene, p. 118. For a fuller analysis of "the family protection act" and the New Right agenda for women, see Jeanne Butterfield, "The New Right: Women's Rights Under Attack," *Radical Religion*, 5:4 (1981), pp. 61-73. For a helpful critique of the moral assumptions of the New Right, including some insightful theological observations, see J. Mark Thomas, "Worshipping a Place That Isn't God," *Christianity and Crisis*, 42:2 (February 15, 1982), pp. 26-29. I do not endorse all of Thomas's suggestions for a "more adequate" theological alternative.
5. *Christian Voice*, as quoted in Greene, p. 252. I do not mean to imply here that all those whom moral majority leaders identify as their followers oppose abortion. One recent controlled study that sampled opinions of regular viewers of new religious Right programming revealed that 34 percent of those surveyed favored legal abortion and 41 percent supported the Equal Rights Amendment. See Donna Day Lower, "Who Is the Moral Majority? A Composite Profile," *Union Theological Seminary Quarterly*, 37:4 (1983), pp. 335-349.
6. Tensions between the Reagan administration and the New Right religious groups have been widely reported. Because of other Reagan administration priorities, cultural issues have not been pressed as fervently as the New Right expected. See Charles Austin, "Religious Right Growing Impatient with Reagan," *New York Times*, August 16, 1982, p. A13.

7. The New Right assault on "humanism" in religion as a sure sign of "godlessness" demonstrates how sharp is the dualistic either/or logic of its position. It is assumed that one reverences either God or man [sic]. The possibility that the love of God and of people are not contraries but dialectically related realities does not occur to New Right adherents. Because God is a "jealous God" who must "own" those who love "Him," love implies possession for this group. In mirroring the structure of love exemplified in patriarchy, a love relationship between higher (male/God) and lower (female/Man) beings must involve ownership, unquestioned loyalty, exclusivity. Of course, Christianity at its best is intrinsically oriented to human well-being. No one should fear such "humanism." The New Right contention that "humanism" is equivalent to "secularism" and that faithfulness to God entails an antihumanistic stance is one I challenge in Chapter 4.

8. Nancy Jay, *Throughout Your Generations Forever: A Sociology of Blood Sacrifice*, unpublished Ph.D. dissertation, Brandeis University, 1981.

9. See Rosemary Radford Ruether, *New Woman/New Earth: Sexist Ideologies and Human Liberation* (New York: Seabury Press, 1975).

10. "Supererogatory" acts are, in the technical language of ethics, those that exceed minimal rationally justified expectations that define obligation. See Rawls, *A Theory of Justice* (Cambridge: Belknap Press, Harvard University Press, 1971), pp. 438-439; 478-479. Rawls defines "supererogatory" acts in a manner characteristic of many contemporary philosophical theories about morals. However, I do not embrace his sharp differentiation between justice and love.

11. An "ontic" distinction is one rooted in the essential structure of things and, therefore, presumably not malleable. Much Christian theology that begins by analyzing the "ontological structure" of reality presumes that the essence of things can be isolated and identified apart from process and relationship. Hence, such theology often stands in continuity with older natural law approaches, even when its method of identifying "essences" is based on more modern philosophical assumptions.

12. The canon is that body of literature that Christians hold to be "authoritative." Different groups of Christians vary in their views about which literature is properly canonical. Concerning the formation of the Christian canon and the problem of canonization, see Brevard S. Childs, *Introduction to the Old Testament as Scripture* (Philadelphia: Fortress Press, 1979), and Hans von Campenhausen, *The Formation of the Christian Bible*, trans. J. A. Baker (London: Black, 1972).

13. Work by female biblical scholars has begun to correct several dimensions of misogyny in biblical studies. See Phyllis Trible, *God and the Rhetoric of Sexuality* (Philadelphia: Fortress Press, 1978); Elisabeth Schüssler Fiorenza, "Women in the Pre-Pauline Churches," *Union Seminary Quarterly Review*, 33, 1978, pp. 153-166; Elisabeth Schüssler Fiorenza, "Word, Spirit and Power: Women in Early Christian Communities," in *Women of Spirit: Female Leadership in Jewish and Christian Traditions*, ed. Rosemary Ruether and Eleanor McLaughlin (New York: Simon & Schuster, 1979); *In Memory of Her: A Feminist Theological Reconstruction of Christian Origins* (New York: Crossroads, 1983). See also Letty M. Russell, ed.,

The Liberating Word: A Guide to Nonsexist Interpretation of the Bible (Philadelphia: Westminster Press, 1976). On the roots of Christian anti-Semitism, see Rosemary Radford Ruether, *Faith and Patricide: The Theological Roots of Anti-Semitism* (New York: Seabury Press, 1974).

14. The widespread recognition that the family is a socio-historical institution that undergoes considerable change, albeit slowly, is now taken for granted by modern historians. See, for example, Jean Louis Flandrin, *Families in Former Times* (Cambridge: The University Press, 1979); Carl N. Degler, *At Odds: Women and the Family in America from the Revolution to the Present* (New York: Oxford University Press, 1980); Sarah B. Pomeroy, *Goddesses, Whores, Wives, and Slaves: Women in Classical Antiquity* (New York: Schocken, 1976); and Page Smith, *Daughters of the Promised Land: Women in American History* (Boston: Little, Brown, 1970).

15. Philippe Ariès traces the emergence of the child-centered family in Europe in *Centuries of Childhood*, trans. Robert Baldick (New York: Vintage, 1965). He argues that the child-centered family could not have been a widespread phenomenon in premodern Europe. Greater longevity and relative economic affluence have extended the years of childhood dramatically over the last two centuries. His thesis is controversial, however, and here I do not presume that nuclear families were unknown earlier. What becomes distinctive of the family in the last two centuries is the severing of economic production from women's domestic roles, hence the socioeconomic disempowerment of women. Cf. Heidi Hartmann, "Capitalism, Patriarchy and Job Segregation by Sex," in Zillah Eisenstein, ed., *Capitalist Patriarchy and the Case for Socialist Feminism* (New York: Monthly Review Press, 1979), pp. 206-247. On the role of social gospel theologians in solidifying piety toward the family, see Janet Forsyth Fishburn, *The Fatherhood of God and the Victorian Family* (Philadelphia: Fortress Press, 1981).

16. "Covenant" is, of course, the more Protestant conception of marriage. Roman Catholic theologians more characteristically interpret marriage under the rubric of a sacramental reality. Compare John Calvin Reed, *Marriage Covenant* (Richmond: John Knox Press, 1967), and Leonardo Boff, "The Sacrament of Marriage," in William Basset and Peter Huizing, eds., *The Future of Christian Marriage* (New York: Herder & Herder, 1973), pp. 22-23. Even those statements that explicitly break with the notion that procreation is the sole or chief goal of sexuality in marriage remain ambivalent about the value of sexuality per se. Ideals of "intimacy" in Christian marriage often are so overstressed that I believe Christian theological teaching bears some responsibility for the degree of disappointment many couples experience. For a probing early challenge to Christian thinking on this issue, see Dorothea Krook, "The Lambeth Conference, 1958: Theology of Sexuality," in *Three Traditions of Moral Thought* (Cambridge: The University Press, 1959), pp. 333-347, App. C.

17. Papal pronouncements, and especially papal speeches addressed to women, exemplify this romanticism. For example, on April 29, 1979,

in a speech to domestic workers Pope John Paul II reiterated Pope Pius XII's 1945 statement that "Each of the sexes must play its part in society according to its nature, its character, its physical, intellectual and moral aptitude. Both have the right and the duty to cooperate for the good of society. But it is clear that if men are by temperament more apt to deal with matters outside the home, in the public domain, women have, generally speaking, more understanding and tact for comprehending and resolving the delicate problems of domestic life, which is the foundation of social life." In addition, he told the assembled women that "Certainly domestic work must be seen not as an implacable and inexorable imposition, as slavery, but as a free choice, conscious and willing, which fully realizes women's nature, and fulfills their needs." About the presence of women in the home, he stated that it "can bring serenity, peace, hope, joy, comfort, and encouragement to good. . . [Women] can be the leaven of goodness in the family." Quoted in *Religious News Service* release of April 30, 1979, p. 10.

18. Even when Jewish religious leaders oppose abortion, they frequently do so for quite different moral reasons than their Christian counterparts. Jewish abortion opponents often fear for the survival of their people, given the history of genocidal treatment of Jews by Christians, or they oppose legal abortion because it fosters other social changes. Only recently have Jews begun to formulate arguments analogous to recent Christian statements about the value of fetal life. On this point, see Annette Daum, "The Jewish Stake in Abortion Rights," *Lilith*, no. 8 (n.d.).

19. The range of modern theological opinion on eschatology and its bearing on the early Christian message is surveyed in Norman Perrin, *The Kingdom of God in the Teaching of Jesus* (London: SCM Press, 1963). However, I do not concur with Perrin's individualistic interpretation of the New Testament ethic.

20. I Corinthians 7:9-10. See John Boswell, *Christianity, Social Tolerance and Homosexuality: Gay People in Western Europe from the Beginning of the Christian Era to the Fourteenth Century* (Chicago: University of Chicago Press, 1980), pp. 104-117. Many book-length discussions of Paul's theology and ethics all but ignore his teaching on sexuality. His counsel on marriage is generally related to his eschatological expectations. On Paul's views on women, see Madeleine Boucher, "The Order of Creation and the Role of Women: From Genesis 1-3 to I Corinthians 11:2-16," unpublished paper presented at the Women in Scripture Consultation, meeting of the Society of Biblical Literature, San Francisco, December 19-22, 1981. For an elaboration of Paul's attitude toward the body, see John A. T. Robinson, *The Body: A Study in Pauline Theology*, Studies in Biblical Theology no. 5 (London: SCM Press, 1952). Also see Fiorenza, *In Memory of Her*, pp. 211-350.

21. Anne L. Barstow, *Married Priests and the Reforming Papacy: The Eleventh Century Debates* (Lewiston, N.Y.: Mellen, 1982).

22. Boswell, pp. 163ff.

23. Ibid. John Boswell's pioneering work is helpful in identifying not only the diversity of scriptural teaching on sexuality but divergences in Christian teaching and practice over a millennium. Unfortunately, Boswell chooses to focus almost exclusively on male homosexual practice, but he does examine this issue in relation to the more exclusive Christian teaching on sexuality. See also Stephen Sapp, *Sexuality, the Bible, and Science* (Philadelphia: Fortress Press, 1977).

24. See Genesis 19 and commentaries on the passage in Isaiah 1:10-23; Ezekiel 16: 48-49; Jeremiah 23:14; and Zephaniah 2:8-11. The original tale of the destruction of Sodom, now associated with the presumed homosexual practice of its citizens, was a powerful symbol of evil-doing and disobedience to God. However, none of the later biblicist references to Sodom pinpoint homosexuality as the "sin of Sodom"; injustice or lack of hospitality to the stranger was the problem. That Lot *offered his daughters* to the Sodomites who wished to "know" the strangers is hardly mentioned by most exegetes. Boswell is skeptical that this text implies anything at all about sexual relations. He does not, however, offer an alternative explanation as to why Lot proposes to offer his daughters to the men in the street rather than expel the strangers from his house. I wish I found his argument more compelling, although he does say that the text reflects "the very low status of female children at the time," p. 95.

25. Exodus 21:22-24. Other scriptural passages yield indirect information about ancient Israelite attitudes toward fetal life. But such texts are not cited by Christian theologians, precisely because they exemplify a characteristic Israelite attitude that life begins at birth. Koheleth, the writer of Ecclesiastes, for example, laments the suffering of the living: "An untimely birth is better off than a living person, for the miscarriage goes into darkness, where its name disappears: it has not seen the light nor known anything, yet it finds rest denied to the living" (Ecclesiastes 6:3-5). In much Hebraic idiom, the disappearance of one's name is equivalent to loss of existence under God. Obviously, fetal life is not here understood as equivalent to a living person.

26. For example, see Exodus 23:26 and Genesis 21:1-7.

27. See, for example, Doug Badger, "Divinely Knit," *Sojourners*, vol. 9, no. 11 (November 1980), pp. 17-18. See also, John A. Rasmussen, "Abortion: Historical and Biblical Perspectives," *Concordia Theological Quarterly*, 43:1 (January 1979), pp. 19-26. Rasmussen cites numerous biblical texts totally unrelated to abortion to "make his case." Of the Old Testament, he says: "One cannot help but see the hand of God at work in the formation of the fetus."

28. An excellent description of a feminist liberation hermeneutic in relation to the tradition is Elisabeth Schüssler Fiorenza's "Discipleship and Patriarchy: Early Christian Ethos and Christian Ethics in a Feminist Theological Perspective," *The Annual*, Society of Christian Ethics (1982), pp. 131-172.

29. Many theologians have argued that some periods of early Israelite

history, and also the early Christian community, were uncharacteristically egalitarian in terms of male/female relations. See Letty M. Russell, *Human Liberation in a Feminist Perspective: A Theology* (Philadelphia: Westminster Press, 1974). Even so, it is clear that the ethos of the early Christian community did not challenge female inequality in the *wider social structure*. Furthermore, our Jewish sisters rightly have cautioned Christian feminists about the dangers of an implicit anti-Semitism in overblown claims for early Christian gender equality. Christian feminists do not always compare adequately the practice of the Christian community in relation to its wider Jewish cultural setting. See Judith Plaskow, "Blaming Jews for Inventing Patriarchy," and Annette Daum, "Blaming Jews for the Death of the Goddess," *Lilith*, no. 7 (1981), pp. 11-13.

30. Bruce Birch and Larry Rasmussen, *The Bible and Ethics in the Christian Life* (Minneapolis: Augsburg Publishing House, 1976); Dennis Nineham, *The Use and Abuse of the Bible: The Study of the Bible in an Age of Rapid Social Change* (London: Macmillan, 1976); Thomas Ogletree, *The Use of the Bible in Christian Ethics* (Philadelphia: Fortress Press, 1983). David H. Kelsey has analyzed the tremendous diversity of uses of scripture in the work of major twentieth-century Protestant theologians. See *The Use of Scripture in Recent Theology* (Philadelphia: Fortress Press, 1975).

31. A work that well characterizes the shift of Roman Catholic moral theology to a more characteristic neoorthodox reliance on a biblical framework for Christian ethics is *The Law of Christ*, vols. 1 and 2, by Bernard Häring, C.S.S.R. (Paramus, N.J.: Newman Press, 1966). (Häring's work went through six printings in Germany prior to its translation into English.)

32. A vast body of literature has developed around the question of the validity of Divine Command ethics. See, for example, Janine Marie Idziak, *Divine Command Morality: Historical and Contemporary Perspective* (Lewiston, N.Y.: Mellen, 1980).

33. Emil Brunner, for example, in his *The Divine Imperative* (Philadelphia: Westminster, 1947), employed the orders of creation notion. Barth preferred to speak of divine decrees and commands. See his *Church Dogmatics*, vol. II/2, ed. G. W. Bromily and T. F. Torrance (Edinburgh: Clark, 1957). Dietrich Bonhoeffer in *Ethics*, ed. Eberhard Bethge (New York: Macmillan, 1955), pp. 130-131, 137ff., introduced the term *mandate* into his analysis. These differences are more than terminological. Barth and Bonhoeffer sought to avoid any simplistic equation of divine will with "natural" categories. Concerning marriage, women's "nature," and procreation, however, there is more continuity than difference among Brunner, Barth, and Bonhoeffer. Even though Bonhoeffer discusses "the right of the body" as a foundational ethical reality, he treats conception undialectically as an act of God and condemns abortion as murder, even when a woman's circumstances make the act comprehensible (Part I/IV).

34. The distinction between this general political orientation and attitudes

toward the family is most acute in Emil Brunner's work. In *Man in Revolt: A Christian Anthropology* (Philadelphia: Westminster, 1947), pp. 352-353, he says of gender differentiation:

> The depth of this division (between spirit and nature) shows how deeply sexuality has been implanted in the nature of man by the Creation. Man is not a sex being in addition to that which he is otherwise, but the sex difference penetrates and determines the whole of human existence. The man is not only man in his sexual function, but he is man in all his thought and feeling. The same is true of the woman in her existence as woman. The differentiation of the biological sexual function in the man and the woman has its exact counterpart in the mental and spiritual nature of both sexes, although — in accordance with what has already been said about the relation between individuality and genius . . . — it recedes in exact proportion to the measure in which the spirit, and the personal spirit in particular, becomes strong. Within this limitation it may be said that also spiritually the man expresses the productive principle and the woman expresses the principle of bearing, tending, and nourishing. The man turns more to the outside world, the woman turns more to the inner realm; the man inclines to be objective, the woman to be subjective; the man seeks the new, the woman preserves the old; the man roams about, the woman makes a home.

See also Brunner's *The Divine Imperative*, pp. 340-383. Brunner insists on the relative legitimacy of the state, but also on its limitations within the orders of creation. Christian participation in politics is essential, but the status of the state remains provisional. Not so with marriage and the role of men and women. Although Barth's position appeals to scripture, not nature, he still feels obligated to develop the theme of woman's subordination to man. See Karl Barth, vol. III/4 (1961), pp. 116-240.

35. A helpful analysis of Protestant *imago dei* discussions as they bear on the abortion question has been written by Ruth Evans, "The Image of God and the Abortion Debate," unpublished manuscript, University of Toronto, 1979.

36. See especially Karl Barth, *The Humanity of God* (Richmond: John Knox Press, 1960). Barth's interest in this theme is, I believe, grounded more in his continuity with earlier German liberalism and Christian socialism than in his neoorthodox correction of liberal theology.

37. See Paul Helm, ed., *Divine Commands and Morality* (New York: Oxford University Press, 1981).

38. For Paul Ramsey's early position, see "The Morality of Abortion: Life or Death Ethics and Options," in Edward Shils et al., eds., *Life or Death: Ethics and Options* (Seattle: University of Washington Press, 1968), pp. 60-93. For his later views, see "Abortion: A Review Article," *Thomist*, vol. 37 (1973) pp. 174-226.

39. Helmut Theilicke, *The Ethics of Sex* (New York: Harper & Row, 1964), pp. 210, 226ff. Theilicke argues that because of the reality of sin, we cannot apply an "orders of creation" argument in a simplistic fashion.

There is an indication here that abortion can be justified in order to save a woman's life, but the identification of biological reproduction with direct, divine blessing is blatant.

40. David M. Kennedy describes the churches' organized opposition to birth control in Chapter 6 of his *Birth Control in America* (New Haven: Yale University Press, 1970).

41. Compare, for example, Paul D. Simmons, "A Theological Response to Fundamentalism on the Abortion Issue," in *Abortion: The Moral Issues,* ed. Edward Batchelor, Jr. (New York: Pilgrim Press, 1982), pp. 175-187, with John Noonan's *A Private Choice: Abortion in America in the Seventies* (New York: Free Press, 1979), p. 169. Simmons's invocation of Barth in support of pro-choice is nuanced, whereas Noonan simply invokes his authority for an anti-abortion position without qualification.

42. Robert T. Handy, ed., *The Social Gospel in America* (New York: Oxford University Press, 1966); Henry F. May, *Protestant Churches in Industrial America* (New York: Octagon Books, 1949).

43. Karl Rahner, "Experiment Man," *Theology Digest,* Sesquicentennial Issue (February 1968), pp. 61ff.

44. Ann Douglas, *The Feminization of American Culture* (New York: Knopf, 1977). I do not concur fully with Douglas's analysis. She seems to verge on insensitivity to the actual values implicit in traditional notions of the feminine. While I share her opposition to the romanticization of women, feminists also need to appreciate the values of women's culture and to be critical of the values operative in so-called public life. Even so, her criticism of the sentimentalization of the nineteenth-century women's movement, involving clergy complicity, is accurate. See also James Reed, *From Private Vice to Public Virtue: The Birth Control Movement and American Society Since 1830* (New York: Basic Books, 1978); Linda Gordon, *Woman's Body, Woman's Right: A Social History of Birth Control in America* (New York: Penguin Books, 1974); and Beverly W. Harrison, "Sexism and the Contemporary Churches: When Evasion Becomes Complicity," in *Sexist Religion and Women in the Church: No More Silence,* ed. Alice L. Hageman (New York: Association Press, 1974), pp. 195-216.

45. Daniel Callahan, *Abortion: Law, Choice, and Morality* (New York: Macmillan, 1970), p. 340. Callahan's book, which was the first study in religious ethics to bring a liberal perspective to the abortion issue, remains a valuable source of information and reflection on abortion. As stated earlier, its greatest strength is its recognition of the religious, cultural, and authentic moral pluralism underlying the abortion debate. His discussion of the moral principles involved is especially useful. A major limitation, however, is Callahan's lack of socio-historical interest in the role abortion plays in women's lives. Although he acknowledges the recent impact of women's rights arguments, he characterizes the moral claim women make as one-dimensional. See pp. 460ff.

46. Mary Meehan, "Will Somebody Please Be Consistent," *Sojourners,* vol. 9, no. 1 (November 1980), p. 14.

47. It is not possible to controvert this claim, because Juli Loesch in "Fetus

Is Latin for Unborn Child," *Sojourners* (November 1980), p. 19, does not document her etymological source.

48. See James W. Douglas, *The Non-Violent Cross: A Theology of Revolution and Peace* (New York: Macmillan, 1968).

49. James W. Douglas, "Patriarchy and the Pentagon Make Abortion Inevitable," *Sojourners*, pp. 14-15.

50. Ibid., p. 15.

51. Jeanne Mager Stellman, *Women's Work, Women's Health: Myths and Realities* (New York: Pantheon, 1977), pp. 144-173.

52. James B. Nelson, *Embodiment: An Approach to Sexuality and Christian Theology* (Minneapolis: Augsburg Publishing House, 1978); Tom F. Driver, *Christ in a Changing World: Toward an Ethical Christology* (New York: Crossroads, 1981). See also Anthony Kosnick, et al., eds., *Human Sexuality: New Directions in American Catholic Thought* (New York: Paulist Press, 1977). A number of Roman Catholic bishops have taken strong exception to this study. For a Roman Catholic revisionist discussion of human sexuality, see André Guindon's *The Sexual Language* (Ottawa: University of Ottawa Press, 1977). Guindon offers a spirited and excellent critique of papal teaching on contraception and other "unnatural" aspects of sexuality (pp. 163-220 and passim). Characteristically, abortion is not mentioned. However, Guindon's treatment of homosexuality is severely flawed. He assumes that there is something called a "homosexual personality" and employs now-discredited psychoanalytic theories of "overmothering" to account for male homosexual development.

53. Christine Gudorf, *Catholic Social Teaching on Liberation Themes* (Washington, D.C.: University Press of America, 1980). This helpful history of papal responses to issues of racial justice, radical economic critique, liberation theological methods, and women's equality makes clear that papal teaching has been most adamant in its unbending attitude toward women's role and "nature."

54. H. Richard Niebuhr, *Social Sources of Denominationalism* (New York: Holt, 1929); *Kingdom of God in America* (Chicago: Willet, Clark, 1937); and *The Meaning of Revelation* (New York: Macmillan, 1937). I have analyzed why Niebuhr's revisioned social anthropology did not result in a more dynamic social ethic. See Beverly W. Harrison, "H. Richard Niebuhr: Towards a Christian Moral Philosophy," unpublished doctoral thesis, Union Theological Seminary, New York, 1974.

55. John MacMurray, *Persons in Relation* (London: Faber and Faber, 1961) and *The Self as Agent* (London: Faber and Faber, 1957).

56. John C. Bennett, *Christian Ethics and Social Policy* (New York: Scribner's, 1946) and *The Radical Imperative: From Theology to Social Ethics* (Philadelphia: Westminster, 1975). See also James Luther Adams, *On Being Human — Religiously: Selected Essays in Religion and Society*, ed. and intro. Max L. Stackhouse (Boston: Beacon Press, 1976). Much of Adams's work appeared as essays in journals, unfortunately not yet republished. See D. B. Robertson, ed., *Voluntary Associations* (Richmond: John Knox Press, 1966) for a discussion of Adams's thought.

57. Reinhold Niebuhr is the theological ethicist most often associated with the challenge to absolute idealism in ethics. He identified moralism and sentimentality as the major shortcomings of theological liberalism. However, he did not reformulate an alternative ethical theory. Instead, he "corrected" moral idealism with "realist" theological and political assumptions in a manner that made it somewhat less than clear what force normative ethical considerations were to have in Christian action. See, for example, *Christian Realism and Political Problems* (New York: Scribner's, 1953). Some readers may be surprised that I do not associate Reinhold Niebuhr with what I identify here as the needed reconstruction of Christian social theory. This is because I believe Niebuhr's thought contained an ambiguity about self-society relations, such that some aspects of our experience, the religious dimension, for example, prescind from social relations. See his *Self and the Dramas of History* (New York: Scribner's, 1955), pp. 23-24, passim.

58. Alfred North Whitehead's integrative cosmology is elaborated in his *Process and Reality: An Essay in Cosmology* (New York: Macmillan, 1929). See also Charles Hartshorne, *A Natural Theology for Our Time* (La Salle, Ill.: Open Court Press, 1967).

59. Teilhard de Chardin, *The Phenomenon of Man* (New York: Harper & Row, 1961).

60. See Daniel Day Williams, "Deity, Monarchy and Metaphysics," in Ivor Le Clerc, ed., *The Relevance of Whitehead* (New York: Macmillan, 1961).

61. See Beverly W. Harrison, "Feminism and Process Thought," *Signs*, 7:3 (Spring 1972), pp. 704-710. See also Sheila Greeve Daveney, ed., *Feminism and Process Thought* (New York: Mellen, 1981).

62. Charles Hartshorne, "Concerning Abortion: An Attempt at a Rational View," *Christian Century*, vol. 98, no. 2 (January 21, 1981). William S. Hamrick, "Abortion: A Whiteheadian Perspective," paper presented at Eastern Philosophical Association, Boston, December 1980. (See Chapter 7, n. 63.)

63. Jean Lambert, "Becoming Human: A Contextual Approach to Decisions About Pregnancy and Abortion," in Daveney, pp. 134-135.

64. Beverly W. Harrison, "When Blessedness and Fruitfulness Diverge," *Religion in Life*, vol. 41 (1972), pp. 480-496.

65. John Hudgins, "Is Birth Control Genocide?" *Black Scholar*, 4:3 (November-December 1972), pp. 34ff.; Kay Lindsey, "Birth Control and the Black Woman," *Essence* (October 1970), pp. 56-57, 70-71; and Nathan Wright, "Black Power vs. Black Genocide," *Black Scholar*, 1:2 (December 1969), pp. 47-52.

66. Ronald Michael Green, *Population Growth and Justice: An Examination of Moral Issues Raised by Rapid Population Growth* (Missoula, Mont.: Scholars Press, 1976).

67. Marie Augusta Neal, "Sociology and Sexuality: A Feminist Perspective," *Christianity and Crisis*, 39:8 (May 14, 1979), pp. 118-122. That I have reservations about much genetic engineering, including the prospects

for reproduction that cloning may open up, should be clear from my discussion in Chapter 2.

4: Toward a Liberating Theological Perspective on Procreative Choice and Abortion

1. I take this assumption to be characteristic of liberation theologies, which emphasize the embodiment of justice in history as dialectically related to one's vision of God. See "To Know God Is to Do Justice," in Gustavo Gutiérrez, *A Theology of Liberation* (Maryknoll, N.Y.: Orbis Books, 1973), pp. 189-202.
2. Gutierrez, pp. 287-308. Elsa Tamez, *Bible of the Oppressed*, trans. Matthew J. O'Connell (Maryknoll, N.Y.: Orbis Books, 1979). I affirm Tamez's general hermeneutic for the interpretation of scripture but regret her failure to acknowledge the structural reality of women's subjugation and racism as significant dynamics of oppression. She subsumes violence against women under an interpretation of exploitation that is basically economic and fails to clarify how poverty interfaces with a system of gender control.
3. "Keep on keeping on" is a phrase originating from the black oral/aural tradition. See La Frances Rodgers-Rose, ed., *The Black Woman* (Beverly Hills: Sage Publications, 1980), p. 10.
4. See Juan Luis Segundo, *The Liberation of Theology*, trans. John Drury (Maryknoll, N.Y.: Orbis Books, 1976), pp. 178-182. I agree with Segundo on the origins of violence in society, but not with his analysis of the relationship between love and violence. I think that he fails to make an adequate distinction between violence, coercion, and moral impact. See pp. 154-165.
5. For a discussion of the meaning of this term in Latin American liberation theology, see Robert McAfee Brown, *Theology in a New Key: Responding to Liberation Themes* (Philadelphia: Westminster, 1978), pp. 60-61.
6. See, for example, James Cone, *A Black Theology of Liberation* (Philadelphia: Lippincott, 1970); Allan Aubrey Boesak, *Farewell to Innocence: A Socio-Ethical Study on Black Theology and Power* (Maryknoll, N.Y.: Orbis Books, 1977); Vine Deloria, Jr., *God Is Red* (New York: Dell, 1975); Rosemary Radford Ruether, *New Woman/New Earth: Sexist Ideologies and Human Liberation* (New York: Seabury Press, 1975); *Theology in the Americas*, Detroit II Conference Papers, Cornell West, Caridad Guidote, and Margaret Coakley, eds. (Maryknoll, N.Y.: Orbis Press, 1981); Cornell West, Caridad Guidote, and Margaret Coakley, eds., *Is Liberation Theology for North America? The Response of First World Churches* (New York: Theology in the Americas, 1978), pp. 21-27; *Asian Christian Theology: Emerging Themes*, ed. Douglas J. Elwood (Philadelphia: Westminster, 1980); *Asian Voices in Christian Theology*, ed. Gerald H. Anderson (Maryknoll, N.Y.: Orbis Books, 1976). See also Gerard Fourez, *Liberation Ethics* (Philadelphia: Temple University Press, 1982).

7. *Your Daughters Shall Prophesy: Feminist Alternatives in Theological Education*, ed. Cornwall Collective (New York: Pilgrim Press, 1981), pp. 38-75.

8. Robert McAfee Brown, *Theology in a New Key*.

9. Isabel Carter Heyward, *The Redemption of God: A Theology of Mutual Relation* (Washington, D.C.: University Press of America, 1982), pp. xv-24. My theological indebtedness to this study is obvious.

10. Karl Marx, *The Economic and Philosophical Manuscripts of 1844*, ed. and intro. Dirk J. Struik, trans. Martin Milligan (New York: International Publishers, 1964); John Dewey, *Human Nature and Conduct* (New York: Holt, 1922); Alfred North Whitehead, *Science and the Modern World* (New York: Macmillan, 1927). On the conception of knowledge and philosophy implicit here, see Richard Rorty, *Philosophy and the Mirror of Nature* (Princeton: Princeton University Press, 1979).

11. For an elaboration of this function of theology, see Younghak Hyun, "Theology as Rumormongering," unpublished lecture delivered at Union Theological Seminary, New York, April 20, 1982.

12. From Adrienne Rich, *On Lies, Secrets, and Silence: Selected Prose, 1966-1978* (New York: Norton, 1979).

13. Henry David Aiken, *Reason and Conduct: New Bearings in Moral Philosophy* (New York: Knopf, 1962). See especially Chapter 8, pp. 134-170.

14. Elisabeth Koltun, ed., *The Jewish Woman: New Perspectives* (New York: Schocken, 1976), and Susanna Heschel, ed., *Towards a Feminist Rejuvenation of Judaism* (New York: Schocken, 1982). Judith Plaskow, "God and Feminism," *Menorah*, 3:2 (1982).

15. See, for example, Mary Daly, *Gyn/Ecology: The Metaethics of Radical Feminism* (Boston: Beacon Press, 1978); Starhawk, *The Spiral Dance: A Rebirth of the Ancient Religion of the Great Goddess* (San Francisco: Harper & Row, 1979); Carol P. Christ, *Diving Deep and Surfacing: Women Writers on Spiritual Quest* (Boston: Beacon Press, 1980); Carol P. Christ and Judith Plaskow, eds., *WomanSpirit Rising: A Feminist Reader in Religion* (San Francisco: Harper & Row, 1979); Naomi Goldenberg, *Changing of the Gods: Feminism and the End of Traditional Religions* (Boston: Beacon Press, 1979). For a compendium of writings on feminist spirituality, see Charlene Spretnak, ed., *The Politics of Women's Spirituality* (New York: Doubleday-Anchor, 1982).

16. Simone Weil's actual statement is stronger: "History, therefore, is nothing but a compilation of the dispositions made by assassins with respect to their victims and themselves." *The Need for Roots* (London: Routledge & Kegan Paul, 1952), p. 225.

17. Starhawk, "Ethics and Justice in Goddess Religion," in Spretnak, p. 416.

18. Nelle Morton, "The Rising of Women's Consciousness in a Male Language Structure," *Andover Newton Quarterly*, 12:4 (March 1972), pp. 177-190.

19. Paulo Freire has elaborated the process of *conscientizacao* in *Cultural Action for Freedom*, published by *Harvard Educational Review* and Center for the Study of Development and Social Change, Monograph Series No. 1 (Cambridge, Mass., 1970). See also Sheila D. Collins, *A*

Different Heaven and Earth (Valley Forge: Judson Press, 1974), and Christ and Plaskow.

20. Sallie McFague, *Metaphorical Theology: Models of God in Religious Language* (Philadelphia: Fortress Press, 1982). An excellent analysis of the requirements of feminist methodology, especially in relation to a *critical* reappropriation of tradition, is found in Elisabeth Schüssler Fiorenza, "Feminist Theology as a Critical Theology of Liberation," *Theological Studies*, 36:4 (December 1975), pp. 605-626.

21. Because process is more fundamental than stasis, our being is not a given from which action proceeds; rather, movement is the given out of which consciousness arises. This way of formulating the matter reverses the usual starting point of ontological theologians. See, for example, Paul Tillich, *The Courage to Be* (New Haven: Yale University Press, 1952).

22. Jules Girardi, "Class Struggle and the Excluded Ones," trans. New York Circus, from *Amos Christiano Y Lucha De Classes* (Sigueme, Spain; 1975).

23. Gutiérrez, pp. 232-230; Jose Porfino Miranda, *Mark and the Bible: A Critique of the Philosophy of Oppression*, trans. John Eagleson (Maryknoll, N.Y.: Orbis Books, 1974), pp. 254ff. Reinhold Niebuhr's polemic against utopianism suffused his writings. For some of these materials, see *Reinhold Niebuhr on Politics: His Political Philosophy and Its Application to Our Age as Expressed in His Writings*, ed. Harry R. Davis and Robert C. Good (New York: Scribner's, 1960), especially Chapters 2 and 3.

24. Valerie C. Saiving, "Androgynous Life: A Feminist Appropriation of Process Thought," in *Feminism and Process Thought*, ed. Sheila Greeve Daveney (New York: Mellen, 1981), pp. 11-31.

25. Dorothee Soelle, *Christ the Representative: An Essay in Theology after the "Death of God"* (Philadelphia: Fortress Press, 1967). See part 1, pp. 17-56.

26. Nancy Jay, "Gender and Dichotomy," *Feminist Studies*, 7:1 (Spring 1981), pp. 39-56.

27. Beverly W. Harrison, "Sexism and the Language of Christian Ethics," unpublished essay, Union Theological Seminary, New York, 1981.

28. This appears to be what Mary Daly proposes. See Beverly W. Harrison, "The Power of Anger in the Work of Love: Christian Ethics for Women and Other Strangers," *Union Seminary Quarterly Review*, vol. 36, supplementary issue (1981), pp. 41-43, 54-57, nn. 1-4, 32.

29. Penelope Washbourn, *Becoming Woman: The Quest for Spiritual Wholeness in Female Experience* (New York: Harper & Row, 1979), and *Seasons of Woman*, ed. Penelope Washbourn (New York: Harper & Row, 1979).

30. Tom F. Driver, *Patterns of Grace: Human Experience as Word of God* (New York: Harper & Row, 1977), pp. 144-169.

31. Susan Griffin, *Woman and Nature: The Roaring Inside Her* (New York: Harper & Row, 1978).

32. Dorothee Soelle, *Beyond Mere Obedience*, trans. Lawrence W. Denef (New York: Pilgrim Press, 1982).
33. Beverly W. Harrison, "Power of Anger," pp. 45-48.
34. Boston Women's Health Book Collective, *Our Bodies, Ourselves* (New York: Simon & Schuster, 1976).
35. See two special issues on "Women: Sex and Sexuality" in *Signs*, 5:4 (Summer 1980), 6:1 (Autumn 1980).
36. Isabel Carter Heyward, "In the Beginning Was the Relation," *Integrity Forum*, 7:2 (1981), pp. 1-6.
37. Sheila Rowbotham, *Woman's Consciousness, Man's World* (Middlesex, England: Penguin Books, 1979), Chapter 3, pp. 26-46.
38. I have used the traditional construct "God" in this work, although I acknowledge the value of using female imagery. Given the history of gender oppression in religion, both terms are inadequate.
39. Marie Augusta Neal, S.N.D. deN., *The Socio-Theology of Letting Go: The Role of a First World Church Facing Third World Peoples* (New York: Paulist Press, 1977).
40. See Rosemary Radford Ruether, *Mary: The Feminine Face of the Church* (Philadelphia: Westminster, 1977); Dorothee Soelle, *Revolutionary Patience*, trans. Rita and Robert Kimber (Maryknoll, N.Y.: Orbis Books, 1977), "Meditation on Luke 1," pp. 51-52.
41. Rachel Conrad Wahlberg, "The Woman and the Fetus: One Flesh?" *Christian Century*, vol. 88 (1971), pp. 1045-1048. Wahlberg argues that women experience fetal life as part of their own bodily processes. Contrary to Wahlberg, I believe that women's subjective experience of pregnancy is shaped by cultural expectations and, therefore, may differ. Nevertheless, it is the case that fetal development is a process and that fetal life survives in interaction with the mother's life system.
42. Paul Lehmann, *Ethics in a Christian Context* (New York: Harper & Row, 1964), pp. 284, 351, passim.
43. See Gene Outka, *Agape: An Ethical Analysis* (New Haven: Yale University Press, 1972).
44. Reginald Stewart Moxon, *Modernism and Orthodoxy: An Appraisal of the Usefulness of the Vincentian Canon* (London: Clarke, 1924).

5: The History of Christian Teaching

1. John Boswell, *Christianity, Social Tolerance, and Homosexuality: Gay People in Western Europe from the Beginning of the Christian Era to the Fourteenth Century* (Chicago: University of Chicago Press, 1980), p. 103.
2. See, for example, E. P. Thompson, *The Making of the English Working Class* (New York: Vintage, 1966). This work places the development of English Methodism within the sort of broad social and cultural framework much needed in religious historiography. Feminist works

that integrate social and intellectual history are cited throughout this book.

3. See, for example, Joseph Pieper, *The Silence of St. Thomas*, trans. John Murray, S. J., and Daniel O'Connor (Chicago: Henry Regnery, 1957). Neither Augustine nor Aquinas figures centrally in the more adequate treatments of the history of abortion, for reasons that will become clear in this chapter.

4. Augustine, of course, was opposed adamantly to any sexuality not aimed at procreation. He viewed contraception as a serious wrong, as perusal of his writings against Manichean "heretics" makes clear. See *On the Morals of the Manichees*, 18:65 in *Writings Against the Manicheans and Against the Donatists*, vol. 4 of *The Nicene and Post-Nicene Fathers* (Grand Rapids, Mich.: Eerdmans, 1956), pp. 86-87 and passim. Even so, when in a few places in his writings he addressed the topic of abortion, he observed the "unformed" and "formed" distinction. Those who used this distinction presumed that fetal life was "merely" animal until spiritually was infused by God. The rational soul required for full humanity emerged at ensoulment; hence, termination of pregnancy prior to ensoulment was not technically homicide, even if it was wrong because it thwarted procreative intent. See Augustine, *The Confession and The Enchiridion*, in *Library of Christian Classics* (Philadelphia: Westminster, 1955), chap. 23, 85, p. 390. He also believed in the probable resurrection of fetuses. See *City of God*, 22:12 and 13, trans. Marcus Dods (New York: Modern Library, 1950), pp. 835-837. Apart from his extreme hostility to the Manichees, John Noonan's account of Augustine's views is generally accurate. John T. Noonan, Jr., *Contraception: A History of Its Treatment by the Catholic Theologians and Canonists* (Cambridge: Harvard University Press, 1966), pp. 119ff.

5. Aristotle, *On the History of Animals*, vol. 4 of *The Works of Aristotle*, and *On the Generation of Animals*, vol. 5 of *The Works of Aristotle*, 1:19-20, pp. 726A-729, trans. J. A. Smith and W. D. Ross (Oxford: Clarendon Press, 1910). See also Books 2-4, pp. 583ff. The first certain use of Aristotle's views in Christian reasoning on abortion can be found in the writings of Aquinas's teacher Albert the Great (1206-1280), *Commentarium MLIV*. Following Aristotle, Albert speculated about fetal development, but, contrary to the implication of Connery's otherwise admirable discussion, I do not read these musings as aimed specifically at assessing the moral value of fetal life. See John R. Connery, *Abortion: The Development of the Roman Catholic Perspective* (Chicago: Loyola University Press, 1977), pp. 107ff.

6. See, for example, Bernard Häring, "A Theological Evaluation," in John T. Noonan, Jr., ed., *The Morality of Abortion: Legal and Historical Perspectives* (Cambridge: Harvard University Press, 1970), pp. 123-145.

7. Connery does justice to this line of moral reasoning in much of his analysis.

8. John T. Noonan, Jr., "An Almost Absolute Value in History," in Noonan, ed., *The Morality of Abortion*, pp. 1-39.

9. Noonan, *Contraception.* I have concentrated so heavily on this work as a counterpoint to my own assessment of the history of Christian teaching on abortion because of its widespread use in scholarly literature and the relative absence of critical perspective on it. Connery objects to some of Noonan's conclusions in notes to his study.

10. John T. Noonan, Jr., *A Private Choice: Abortion in America in the Seventies* (New York: Free Press, 1979).

11. This is the implicit if not explicit assumption of nearly all historical treatments of Christian teaching on abortion. Even Connery implies it at points. Others, such as Noonan, use texts unrelated to abortion to establish Christian pronatalism and reverence for children as a context for discussion of anti-abortion texts and then fail to isolate the actual logic of these texts against abortion. Thereby, the reader is invited to assume that the line of moral reasoning involved concerns the moral value of fetal life. See, for example, Germain C. Grisez, *Abortion: The Myths, Realities, and the Arguments* (Washington, D.C.: Corpus Books, 1969).

12. Noonan, *Contraception,* pp. 56-106 and passim, and John R. Connery, "Abortion: Roman Catholic Perspectives," *Encyclopedia of Bioethics,* vol. 1 (New York: Free Press, 1978), p. 11. I have already noted the ease with which Christian writers glibly relegate groups in which women have a central role to the "pagan" category. Noonan does this and, unfortunately, so does Connery. The point is that by reducing practices they disapprove of to "paganism," these writers avoid the necessity of asking why abortion practices, teaching, and attitudes differed among Christians.

13. Noonan, "An Almost Absolute Value," pp. 4-5, and *Contraception,* pp. 13, 18.

14. For a new translation of sections of the Hippocratic corpus, written by a number of physicians in the fourth and fifth centuries B.C.E., see "Hippocrates: Diseases of Women, I," translated and with a headnote by Ann Ellis Hanson in *Signs,* 1:2 (Winter 1975), pp. 567-584.

15. Ibid., p. 567.

16. Connery, *Abortion,* pp. 33-45.

17. This is especially so in Connery's sometimes critical review of Grisez's work. He says of Grisez's historical account: "Although I would have appreciated a little more theological precision at times, and though I experienced a little uneasiness with some of the interpretations, I found the study generally satisfactory" ("Grisez on Abortion," *Theological Studies,* vol. 31 (1970), p. 174). If anything, Grisez's account is more adamantly an ideological overreading of the evidence than Noonan's.

18. Häring, p. 128, n. 10.

19. Noonan's data actually frequently support my thesis here, but because he does not object to the pervasive correlation of abortion with promiscuity, he does not grasp the textual significance of the evidence he marshals. Note, among numerous examples, his citation from John Chrysostom:

Why do you sow where the field is eager to destroy the fruit? Where there are medicines of sterility? Where there is murder before birth? You do not even let a harlot remain only a harlot, but you make her a murderess as well. Do you see that from drunkenness comes fornication, from fornication adultery, from adultery murder? Indeed, it is something worse than murder and I do not know what to call it; for she does not kill what is formed but prevents its formation. What then? Do you condemn the gift of God, and fight with His laws? What is a curse, do you seek as though it were a blessing? Do you make the anteroom of birth the anteroom of slaughter? Do you teach the woman who is given to you for the procreation of offspring to perpetrate killing? That she may always be beautiful and lovable to her lovers, and that she may rake in more money, she does not refuse to do this, heaping fire on your head; and even if the crime is hers, you are the cause. Hence also arise idolatries. To look pretty many of these women use incantations, libations, philtres, potions, and innumerable other things. Yet after such turpitude, after murder, after idolatry, the matter still seems indifferent to many men — even to many men having wives. In this indifference of the married men there is greater evil filth; for then poisons are prepared, not against the womb of a prostitute, but against your injured wife. Against her are these innumerable tricks, invocations of demons, incantations of the dead, daily wars, ceaseless battles, and unremitting contentions (St. John Chrysostom, *Homily 24 on the Epistle to the Romans*, PG 60:626-627, quoted in Noonan, *Contraception*, p. 98).

20. Noonan, *Contraception*, p. 85.
21. Ibid., p. 22.
22. Ibid., p. 26. Noonan may be mistaken here. From time to time there were laws against abortion under some emperors, but these were always part of efforts to strengthen the laws of *paterfamilias*, or father's rule over his household. The concern here was not related to positive assessments of fetal life. Perhaps Noonan means to suggest that no *criminal* law on abortion existed. If so, this is true.
23. Noonan, *A Private Choice*, pp. 53ff.
24. Susan Teft Nicholson, *Abortion and the Roman Catholic Church, Journal of Religious Ethics,* Studies in Religious Ethics/II, ed. James Childress (Knoxville: Religious Ethics, 1978), pp. 3-4.
25. Ibid., p. 12.
26. Ibid., p. 13.
27. She concludes: "The Roman Catholic condemnation of abortion as a sin of killing is thus presented as a conclusion validly derived from a moral principle common to our Judaeo-Christian society and a factual premise well established by the scientific developments of the past century" (p. 15). As we will see, the intertwining of the antikilling ethic with the anti-abortion ethic in Christianity was never linked to consideration of fetal life per se. Because Nicholson reads modern scientific evidence in a manner characteristic of those who already morally object to abortion, and because she does not review the historical materials

herself, she misses the conflation. The antikilling ethic surely has "common" support in our society. The debate as to whether it relates to abortion is a far more complex matter than her analysis acknowledges, however. See Chapter 7.

28. Much of the early motivation for this asceticism, it should be stressed, came from charges by Christianity's opponents that Christians were licentious. The ascetic wing of Christianity was the group that responded by adopting rigorism. As early as the second century, Justin Martyr urged Christian male youth to accept castration rather than be accused of licentiousness. Justin and his disciple Tatian provide some of the earliest, fragmentary literary evidences of antisexual, pro-creative-functional phobia. See St. Justin Martyr, *First Apology*, in Cyril Richardson, ed., *Early Christian Fathers*, vol. 1 (Philadelphia: Westminster Press, 1957), pp. 258-260.

29. Pius XI, *Casti Connubi*, in Claudia Carlen, ed., *The Papal Encyclicals: 1740-1981*, vol. 3 (Wilmington, N.C.: McGroth Publishing Co., 1930), pp. 391-414. Paul VI, *Humanae Vitae*, in Carlen, vol. 5 (1968), pp. 223-236. Pope John Paul II's viewpoint reaffirms the intimate connection between the role of procreation in marital sexuality and the condemnation of abortion. Publicly decrying both divorce and abortion, on November 2, 1982, he admonished Catholics in Madrid to live in "indissoluble unions" and quoted Paul VI, who said that "every conjugal act must remain open to the transmission of life." In response to the Spanish government's plans to liberalize abortion to save the life of the endangered mother and to terminate the pregnancy of a rape victim or the gestation of an abnormal fetus, John Paul II said: "I speak on the absolute respect for human life . . . Therefore, whoever denies defense to the most innocent and frailest human person, to the human person conceived but not yet born, commits a most grave violation of the moral order." See Henry Kamm, "Pope, in Spain, Condemns All Abortions," *New York Times*, November 3, 1982, p. A3.

30. The *Decretum* of Buchard, written in the eleventh century, uses this text from Caesarius. See Nicholson, p. 7.

31. *The Pastoral Constitution on the Church and the Modern World*, N.51 (New York: Paulist Press, 1967), p. 161. This is, of course, a reforming document from the Second Vatican Council, but the sections on marriage and procreation continue to reflect older readings of natural law (see pp. 117ff.).

32. *The Didache*, in *Christian Ethics: Sources of the Living Tradition*, ed. Waldo Beach and H. Richard Niebuhr (New York: Ronald Press, 1955), pp. 58-59. Many translators, believing that the reference to "child in the womb" is not an accurate rendering of the original, translate it simply as "child." See Richardson, *Early Christian Fathers*, pp. 111-179.

33. Noonan, "An Almost Absolute Value," p. 18.

34. It should be emphasized that Tertullian's teaching is always the first elaborated, not merely cited, as anti-abortionist, because, given his "traducian" theory (as explained later in the text), he penned the only extended literary example of reasoning about the *origins* of "full hu-

manity." That his reasoning was not aimed at assessing fetal life, but at speculating about soul/body unity, is ignored. See Tertullian, *Apologetical Works and Minueus Felix Octavius*, 9:8 (New York: Fathers of the Church, 1950), p. 32. In this passage, Tertullian inveighs against human blood sacrifice rituals.

35. I say "may" because the authenticity of the relevant text is disputed. See Tertullian, *De Anima*, 25.4 (Amsterdam: Meulenhoff, 1947), pp. 35-36 and also pp. 324-326. Along with Justin, Clement, Augustine, and Jerome, Tertullian believed that sexual activity was only for procreation; otherwise, it was sensuous, and therefore violated God's spirit. See his *Treatises On Marriage and Remarriage* (Westminster, Md.: Newman Press, 1951), pp. 70-71 and passim.

36. Tertullian, *De Anima*.

37. On Justin, see n. 28, above. Clement believed that abortion was an unspeakable evil, evidently for two reasons: (1) it wasted "the seed" God meant to come to fruition and (2) it was practiced invariably by women to hide sexual infidelity. See Clement of Alexandria, *Le Pedagogue*, Livre 4, 10:84 and 91 (Paris: Les Edition des Cerf, 1965), pp. 162-168 and 176. Jerome and Chrysostom believed that ascetic, virginal women could overcome women's fallen state. The former commended women for abandoning their children for the monastic life. See Elizabeth A. Clark, *Jerome, Chrysostom, and Friends: Essays and Translations* (Lewiston, N.Y.: Mellen, 1979), pp. 51ff.

38. Connery, *Abortion*, pp. 17-21. See also Connery, *Encyclopedia of Bioethics*, p. 9.

39. Augustine, *Letters*, 4:165-203, trans. Sister W. Parsons (New York: Fathers of the Church, 1955), p. 279.

40. *Anti-Pelagian Works of St. Augustine, The Works of Aurelius Augustine*, vol. 12, bk. 1, 8-14, pp. 104-113; bk. 2, pp. 38-43, 80-86 (Edinburgh: Clark, 1885). This material is part of Augustine's anti-Pelagian polemic. It is important to notice, however, that Augustine never used the rhetorical invocation of "homicide" and "murder" in relation to abortion as did some of his contemporaries, such as Jerome.

41. The sixth-century Bishop of Arles Caesarius makes clear that sexual permissiveness was the reason abortion was wrong:

    Who is he who cannot warn that no woman may take a potion so that she is unable to conceive or condemns in herself the nature which God willed to be fecund. *As often as she could have conceived or given birth, of that many homicides she will be held guilty,* and, unless she undergoes suitable penance, she will be damned by eternal death in hell. If a woman does not wish to have children, let her enter into a religious agreement with her husband; for chastity is the sole sterility of a Christian woman. (Italics mine)

    As Nicholson notes, Caesarius's teaching was the basic one shaping official canons until 1917, p. 7.

42. George Hunston Williams, "Religious Residues and Presuppositions, in the American Debate on Abortion," *Theological Studies*, vol. 31, (1970), p. 33.

43. There were, of course, a number of variants of the "sire-centered" view, in which women contributed something to the process of pregnancy, but all views presupposed the male role as the primary generative one. George II. Williams, for all the inadequacies of his essays on the subject of abortion, has written the best résumé of these perspectives. Ibid., pp. 14ff. See note 4, p. 286 above.

44. See Connery, *Abortion*, p. 53, who suggests that Jerome's views on abortion are not entirely consistent, that he sometimes equates sterilization and abortion as "homicide" and at other points observes the distinction between the formed and unformed fetus. Such inconsistencies are typical of Jerome. In any case, his hostility to all sexuality except procreative functionalism (acceptable if it produced virgin ascetics) and women is well known. See J. N. D. Kelly, *Jerome, IIis Life, Writings and Controversies* (London: Duckworth, 1975), pp. 102-103, 104-106, and passim.

45. Kelly, pp. 179-194ff., 277-282.

46. Compare Augustine, *Against the Pelagians*, n. 40, p. 290. See also *Against the Donatists*, pp. 403-651. It is important to observe how much of the fragmentary discussion of abortion was implicated in polemical debate over whose morality was superior. In the earlier Christian writings, this polemic was defensive vis-à-vis Jewish non-Christian rigorism and Roman "enlightened secular" slander. But from the late third century C.E. onward, these polemics were largely internal to the Christian movement.

47. In a book deeply sympathetic to Augustine's teaching on the body, Margaret Miles, *Fullness of Life: IIistorical Foundations for a New Asceticism* (Philadelphia: Westminster Press, 1981), pp. 62-78, has argued that Augustine was, by contrast to his contemporaries, body-affirming. This is true if one compares Augustine to his theological and late IIellenistic, philosophical contemporaries, but the pervasiveness of body-spirit dualism among intellectuals was so pronounced that only in the context of other intellectual elites does he appear to affirm the body.

48. Samuel Laeuchli, *Power and Sexuality: The Emergence of Canon Law at the Synod of Elvira* (Philadelphia: Temple University Press, 1972), pp. 88-113 and passim.

49. Canon 63, as translated by Samuel Laeuchli in *Power and Sexuality*, Appendix, p. 133:
    If a woman, while her husband is away, conceives by adultery and after that crime commits abortion, she shall not be given communion even at the end, since she has doubled her crime.

50. Ibid., canon 68, p. 134:
    A catechumen, if she has conceived a child in adultery and then suffocated it, shall be baptized at the end.

51. See a standard English reference work widely used in the early decades of the twentieth century, such as the Rev. Edward II. Landon, ed., *A Manual of Councils of the IIoly Catholic Church* (Edinburgh: John Grant, 1909), pp. 23ff. Landon's itemization of Ancrya's canons does not mention abortion. IIe stresses the concern with adultery (canon 20).

He does not mention canon 21, in which abortion to hide adultery appears to be condemned. Another moral reason for the condemnation of abortion was that it involved using soothsaying and following the customs of the Gentiles (canon 24). The twenty-fourth canon's authenticity has long been challenged, however. (Landon, p. 25, n. 1).

52. Connery correctly summarizes Ancrya's "more lenient" attitude to abortion as compared with Elvira's in his *Abortion*, pp. 48ff. Evidently a century passed before abortion to hide adultery was condemned again by a council, this time by the sex-phobic bishops of Spain at the Council of Lerida, 524 C.E. A standard Roman Catholic interpretation of Canon Law on abortion treats the Elvira, Ancrya, and Lerida pronouncements as part of a consistent, established tradition, predicated on concern for "the protection and vindication of infant life." Its author concedes that the Council of Elvira and Lerida were aimed at condemning abortion to hide adultery but insists that the Ancrya Canon was not! The disputed text of Canon 21 quoted in this work explicitly condemns "women who prostitute themselves" and therefore have abortions. Like Noonan, this author quotes these misogynist texts without computing their meaning. Not one word regarding the value of fetal or "infant" life in relation to abortion appears in *any* material cited in the work. Roger John Huser, O.F.M., *The Crime of Abortion in Canon Law* (Washington, D.C.: The Catholic University Press of America, 1942), p. 19 and passim.

53. Even Connery adopts this logic — the distinction between the "normative" theological ethical tradition and the more morally "permissive" canonical tradition. I hold an alternative view, namely, that Church canons if they are less "rigorist" than the anathemas of individual theologians should be viewed as evidence of lack of moral consensus among Christians, not as lesser morality. Samuel Laeuchli's thesis about the use of hierarchical power to enforce sexual conformity at Elvira also implies that, at least with respect to sexuality, rigorist councils should be read as *imposing* homogeneous practice where diversity prevailed. The use of external power to impose sexual morality suggests lack of agreement from those affected. See Connery, "Abortion: Roman Catholic Perspectives," in *Encyclopedia of Bioethics*, pp. 9-13.

54. Jean Danielou and Henri Marrou, *The First Centuries*, trans. Vincent Cronin (London: Darton, Longman and Todd, 1964), pp. 149-151.

55. Connery, *Abortion*, pp. 91ff.

56. Magister Rufinus (d. 1190), *Summa Decretorum* as cited in Connery, *Abortion*, pp. 93ff.

57. Aquinas's references to abortion are few and his lack of animosity to women, whom he deemed to be "by nature" inferior to males, is striking. See his *Summa Theologica*, vol. 38 (New York: McGraw Hill, in conjunction with Blackfriars, 1975), p. 47. Here he makes clear that he assumed the formed/unformed distinction, 2.2., 64.a.8. Evidently in his day some argued that, because of the necessity of baptism the mother's uterus could be opened to permit fetal baptism. Aquinas disagreed. *Summa Theologica*, 3.q., 68.a.11; 3, vol. 57, pp. 115, 117.

58. This demonstrates how completely Aquinas equated "natural" and procreative sex. All noncoital sex acts were, in his schema, unnatural, since rape involves coitus, it is natural!

59. Connery, *Abortion*, pp. 124ff. Earlier, John of Naples had embraced therapeutic abortions to save the life of the mother. However, this "permissive" attitude was soon under attack.

60. Ibid., pp. 105-313.

61. Sixtus V died in 1590. Even John Noonan recognizes that his reforms were "draconian." See his *Contraception*, pp. 362ff. Noonan does not connect Sixtus's arbitrary use of power with his hostility to nonprocreative sex, contraception, and abortion, however.

62. Technically, this distinction is part of a wider moral reasoning in Catholic ethics called "the principle of double effect." The "principle of double effect" aims to differentiate acts that are morally negative but that occur as an effect of a morally good act. Criteria derived from this distinction are often employed to analyze when therapeutic abortion is morally justified. See Charles Curran, "Abortion: Contemporary Debate in Philosophical and Religious Ethics," *Encyclopedia of Bioethics*, pp. 23ff.

63. Williams, "Religious Residues," p. 53. See also his "The Sacred Condominium," in Noonan, *The Morality of Abortion*.

64. Williams, "Religious Residues," p. 34.

65. Ibid., p. 44.

66. See James Nelson, "Abortion: Protestant Perspectives," in *Encyclopedia of Bioethics*, vol. 1, p. 14. See also Williams, "Religious Residues," pp. 35ff.

67. E. William Monter, "Women in Calvinist Geneva (1550-1800)," *Signs*, 6:2 (Winter 1980), pp. 189-209.

68. Noonan concedes the length of time it took for theologians to begin to invoke this new "medical" opinion about human ensoulment against the "formed" and "unformed" distinction. One must also put the term *medical* in quotes, because these opinions of the Italian doctors were unrelated to anything we would recognize as modern embryology. They were, in point of fact, still embroiled in theological speculation. And their bias was that men were the real possessors of generative procreative power, women being passive in the process. See Noonan, *Contraception*, pp. 365ff.

69. Williams, "Religious Residues," p. 42.

70. This contention has been documented in the work of legal scholar Cyril C. Means, Jr. See, for example, "The Law of New York Concerning Abortion and the Status of the Foetus, 1664-1968," *New York Law Forum*, vol. 14 (1968), pp. 411-515. Means's claims about the British common law tradition have been dismissed summarily by J. M. Finnis in "Abortion: Legal Aspects," in *Encyclopedia of Bioethics*, vol. 1, pp. 26-32.

71. On the shifts of Anglican practice, see G. R. Quaife, *Wanton Witches and Wayward Wives: Peasants and Illicit Sex in Early 17th Century England* (New Brunswick, N.J.: Rutgers University Press, 1929), pp. 244ff.

72. Noonan, *A Private Choice,* pp. 5ff., 47-68, and passim.
73. Ibid., especially pp. 5ff.
74. Williams, "Religious Residues," p. 50.
75. James Nelson, "Abortion: Protestant Perspectives," pp. 13-17.
76. James Mohr, *Abortion in America: The Origins and Evolution of Public Policy* (New York: Oxford University Press, 1979).
77. Beverly W. Harrison, "Sexism and the Churches: When Evasion Becomes Complicity," in Alice Hageman, ed., *Sexist Religion and Women in the Church: No More Silence* (New York: Association Press, 1974), pp. 195-217.
78. See David M. Kennedy, *Birth Control in America* (New Haven: Yale University Press, 1970), Chapter 6, pp. 136-171. Some additional data may be found in Linda Gordon's *Woman's Body, Woman's Right: A Social History of Birth Control in America* (New York: Penguin Books, 1974), and in James Reed, *From Private Vice to Public Virtue: The Birth Control Movement and American Society Since 1830* (New York: Basic Books, 1978).

6: Notes Toward a Feminist Perspective

1. Samuel Laeuchli, *Power and Sexuality: The Emergence of Canon Law at the Synod of Elvira* (Philadelphia: Temple University Press, 1972), p. 92.
2. Ibid., pp. 103-104.
3. The life expectancy of women, now greater than that of men in advanced industrial societies, was once lower than men's, in part because of the high incidence of death in childbearing. Few pause to note how recent is this shift and that it is definitely related to contraception and adequate prenatal health care.
4. This line of speculation is developed by Ross S. Kraemer in "The Conversion of Women in Ascetic Forms of Christianity," *Signs,* 6:2 (Winter 1980), pp. 298-307.
5. See Mary O'Brien, *The Politics of Reproduction* (London: Routledge & Kegan Paul, 1981), and Sandra Schwartz Tangri, "A Feminist Perspective on Some Ethical Issues in Population Programs," *Signs,* 1:4 (Summer 1976), pp. 895-904.
6. Gerda Lerner, "Placing Women in History: Problems and Challenges," *Feminist Studies,* 3/2 (Fall 1975), pp. 10, 11, 14. These quotations are excerpted from a wider discussion of the methodological problems of women's history.
7. See, for example, Elise Boulding, *The Underside of History: A View of Women Through Time* (Boulder, Colo.: Westview Press, 1976), and Berenice A. Carroll, ed., *Liberating Women's History: Theoretical and Critical Essays* (Chicago: University of Illinois Press, 1976).
8. Louise Kapp Howe, *Pink Collar Workers: Inside the World of Women's Work* (New York: Putnam's, 1977).
9. Union of Radical Political Economists, *U.S. Capitalism in Crisis* (New York, 1978). Another source for understanding some of these dynamics

298 Our Right to Choose

is David Cooper's *Death of the Family* (New York: Pantheon, 1970), although I do not agree with the ideological assumptions of his analysis.

10. The growing economic vulnerability of women in this new phase of our political-economic life has been obscured by two factors: (1) the movement into middle-income, professional-strata employment of a few women, whose income level has increased the per capita wages of women and (2) the increased cumulative family income level that follows upon a woman's earning a second paycheck in a family. See Beverly W. Harrison, "Effet De L'Industrialisation sur le Role des Femmes dans la Societé," *Concilium* III (1976), pp. 91-103, and Eli Zaretsky, *Capitalism, the Family, and Personal Life* (New York: Harper & Row, 1976).

11. Scott Burns, *The Household Economy: Its Shape, Origins, and Future* (Boston: Beacon Press, 1975).

12. Margaret Llewelyn Davies, ed., *Maternity: Letters from Working Women* (New York: Norton, 1978), passim.

13. Peter Filene, *Him/Herself: Sex Roles in Modern America* (New York: Harcourt Brace Jovanovich, 1974), and G. J. Barker-Benfield, *The Horrors of the Half-Known Life: Male Attitudes Toward Women and Sexuality in Nineteenth Century America* (New York: Harper & Row, 1976). On the male role viewed historically, see also Elizabeth H. and Joseph H. Pleck, *The American Man* (Englewood Cliffs, N.J.: Prentice-Hall, 1980). On sex-role theory in relation to the male role, see Joseph H. Pleck, *The Myth of Masculinity* (Cambridge, Mass.: MIT Press, 1981).

14. The emergent fragmentary historiography relating to women's lives from earlier periods tends, in passing, to confirm this view. See, for example, Frances and Joseph Gies, *Women in the Middle Ages* (New York: Barnes & Noble, 1978), pp. 156-157ff. See also Emily Coleman, "Infanticide in the Early Middle Ages," pp. 47-70, and Jo-Ann McNamara and Suzanne F. Wemple, "Marriage and Divorce in the Frankish Kingdom," pp. 95-124, in *Women in Medieval Society*, ed. Susan Mosher Stuard (Philadelphia: University of Pennsylvania Press, 1976).

15. See John T. Noonan, Jr., *Contraception: A History of Its Treatment by the Catholic Theologians and Canonists* (Cambridge: Harvard University Press, 1966). See also Noonan, *A Private Choice: Abortion in America in the Seventies* (New York: Free Press, 1979).

16. See Chapter 2, pp. 42ff.

17. See Christopher Tietze, *Induced Abortion: A World Review* (New York: Population Council, 1981).

18. Medical opinion on the safety to a woman of having repeated abortions varies widely. Much depends on whether the abortions are performed early and under optimal medical conditions. In any case, illegal abortions are statistically less safe. For an interesting pioneering discussion of criminal abortion, see Alan F. Guttmacher, *Babies by Choice or by Chance* (New York: Avon, 1961), especially pp. 136-170.

19. See Malcom Potts, Peter Diggory, and John Peel, *Abortion* (Cambridge: The University Press, 1977), Chapter 5, pp. 154-175.

20. On the deterioration of women's role in Hinduism and the effects of religion on women's role, see Doranne Jacobson, "The Women of North

and Central India: Goddesses and Wives," in *Many Sisters: Women in Cross-Cultural Perspective*, ed.Carolyn J. Matthiasson (New York: Free Press, 1974), pp. 99-175. See also Lois Beck and Nikki Reddie, *Women in the Muslim World* (Cambridge: Harvard University Press, 1978), and Fatima Mernissi, "Virginity and Patriarchy," *Women's Studies International Forum*, 5:2 (1982). On male sexuality and "the cult of masculine honor," see Marshall G. Hodgson, *The Venture of Islam*, vol. 2 (Chicago: University of Chicago Press, 1974), pp. 140ff. See also Chapter 1, n. 28, above.

21. See Chapter 1, n. 23, above.

22. Both genders now bring "companionate expectations" to marriage. However, sociologist Jessie Bernard has documented the extent to which the expectations and gratification of men and women within marriage continue to differ. See *The Future of Marriage* (New York: Bantam, 1972). It is clear that the development of expectations about personal intimacy in marriage is related somewhat to class location and educational levels. See Mira Komarovsky, *Blue Collar Marriage* (New York: Vintage, 1964).

23. Potts, Diggory, and Peel, pp. 119ff. See also Joseph Chamie, *Religion and Fertility: Arab Christian-Muslim Differentials* (Cambridge: The University Press, 1981).

24. Laila Williamson, "Infanticide: An Anthropological Analysis," in *Infanticide and the Value of Life*, ed. Marvin Kohl (Buffalo, N.Y.: Prometheus Books, 1978), pp. 61-75.

25. A good source for discussions of theory that should inform cross-cultural studies of women is *Women, Culture, and Society*, ed. M. Z. Rosaldo and Louis Lamphere (Stanford: Stanford University Press, 1974).

26. In addition to texts cited in Chapter 2, n. 8, above, see Richard W. and Dorothy C. Wentz, *Lying In: A History of Childbirth in America* (New York: Schocken, 1977).

27. Ibid. See also Jane B. Donegan, *Women and Men Midwives: Medicine, Morality, and Misogyny in Early America* (Westport, Conn.: Greenwood Press, 1978).

28. Wertz and Wertz, p. x.

29. Noonan's *Contraception* does contain a useful review of the range of contraceptive techniques. See also Guttmacher, Chapters 3 and 6.

30. See Potts, Diggory, and Peel, Chapter 2. The frequency of spontaneous abortion, especially in the first two weeks of pregnancy, has been a major reason for the recent shift in moral theology toward endorsing the implantation of the genetic code as the point where "truly human" life begins. Several studies suggest that only 42 percent of fertilized ova survive until the twelfth day of pregnancy (p. 59). Potts, Diggory, and Peel conclude that "in sum, embryonic development is an inaccurate and unreliable process" (p. 60).

31. It should be noted that the rate of illegal abortions in Latin America is also high. See Potts, Diggory, and Peel, pp. 95ff.

32. I have been unable to find literary documentation for this practice, reported orally by several observers to be frequent in poorer nations.

33. Noonan, *A Private Choice*, p. 51.

34. The usual way of citing data regarding the reliability of barrier birth

control methods is often highly misleading when percentages of reliability are offered. To say, for example, that a diaphragm is 95 percent
reliable does *not* mean that it always works effectively all of the time
for 95 percent of the female population using it. Rather, it means that
5 percent of the users become pregnant while using the diaphragm during
a specific period of time, often one year. The rate of unintended pregnancy from all barrier methods is fairly high, although proper use
increases effectiveness. Furthermore, for some women, barrier methods
are highly unreliable, even when used properly. Nevertheless, in the
ethics of abortion literature there is a growing number of pejorative
comments about women who have multiple abortions, as if they were
"repeat offenders." This suggests that many writers assume that women
are largely responsible for "unwanted pregnancy" and that one "mistake"
might be forgivable, but not a number. Unfortunately, where effectiveness of contraception is concerned, some women are simply at far
greater risk than others. The new "environment of blame" toward women
regarding abortions is uninformed by any awareness of this reality. There
are positive advantages to the use of barrier methods having to do with
minimizing infection, and one study, a statistical analysis that correlated
both effectiveness and health effects of contraception, "showed that
the safest approach to contraception is the use of a barrier method,
with early abortion as a backup if the method should fail to prevent
pregnancy." See Jane E. Brody, " 'Barrier' Methods of Birth Control,"
New York Times, December 31, 1980, p. 11. See also *Draper Fund
Report*, no. 6 (Summer 1978).
35. Linda Gordon, *Woman's Body, Woman's Right: A Social History of Birth
Control in America* (New York: Penguin Books, 1974).
36. Wertz and Wertz, p. 206.
37. Ibid., pp. 204–206.
38. Ibid., pp. 201–233.
39. Ibid., p. 208.
40. The evidence is, of course, somewhat speculative. From literary sources
we know that the onset of menstruation as late as age sixteen was not
unusual a few centuries ago. In the last three decades, the typical age
of menarche appears to have dropped by two years. This may be a factor
in the rising incidence of childhood pregnancies. See Carlo M. Cipolla,
The Economic History of World Population (New York: Penguin Books,
1978). See also Potts, Diggory, and Peel, pp. 30ff.
41. Carl Djerassi, *The Politics of Contraception* (New York: Norton, 1979),
p. 13.
42. Djerassi, pp. 10ff.
43. Lisa Leghorn and Mary Roodkowsky, *Who Really Starves? Women and
World Hunger* (New York: Friendship Press, 1977).
44. The most conspicuous example of corporate involvement in contraceptive failure was the famous Dalkon Shield scandal. The manufacturer
of the Dalkon Shield is still dumping its dangerous and ineffective
product on family-planning programs of so-called third-world
(overexploited) countries. On the issue of the safety of contraceptives,
especially the pill, see Djerassi.

45. Beverly W. Harrison, "When Blessedness and Fruitfulness Diverge," *Religion in Life*, vol. 41, no. 4 (1972), pp. 480-496.
46. Djerassi, pp. 183-213. On Chinese policy, see Potts, Diggory, and Peel, pp. 77ff. and passim, and *Draper Fund Report*, no. 8 (March 1980), Washington, D.C. For data on Mexico, see B. R. Ordonez, "Induced Abortion in Mexico City," in *Epidemiology of Abortion and Practices of Fertility Regulation in Latin America* (Washington, D.C.: Pan American Health Organization, 1975), pp. 26-29.
47. For data on Latin America and Africa, see Tietze, pp. 22, 25. An article that denies this interpretation of the Latin American situation, Maria Eugenia de Guerrero and Oscar I. Rojas, M.D., "Abortion in Latin America," in *New Perspectives on Abortion*, ed. Thomas W. Hilgers et al. (Frederick, Md.: Alethia Press, 1981), pp. 466-485. Again, gross generalizations are difficult on this point. In Latin America, Africa, and the United States, poverty and high incidence of abortion appear to be correlated, but not in India. Evidently the poverty factor correlates with increased abortion when urbanization occurs. See Potts, Diggory, and Peel, pp. 111-118, and Tietze, pp. 39-40.
48. A new journal, containing Russian women's reflections on sexism and especially women's oppression around reproductive and childrearing issues, dramatically attests to the suffering of Soviet women. See *Women and Russia*, ed. Tatyana Mamanova (Boston: Beacon Press, 1983).
49. Potts, Diggory, and Peel repeatedly observe that women seek abortions regardless of whether their societies approve or disapprove. Furthermore, they imply that women do so even when they express the opinion that abortion is wrong. They also confirm data cited earlier that religion has little or no effect on whether women resort to abortion. *Abortion*, pp. 3ff., 119ff., 132ff., and passim.
50. Oral reports that I have frequently received from black women are confirmed by the most recent official statistics collected on abortion. Recent Population Council reports suggest that abortion rates among black women are now almost three times as high as the rate among white women: 60.9 per 1,000 black women; 22.7 per thousand white women. From 1963 to 1965, white women appear to have had more abortions, and from 1966 to 1968 the comparative rate equalized. It should be recalled, however, that prior to legislation, statistics were more speculative. See Tietze, pp. 34-35.
51. Eugene Turner, "Racial-Ethnic Perspectives on Abortion," lecture given at the Seamen's Church Institute, New York, September 1979.
52. This is a frequently made claim, but it is difficult to substantiate. Probably it would be more accurate to say that abortion is the most widely used means of *artificial* birth control. Because abortion is resorted to only when other modes of contraception fail, comparative statistics neglect women's use of rhythm, sexual abstinence, and the like. Djerassi ranks abortion after the pill and lactation as the major means of contraception, pp. 22ff.
53. Djerassi, p. 30. See also Tietze, p. 19; his global estimate is 7 percent.

54. Tietze, p. 44.
55. Although Tietze claims a worldwide reduction in the incidence of abortion among married women, his data is drawn only from western countries.
56. On the problems of estimating illegal abortions, see Colin Francome, "Estimating the Number of Illegal Abortions," *Journal of Biosocial Science*, vol. 9 (1977), pp. 467-479.
57. Djerassi, pp. 120-181. See also William J. Bremmer and David M. de Krester, "Contraceptives for Males," *Signs*, 1:2 (Winter 1975), pp. 387-396.
58. The National Conference of Catholic Bishops has made curtailment of federal funding for contraceptive research a major priority. See Kenneth A. Briggs, "Catholics Beginning an Expanded Drive Against Abortions," *New York Times*, vol. 126, no. 43670, 1977, pp. 13, 20.
59. See Alan Crawford, *Thunder on the Right: The "New Right" and the Politics of Resentment* (New York: Pantheon, 1980), and Andrew H. Merton, *Enemies of Choice: The Right-to-Life Movement and Its Threat to Abortion* (Boston: Beacon Press, 1981).
60. Boyce Rensberger, "Lag in Research on Birth Control Found Despite Increasing Need," *New York Times*, November 17, 1976. This report on the Ford Foundation's study on contraception research projected that to maintain the 1976 levels of research, which cost less than $150 million, by 1980 a half billion dollars would be required worldwide. Expenditures have not increased markedly since then.
61. For a sociological study that illumines women's real experience, see Ann Oakley's *Women Confined: Towards a Sociology of Childbirth* (New York: Schocken, 1980). Oakley identifies the major, and severe, strains of childbearing to inhere in the present structural opposition between work and family. Childbearing involves extreme identity loss because it makes a woman dependent — on doctors, on spouses, on family. She rightly insists that this social confinement is due to changeable social conditions that would enhance the gratifications of childbearing. See pp. 290-300.
62. See Gloria Steinem, "The Verbal Karate of Florynce R. Kennedy, Esq.," *Ms.*, vol. 1, no. 9 (1973), pp. 54-55, 59.
63. James Reed, *From Private Vice to Public Virtue: The Birth Control Movement and American Society Since 1830* (New York: Basic Books, 1978).
64. See Adrienne Rich, *Of Woman Born: Motherhood as Experience and Institution* (New York: Norton, 1976), pp. 259-265. See also Marvin Kohl, ed., *Infanticide and the Value of Life* (Buffalo, N.Y.: Prometheus Books, 1978).
65. Laila Williamson, "Infanticide: An Anthropological Analysis," in Kohl, pp. 61-75.
66. The practice of embryotomy or killing of the fetus in the womb, usually involved craniotomy. This destruction of the fetal head induced stillbirth. The important issue with regard to this technique was that it resulted in deliveries that were life-threatening to the mother. Roman Catholic

official teaching differed on the moral acceptability of such options, and, in fact, some discussion of abortion turned on the question of their use. That Roman Catholic opinion was diverse, however, is a conclusion contrary to the interpretation of T. J. O'Donnell in "Abortion: II (Moral Aspect)," in *The New Catholic Encyclopedia* (New York: McGraw-Hill, 1967), pp. 28ff.

67. Magda Denes, *In Necessity and Sorrow* (Middlesex, England: Penguin Books, 1977), pp. xv–xvi.

68. This point must be insisted on in light of two realities: (1) Oral contraceptives frequently function as abortifacients. They do not always prevent fertilization of the ovum; rather, they prevent implantation of a fertilized ovum in the uterine wall. The IUD also functions to prevent not conception but implantation of the fertilized ovum. (2) As noted, only about 50 percent of fertilized ova actually result in pregnancy; "natural" abortions are frequent. See Chapter 7, n. 30, below.

69. This statement appeared as part of an Ellen Willis commentary in the *Village Voice*, December 31-January 6, 1981, p. 28.

7: Evaluating the Act of Abortion

1. The phrase is Peter Steinfels's, used to characterize the entire pro-choice movement, in his "The Search for an Alternative," *Commonweal*, 108:21 (November 20, 1981), p. 663. This accusation, whether implicit or explicit, is widespread in the abortion literature. See, for example, J. Robert Nelson, "What Does Theology Say About Abortion?" in *Abortion: The Moral Issues*, ed. Edward Batchelor, Jr. (New York: Pilgrim Press, 1982), pp. 55–72. It will become clear as I proceed that anyone who appeals to "science" as the source of unambiguous fact for determining when a human life begins will find the rest of us, by definition, oblivious to science or biology.

2. Charles Curran formulates a less pejorative criticism of those whose views of fetal life do not fall into what he classifies as the "individual-biological criterion" position. Of those who stand outside this category, he states, "Biological data are given little or no importance." It would be fairer, I argue here, to say that those of us who do not fall into this individual-biological classification relate biological and moral criteria differently. See Charles Curran, "Abortion: Contemporary Debate in Philosophical and Religious Ethics," In *Encyclopedia of Bioethics* (Washington, D.C.: Georgetown University Press, 1978), vol. 1, p. 22.

3. The phrase is Ruth Hubbard's in "The Fetus as Patient," *Ms.* (October 1982), pp. 28 and 32.

4. Robert M. Veatch, "Abnormal Newborns and the Physician's Role," in *Decision Making and the Defective Newborn*, ed. Chester A. Swinyard (Springfield, Ill.: Charles C. Thomas, 1978), p. 178. Veatch here questions the moral adequacy of using physiological criteria as indices for determining when therapy for defective newborns is to be undertaken, characterizing this approach as "technicalizing the decision."

I do not know if he would raise the same objection to the use of physiological criteria vis-à-vis the characterization of fetal life.

5. Hubbard, p. 32. See also her "Legal and Policy Implications of Recent Advances in Prenatal Diagnosis and Fetal Therapy," *Women's Legal Rights Reporter*, 7:3 (1983), pp. 201-228.

6. Fenton presented his findings at the Political Studies Association's American Politics Group. I am dependent on Bob O'Keefe's report "Life Line: Life, Not Choice, Is the Issue," *Commonweal*, 108:21 (November 20, 1981), p. 658.

7. See Chapter 2, n. 5 above, and the *Voting Index of the New York Civil Liberties Union* (September 1982), which shows a high correlation between opposition to Medicaid funding for abortions and minors' abortion rights and support for the death penalty among New York State legislators.

8. These studies are being conducted by a group of psychologists at Bowling Green University, including Thomas Rywick, Richard Allgeier, and Elizabeth Rice Allgeier. Their first study, "Abortion: Reward for Conscientious Use?" is available from the authors. Elizabeth Allgeier presented further findings of the group in a paper entitled "The Abortion Dilemma: Assessing Public Decisions" at the Eastern Regional Meeting of the Society for the Scientific Study of Sex, Philadelphia, April 1981.

9. The title of Bob O'Keefe's essay, n. 6, above, should make clear the use to which he puts Fenton's research.

10. For such an argument see the quotation from Marilyn Frye, n. 55, below.

11. I have already pointed out that many moralists agree that "willingness to give reasons" or to enter into public discourse regarding justifications for our actions is constitutive of "the moral point of view." Secrecy or arbitrary appeals to authority, unless justified by moral considerations, are contrary to the nature of morality. Although I have made this and analogous points in the preceding material, I stress it again because this normative equation of willingness to communicate and what it means to be a "moral person" is so often missed.

12. This insight that a theistic ethic presumes such "a center of value" has been advanced by H. Richard Niebuhr in "Value-Theory and Theology," in *The Nature of Religious Experience*, ed. J. S. Bixler and R. L. Calhoun (New York: Harper Brothers, 1937), pp. 93-116, and in his "The Center of Value," in *Radical Monotheism and Western Culture* (New York: Harper & Row, 1960), pp. 100-111.

13. Another way to put this point is to acknowledge that the moral point of view presupposes a clear humanistic commitment. This is, I believe, an important and irreducible point, one that theists who wish to avoid "humanism" obscure. Those who maintain that modern morality is "thin" because it is "merely" humanistic fail to appreciate that theistic ethics have often been less, not more, than humane. If our morals are not at least humanistic, they are not moral. Complaints against humanism in ethics have recently arisen from another quarter. Some environmentalists rightly insist that an androcentric ethics can legitimate human abuses of the rest of nature. However, in my view, the argument does not discredit authentic humanism. The way to an ethic that precludes

the exploitation of nature is to recognize that in addition to our obligations to human beings we have analogous obligations to the rest of nature. See also my discussions of "intrinsic value" in Chapters 1 and 4, pp. 16, 111-112.

14. See my discussion of the "killing ethic" in Chapter 5, pp. 128ff.

15. Malcolm Potts, Potter Diggory, and John Peel, *Abortion* (Cambridge: The University Press, 1977), p. 20.

16. Ibid., pp. 20-29.

17. It is important to note that the abortion laws of most western nations have been framed "therapeutically," thereby placing decisions about abortion in the hands of medical professionals. Not all nations that have "medicalized" abortion via law, however, have neglected the wider moral issues relevant to abortion. Canada, for example, which severely medicalizes abortion, nevertheless has sponsored very probing studies aimed at illuminating the genuine questions that must be faced if abortion is to be minimized. See the excellent and extensive *Report on the Committee on the Operation of the Abortion Law* (Ottawa: Ministry of Supply and Services, 1977).

18. I say "seem to deny" because many writers cited here, such as John Noonan, John Rassmussen, Robert Nelson, Joseph Mangan, Helmut Theilicke, James Burtchaell, and several other authors in *Abortion: Catholic Perspectives* ed. John Garvey and Frank Morris (Chicago: Thomas More Press, 1979), and in *New Perspectives on Human Abortion* ed. Thomas W. Hilgers, Dennis J. Horan, and David Mall (Frederick, Md.: Alethia Press, 1981), all write as though abortion were such an unspeakable crime that, by implication, exceptions appear unthinkable. Their tenor, however, may only reflect the heat of battle.

19. I know of no defender of the morality of elective abortion who would deny that *some* elective abortions are morally dubious. There are discussions of "frivolous reasons" for abortion in the pro-choice philosophical literature. See, for example, Jane English, "Abortion and the Concept of the Person," reprinted from the *Canadian Journal of Philosophy* 5 in *Feminism and Philosophy*, ed. Mary Vetterling-Braggin, Frederick A. Elliston, and Jane English (Totowa, N.J.: Littlefield, Adams, 1978), pp. 417-428. See especially p. 427. English's assessment is impressive, and, as will be apparent, has affinities with my own. Nevertheless, I believe she fails to appreciate the full force of philosophical arguments that locate "personhood" within social relations. At least one male philosopher has recognized how many reasons for abortion are *not* "frivolous." See Howard Cohen, "Abortion and the Quality of Life," in Vetterling-Braggin, Elliston, and English, pp. 429-440. Another essay that formulates an argument for the principle of women's right to choose as a *moral* right is Alison Jaggar's "Abortion and a Woman's Right to Decide," in *Women and Philosophy: Toward a Theory of Liberation*, ed. Carol C. Gould and Max W. Wartofsky (New York: Putnam's, 1976), pp. 347-359. Although I concur with Jaggar that the question of who should choose is a principled moral issue, I disagree strenuously with her rejection of body-right as a moral claim. I also believe she dismisses utilitarian claims on behalf of women, especially women as a class, too readily.

20. See Chapters 2 and 4, pp. 20, 108-112, and n. 26, below.
21. Several briefs now pending before the courts do apply common law claims and precedents against bodily invasion to women's reproductive capacity. Some await legal decision by the Supreme Court. See Supreme Court Briefs, Nos. 81-185, 81-746, 81-1172, 81-1255, and 81-1623. See also, New Jersey Medicaid Abortion Brief. For the legal theory involved, see Donald H. Regan, "Rewriting *Roe v. Wade*," *Michigan Law Review*, 77 (1979), pp. 1569, 1583-1588, 1622-1623, and Norman L. Cantor, "A Patient's Decision to Decline Lifesaving Medical Treatment: Bodily Integrity Versus the Preservation of Life," *Rutgers Law Review*, 228 (1973).
22. An excellent collection of essays on various philosophical views of "rights" is contained in David Lyons, ed., *Rights* (Belmont, Calif.: Wadsworth, 1979). See also L. W. Sumner, *Abortion and Moral Theory* (Princeton: Princeton University Press, 1981), pp. 41ff., 85-88. Sumner's definition of rights is defective, in my opinion, because it does not incorporate specifically the notion that rights are *reciprocal* accountabilities.
23. See Gene Outka, *Agape: An Ethical Analysis* (New Haven: Yale University Press, 1972), and Thomas E. Hill, Jr., "Servility and Self-Respect," *The Monist*, 57:1 (January 1973), pp. 87-104. (Also reprinted in Lyons, pp. 111-124.)
24. John Rawls's *A Theory of Justice* (Cambridge: Harvard University Press, 1971) is, in a formal sense, a work of consummate "liberalism" in that concern for liberty is central to his argument. His position is uncharacteristic of much liberalism, however, in its integral linking of liberty with justice, such that "equal liberty" becomes the operative moral principle. It is this integration of liberty and equality that gives Rawls's work its suggestively post-liberal thrust. See pp. 195-303. A philosophical effort to make "liberty" the central principle of a "moral" system was developed to counter Rawls by Robert Nozick, *Anarchy, State, and Utopia* (New York: Basic Books, 1974). Obviously, in insisting that liberty per se is morally neutral, I am placing myself at the greatest possible distance from Nozick's approach. Rawls's "correction" of liberalism is, in my view, a condition for liberalism's continued claim to moral legitimacy. In our world only the affluent and powerful experience society as "liberty-filled"; hence they are threatened by governmental actions aimed at moderating the effects of unregulated economic activity.
25. This developing legal theory (see n. 21), rooted in common law tradition, has not yet been established as relevant to the issue of procreation. If my analysis here is correct, the mainstream of legal opinion may be slow in acknowledging any connections between legal rights to "bodily integrity" and women's role as procreators.
26. In his "Rules for Abortion Debate" (Batchelor, pp. 27-37), Richard A. McCormick, S. J., in a section of the essay entitled "Avoid the Use of Slogans," says:
   Slogans are the weapons of the crusader, one who sees his or her role as warfare, generally against those sharply defined as

"the enemy." Fighting for good causes clearly has its place, as do slogans. The political rally or the protest demonstration are good examples. But slogans are not very enlightening conversational tools, simply because they bypass and effectively subvert the process of communication.

I have in mind two current examples. One is the use of the word murder to describe abortion. "Murder" is a composite value term that means (morally) unjustified killing of another person. There are also legal qualifiers to what is to count as murder. To use this word does not clarify an argument if the very issue at stake is justifiability. Rather, it brands a position and, incidentally, those who hold it. It is a conversation-stopper. Moreover, the word murder is absolutely unnecessary in the defense of the traditional Christian position on abortion.

The other example is "a woman has a right to her own body." This is not an argument; it is the conclusion of an often unexamined argument and therefore a slogan with some highly questionable assumptions. For instance: that the fetus is, for these purposes, a part of the woman's body; that rights over one's body are absolute; that abortion has nothing to do with a husband, etc. To rattle some of these assumptions, it is sufficient to point out that few would grant that a woman's rights over her own body include the right to take thalidomide during pregnancy. The U.S. Supreme Court has gone pretty far in endorsing some of these assumptions. But even justices not above the use of a little "raw judicial power" would choke, I think, on the above slogan as an apt way to summarize the issue (pp. 29-30).

McCormick counsels anti-abortionists against the use of an inapt word — *murder* — to describe abortion. His criticism of the pro-choice position, however, involves not merely the rejection of a slogan but of a serious moral claim. By paralleling these two criticisms, he appears evenhanded, but his criticisms are hardly analogous. Not surprisingly, a few pages later, he concludes that "the core issue is, therefore, the evaluation of nascent life" (p. 31). Later he acknowledges:

Nothing in femaleness as such makes women more or less vulnerable to error or bias in moral discourse than men, yet when all is shrieked and done, the basic point remains valid: The abortion discussion proceeds at its own peril if it ignores women's perspectives (p. 36).

The problem, of course, is that if the "shriekers" insist on the bodily integrity argument, his own way of formulating the issues already precludes his hearing of it. McCormick is not atypical of so-called moderates on this question. An analogous dismissal of this "slogan" is found in Stanley Hauerwas, "Abortion: Why the Arguments Fail," in *Abortion Parley*, ed. James T. Burtchaell (New York: Andrews and McMeel, 1979), pp. 325-352.

27. See Liam Hudson, *The Cult of Fact* (New York: Harper & Row, 1972); Theodosius Dobzhansky, *The Biological Basis of Human Freedom*

(New York: Columbia University Press, 1956); *Dialectics of Biology Group, Against Biological Determinism*, ed. Steven Rose (New York: Allison & Busby, 1982) and *Towards a Liberatory Biology*, ed. Steven Rose (New York: Allison & Busby, 1982). On the development of early differing theories of nature among western scientists, and in relation to conceptions of women, see Carolyn Merchant, *The Death of Nature: Women, Ecology, and the Scientific Revolution* (New York: Harper & Row, 1980). See especially Chapter 6, pp. 149-163.

28. E. Blechschmidt, "Human Being from the Very First," in Hilgers, Horan, and Mall, pp. 6-28, and Germain G. Grisez, *Abortion: The Myth, the Realities and the Arguments* (Washington, D.C.: Corpus Books, 1969). Joseph T. Mangan, S. J. uses potentiality as equivalent to "virtually human," (p. 128). See Mangan, "The Wonder of Myself: Ethical-Theological Aspects Of Direct Abortion," *Theological Studies*, vol. 31 (1970), pp. 125-148, especially p. 128.

29. It should be emphasized that many definitions of natural-law ethics have rejected these older "organic" theories. See, for example, Anthony Battaglia, *Toward a Reformulation of Natural Law* (New York: Seabury Press, 1981), and Daniel Maguire, *The Moral Choice.* (N.Y.: Doubleday, 1978.) On attitudes toward change in papal teaching, see Christine Gudorf, *Catholic Social Teaching on Liberation Themes* (Washington, D.C.: University Press of America, 1980).

30. Battaglia, pp. 8, 9.

31. Among traditional Thomists, the limits set by this theory of organism often exempt specific "higher" functions of human reason. Nevertheless, rational action remains constricted by the logic of the argument, which always moves from lower to higher organic levels. The natural "end" of action is determined by its organic structure. Hence, Germain Grisez in *Contraception and the Natural Law* (Milwaukee: Bruce Publishing, 1964) begins his discussion of the immorality of contraception by affirming:

> The second consideration which shows that the procreative good is the object of a basic natural inclination is the fact that from a biological point of view the work of reproduction is the fullest organic realization of the living substance...
>
> One of these is the organic system of nutrition, growth, and reproduction. This system is not isolated from the rest of man. Indeed, as psychosomatics show, there are all manners of intimate relationships between it and the higher psychic and intellectual planes of man's being. Nevertheless, the organic system does have its own unity and distinctness. And for it all achievements center on reproduction. Reproduction is the act of maturity and full power. It is the act which uses the best resources of the organism. It is the act after the completion of which the life of many organisms is finished.
>
> To the extent that man truly is an organism rather than a pure spirit using a bodily medium of expression, the basic organic plane of his being inclines him to the attainment of its appropriate per-

fection in the good of procreation. One can explain many human interests and tendencies, but it is impossible to explain the fact that having children is practically universal except by observing that it is natural for a man as an organism to reproduce (pp. 79-80). In a continuation of this argument, Grisez "demonstrates" that nothing concrete or contingent may count against this "organic system"; hence all contraception is wrong, especially Chapter 4, pp. 76-106.

32. Blechschmidt, pp. 6, 7, 8.
33. On the function of the temporal frame of the future in ethical reflection, see Gibson Winter, *Elements for a Social Ethic* (New York: Macmillan, 1966), pp. 66-70.
34. Philosophical arguments regarding freedom and determinism lie outside my interest here. I simply want to stress that we have no need for morality where determinism reigns. On this issue, see Ralph Ross, *Obligation: A Social Theory* (Ann Arbor: University of Michigan Press, 1970), pp. 1ff., 37, 54-61.
35. There is a long history of discussion of the "naturalistic fallacy" in ethics. Obviously, I do not agree with some theorists that all theological reasoning is "naturalistically" fallacious. However, I do believe that *all* appeals to simple "fact" as logically implying obligation or value are gross forms of this fallacy. On the naturalistic fallacy, see Kai Nielsen, "Ethics, Problems of" in *Encyclopedia of Philosophy*, especially pp. 100-106, and Jonathan Harrison, "Ethical Naturalism," Ibid., pp. 69-71.
36. J. Phillip Wogaman, "Abortion as a Theological Issue," reprinted from the *Washington Post*, August 16, 1977, by the Religious Coalition for Abortion Rights, Washington, D.C.
37. Mary Meehan, "Catholic Liberals and Abortion," *Commonweal*, 108:21 (November 20, 1981), p. 650.
38. James Burtchaell, "A Call and a Reply," *Christianity and Crisis*, 37:17 (November 14, 1977), p. 270.
39. For a discussion of the range of positions on "person" in moral parlance, see Joel Feinberg, "Abortion," in Thomas Regan, ed., *Matters of Life and Death: New Introductory Essays in Moral Philosophy* (New York: Random House, 1980), pp. 183-217. See also John MacMurray, *The Self as Agent* (London: Faber and Faber, 1957), and *Persons in Relation* (London: Faber and Faber, 1961).
40. See nn. 1, 37, 38. See also James Burtchaell, "Continuing the Discussion: How to Argue About Abortion: II," *Christianity and Crisis*, 37:21 (December 26, 1977), pp. 73-81. A more sophisticated philosophical repudiation of these distinctions, flawed by the impact, if partial, analogy between "Negroes" and fetuses, is Roger Wertheimer's "Understanding the Abortion Argument," in *The Problem of Abortion*, Joel Feinberg ed. (Belmont, Calif.: Wadsworth, 1973), pp. 33-51.
41. See MacMurray, *Self as Agent* and *Persons in Relation*; Mary Anne Warren, "On the Moral and Legal Status of Abortion," in *Philosophy and Women*, ed. Sharon Bishop and Marjorie Weinzweig (Belmont, Calif.: Wadsworth, 1979), pp. 216-236; Charles Hartshorne, "Concerning Abortion: An Attempt at a Rational View," *Christian Century*, vol. 98,

no. 2 (January 21, 1981), pp. 43-46. The best source on the historical background and abuse of notions of the person in the abortion debate is Rosalind Pollack Petchesky's "Statement on the Meaning of the Person," submitted to the U.S. Senate Judiciary Committee on the Separation of Powers, May 1, 1981. Marvin Kohl, "Abortion and the Argument from Innocence," in Feinberg, *The Problem of Abortion*, pp. 28-32, offers a justification of the relevant distinctions, predicated on standard usage of the English language. A much discussed and strongly criticized position on "moral personhood" is Michael Tooley's "A Defense of Abortion and Infanticide," in Feinberg, *The Problem of Abortion*, pp. 51-91. Although Tooley's essay is much maligned, his distinction between "person" and human being makes perfect sense to me. While I do not agree with his limited defense of infanticide, I believe objections to this aspect of his argument can be formulated without violating the basic logic of his position. A sound proposal for strengthening Tooley's argument is S. I. Benn's "Abortion, Infanticide, and Respect for Persons," in Feinberg, *The Problem of Abortion*, pp. 92-104.

42. On theological objections to this assumption, see Chapters 3 and 4, pp. 76-77, 112-117.

43. The notion of "reification" was articulated by Marx to explain the effects of alienated labor on human consciousness. The concept has been developed more systematically by Henri Lukacs to account for the reduction of human relationships to "objectified" or "use" relations.

44. Not all these writers are precise about this point, but genetic data seem to be most relevant. Paul Ramsey in his "Reference Points in Deciding about Abortion," in John T. Noonan, Jr., ed. *Morality of Abortion: Legal and Historical Perspectives* (Cambridge: Harvard University Press, 1970, pp. 60-100, says:
    In a remarkable way, modern genetics seems to teach — with greater precision and assurance than theology could ever muster — that there are "formal causes," immanent principles or constitutive elements. . . These minute formal elements are already determining the organic life to be not only generally "human" but also the unique individual human being it is to be (p. 67).
    See also Charles E. Curran, "Abortion: Its Moral Aspects," in Batchelor, pp. 115-128. Curran is uncharacteristically subtle, however, in distinguishing an individuated life from a "person" (see p. 125).

45. Again, the important point is that what one takes to be the theoretical assumptions of biology differ. For example, the "genetic-code" proponents use as biological criteria data regarding the fetus in isolation from the pregnant woman's body. For persons like myself who assume that embryology involves relational and functional developmental analysis, such positions use biology reductionistically.

46. The "social construction of reality" is a standard phrase in sociology, popularized by Peter L. Berger and Thomas Luckmann in *The Social Construction of Reality: A Treatise in the Sociology of Knowledge* (New York: Doubleday, 1966). Their treatment of the process of the "construction" of society is highly voluntaristic and subjective. To a great extent, they ignore structural power factors in the process, both

in terms of the effects of power on consciousness and the objective differences between dominant and suppressed groups' capacity to legitimate their world views.

47. Feinberg, *The Problem of Abortion*, pp. 3-5.

48. Ibid., pp. 1-9.

49. For example, see Elizabeth Rapaport and Paul Sagal, "One Step Forward, Two Steps Backward: Abortion and Ethical Theory," in Vetterling-Braggin, Elliston, and English, p. 414. Feinberg uses the term "extremely permissive liberal" in his introduction to *The Problem of Abortion*, p. 3.

50. "The zygote does have this power to reproduce itself," from Mangan, pp. 125-148. Needless to say, all writers who regularly speak of "the child in the womb" are, by virtue of that language, imputing agency to a zygote, embryo, or early-gestating fetus.

51. The phrase is Curran's, used to describe other Catholic positions. See Curran, "Abortion: Contemporary Debate in Philosophical and Religious Ethics," in *Encyclopedia of Bioethics*, vol. 1, p. 18.

52. I say "apparently" because, since the focus of such positions is on fetal development in abstraction from the mother's body, ignoring relationality as intrinsic to biological perspective, I contend that the embryology implied is itself not terribly sophisticated. Compare the biological perspectives developed in Steven Rose, ed., *Towards a Liberatory Biology*.

53. Curran, "Abortion: Contemporary Debate," pp. 19-20.

54. Thomas S. Szasz, "The Ethics of Abortion," *The Humanist*, vol. 26 (1966), p. 148. This position is sometimes satirized. It is often ascribed to those of us who believe early fetal life is human tissue. We are charged with reducing the value of the fetus to that of an appendix.

55. Judith Jarvis Thompson, "A Defense of Abortion," in Bishop and Weinzweig, pp. 207-216. Neither Thompson's "unjust aggressor" nor the "innocent child" analogy is appropriate because they both violate the criteria above. Another analogy sometimes used on the pro-choice side is that the fetus is a "parasite" in relation to the woman's body. I doubt the moral wisdom of the analogy, even though it does not suffer from the same projectional inaptness that these other analogies exemplify. Marilyn Frye, in "Some Reflections on Separatism and Power," *Sinister Wisdom*, no. 6 (Summer 1975), pp. 30-39, uses this analogy to suggest a parallel between the fetus and the social (I would add, emotional) parasitism of men on women:

> The parasitism of males on females is, as I see it, demonstrated by the panic, rage, and hysteria generated in so many of them by the thought of being abandoned by women . . .

> The fetus lives parasitically. It is a distinct animal surviving off the life (the blood) of another animal creature. It is incapable of surviving on its own resources, of independent nutrition; incapable even of symbiosis. If it is true that males live parasitically upon females, it seems reasonable to suppose that many of them and those loyal to them are in some way sensitive to the parallelism between their situation and that of the fetus. They could easily

identify with the fetus. The woman who is free to see the fetus
as a parasite might be free to see the man as a parasite...
    ...They do not worry about murder and involuntary steriliza-
tion in prisons, nor murder in war, nor murder by pollution and
industrial accidents. Either these are not real to them or they cannot
identify with the victims; but anyway, killing in general is not what
they oppose. They worry about the rejection *by women, at women's
discretion*...
    I discuss abortion here because it seems to me to be the most
publicly emotional and most physically dramatic ground on which
the theme of separation and male parasitism is presently being
played out...
    Male parasitism means that males *must* have access to women;
it is the Patriarchal Imperative. But feminist no-saying is more than
a substantial removal (re-direction, re-allocation) of goods and
services because Access is one of the faces of Power. Female denial
of male access to females substantially cuts off a flow of benefits,
but it has also the form and full portent of assumption of power.
    Differences of power are always manifested in asymmetrical
access (pp. 33-35).

It should be clear that I emphathize with Frye's social analysis. My reser-
vation about the moral aptness of the fetal analogy holds, however.

56. See, for example, Sumner, pp. 65-73, 111-127, and Benn, pp. 92-104.
     See also James P. Sterba, *The Demands of Justice* (Notre Dame:
     University of Notre Dame Press, 1980), especially pp. 126-150. Sterba
     uses a Rawlsian "justice as fairness" argument to show that Judith Jarvis
     Thompson, along with any other liberal, is inconsistent as a liberal in
     not recognizing the fetus's right to life. Sterba's application of Rawls
     in raising questions about some (most?) abortions is an example of
     abstractionism run wild and, in my view, is also an abuse of Rawls.
     All historical concreteness is lost in Sterba's "principled speculation."
     Perhaps Rawls's approach opens the way to such "dehistoricizing" of
     reality. Nevertheless, as my own effort to combine a social contractual
     argument for the justice of procreative choice with historical and
     utilitarian arguments for women's disadvantaged situation as a class
     makes clear, I do not believe arguments about principles of rational
     choice need to cut us off from reality. They have functioned in this way
     for Sterba, however, at least on the abortion question. For a critique
     of the entire tradition of moral reasoning utilized by Thompson, see
     Kathryn Pyne Parsons, "Moral Revolution," in Julia A. Sherman and
     Evelyn Torton Beck, eds., *The Prism of Sex: Essays in the Sociology
     of Knowledge* (Madison: University of Wisconsin Press, 1979),
     pp. 189-227.
57. See, for example, John Finnis, "The Rights and Wrongs of Abortion,"
     in *The Rights and Wrongs of Abortion*, ed. Marshall Cohen, Thomas
     Nagel, and Thomas Scanlon (Princeton: Princeton University Press,
     1974). Judith Jarvis Thompson's reply is contained on pp. 114-127.
58. For a defense of brain-wave criteria, see Baruch Barody, "Fetal Hu-

manity and the Theory of Essentialism," in *Philosophy and Sex*, ed. Robert Baker and Frederick Elliston (Buffalo, N.Y.: Prometheus Books, 1975). For a review of the "developmentalist" criteria, see Daniel Callahan, *Abortion: Law, Choice and Morality* (New York: Macmillan, 1970), pp. 384-390. Sumner articulates and defends a "sentience" position, though without very clear justification for sentience other than that it yields a "moderate" position. See pp. 141-154. I find Sumner neither clear nor consistent; for while he appeals to sentience throughout his argument, he also says that development of the brain to an operational level is a decisive indicator for sentience. Hence his actual position seems to approximate my own, namely, that third-trimester gestating fetuses deserve our respect from a moral point of view (p. 149). I would be less critical of Sumner's views if he were not so contemptuous toward others' positions.

59. I want to emphasize that I am not appealing here to a woman's subjective relation to the fetus, which conversations with many women suggest vary greatly. The relationality at issue here is specific biological differentiation and the existence of a genuinely operational human biosystem.

60. Hartshorne, p. 43.

61. See, for example, Steinfels, p. 661. Steinfels's so-called biological criteria ignore all interactional and systemic functional considerations, however.

62. Feinberg, *The Problem of Abortion*, pp. 3-4.

63. William S. Hamrick, "Abortion in Whiteheadian Perspective," paper delivered at the Eastern Philosophical Association, Boston, December 1980. In an interesting letter, Professor Hamrick noted that discussion of his paper focused on whether a Whiteheadian scheme, concerned with realization of value, can yield a notion of rights. My view here, of course, is that rights as a moral category may be justified by several moral arguments interrelating claims of value and obligation. Consequently, I have no objections to Professor Hamrick's use of the category, even if not warranted by Whitehead's views.

64. My point here is twofold: first, that early "viability" criteria are still debatable in terms of relational differentiation of the fetus and its functional equivalence to a human life and, second, that "person" is an intrinsically "moral" notion not applicable to simplest species differentiation.

65. Warren, p. 222.

66. Curran, "Abortion: Contemporary Debate," pp. 20-21, and Feinberg, *The Problem of Abortion*, pp. 3-4.

67. Rapaport and Sagal, pp. 409-410.

68. Warren, pp. 225-226. My own view is that infanticide is more morally dubious than late-stage abortion, precisely because the life of the neonate can be differentiated from the mother in a way not possible before birth. It is true, as many have argued, that the position I endorse — which differentiates a fetal life form worthy of respect, a human life, and moral personhood — does not draw a sharp line between late-stage abortion and infanticide. But why is a sharp line necessary? A good society will seek to find ways to care for babies born into it, even

though they are technically only "potential persons." It is morally wise to err on the side of imputing "personhood" to a neonate, just as it is morally wise to impute respect to late-gestating fetuses. I have already observed that in the developmental process, no classificatory distinction is overwhelmingly persuasive. I would also acknowledge that infanticide may be justified in some situations, without believing that it is a morally indifferent act.

69. The phrase is John MacMurray's. See his *The Self as Agent*, pp. 1-38.
70. Ibid., p. 219.
71. MacMurray, *Persons in Relation*, p. 48.
72. Ibid., pp. 48, 49, 50, 51.
73. Janet Gallagher, *Ms.*, April 1983.
74. Feinberg, *The Problem of Abortion*, pp. 7-9.
75. See Christopher Tietze, *Induced Abortion: A World Review* (New York: Population Council, 1981). In Sweden, the mean duration of pregnancies before abortion dropped from 14.1 weeks in 1968 to 9.9 in 1979 (p. 66).
76. Ibid., pp. 66-67. New York's permissive law and the availability of many clinics that perform abortions mean that numerous abortions are performed on nonresidents there. Tietze notes the trend toward earlier abortions among New York State residents. On the effects of legalization on early abortion in New York State from 1970 onward, see Alan F. Guttmacher, M.D., "The Genesis of Liberalized Abortion in New York: A Personal Insight," in David F. Wahlbert and J. Douglas Butler, eds., *Abortion, Society and Law* (Cleveland: Press of Case Western Reserve, 1973), pp. 63-87.
77. Tietze, pp. 66-67.
78. This phrase is from Dietrich Bonhoeffer's *Letters and Papers from Prison* (London: SCM Press, Fontana Books, 1953), pp. 106-110.

8: Conclusion

1. See Mary Seeger's contribution to the Christianity and Crisis symposium, "Does the First Amendment Bar the Hyde Amendment?," *Christianity and Crisis*, 39:3 (March 5, 1979), pp. 36-38. Compare with Peter Steinfels, "The Search for an Alternative," *Commonweal*, pp. 108:21 (November 20, 1981).
2. See, for example, Chapter 7, nn. 1 and 38, pp. 300-306.
3. This is the characterization used not only by Joel Feinberg, ed., in *The Problem of Abortion* (Belmont, Calif.: Wadsworth, 1973), but by a majority of moral theologians and philosophers cited in Chapter 7 — Sumner, Curran, and Ramsey, among others.
4. For a helpful summary of early reform efforts as well as an excellent history of recent legal and legislative action on abortion, see Eva R. Rubin, *Abortion, Politics and the Courts: Roe-Wade and Its Aftermath* (Westport, Conn.: Greenwood Press, 1982), pp. 9-28. On abortion law reform legislation prior to the Roe-Wade decision, see B. James George, Jr., "The Evolving Law of Abortion," in David F. Wahlbert and J. Douglas Butler, eds., *Abortion, Society and Law* (Cleveland: Press of Case Western Reserve, 1973), pp. 3-62.

5. Rubin, pp. 17ff.
6. Ibid., p. 21. See also n. 4, above.
7. Rubin, pp. 22-23.
8. I say "apparently" because she seems to me to imply reservations about the use of litigation to establish political goals. Ibid., pp. 1-7, p. 29, pp. 57-62. Even so, her account of the legal history of the issue and of legislative response to *Roe v. Wade* is exemplary. Unfortunately, she charges "extremists" on both sides with excess emotionality without documenting her complaints. See p. 92.
9. Ibid., p. 82.
10. Ibid., p. 63. See also Bob Woodward and Scott Armstrong, *The Brethren* (New York: Simon & Schuster, 1979), pp. 230ff.
11. Rubin, p. 64.
12. For Blackmun's account of this, a decade after the decision, see John A. Jenkins, "A Candid Talk with Justice Blackmun," *The New York Times Magazine*, February 20, 1983.
13. For example, see John Noonan, *A Private Choice: Abortion in America in the Seventies* (New York: Free Press, 1981), pp. 1-58. See also Donald II. Regan, "Rewriting *Roe v. Wade*," *Michigan Law Review*, 77 (1979).
14. Rubin, pp. 57-62.
15. Rubin, pp. 57-62. See also Woodword and Armstrong, pp. 230ff.
16. This feminist perspective is well developed in Lucinda Cisler, "Abortion Law Repeal (Sort of): A Warning to Women," in *Radical Feminism: An Anthology*, ed. Anne Koedt, Ellen Levine, and Anita Rapone (New York: Quadrangle Books, 1973), pp. 151-164.
17. See *Roe v. Wade in Law and Bioethics: Texts with Commentary on Major U.S. Court Decisions*, ed. Thomas A. Shannon and Jo Ann Manfra (New York: Paulist Press, 1982), pp. 7-41.
18. Ibid. See also Rubin, pp. 62-83.
19. Rubin's quotations on women's movement reactions come from articles written before *Roe v. Wade*, such as Lucinda Cisler's "Unfinished Business: Birth Control and Women's Liberation," in Robin Morgan, ed., *Sisterhood Is Powerful* (New York: Vintage, 1970), pp. 273-274.
20. The term "religious anarchist" here is not pejorative. Many religious people doubt the legitimacy of state interference in matters relating to morality. Catholic spirituality has a strong tradition of this sort, which is why no one should be surprised that at least as many, perhaps slightly more, Catholics than Protestants (in one survey 20 percent to 19 percent) believe the government should not regulate abortion at all.
21. At the risk of redundancy, I want to stress once more that this thesis is a standard principle of interpretation in most, not just some, feminist social theory.
22. See James Kelly, "Beyond the Stereotypes: Interviews with Right-to-Life Pioneers," *Commonweal*, 108:21 (November 20, 1981), pp. 654-657.
23. Noonan's recent diatribe, *A Private Choice*, is characteristic in its implication that until the Supreme Court engaged the issue, creating a new liberty by fiat, the social consensus on abortion was clear, firm, and incontrovertible.

24. It is one of the many virtues of Rubin's book that she recognizes the unparalleled character of the Catholic bishops' action in supporting civil disobedience on abortion. Rubin, pp. 88ff.

25. Ibid., pp. 87-100.

26. Beverly W. Harrison, "Continuing the Discussion: How to Argue about Abortion: II," *Christianity and Crisis*, 37:21 (December 26, 1977), especially p. 313.

27. James T. Burtchaell, "A Call and a Reply," *Christianity and Crisis* (November 14, 1977), p. 270. It is important to recall the point made earlier that it was not the bishops' involvement, but the substance of the politics they endorsed, that led to many of us signing "Call to Concern." See Chapter 1, n. 9. See also, "Pastoral Plan for Pro-Life Activities" (Washington, D.C.: National Catholic Conference).

28. How much the outcome of the 1980 senatorial elections was a result of anti-abortion efforts has been widely debated. Certainly, the defeat in 1980 of numerous liberal senators by conservatives was a massive setback for public moral sensibility, as the Catholic bishops must by now realize, as they confront opposition from such senators to their current efforts to give constructive leadership in relation to nuclear policy and U.S. foreign policy in Latin America.

29. George C. Higgins, Chapter 1, n. 34. James Breshnahan has analyzed a range of options open to Catholics on the question of social policies regarding abortion in "The Interaction of Religion and Law: Post-Vatican II Roman Catholic Perspectives," *The Hastings Journal of Law*, 29:6 (1978), pp. 1361-1382.

30. See Rosalind Pollack Petchesky, "Antiabortion, Antifeminism and the Rise of the New Right," *Feminist Studies*, 7:2 (Summer 1981), pp. 206-246. See also Chapter 2, n. 1, Chapter 3, nn. 3-5.

31. Rubin, p. 141, also pp. 138-146.

32. This amendment was named after its sponsor, Senator Orrin Hatch of Utah, who proposed the alternative when it became clear that the various versions of a Human Life Amendment, which he originally supported, would not win Senate approval.

33. Rubin, pp. 116, 126.

34. Ibid., p. 117.

35. In *Planned Parenthood of Central Missouri v. Danforth*, 428 U.S. 52 (1976), reprinted in Shannon and Manfra, pp. 42-69. See Rubin, pp. 130-136, especially p. 131.

36. The status of parental consent laws relating to minors was confused, because in the case cited in n. 35, parental consent requirements were struck. At the same time, the Court heard, but waited three years to invalidate, Massachusetts' minor consent requirements in *Bellotti v. Baird*, 443 U.S. 622 (1979), reprinted in Shannon and Manfra, pp. 100-120. Even so, minors' consent requirements are still in force in many areas. See, for example, the Akron, Ohio, ordinance to be reviewed by the Supreme Court this term. See Rubin, p. 137.

37. See Nadine Brozan, "Birth-Control Rule: Clinics Ponder Effects," *New York Times*, January 29, 1983, p. B11.

38. *Beal v. Doe*, 45, U.S.L.W. 4781 (1977), and *Maher v. Roe*, 45, U.S.L.W. 4787 (1077), reprinted in Shannon and Manfra, pp. 70-99. See also Rubin, pp. 126-129, 151-157. It was, of course, the Hyde Amendment that shut off federal funding for abortions. For a helpful objection to this position, see Mary C. Segers, "Abortion and the Supreme Court: Some Are More Equal Than Others," Institute of Society, Ethics and the Life Sciences, *Hastings Center Report* (August, 1977), pp. 5-6.
39. Rubin, p. 136.
40. Ibid., p. 137.
41. Ibid., pp. 106-113. Rubin rightly observes that pro-choice groups actually played down abortion politics in the period prior to 1977, in the hope that *Roe v. Wade* would gain acceptance. Her quite accurate assessment belies charges of equal "extremism" on both sides.
42. Steinfels, especially pp. 663-664.
43. Beverly W. Harrison, "A Fresh Paradigm of Human Sexuality," *Journal of Presbyterian History*, 61:1 (Spring 1983).
44. See Chapter 1, n. 10. It should be stressed that strong elements within the so-called right-to-life movement oppose the legality of amniocentesis as a method for testing for genetic defects. An effort to withdraw public funds for amniocentesis nearly passed the Utah legislature in 1981. See *Options*, published by the Religious Coalition for Abortion Rights (April 1981), p. 9.
45. On the psychology of avoiding birth control precautions, see Kirstin Luker, *Taking a Chance: Abortion and the Decision Not To Contracept* (Berkeley: University of California Press, 1976).
46. Studies cited throughout this book on public attitudes toward abortion indicate high support, 80-95 percent, for legal abortion when rape or incest is involved.
47. See, for example, James T. Burtchaell, "Continuing the Discussion: How to Argue about Abortion: II," *Christianity and Crisis*, 37:21 (Dec. 26, 1977), p. 314.
48. Murray A. Straus, "Wife Beating: How Common and Why?" *Victimology: An International Journal*, 2:3, 4 (1977), pp. 443-458. His estimate is that 28 percent of all women experience battering. Other estimates go as high as 50 percent. See also Nancy Gager and Cathleen Schurr, *Sexual Assault: Confronting Rape in America* (New York: Grosset & Dunlap, 1976).
49. In a new study, Diana Russell reports that 19 percent of the women she interviewed acknowledged experiences of marital rape. See *Rape in Marriage* (New York: Macmillan, 1982).
50. FBI estimates are that well over half a million rapes of women occur in the United States per year. The FBI presumes, however, that only one out of ten rapes are reported.
51. Janet Radcliffe Richards has argued that it is philosophically inconsistent to support abortion in the case of rape if one does not support elective abortion, because the fetus involved has the same status in either case. The widespread willingness to "exempt" strictures against abortion in

the case of rape, she claims, derives from the "ingrained habit [of thinking] that abortion is bad, tempered by the charitable idea that it is really not fair to add to the unmerited suffering of a woman who has gone through so much already." She suggests that this attitude is evidence of how pivotal the issue of retribution against erring women is in abortion reasoning. I agree. See Janet Radcliffe Richards, *The Sceptical Feminist: A Philosophical Inquiry* (London: Routledge & Kegan Paul, 1980), pp. 221-226.

52. On this sort of argument, see Warren Reich, "Life: Quality of Life," *The Encyclopedia of Bioethics*, vol. 2 (Washington, D.C.: Georgetown University Press, 1978), pp. 829-840.

53. See Daniel Callahan, *Abortion: Law, Choice, and Morality* (New York: Macmillan, 1970), pp. 253-277 and passim.

54. As is the case in Sweden, cited above in Chapter 7, n. 75.

55. On this point, I agree strongly with Thomas E. Hill, Jr. See his "Servility and Self-Respect." *The Monist* (January 1973).

56. Several of the authors in *Abortion and the Unwanted Child*, ed. Carl Reiterman (New York: Springer, 1971) have studied the effects of unwanted pregnancy on women and children. No one who assesses the moral meaning of abortion should neglect this question.

57. This is why feminist historiographers often disagree about how greatly the antifeminism of the 1920s and the Great Depression set back women's progress. Writers who attend to indices of public change see a watershed and perceive regressive trends. Those who monitor cultural change in women's lives do not always agree. We do know that women's personal freedoms — in dress, social and cultural involvements, and so on — continued to grow even when political and economic change slowed or was reversed.

58. Harrison, "Continuing the Discussion." In my opinion, those on the "pro-life" side who believe that church agencies can adequately support women through "unwanted pregnancies" are ignoring the bitter truth about how such agencies functioned prior to the legalization of abortion. See Diana Schulder and Florynce Kennedy, *Abortion Rap* (New York: McGraw-Hill, 1971), pp. 6-20 and passim. One Catholic moral theologian has recognized the weakness of Roman Catholic social ethics in treating "the right of procreation" abstractly, in isolation from other social values. David Hollenbach, S. J., *The Right to Procreate and Its Social Limitation*, Unpublished dissertation, Yale University, 1975, university microfilm, no. 75, 25-26, 389.

59. Charles Hartshorne, "Concerning Abortion: An Attempt at a Rational View," *Christian Century*, vol. 98, no. 2 (January 21, 1981), p. 44.

60. Pauli Murray, from "Dark Testament" in *Dark Testament and Other Poems* (Norwalk, Conn.: Silvermine Publishers, 1970), p. 17.

61. Adrienne Rich, "Natural Resources," 13; 14 in *The Dream of a Common Language: Poems 1974-1977* (New York: Norton, 1978), pp. 66, 67.

62. Dorothee Soelle, "Play Me a Song about Rosa, Anna, and Rosa" in *Of War and Love*, trans. from the German by Rita and Robert Kimber (Maryknoll, N.Y.: Orbis Books, 1983), pp. 53-54.

Index

Reproductive engineering, 270n9-271

Rich, Adrienne, *The Dream of a Common Language; Poems 1974-1977*, 318n62; *On Lies, Secrets, and Silences: Selected Prose*, 286n12; *A Wild Patience Has Taken Me This Far: Poems 1978-1981*, 318n61; *Of Woman Born: Motherhood as Experience and Institution*, 270n6, 302n64

Richards, Janet Radcliffe, *The Sceptical Feminist: A Philosophical Inquiry*, 317n51-318

Richardson, Cyril, *Early Christian Fathers*, 292n28,n32

Rights(s), 274n33; of bodily integrity, 198-199; conflict of, 200; human, 196-197; in moral sense, 51, 197; political, 198; social character of, 199

Robertson, D. B., ed., *Voluntary Associations*, 283n56

Robinson, John A. T., *The Body: A Study in Pauline Theology*, 278n20

Rodgers-Rose, La Frances, ed., *The Black Woman*, 285n3

Roe v. Wade, 53, 149, 231-244 passim, 249, 252, 253-254

Roodkowsky, Mary, *Who Really Starves? Women and World Hunger* (with L. Leghorn), 300n43

Rorty, Richard, *Philosophy and the Mirror of Nature*, 286

Rosaldo, M. Z., ed., *Women, Culture, and Society* (with L. Lamphere, ed.), 270n6, 299n25

Rose, Steven: ed., *Against Biological Determinism*, 307n27-308; ed., *Towards a Liberatory Biology*, 307n27-308, 311n52

Ross, Ralph, *Obligation: A Social Theory*, 309n34

Ross, W. D., 289n5

Rowbotham, Sheila, *Woman's Con-sciousness, Man's World*, 263n2, 269n4, 288n37

Rubin, Eva R., 233, 235-236, 240, 242-243; *Abortion, Politics and the Courts: Roe-Wade and Its Aftermath*, 314n4, 316n24, n35, 317n41

Ruether, Rosemary Radford: ed., *Women of Spirit: Female Leadership in Jewish and Christian Traditions* (with E. McLaughlin, ed.), 276n13; *Faith and Patricide: The Theological Roots of Anti-Semitism*, 276n13-277; *Mary: The Feminine Face of the Church*, 288n40; *New Woman/New Earth: Sexist Ideologies and Human Liberation*, 276n9, 285n6

Rufinus, Magister, 142; *Summa decretorum*, 295n56

Rules and principles, 12-13, 122, 255

Russell, Diana, *Rape in Marriage*, 317n49

Russell, Frederick R., *The Just War in the Middle Ages*, 272n21

Russell, Letty M.: ed., *The Liberating Word: A Guide to Nonsexist Interpretation of the Bible*, 276n13-277; *Human Liberation in a Feminist Perspective: A Theology*, 279n29-280

Sacredness and intrinsic value, 112-113

Sanger, Margaret, 171

Sapp, Stephen, *Sexuality, the Bible, and Science*, 279n23

Sargent, Alice G., ed., *Beyond Sex Roles*, 271n12

Scanlon, Thomas, ed., *The Rights and Wrongs of Abortion* (with M. Cohen and T. Nagel, eds.), 312n57

Schulder, Diana, *Abortion Rap* (with F. Kennedy), 318n58

Schurr, Cathleen, *Sexual Assault:*